Conference of the North American Chapter of the Association for Computational Linguistics: Human Language Technologies (NAACL HLT 2019)

Student Research Workshop

Minneapolis, Minnesota, USA
2 – 7 June 2019

ISBN: 978-1-5108-8756-5

NAACL HLT 2019

**The 2019 Conference of the
North American Chapter of the
Association for Computational Linguistics:
Human Language Technologies**

Proceedings of the Student Research Workshop

June 3 - 5, 2019
Minneapolis, Minnesota

This workshop is supported by the National Science Foundation under Grant No. 1907573. Any opinions, findings, and conclusions or recommendations expressed in this material are those of the authors and do not necessarily reflect the views of the National Science Foundation.

Introduction

Welcome to the NAACL-HLT 2019 Student Research Workshop! This year's submissions were organized in two tracks: research papers and thesis proposals.

- Research papers may describe completed work, or work in progress with preliminary results. For these papers, the first author must be a current graduate or undergraduate student.

- Thesis proposals are geared towards students who have decided on a thesis topic and wish to get feedback on their proposal and broader ideas for their continuing work.

This year, we received a total of 54 submissions: 50 of these were research papers, and 4 were thesis proposals. We accepted 22 research papers and 2 thesis proposals, resulting in an overall acceptance rate of 44%. The main authors of the accepted papers represent a variety of countries: Australia, Canada, India (6 papers), Ireland, Japan (2 papers), Hong Kong, South Korea, Taiwan, USA (10 papers). These papers span topics across a wide range of subdisciplines and topics within NLP and CL.

Accepted research papers will be presented as either talks or posters within the NAACL main conference. We have 9 accepted papers being presented as talks and 14 as posters.

Following previous editions of the Student Research Workshop, we have offered students the opportunity to get mentoring feedback before submitting their work for review. Each student that requested pre-submission mentorship was assigned to an experienced researcher who read the paper and provided some comments on how to improve the quality of writing and presentation of the student's work. A total of 22 students participated in the mentorship program. During the workshop itself, we will also provide an on-site mentorship program. Each mentor will meet with their assigned students to provide feedback on their poster or oral presentation, and to discuss their research careers.

We would like to express our gratitude for the financial support from the National Science Foundation (NSF), the Computing Research Association Computing Community Consortium (CRA-CCC), the National Research Council (NRC) Canada, and Google. Thanks to their support, this year's SRW is able to assist students with their registration, travel, and lodging expenses.

We would like to thank the mentors for dedicating their time to help students improve their papers prior to submission, and we thank the members of the program committee for the constructive feedback they have provided for each submitted paper.

This workshop would not have been possible without the help from our faculty advisors, and we thank them for their guidance along this year of workshop preparation. We also thank the organizers of NAACL-HLT 2019 for their continuous support. Finally, we would like to thank all students who have submitted their work to this edition of the Student Research Workshop. We hope our collective effort will be rewarded in the form of an excellent workshop!

Student Chairs:

Sudipta Kar, University of Houston (USA)
Farah Nadeem, University of Washington (USA)
Laura Burdick, University of Michigan (USA)

Faculty Advisers:

Greg Durrett, University of Texas at Austin (USA)
Na-Rae Han, University of Pittsburgh (USA)

Mentors:

Mohit Bansal, University of North Carolina at Chapel Hill
Micha Elsner, The Ohio State University
Katrin Erk, University of Texas at Austin
Jonathan Kummerfeld, University of Michigan
Junyi Jessy Li, University of Texas at Austin
Yang Liu, Liulishuo Inc.
Marie de Marneffe, The Ohio State University
Saif Mohammed, National Research Council Canada
Mari Ostendorf, University of Washington
Verónica Pérez-Rosas, University of Michigan
Swapna Somasundaran, Educational Testing Service

Program Committee:

Gustavo Aguilar, University of Houston
Bharat Ram Ambati, Apple
Antonios Anastasopoulos, Carnegie Mellon University
Maria Antoniak, Cornell University
Rachel Bawden, University of Edinburgh
Jifan Chen, University of Texas at Austin
Volkan Cirik, Carnegie Mellon University
Ahmed Elgohary, University of Maryland, College Park
Hady Elsahar, Université de Lyon
Saadia Gabriel, University of Washington
David Gaddy, University of California, Berkeley
Kevin Gimpel, Toyota Technological Institute at Chicago
Alvin Grissom II, Ursinus College
Na-Rae Han, University of Pittsburgh
Ji He, Citadel
Eric Holgate, University of Texas at Austin
Dirk Hovy, Bocconi University
Aaron Jaech, Facebook Research
Labiba Jahan, Florida International University
Youxuan Jiang, University of Michigan

Daniel Khashabi, University of Pennsylvania
Philipp Koehn, Johns Hopkins University
Jasy Suet Yan Liew, Universiti Sains Malaysia
Angela Lin, University of Texas at Austin
Kevin Lybarger, University of Washington
Suraj Maharjan, Capital One
Amita Misra, IBM Watson
Kenton Murray, University of Notre Dame
Denis Newman-Griffis, The Ohio State University
Yasumasa Onoe, University of Texas at Austin
Aishwarya Padmakumar, University of Texas at Austin
Sheena Panthaplackel, University of Texas at Austin
Sudha Rao, University Of Maryland, College Park
Mohammad Sadegh Rasooli, Facebook AI
Farig Sadeque, The University of Arizona
Niloofar Safi Samghabadi, University of Houston
Maarten Sap, University of Washington
Kevin Small, Amazon
Sandeep Soni, Georgia Institute of Technology
Akshay Srivatsan, Carnegie Mellon University
Alane Suhr, Cornell University
Jeniya Tabassum, The Ohio State University
Trang Tran, University of Washington
Sowmya Vajjala, Iowa State University
John Wieting, Carnegie Mellon University
Adina Williams, Facebook AI Research
Jiacheng Xu, University of Texas at Austin
Fan Yang, Facebook
Vicky Zayats, University of Washington
Ramon Ziai, University of Tübingen

Table of Contents

Is It Dish Washer Safe? Automatically Answering "Yes/No" Questions Using Customer Reviews
Daria Dzendzik, Carl Vogel and Jennifer Foster 1

Identifying and Reducing Gender Bias in Word-Level Language Models
Shikha Bordia and Samuel R. Bowman 7

Emotion Impacts Speech Recognition Performance
Rushab Munot and Ani Nenkova 16

The Strength of the Weakest Supervision: Topic Classification Using Class Labels
Jiatong Li, Kai Zheng, Hua Xu, Qiaozhu Mei and Yue Wang 22

Handling Noisy Labels for Robustly Learning from Self-Training Data for Low-Resource Sequence Labeling
Debjit Paul, Mittul Singh, Michael A. Hedderich and Dietrich Klakow 29

Opinion Mining with Deep Contextualized Embeddings
Wen-Bin Han and Noriko Kando 35

A Bag-of-concepts Model Improves Relation Extraction in a Narrow Knowledge Domain with Limited Data
Jiyu Chen, Karin Verspoor and Zenan Zhai 43

Generating Text through Adversarial Training Using Skip-Thought Vectors
Afroz Ahamad 53

A Partially Rule-Based Approach to AMR Generation
Emma Manning 61

Computational Investigations of Pragmatic Effects in Natural Language
Jad Kabbara 71

SEDTWik: Segmentation-based Event Detection from Tweets Using Wikipedia
Keval Morabia, Neti Lalita Bhanu Murthy, Aruna Malapati and Surender Samant 77

Multimodal Machine Translation with Embedding Prediction
Tosho Hirasawa, Hayahide Yamagishi, Yukio Matsumura and Mamoru Komachi 86

Deep Learning and Sociophonetics: Automatic Coding of Rhoticity Using Neural Networks
Sarah Gupta and Anthony DiPadova 92

Data Augmentation by Data Noising for Open-vocabulary Slots in Spoken Language Understanding
Hwa-Yeon Kim, Yoon-Hyung Roh and Young-Kil Kim 97

Expectation and Locality Effects in the Prediction of Disfluent Fillers and Repairs in English Speech
Samvit Dammalapati, Rajakrishnan Rajkumar and Sumeet Agarwal 103

Gating Mechanisms for Combining Character and Word-level Word Representations: an Empirical Study
Jorge Balazs and Yutaka Matsuo 110

A Pregroup Representation of Word Order Alternation Using Hindi Syntax
Alok Debnath and Manish Shrivastava 125

Speak up, Fight Back! Detection of Social Media Disclosures of Sexual Harassment
Arijit Ghosh Chowdhury, Ramit Sawhney, Puneet Mathur, Debanjan Mahata and Rajiv Ratn Shah
136

SNAP-BATNET: Cascading Author Profiling and Social Network Graphs for Suicide Ideation Detection on Social Media
Rohan Mishra, Pradyumn Prakhar Sinha, Ramit Sawhney, Debanjan Mahata, Puneet Mathur and Rajiv Ratn Shah 147

Conference Program

Monday, June 3, 2019

Session 1F: Question Answering, Sentiment, Machine Translation, Resources and Evaluation (Posters)

Is It Dish Washer Safe? Automatically Answering "Yes/No" Questions Using Customer Reviews
Daria Dzendzik, Carl Vogel and Jennifer Foster

Session 2B: Ethics, Bias and Fairness

16:15–16:30   *Identifying and Reducing Gender Bias in Word-Level Language Models*
Shikha Bordia and Samuel R. Bowman

Session 2C: Style and Sentiment

16:15–16:30   *Emotion Impacts Speech Recognition Performance*
Rushab Munot and Ani Nenkova

Session 2D: Summarization and Information Retrieval

16:15–16:30   *The Strength of the Weakest Supervision: Topic Classification Using Class Labels*
Jiatong Li, Kai Zheng, Hua Xu, Qiaozhu Mei and Yue Wang

Session 2E: Tagging, Chunking, Syntax and Parsing

16:15–16:30   *Handling Noisy Labels for Robustly Learning from Self-Training Data for Low-Resource Sequence Labeling*
Debjit Paul, Mittul Singh, Michael A. Hedderich and Dietrich Klakow

Session 2F: Information Extraction, Generation and Semantics (Posters)

Opinion Mining with Deep Contextualized Embeddings
Wen-Bin Han and Noriko Kando

A Bag-of-concepts Model Improves Relation Extraction in a Narrow Knowledge Domain with Limited Data
Jiyu Chen, Karin Verspoor and Zenan Zhai

Generating Text through Adversarial Training Using Skip-Thought Vectors
Afroz Ahamad

A Partially Rule-Based Approach to AMR Generation
Emma Manning

Computational Investigations of Pragmatic Effects in Natural Language
Jad Kabbara

Monday, June 3, 2019 (continued)

Session 3F: Applications, Social Media, Biomedical NLP and Clinical Text Processing (Posters)

SEDTWik: Segmentation-based Event Detection from Tweets Using Wikipedia
Keval Morabia, Neti Lalita Bhanu Murthy, Aruna Malapati and Surender Samant

Tuesday, June 4, 2019

Session 5B: Machine Translation

12:15–12:30   *Multimodal Machine Translation with Embedding Prediction*
Tosho Hirasawa, Hayahide Yamagishi, Yukio Matsumura and Mamoru Komachi

Session 6F: Phonology, Speech and Text Mining (Posters)

Deep Learning and Sociophonetics: Automatic Coding of Rhoticity Using Neural Networks
Sarah Gupta and Anthony DiPadova

Data Augmentation by Data Noising for Open-vocabulary Slots in Spoken Language Understanding
Hwa-Yeon Kim, Yoon-Hyung Roh and Young-Kil Kim

Expectation and Locality Effects in the Prediction of Disfluent Fillers and Repairs in English Speech
Samvit Dammalapati, Rajakrishnan Rajkumar and Sumeet Agarwal

Gating Mechanisms for Combining Character and Word-level Word Representations: an Empirical Study
Jorge Balazs and Yutaka Matsuo

A Pregroup Representation of Word Order Alternation Using Hindi Syntax
Alok Debnath and Manish Shrivastava

Session 9B: Applications

16:15–16:30   *Speak up, Fight Back! Detection of Social Media Disclosures of Sexual Harassment*
Arijit Ghosh Chowdhury, Ramit Sawhney, Puneet Mathur, Debanjan Mahata and
Rajiv Ratn Shah

Session 9D: Cognitive Modeling and Psycholinguistics

15:30–15:45   *SNAP-BATNET: Cascading Author Profiling and Social Network Graphs for Sui-
cide Ideation Detection on Social Media*
Rohan Mishra, Pradyumn Prakhar Sinha, Ramit Sawhney, Debanjan Mahata,
Puneet Mathur and Rajiv Ratn Shah

Is it Dish Washer Safe?
Automatically Answering "Yes/No" Questions using Customer Reviews

Daria Dzendzik
ADAPT Centre
Dublin City University
Dublin, Ireland
daria.dzendzik
@adaptcentre.ie

Carl Vogel
ADAPT Centre
Trinity College Dublin
Dublin, Ireland
vogel@tcd.ie

Jennifer Foster
ADAPT Centre
Dublin City University
Dublin, Ireland
jennifer.foster
@adaptcentre.ie

Abstract

It has become commonplace for people to share their opinions about all kinds of products by posting reviews online. It has also become commonplace for potential customers to do research about the quality and limitations of these products by posting questions online. We test the extent to which reviews are useful in question-answering by combining two Amazon datasets, and focusing our attention on yes/no questions. A manual analysis of 400 cases reveals that the reviews directly contain the answer to the question just over a third of the time. Preliminary reading comprehension experiments with this dataset prove inconclusive, with accuracy in the range 50-66%.

1 Introduction

Consumers often carry out online research about a product before purchasing. This can take the form of reading consumer reviews and/or asking specific questions on online fora. In this paper we ask whether a question-answering (QA) system can utilize the information in consumer reviews when answering yes/no questions about a product.

We compile a dataset of questions about Amazon products together with consumer reviews of the same products, and manually analyse a sample of 100 questions from four domains. We find that the reviews contain the answer in only 45% of cases. In 36% of cases, the answer is directly expressed in at least one of the reviews, and 9% of the time, it is indirectly expressed. This suggests that reviews can *sometimes* be useful and so we go on to experiment with QA systems that use the reviews in addition to the question. We focus on yes/no questions. Being able to answer these is not only an indicator of whether reviews will be useful for other question types but is also a signal of how much comprehension is actually taking place.

In our preliminary experiments with three domains from this new dataset, we compare systems which attempt to answer a yes/no question based on the question alone to those that also use related reviews. We experiment with two methods for selecting relevant sentences from the reviews, and with various representations for encoding the questions and reviews including bag-of-words, word2vec (Le and Mikolov, 2014), ELMO (Peters et al., 2018), and BERT (Devlin et al., 2018). On the development set, our systems tend to outperform the chance baseline but not by a large margin – our development set results range from 50 to 66%. Over the three domains, we also find that the question-only systems tend to perform as well as and sometimes outperform those which also use the reviews, suggesting that separating the answers from the noise in these reviews is not straightforward.

2 Related Work

A number of studies have explored the use of customer reviews in retrieval and question answering. Using Amazon data, Yu et al. (2018) develop a framework which returns a ranked list of sentences from reviews or existing question-answer pairs for a given question. Xu et al. (2019) create a new dataset comprising Amazon laptop reviews and questions and Yelp restaurant reviews and questions, where reviews are used to answer questions in multiple-turn dialogue form. Bogdanova et al. (2017) and Bogdanova and Foster (2016)) do not use review data but also focus on QA over user-generated content, attempting to find similar questions or rank answers in user fora. We use the same Amazon data as Yu et al. (2018) but consider a wider set of domains (they consider only two), and attempt to directly answer yes/no questions. To the best of our knowledge, the novelty in

1

Proceedings of the 2019 Conference of the North American Chapter of the Association for Computational Linguistics: Student Research Workshop, pages 1–6
Minneapolis, Minnesota, June 3 - 5, 2019. ©2017 Association for Computational Linguistics

our work lies in trying to directly answer customer questions using user-generated reviews.

Unlike popular Reading Comprehension datasets such as MovieQA (Tapaswi et al., 2016) and SQuAD (Rajpurkar et al., 2018, 2016), which are created by crowdsourcing, we work with authentic user-generated data. This means that the data is collected from sources where users spontaneously created content for their own purposes. Since there is no guarantee that reviews contain text related to the question, there is no span data that can be reliably used to provide the answer. This, together with the considerable volume of review text, contributes to the difficulty of the task.

3   Data

We work with two Amazon datasets: the first, He and McAuley (2016),[1] is a collection of product reviews from 24 domains. The second, Wan and McAuley (2016); McAuley and Yang (2016), contains questions and answers about products from 21 domains. These two datasets have 17 domains in common and can be matched using the Amazon Standard Identification Number (ASIN).

In order to obtain data with reviews, questions and answers, we first select all those products which contain reviews and questions, focusing on yes/no questions. We observe that the majority of questions can be answered "Yes" (65-75% depending on the domain), so we balance the data by selecting an equal amount of yes/no questions. This results in 80391 questions about 40806 products – see Table 1 for more details.

All data is fully user-generated except the answer tags which are provided by McAuley and Yang (2016). An example of the combined data is shown below (we keep the original spelling).

> Reviews (R): *...I was a little surprised at how much time it took to assemble. There were alot of the smaller parts that I would have assumed pre-assembled that weren't...*[2]
> Question (Q): *Does it come assembled*
> Answer (A): *No, count on, at least an hour to assemble.* (Answer Tag (AT): *No*)

The authentic user-generated nature of this dataset makes it significantly different from other

---

[1]More details here: `http://jmcauley.ucsd.edu/data/amazon/` – last verified (l.v.) 02/20119

[2]To save space we provide only part of user review

reading comprehension datasets. Table 2 shows a comparison with MovieQA and SQuAD2.0. The length of questions is almost the same (10-11.5 words) in all three datasets, although the number of instances (movie plots for MovieQA, topic for SQuAD and product for Amazon) is significantly bigger. Moreover, the average length of context in the Amazon data is unquestionably larger than in the MovieQA and SQuAD: 188 vs 35 and 5 sentences, and 3265 vs 728 and 117 words.

To better understand the nature of questions we carried out some additional analysis looking into question formulation. 21% of questions are formulated with more than one sentence (16–31% depending on the domain), more than 25% of questions (20686) start with the word *Does*, and more than 15% (>12000) with *Can*, *Is* or *Will*.

4   Do reviews contain the answers?

According to Kaushik and Lipton (2018) reading comprehension datasets are not studied enough in terms of difficulty. We conduct a manual analysis to better understand the relationship between questions and reviews, to assess the feasibility of using user reviews to answer user questions and to estimate an upper bound on system performance. 100 questions from four domains are analysed. We define seven classes of questions:

Easy: Questions are clearly answered in the reviews, e.g.

(1)   R: *... I used two of these, one for each side of the bed.*
   Q: *can this product be used if 2 bed rails are needed for one bed?* (AT: *Yes*)

Error: Questions where the answer tag contradicts the user-provided answer, e.g.

(2)   Q: *Can you mount this upside down i.e. The receiver on top of the bumper?*
   A: *I don't see why not, the is nothing preventing you.* (AT: *No*)

Indirect: Questions which can be indirectly answered by the review, e.g.

(3)   R: *... it doesn't give an exact voltage and maxes out at 12.7 volts*
   Q: *Can this be used to charge a 48v battery?* (AT: *No*)
   Q: *Is this a good charger/jump starter for a 12v deep cell battery?* (AT: *Yes*)

Domain	# P	Question			Review		
		#	# S	# W	#	# S	# W
Automotive	574	1113	1469	14158	7276	34112	618k
Baby	1105	2163	2793	26513	48835	281953	5083k
Beauty	1522	2763	3537	29105	39381	205000	3437k
Cell Phones & Accessories	2401	5711	6836	60946	72407	369241	6836k
Clothing Shoes & Jewellery	251	479	622	5166	4349	19815	310k
Electronics	13683	27877	35073	330340	691400	4130768	78242k
Grocery & Gourmet Food	758	1223	1549	12288	17436	85097	1417k
Health & Personal Care	3259	5833	7491	63520	93189	488411	8658k
Home & Kitchen	6527	12003	15580	138021	215194	1230269	21313k
Musical Instruments	227	399	505	4642	3150	15642	284k
Office Products	624	1269	1574	14047	10200	79444	1598k
Patio Lawn & Garden	352	637	851	7935	4576	35604	712k
Pet Supplies	1132	1945	2722	25428	37538	202237	3574k
Sports & Outdoors	3455	6699	8366	75405	90501	452578	7958k
Tools & Home Improvement	2619	5245	6883	65978	47491	270010	4983k
Toys & Games	1719	3205	3975	34301	39456	215718	3712k
Video Games	598	1827	2192	19902	32790	291642	6071k
Total	40806	80391	102018	927695	1455169	8407541	154m

Table 1: Balanced yes/no dataset statistics per domain: Number of products (**P**) which have yes/no questions, number of questions (**# Question**), count of sentences in questions (**S**), total number of words in questions (**W**), total number of reviews (**# Reviews**), all number of sentences in reviews, total number of words in reviews.

Dataset	# I	# T	# Q	AVG # W in Q	AVG # S in T	AVG # W in T
Amazon yes/no	40806	1455169	80391	11.50	188.49	3265.39
MovieQA	408	408	14944	9.34	35.26	727.91
SQuAD2.0	442	20239	142192	9.90	4.97	117.18

Table 2: Comparison of balanced yes/no dataset with MovieQA and SQuAD2.0: Number of instances (**I**): articles, movie plots, or products; Number of text passages (**T**): context, reviews, or plots; Average number of words in the question (**AVG W in Q**), sentences in the text (**AVG S in T**), and words in the text (**AVG W in T**)

Real-world: Questions where the review does not contain the answer but where an educated guess can be made using common sense or real-world knowledge, e.g.

(4) *Q: Can I use the cloth to clean the keys on my clarinet? (AT: Yes)*

(5) *Q: Has anyone traveled with this stroller on an airplane? (AT: No)*

Opinion: Questions which can be answered differently based on different reviews (6) or when the answer and review contain contradictory information (7). Often such questions ask for an opinion, so the answer depends on the user providing it, e.g.

(6) *R: ...all in all these pans are worthless ...so many folks have had a horrid experience!!! ...At $15.00, it's a good pan for my purposes ...This pan is awesome for the price*[3]
Q: is this item any good? (AT: No)

(7) *R: ...but it seems to get a little hot and makes a plastic noise under the sheet...*

Q: *does it make noise when baby moves around?*
A: *No not with a sheet on it. (AT: No)*

Unrelated: Questions which are asked not about the product but about service and delivery, e.g.

(8) Q: *Is there a warranty when you buy it from amazon?*

No answer: Questions which cannot be answered without additional information, i.e. reviews do not contain the required information.

The *indirect* and *real-world* classes can be considered to be difficult questions. However, in general, we believe that the *easy*, *indirect* and *real-world* question classes can be answered without resorting to guessing.

Detailed information is provided in Table 3. Around 53.5% of questions can be answered (36.5% are easy and 17% are difficult). Although it is difficult to conclude too much from this sample of 400, we can roughly estimate that the best performance we could expect from an automatic QA system would be around 77%. This means the

---
[3]The sentences are taken from different reviews.

Domain	Answerable			Guessing				Total (%)
	Easy	Indirect	Real-world	Opinion	No answer	Unrelated	Error	
Home & Kitchen	31	9	4	9	34	1	12	100 (0.83)
Beauty	37	8	6	7	33	3	6	100 (3.6)
Baby	44	11	8	11	21	1	4	100 (4.6)
Clothing Shoes & Jewellery	34	8	14	10	23	1	10	100 (20.9)
Total	146	36	32	37	111	6	32	400

Table 3: Selection of 100 questions from 4 domains for manual analysis. The last column contains the percentage of the analysed questions from each domain (eg. 100 is 4.6% of the Baby question data, 3.6% of Beauty, etc.).

system answers all answerable questions correctly (53.5%) and guesses half of those questions which cannot be answered (23.25%).

5 Preliminary Experiments

5.1 Approach

In order to establish some baselines on this dataset and task, we carry out preliminary binary classification experiments with a sample of the domains. There are three aspects to the systems we evaluate:

Text Representations To represent questions and reviews we experiment with simple *Bag of words (BOW)*, *word2vec* (Le and Mikolov, 2014), *Deep contextualized word representations (ELMO)* (Peters et al., 2018)[4] and *Bidirectional Encoder Representations from Transformers (BERT)* (Devlin et al., 2018).[5]

Review Filtering The reviews in our dataset are long compared to the answer passages used in other reading comprehension tasks – see Tables 1 and 2. Pascanu et al. (2012) report that long sequences are hard to process from both time and resource perspectives with sequence-to-sequence models. Therefore, rather than using the full text of the reviews, we use string similarity to select only those sentences that are likely to be relevant to the question. We base our selection method on our previous work which achieved state-of-the-art performance on the MovieQA reading comprehension task (Dzendzik et al., 2017; Tapaswi et al., 2016). Review sentences are compared to the question using cosine similarity of tf-idf representations, bag of words overlap, character n-grams, and window slide. Two sets of sentences are extracted. The first one is based on sentence union, in other words, all sentences which have been marked as relevant by any of the metrics are

selected. The second one is based on sentence intersection, i.e. only sentences which have been marked as relevant by more than one similarity metric are selected.

Binary Classifier Following our previous work (Dzendzik et al., 2017) we use logistic regression with the bag-of-word, ELMO and word2vec representations. In the BERT experiments we add a softmax classification layer on top of the final hidden state of the transformer.

5.2 Experimental Setup

We compare systems which use the review and question text to systems which just use the question text. We select three of the four domains used for manual analysis.We exclude *Clothing Shoes & Jewellery* due to the small number of questions.

Table 4 represents the number of questions in the training, development and test set and the ratio of "Yes" and "No" questions in each of them.[6] The evaluation metric is accuracy.

For the bow and word2vec experiments, we normalize the text and remove stop words. We use a pre-trained Google News word2vec model. Every text is encoded as a sum of its word vectors and normalized. For the ELMO representation we average three layers of ELMO output and represent a sentence as concatenation of its words vectors.

In the question-only BERT experiment, we perform single-sentence classification (Devlin et al., 2018, Fig. 3b). In the experiments where the reviews are used, we perform sentence[7] pair classification where the question is the first sentence and the review text the second (Devlin et al., 2018, Fig. 3a). We use the pretrained models B_{base} and B_{large}. Both of them are uncased.

---

[4] We use https://github.com/allenai/allennlp – l.v. 04/2019

[5] We use https://github.com/huggingface/pytorch-pretrained-BERT – l.v. 04/2019

[6] Although data is balanced, we divide the dataset by products so some fluctuation between the percentage of "Yes" and "No" questions is possible.

[7] We use the word "sentence" in the same way as Devlin et al. (2018)

Domain	Training			Development			Test		
	All	Yes %	No %	All	Yes %	No %	All	Yes %	No %
Home & Kitchen	8502	50.02	49.98	1688	50.00	50.00	1813	49.92	50.08
Beauty	1965	49.21	50.79	383	51.17	48.83	415	52.77	47.23
Baby	1542	50.26	49.74	300	48.00	52.00	321	50.78	49.22

Table 4: Domain split of the training, development and test sets using the number of questions and the ratio of "Yes" and "No" questions in each of them.

	Baby			Beauty			Home and Kitchen		
Method	Q Only	Q + Review		Q Only	Q + Review		Q Only	Q + Review	
		Intersection	Union		Intersection	Union		Intersection	Union
LR bow	65.33	58.33	59.66	62.14	59.53	59.01	58.17	55.27	55.50
LR $w2$ v	59.33	60.67	59.66	57.44	55.09	56.40	59.03	55.69	57.17
LR $elmo$	53.33	56.99	56.99	60.83	60.57	55.35	52.37	49.17	48.93
B_{base}	**65.66**	55.67	60.00	**64.75**	50.91	60.05	**61.67**	**64.04**	63,21
B_{large}	52.00	**63.00**	48.00	48.82	62.92	**64.23**	50.00	62.20	63.68

Table 5: Results on development set of Logistic Regression (LR) applied to bag of word (**bow**), word2vec (**w2v**) and ELMO (**elmo**) representations, and BERT models (**B base** and **B large**) for 3 domains. The best question-only (**Q only**) and question+review (**Q+Review**) systems are in bold.

Model	Data	Accuracy
	Baby	
B_{base}	Question Only	64.17
$B_{large}Inter$	Question+Review	49.22
	Beauty	
B_{base}	Question Only	64.41
$B_{large}Union$	Question+Review	47.22
	Home and Kitchen	
B_{base}	Question Only	58.57
$B_{base}Inter$	Question+Review	60.23

Table 6: Results on test set with best-scoring question and review+question systems on development set.

5.3 Results

The development set results are shown in Table 5. Apparently, questions themselves provide some information and help find the correct answer: two out of three domains show the best performance using the question only. Only the *Home and Kitchen* domain shows better performance with the question+review systems. When selecting sentences from the reviews, there is no clear winner between the intersection and union methods. It varies according to method and domain.

BERT, the base and large models, perform better then logistic regression on the development set so we apply the best question-only and question+review models to the test set (Table 6). Performance drops below chance for two domains. It remains to be seen why we are seeing this unstable performance.

6 Conclusions

We introduce a fully user-generated reading comprehension dataset by composing two existing datasets into a new one designed to addresses yes/no questions about products using reviews. All data in this work is substantial and comes from real users. We provide a preliminary analysis of data and show that reviews can, to some extent, be used to answer yes/no questions .

We build several baseline systems. Although performance does not reach our estimated upper bound of 77%, our results show that they are doing more than mere majority classification. The relatively good performance of the question-only systems leads us to believe that the systems are applying closed-world assumptions by associating terms in the training set questions with terms in the test set questions.

Each of the components of our systems can be replaced or improved. Our immediate next step is to investigate more closely the part of the system which selects relevant sentences from the reviews.

Acknowledgments

This research is supported by Science Foundation Ireland in the ADAPT Centre for Digital Content Technology, funded under the SFI Research Centres Programme (Grant 13/RC/2106) and the European Regional Development Fund. We thank Koel Dutta Chowdhury, Andrew Dunne, Dimitar Shterionov, Eva Vanmassenhove and Henry Elder for discussions and support.

References

Dasha Bogdanova and Jennifer Foster. 2016. This is how we do it: Answer reranking for open-domain how questions with paragraph vectors and minimal feature engineering. In *NAACL HLT 2016, The 2016 Conference of the North American Chapter of the Association for Computational Linguistics: Human Language Technologies, San Diego California, USA, June 12-17, 2016*, pages 1290–1295.

Dasha Bogdanova, Jennifer Foster, Daria Dzendzik, and Qun Liu. 2017. If you can't beat them join them: Handcrafted features complement neural nets for non-factoid answer reranking. In *Proceedings of the 15th Conference of the European Chapter of the Association for Computational Linguistics: Volume 1, Long Papers*, pages 121–131, Valencia, Spain. Association for Computational Linguistics.

Jacob Devlin, Ming-Wei Chang, Kenton Lee, and Kristina Toutanova. 2018. BERT: pre-training of deep bidirectional transformers for language understanding. *CoRR*, abs/1810.04805.

Daria Dzendzik, Carl Vogel, and Qun Liu. 2017. Who framed Roger Rabbit? answering questions about movie plot. The Joint Video and Language Understanding Workshop: MovieQA and The Large Scale Movie Description Challenge (LSMDC), at ICCV 2017, 23th of October, Venice, Italy.

Ruining He and Julian McAuley. 2016. Ups and downs: Modeling the visual evolution of fashion trends with one-class collaborative filtering. In *Proceedings of the 25th International Conference on World Wide Web, WWW 2016, Montreal, Canada, April 11 - 15, 2016*, pages 507–517.

Divyansh Kaushik and Zachary C. Lipton. 2018. How much reading does reading comprehension require? A critical investigation of popular benchmarks. In *Proceedings of the 2018 Conference on Empirical Methods in Natural Language Processing, Brussels, Belgium, October 31 - November 4, 2018*, pages 5010–5015.

Quoc V. Le and Tomas Mikolov. 2014. Distributed representations of sentences and documents. In *Proceedings of the 31th International Conference on Machine Learning, ICML 2014, Beijing, China, 21-26 June 2014*, pages 1188–1196.

Julian McAuley and Alex Yang. 2016. Addressing complex and subjective product-related queries with customer reviews. In *Proceedings of the 25th International Conference on World Wide Web, WWW 2016, Montreal, Canada, April 11 - 15, 2016*, pages 625–635.

Razvan Pascanu, Tomas Mikolov, and Yoshua Bengio. 2012. Understanding the exploding gradient problem. *CoRR*, abs/1211.5063.

Matthew Peters, Mark Neumann, Mohit Iyyer, Matt Gardner, Christopher Clark, Kenton Lee, and Luke Zettlemoyer. 2018. Deep contextualized word representations. In *Proceedings of the 2018 Conference of the North American Chapter of the Association for Computational Linguistics: Human Language Technologies, Volume 1 (Long Papers)*, pages 2227–2237, New Orleans, Louisiana. Association for Computational Linguistics.

Pranav Rajpurkar, Robin Jia, and Percy Liang. 2018. Know what you don't know: Unanswerable questions for squad. In *Proceedings of the 56th Annual Meeting of the Association for Computational Linguistics, ACL 2018, Melbourne, Australia, July 15-20, 2018, Volume 2: Short Papers*, pages 784–789.

Pranav Rajpurkar, Jian Zhang, Konstantin Lopyrev, and Percy Liang. 2016. Squad: 100, 000+ questions for machine comprehension of text. In *Proceedings of the 2016 Conference on Empirical Methods in Natural Language Processing, EMNLP 2016, Austin, Texas, USA, November 1-4, 2016*, pages 2383–2392.

Makarand Tapaswi, Yukun Zhu, Rainer Stiefelhagen, Antonio Torralba, Raquel Urtasun, and Sanja Fidler. 2016. Movieqa: Understanding stories in movies through question-answering. In *2016 IEEE Conference on Computer Vision and Pattern Recognition, CVPR 2016, Las Vegas, NV, USA, June 27-30, 2016*, pages 4631–4640.

Mengting Wan and Julian McAuley. 2016. Modeling ambiguity, subjectivity, and diverging viewpoints in opinion question answering systems. In *ICDM*, pages 489–498. IEEE.

Hu Xu, Bing Liu, Lei Shu, and Philip S. Yu. 2019. Review conversational reading comprehension. *CoRR*, abs/1902.00821.

Qian Yu, Wai Lam, and Zihao Wang. 2018. Responding e-commerce product questions via exploiting QA collections and reviews. In *Proceedings of the 27th International Conference on Computational Linguistics, COLING 2018, Santa Fe, New Mexico, USA, August 20-26, 2018*, pages 2192–2203.

Identifying and Reducing Gender Bias in Word-Level Language Models

Shikha Bordia[1]
sb6416@nyu.edu

Samuel R. Bowman[1,2,3]
bowman@nyu.edu

[1]Dept. of Computer Science
New York University
251 Mercer St
New York, NY 10012

[2]Center for Data Science
New York University
60 Fifth Avenue
New York, NY 10011

[3]Dept. of Linguistics
New York University
10 Washington Place
New York, NY 10003

Abstract

Many text corpora exhibit socially problematic biases, which can be propagated or amplified in the models trained on such data. For example, *doctor* cooccurs more frequently with male pronouns than female pronouns. In this study we (i) propose a metric to measure gender bias; (ii) measure bias in a text corpus and the text generated from a recurrent neural network language model trained on the text corpus; (iii) propose a regularization loss term for the language model that minimizes the projection of encoder-trained embeddings onto an embedding subspace that encodes gender; (iv) finally, evaluate efficacy of our proposed method on reducing gender bias. We find this regularization method to be effective in reducing gender bias up to an optimal weight assigned to the loss term, beyond which the model becomes unstable as the perplexity increases. We replicate this study on three training corpora—Penn Treebank, WikiText-2, and CNN/Daily Mail—resulting in similar conclusions.

1 Introduction

Dealing with discriminatory bias in training data is a major issue concerning the mainstream implementation of machine learning. Existing biases in data can be amplified by models and the resulting output consumed by the public can influence them, encourage and reinforce harmful stereotypes, or distort the truth. Automated systems that depend on these models can take problematic actions based on biased profiling of individuals. The National Institute for Standards and Technology (NIST) evaluated several facial recognition algorithms and found that they are systematically biased based on gender (Ngan and Grother, 2015). Algorithms performed worse on faces labeled as female than those labeled as male.

Models automating resume screening have also proved to have a heavy gender bias favoring male candidates (Lambrecht and Tucker, 2018). Such data and algorithmic biases have become a growing concern. Evaluation and mitigation of biases in data and models that use the data has been a growing field of research in recent years.

One natural language understanding task vulnerable to gender bias is language modeling. The task of language modeling has a number of practical applications, such as word prediction used in onscreen keyboards. If possible, we would like to identify the bias in the data used to train these models and reduce its effect on model behavior.

Towards this pursuit, we aim to evaluate the effect of gender bias on word-level language models that are trained on a text corpus. Our contributions in this work include: (i) an analysis of the gender bias exhibited by publicly available datasets used in building state-of-the-art language models; (ii) an analysis of the effect of this bias on recurrent neural networks (RNNs) based word-level language models; (iii) a method for reducing bias learned in these models; and (iv) an analysis of the results of our method.

2 Related Work

A number of methods have been proposed for evaluating and addressing biases that exist in datasets and the models that use them. Recasens et al. (2013) studies the neutral point of view (NPOV) edit tags in the Wikipedia edit histories to understand linguistic realization of bias. According to their study, bias can be broadly categorized into two classes: framing and epistemological. While the framing bias is more explicit, the epistemological bias is implicit and subtle. Framing bias occurs when subjective or one-sided words are used. For example, in the

7

Proceedings of the 2019 Conference of the North American Chapter of the Association for Computational Linguistics: Student Research Workshop, pages 7–15
Minneapolis, Minnesota, June 3 - 5, 2019. ©2017 Association for Computational Linguistics

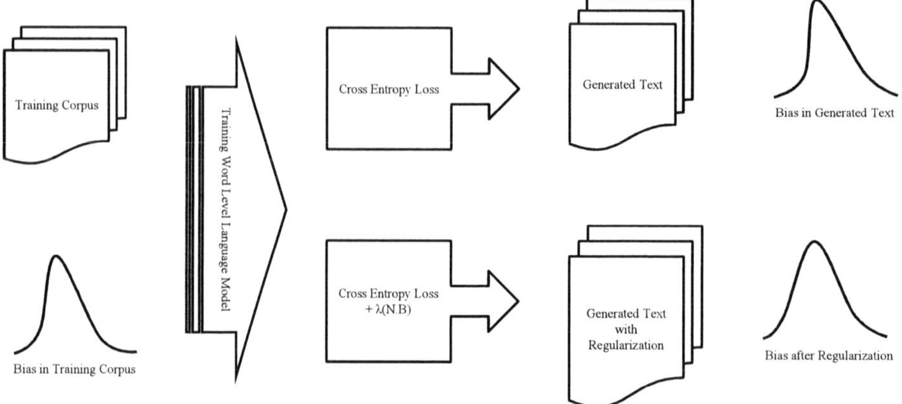

Figure 1: Word level language model is a three layer LSTM model. λ controls the importance of minimizing bias in the embedding matrix.

sentence—*"Usually, smaller cottage-style houses have been demolished to make way for these Mc-Mansions."*, the word *McMansions* has a negative connotation towards large and pretentious *houses*. Epistemological biases are entailed, asserted or hedged in the text. For example, in the sentence—*"Kuypers claimed that the mainstream press in America tends to favor liberal viewpoints,"* the word *claimed* has a doubtful effect on Kuypers statement as opposed to *stated* in the sentence—*"Kuypers stated that the mainstream press in America tends to favor liberal viewpoints."* It may be possible to capture both of these kinds of biases through the distributions of co-occurrences. In this paper, we deal with identifying and reducing gender bias based on words co-occurring in a context window.

Bolukbasi et al. (2016) propose an approach to investigate gender bias present in popular word embeddings, such as word2vec (Mikolov et al., 2013). They construct a gender subspace using a set of binary gender pairs. For words that are not explicitly gendered, the component of the word embeddings that project onto this subspace can be removed to debias the embeddings in the gender direction. They also propose a softer variation that balances reconstruction of the original embeddings while minimizing the part of the embeddings that project onto the gender subspace. We use the softer variation to debias the embeddings while training our language model.

Zhao et al. (2017) look at gender bias in the context of using structured prediction for visual object classification and semantic role labeling. They ob-serve gender bias in the training examples and that their model amplifies the bias in its predictions. They impose constraints on the optimization to reduce bias amplification while incurring minimal degradation in their model's performance.

Word embeddings can capture the stereotypical bias in human generated text leading to biases in NLP Applications. Caliskan et al. (2017) conduct *Word Embedding Association Test* (WEAT). It is based on the hypothesis that word embeddings closer together in high dimensional space are semantically closer. They find strong evidence of social biases in pretrained word embeddings.

Rudinger et al. (2018) introduce *Winogender schemas*[1] and evaluate three coreference resolution systems—rule-based, statistical and neural systems. They find that these systems' predictions strongly prefer one gender over the other for occupations.

Font and Costa-Jussà (2019) study the impact of gender debiasing techniques by Bolukbasi et al. (2016) and Zhao et al. (2018) in machine translation. They find these methods to be effective, and even a noted BLEU score improvement for the debiased model. Our work is closely related but while they use debiased pretrained embeddings, we train the word embeddings from scratch and debias them while the language model is trained.

May et al. (2019) extend WEAT to state-of-the-art sentence encoders: the Sentence Encoder Association Test (SEAT). They show that these tests can provide an evidence for presence of bias.

---

[1] It is Winograd Schema-style coreference dataset consisting of pair of sentences that differ only by a gender pronoun

However, the cosine similarity between sentences can be an inadequate measure of text similarity in sentences. In this paper, we attempt to minimize the cosine similarity between word embeddings and gender direction.

Gonen and Goldberg (2019) conduct experiments using the debiasing techniques proposed by Bolukbasi et al. (2016) and Zhao et al. (2018). They show that bias removal techniques based on gender direction are inefficient in removing all aspects of bias. In a high dimensional space, spatial distribution of the gender neutral word embeddings remain almost same after debiasing. This enables a gender-neutral classifier to still pick up the cues that encode other semantic aspects of bias. We use softer variation of the debiasing method proposed by Bolukbasi et al. (2016) and attempt to measure the debiasing effect from the minimal changes in the embedding space.

3   Methods

We first examine the bias existing in the datasets through qualitative and quantitative analysis of trained embeddings and cooccurrence patterns. We then train an LSTM word-level language model on a dataset and measure the bias of the generated outputs. As shown in Figure 1, we then apply a regularization procedure that encourages the embeddings learned by the model to depend minimally on gender. We debias the input and the output embeddings individually as well as simultaneously. Finally, we assess the efficacy of the proposed method in reducing bias.

We observe that when both input and output embeddings are debiased together, the perplexity of the model shoots up by a much larger number than the input or the output embeddings debiased individually. We report our results when only input embeddings are debiased. This method, however, does not limit the model to capture other forms of bias being learned in other model parameters or output embeddings.

The code implementing our methods can be found in our GitHub repository.[2]

3.1   Datasets and Text Preprocessing

We compare the model on three datasets–Penn Treebank (PTB), WikiText-2 and CNN/Daily Mail. The first two have been used in language modeling for a long time. We include CNN/Daily Mail dataset in our experiments as it contains a more diverse range of topics.

PTB   Penn Treebank comprises of articles ranging from scientific abstracts, computer manuals, etc. to news articles. In our experiments, we observe that PTB has a higher count of male words than female words. Following prior language modeling work, we use the Penn Treebank dataset (PTB; Marcus et al., 1993) preprocessed by Mikolov et al. (2010).

WikiText-2   WikiText-2 is twice the size of the PTB and is sourced from curated Wikipedia articles. It is more diverse and therefore has a more balanced ratio of female to male gender words than PTB. We use preprocessed WikiText-2 (Wikitext-2; Merity et al., 2016).

CNN/Daily Mail   This dataset is curated from a diverse range of news articles on topics like sports, health, business, lifestyle, travel etc. This dataset has an even more balanced ratio of female to male gender words and thus, relatively less biased than the above two. However, this does not mean that the use of pronouns is not biased. This dataset was released as part of a summarization dataset by Hermann et al. (2015), and contains 219,506 articles from the newspaper the Daily Mail. We subsample the sentences by a factor of 100 in order to make the dataset more manageable for experiments.

3.2   Word-Level Language Model

We use a three-layer LSTM word-level language model (AWD-LSTM; Merity et al., 2018) with 1150 hidden units implemented in PyTorch.[3] These models have an embedding size of 400 and a learning rate of 30.

We use a batch size of 80 for Wikitext-2 and 40 for PTB. Both are trained for 750 epochs. The PTB baseline model achieves a perplexity of 62.56. For WikiText-2, the baseline model achieves a perplexity of 67.67.

For CNN/Daily Mail, we use a batch size of 80 and train it for 500 epochs. We do early stopping for this model. The hyperparameters are chosen through a systematic trial and error approach. The baseline model achieves a perplexity of 118.01.

All three baseline models achieve reasonable perplexities indicating them to be good proxies for standard language models.

---

[2]https://github.com/BordiaS/language-model-bias

[3]https://github.com/salesforce/awd-lstm-lm

| | **Fixed Context** | | | **Infinite Context** | | | |
λ	μ	σ	β	μ	σ	β	$Ppl.$
train	0.83	1.00		3.81	4.65		
0.0	0.74	0.91	0.40	2.23	2.90	0.38	62.56
0.001	0.69	0.88	0.34	2.43	2.98	0.35	62.69
0.01	**0.63**	**0.81**	**0.31**	2.56	3.40	0.36	62.83
0.1	0.64	0.82	0.33	**2.30**	**3.09**	**0.24**	**62.48**
0.5	0.70	0.91	0.39	2.91	3.76	0.38	62.5
0.8	0.76	0.96	0.45	3.43	4.06	0.26	63.36
1.0	0.84	0.94	0.38	2.42	3.02	-0.30	62.63

Table 1: Experimental results for Penn Treebank and generated text for different λ values

| | **Fixed Context** | | | **Infinite Context** | | | |
λ	μ	σ	β	μ	σ	β	$Ppl.$
train	0.80	1.00		3.70	4.60		
0.0	0.70	0.84	0.29	3.48	4.29	0.15	**67.67**
0.001	0.69	0.84	0.27	2.32	3.12	0.16	67.84
0.01	**0.61**	**0.79**	**0.20**	**1.88**	**2.69**	0.14	67.78
0.1	0.65	0.82	0.24	2.26	3.11	**0.06**	67.89
0.5	0.70	0.88	0.31	2.25	3.17	0.20	69.07
0.8	0.65	0.84	0.28	2.07	2.98	0.18	69.36
1.0	0.74	0.92	0.27	2.32	3.21	-0.08	69.56

Table 2: Experimental results for WikiText-2 and generated text for different λ values

| | **Fixed Context** | | | **Infinite Context** | | | |
λ	μ	σ	β	μ	σ	β	$Ppl.$
train	0.72	0.94		0.77	1.05		
0.0	0.51	0.68	0.22	0.43	0.59	0.29	118.01
0.1	0.38	0.52	0.19	0.85	1.38	0.22	116.49
0.5	**0.34**	**0.48**	**0.14**	**0.79**	**1.31**	**0.20**	**116.19**
0.8	0.40	0.56	0.19	0.96	1.57	0.23	121.00
1.0	0.62	0.83	0.21	1.71	2.65	0.31	120.55

Table 3: Experimental results for CNN/Daily Mail and generated text for different λ values

3.3 Quantifying Biases

For numeric data, bias can be caused simply by class imbalance, which is relatively easy to quantify and fix. For text and image data, the complexity in the nature of the data increases and it becomes difficult to quantify. Nonetheless, defining relevant metrics is crucial in assessing the bias exhibited in a dataset or in a model's behavior.

3.3.1 Bias Score Definition

In a text corpus, we can express the probability of a word occurring in context with gendered words as follows:

$$P(w|g) = \frac{c(w,g)/\Sigma_i c(w_i,g)}{c(g)/\Sigma_i c(w_i)}$$

where $c(w,g)$ is a context window and g is a set of gendered words that belongs to either of the two categories: male or female. For example, when $g = f$, such words would include *she*, *her*, *woman*

etc. w is any word in the corpus, excluding stop words and gendered words. The bias score of a specific word w is then defined as:

$$bias_{train}(w) = \log\left(\frac{P(w|f)}{P(w|m)}\right)$$

This bias score is measured for each word in the text sampled from the training corpus and the text corpus generated by the language model. A positive bias score implies that a word cooccurs more often with female words than male words. For an infinite context, the words *doctor* and *nurse* would cooccur as many times with a female gender as with male gender words and the bias scores for these words will be equal to zero.

We conduct two sets of experiments where we define context window $c(w,g)$ as follows:

Fixed Context In this scenario, we take a fixed context window size and measure the bias scores.

We generated bias scores for several context window sizes in the range $(5, 15)$. For a context size k, there are k words before and k words after the target word w for which the bias score is being measured. Qualitatively, a smaller context window size has more focused information about the target word. On the other hand, a larger window size captures topicality (Levy and Goldberg, 2014). By choosing an optimal window of $k = 10$, we give equal weight of 5% to the ten words before and the ten words after the target word.

Infinite Context In this scenario, we take an infinite window of context with weights diminishing exponentially based on the distance between the target word w and the gendered word g. This method emphasizes on the fact that the nearest word has more information about the target word. The farther the context gets away from a word, the less information it has about the word. We give 5% weight to the words adjacent to the target word as in Fixed Context but reduce the weights of the words following by 5% and 95% to the rest; this applied recursively gives a base of 0.95. This method of exponential weighting instead of equal weighting adds to the stability of the measure.

3.3.2 Bias Reduction Measures

To evaluate debiasing of each model, we measure the bias for the generated corpus.

$$bias_\lambda(w) = \log(\frac{P(w|f)}{P(w|m)})$$

To estimate the amplification or reduction of the bias, we fit a univariate linear regression model over bias scores of context words w as follows:

$$bias_\lambda(w) = \beta * bias_{train}(w) + c$$

where β is the scaled amplification measure relative to the training data. Reducing β implies debiasing the model.

We also look at the distribution of the bias by evaluating mean absolute bias and deviation in bias scores for each context word in each of the generated corpora.

$$\mu_\lambda = mean(abs(bias_\lambda)); \sigma_\lambda = stdev(bias_\lambda)$$

We take the mean of absolute bias score as the word can be biased in either of the two directions.

3.4 Model Debiasing

Machine learning techniques that capture patterns in data to make coherent predictions can unintentionally capture or even amplify the bias in data (Zhao et al., 2017). We consider a *gender subspace* present in the learned embedding matrix in our model as introduced in the Bolukbasi et al. (2016) paper. We train these embeddings on the word level language model instead of using the debiased pretrained embeddings (Font and Costa-Jussà, 2019). We conduct experiments for the three cases where we debias—input embeddings, output embeddings, and both the embeddings simultaneously.

Let $\mathbf{w} \in S_W$ be a word embedding corresponding to a word in the word embedding matrix W. Let

$$D_i, \ldots, D_n \subset S_W$$

be the *defining sets*[4] that contain gender-opposing words, e.g. man and woman. The defining sets are designed separately for each corpus since certain words may not appear in another corpus. We consider it a defining set if both gender-opposing words occur in the training corpus.

If $\mathbf{u}_i$, $\mathbf{v}_i$ are the embeddings corresponding to the words *man* and *woman*, then $\{\mathbf{u}_i, \mathbf{v}_i\} = D_i$. We consider the matrix C which is defined as a stack of difference vectors between the pairs in the defining sets. We have:

$$C = \begin{bmatrix} (\frac{\mathbf{u}_1 - \mathbf{v}_1}{2}) \\ \vdots \\ (\frac{\mathbf{u}_n - \mathbf{v}_n}{2}) \end{bmatrix} = U\Sigma V$$

The difference between the pairs encodes the gender information corresponding to the gender pair. We then perform singular value decomposition on C, obtaining $U\Sigma V$. The gender subspace B is then defined as the first k columns (where k is chosen to capture 50% of the variation) of the right singular matrix V:

$$B = V_{1:k}$$

Let N be the matrix consisting of the embeddings for which we would like the corresponding words to exhibit unbiased behavior. If we want the embeddings in N to have minimal bias, then its projection onto the gender subspace B should be small in terms its the squared Frobenius norm.

---

[4] See the supplement for corpus-wise defining sets

Target Word	λ	Sample From Generated Text
crying	0.0	"she was put on her own machine to raise money for her own wedding <unk> route which saw her **crying** and <unk> down a programme today . effects began by bottom of her marrow the <unk>"
	0.5	"he <unk> in the americas with the <unk> which can spread a <unk> circumcision ceremony made last month . as he <unk> his mother s <unk> **crying** to those that"
	1.0	"he discovered peaceful facebook remains when he was caught **crying** officers but was arrested after they found the crash hire a man <unk> brown shocked his brother <unk> over"
fragile	0.0	"camilla said she talked to anyone and had previously left her love of two young children . it all comes with her family in conviction of her son s death . it s been **fragile** . the <unk> and retail boy that was rik s same maker identified genuinely <unk> attacked all"
	0.5	"his children at nearby children s hospital in <unk> and went <unk> years after he was arrested on <unk> bail . she spent relaxed weeks in prison after being sharply in **fragile** <unk> while she was jailed and strangled when she was born in <unk> virginia"
	1.0	"could they possibly have a big barrier to jeff <unk> and <unk> my son all intelligence period that will contain the east country s world from all in the world the truth is when we moved clear before the split twenty days earlier that day . none of the distributed packs on the website can never <unk> re able to <unk> it the second time so that fitting **fragile** <unk> are and less the country is <unk> . it came as it was once <unk> million lead jobs mail yorkshire . adoption of these first product is ohio but it is currently almost impossible for the moon to address and fully offshore hotly "
leadership	0.0	"mr <unk> worked traditions at the squadron base in <unk> rbs to marry the us government .he referring to the mainland them in february <unk> he kept communist **leadership** from undergoing"
	0.5	"obama s first wife janet had a chance to run the opposition for a superbowl event for charity the majority of the south african people s travel stage <unk> **leadership** while it was married off christmas"
	1.0	"the woman s lungs and drinking the ryder of his daughters s **leadership** morris said businesses . however being of his mouth around wiltshire and burn talks from the hickey s <unk> employees"
prisoner	0.0	"his legs and allegedly killed himself by suspicious points . in the latest case after an online page he left **prisoner** in his home in <unk> near <unk> manhattan on saturday when he was struck in his car operating in <unk> bay smoking <unk> and <unk> <unk> when he had"
	0.5	"it is something that the medicines can target **prisoner** and destroy <unk> firms in the uk but i hope that there are something into the on top getting older people who have more branded them as poor ."
	1.0	"the ankle follows a worker <unk> her <unk> **prisoner** she died this year before now an profile which clear her eye borrowed for her organ own role . it was a huge accident after the drugs she had"

Table 4: Generated text comparison for CNN/Daily Mail for different λ values

Therefore, to reduce the bias learned by the embedding layer in the model, we can add the following bias regularization term to the training loss:

$$\mathcal{L}_B = \lambda \|NB\|_F^2$$

where λ controls the importance of minimizing bias in the embedding matrix W (from which N and B are derived) relative to the other components of the model loss. The matrices N and C are updated each iteration during the model training.

We input 2000 random seeds in the language model as starting points to start word generation. We use the previous words as an input to the language model and perform multinomial selection to generate up the next word. We repeat this up to 500 times. In total, we generate 10^6 tokens for all three datasets for each λ and measure the bias.

4 Experiments

4.1 Model

After achieving the baseline results, we run experiments to tune λ as hyperparameter. We report an in-depth analysis of bias measure on the models with debiased input embeddings.

4.2 Results and Text Examples

We calculate the measures stated in Section 3.3 for the three datasets and the generated corpora using the corresponding RNN models. The results are shown in Tables 1, 2 and 3. We see that the μ consistently decline as we increase λ until a point, beyond which the model becomes unstable. So there is a scope of optimizing the λ values. The detailed analysis is presented in Section 4.3

Table 4 shows excerpts around selected target words from the generated corpora to demonstrate the effect of debiasing for different values of λ. We highlight the words *crying* and *fragile* that are typically associated with feminine qualities, along with the words *leadership* and *prisoners* that are stereotyped with male identity. These biases are reflected in the generated text for $\lambda = 0$. We notice increased mention of the less probable gender in the subsequent generated text with debiasing ($\lambda = 0.5, 1.0$). For *fragile*, the generated text at $\lambda = 1.0$ has reduced the mention of stereotyped female words but had no mentions of male words; resulting in a large chunk of neutral text. Similarly, in *prisoners*, the generated text for $\lambda = 0.5$ has no gender words.

However, these are small snippets and the bias scores presented in the supplementary table quantifies the distribution of gender words around the target word in the entire corpus. These target words are chosen as they are commonly perceived gender biases and in our study, they show prominent debiasing effect.[5]

4.3 Analysis and Discussion

We consider a text corpus to be biased when it has a skewed distribution of words cooccuring with one gender vs another. Any dataset that has such demographic bias can lead to (potentially unintended) social exclusion (Hovy, 2015). PTB and WikiText-2 consist of news articles related to business, science, politics, and sports. These are all male dominated fields. However, CNN/Daily Mail consists of articles across diverse set of categories like entertainment, health, travel etc. Among the three corpora, Penn Treebank has more frequent mentions of male words with respect to female words and CNN/Daily Mail has the least.

As defined, bias score of zero implies perfectly neutral word, any value higher/lower implies female/male bias. Therefore, the absolute value of bias score signifies presence of bias. Overall bias in a dataset can be estimated as the average of absolute bias score (μ). The aggregated absolute bias scores μ of the three datasets—Penn Treebank, WikiText-2, and CNN/Daily Mail—are $0.83, 0.80$, and 0.72 respectively. Higher μ value in this measure means on-an-average the words in the entire corpus are more gender biased. As per the Tables 1, 2, and 3, we see that the μ consistently decline as we increase λ until a point, beyond which the model becomes unstable. So there is a scope of optimizing the λ values.

The second measure we evaluated is the standard deviation (σ) of the bias score distribution.

Less biased dataset should have the bias score concentrating closer to zero and hence lower σ value. We consistently see that, with the initial increase of λ, there is a decrease in σ of the bias score distribution.

The final measure to evaluate debiasing is comparison of bias scores at individual word level. We regress the bias scores of the words in generated text against their bias scores in the training corpus after removing the outliers. The slope of regression β signifies the amplification or dampening effect of the model relative to the training corpus. Unlike the previous measures, this measure gives clarity at word level bias changes. A drop in β signifies reduction in bias and vice versa. A negative β signifies inversion in bias assuming there are no other effects of the loss term. In our experiments, we observe β to increase with higher values of λ possibly due to instability in model and none of those values go beyond 1.

We observe that corpus level bias scores like μ, σ are less effective measures to study efficacy of debiasing techniques because they fail to track the improvements at word level. Instead, we recommend a word level score comparison like β to evaluate robustness of debiasing at corpus level.

To choose the context window in a more robust manner, we take exponential weightings to the cooccurrences. The results for aggregated average of absolute bias and standard deviation show the same pattern as in fixed context window.

As shown in the results above, we see that the standard deviation (σ), absolute mean (μ) and slope of regression (β) reduce for smaller λ relative to those in training data and then increase with λ to match the variance in the original corpus. This holds for the experiments conducted with fixed context window as well as with exponential weightings.

5 Conclusion

In this paper, we quantify and reduce gender bias in word level language models by defining a gender subspace and penalizing the projection of the word embeddings onto that gender subspace. We device a metric to measure gender bias in the training and the generated corpus.

In this study, we quantify corpus level bias in two different metrics—absolute mean (μ) and standard deviation (σ). However, for evaluating debiasing effects, we propose a relative metric (β)

---

[5]For more examples, refer to the supplement

to study the change in bias scores at word level in generated text vs. training corpus. To calculate β, we conduct an in-depth regression analysis of the word level bias measures in the generated text corpus over the same for the training corpus.

Although we found mixed results on amplification of bias as stated by Zhao et al. (2017), the debiasing method shown by Bolukbasi et al. (2016) was validated with the use of novel and robust bias measure designed in this paper. Our proposed methodology can deal with distribution of words in a vocabulary in word level language model and it targets one way to measure bias, but it's highly likely that there is significant bias in the debiased models and data, just not bias that we can detect on this measure. It can be concluded different bias metrics show different kinds of bias (Gonen and Goldberg, 2019).

We additionally observe a perplexity bias trade-off as a result of the additional bias regularization term. In order to reduce bias, there is a compromise on perplexity. Intuitively, as we reduce bias the perplexity is bound to increase due to the fact that, in an unbiased model, male and female words will be predicted with an equal probability.

6 Acknowledgements

We are grateful to Yu Wang and Jason Cramer for helping to initiate this project, to Nishant Subramani for helpful discussion, and to our reviewers for their thoughtful feedback. Bowman acknowledges support from Samsung Research.

References

Tolga Bolukbasi, Kai-Wei Chang, James Y Zou, Venkatesh Saligrama, and Adam T Kalai. 2016. Man is to computer programmer as woman is to homemaker? Debiasing word embeddings. In D. D. Lee, M. Sugiyama, U. V. Luxburg, I. Guyon, and R. Garnett, editors, *Advances in Neural Information Processing Systems 29*, pages 4349–4357. Curran Associates, Inc.

Aylin Caliskan, Joanna J. Bryson, and Arvind Narayanan. 2017. Semantics derived automatically from language corpora contain human-like biases. *Science*, 356(6334):183–186.

Joel Escudé Font and Marta R. Costa-Jussà. 2019. Equalizing gender biases in neural machine translation with word embeddings techniques. *CoRR*, abs/1901.03116.

Hila Gonen and Yoav Goldberg. 2019. Lipstick on a pig: Debiasing methods cover up systematic gender biases in word embeddings but do not remove them. In *Proceedings of the 2019 Conference of the North American Chapter of the Association for Computational Linguistics: Human Language Technologies*. Association for Computational Linguistics.

Karl Moritz Hermann, Tomas Kocisky, Edward Grefenstette, Lasse Espeholt, Will Kay, Mustafa Suleyman, and Phil Blunsom. 2015. Teaching machines to read and comprehend. In C. Cortes, N. D. Lawrence, D. D. Lee, M. Sugiyama, and R. Garnett, editors, *Advances in Neural Information Processing Systems 28*, pages 1693–1701. Curran Associates, Inc.

Dirk Hovy. 2015. Demographic factors improve classification performance. In *Proceedings of the 53rd Annual Meeting of the Association for Computational Linguistics and the 7th International Joint Conference on Natural Language Processing (Volume 1: Long Papers)*, volume 1, pages 752–762.

Anja Lambrecht and Catherine E Tucker. 2018. Algorithmic bias? an empirical study into apparent gender-based discrimination in the display of stem career ads. *Social Science Research Network (SSRN)*.

Omer Levy and Yoav Goldberg. 2014. Dependency-based word embeddings. In *Proceedings of the 52nd Annual Meeting of the Association for Computational Linguistics (Volume 2: Short Papers)*, volume 2, pages 302–308.

Mitchell P. Marcus, Beatrice Santorini, and Mary Ann Marcinkiewicz. 1993. Building a large annotated corpus of english: The penn treebank. *Computational Linguistics*, 19(2):313–330.

Chandler May, Alex Wang, Shikha Bordia, Samuel R. Bowman, and Rachel Rudinger. 2019. On measuring social bias in sentence encoders. In *Proceedings of the 2019 Conference of the North American Chapter of the Association for Computational Linguistics: Human Language Technologies*. Association for Computational Linguistics.

Stephen Merity, Nitish Shirish Keskar, and Richard Socher. 2018. Regularizing and optimizing LSTM language models. In *International Conference on Learning Representations*.

Stephen Merity, Caiming Xiong, James Bradbury, and Richard Socher. 2016. Pointer sentinel mixture models. *arXiv preprint arXiv:1609.07843*.

Tomas Mikolov, Martin Karafiát, Lukás Burget, Jan Cernocký, and Sanjeev Khudanpur. 2010. Recurrent neural network based language model. In *INTERSPEECH*, pages 1045–1048. ISCA.

Tomas Mikolov, Ilya Sutskever, Kai Chen, Greg S Corrado, and Jeff Dean. 2013. Distributed representations of words and phrases and their compositionality. In *Advances in neural information processing systems*, pages 3111–3119.

Mei Ngan and Patrick Grother. 2015. *Face recognition vendor test (FRVT) performance of automated gender classification algorithms*. US Department of Commerce, National Institute of Standards and Technology.

Marta Recasens, Cristian Danescu-Niculescu-Mizil, and Dan Jurafsky. 2013. Linguistic models for analyzing and detecting biased language. In *Proceedings of the 51st Annual Meeting of the Association for Computational Linguistics (Volume 1: Long Papers)*, volume 1, pages 1650–1659.

Rachel Rudinger, Jason Naradowsky, Brian Leonard, and Benjamin Van Durme. 2018. Gender bias in coreference resolution. In *Proceedings of the 2018 Conference of the North American Chapter of the Association for Computational Linguistics: Human Language Technologies*, New Orleans, Louisiana. Association for Computational Linguistics.

Jieyu Zhao, Tianlu Wang, Mark Yatskar, Vicente Ordonez, and Kai-Wei Chang. 2017. Men also like shopping: Reducing gender bias amplification using corpus-level constraints. In *EMNLP*, pages 2979–2989. Association for Computational Linguistics.

Jieyu Zhao, Yichao Zhou, Zeyu Li, Wei Wang, and Kai-Wei Chang. 2018. Learning gender-neutral word embeddings. In *Proceedings of the 2018 Conference on Empirical Methods in Natural Language Processing*, pages 4847–4853. Association for Computational Linguistics.

Emotion Impacts Speech Recognition Performance

Rushab Munot,
University of Pennsylvania
rushab@cis.upenn.edu

Ani Nenkova,
University of Pennsylvania
nenkova@cis.upenn.edu

Abstract

It has been established that the performance of speech recognition systems depends on multiple factors including the lexical content, speaker identity and dialect. Here we use three English datasets of acted emotion to demonstrate that emotional content also impacts the performance of commercial systems. On two of the corpora, emotion is a bigger contributor to recognition errors than speaker identity and on two, neutral speech is recognized considerably better than emotional speech. We further evaluate the commercial systems on spontaneous interactions that contain portions of emotional speech. We propose and validate on the acted datasets, a method that allows us to evaluate the overall impact of emotion on recognition even when manual transcripts are not available. Using this method, we show that emotion in natural spontaneous dialogue is a less prominent but still significant factor in recognition accuracy.

1 Introduction

Alexa and Google Home are becoming increasingly popular, their use spanning a range of applications from reducing loneliness in the elderly (Reis et al., 2017; Ferland et al., 2018) to child entertainment and education (Druga et al., 2017). As these conversational agents become commonplace, people are likely to express emotion during their interactions, either because of their perception of the agent or because of the emotion-eliciting situations in which the agent is deployed.

In this paper, we set out to study the extent to which emotional content in speech impacts speech recognition performance *of commercial systems*. Similar studies have been conducted in the past to study how recognition varies with gender and dialect (Adda-Decker and Lamel, 2005; Tatman, 2017), lexical content (Goldwater et al., 2010), topical domain (Traum et al.,

2015) and delivery style (Siegler and Stern, 1995; Nakamura et al., 2008). A number of studies have studied the impact of stress (Hansen and Patil, 2007; Bou-Ghazale and Hansen, 2000; Steeneken and Hansen, 1999; Hansen, 1996) and emotional factors (Polzin and Waibel, 1998; Kostoulas et al., 2008; Benzeghiba et al., 2007) on speech recognition. Multiple studies (Byrne et al., 2004; Athanaselis et al., 2005; Pan et al., 2006; Meng et al., 2007; Ijima et al., 2009; Sun et al., 2009; Sheikhan et al., 2012) tried to improve upon speech recognition accuracies for emotional speech. However, these studies were carried out with older recognition systems. Recently automatic speech recognition has seen unprecedented gains in accuracy. Yet our work shows that emotional content still poses problems to speech recognition systems.

In our work we seek to quantify the influence of emotion on recognition accuracy for three commercial systems, on several datasets. We start out with two datasets of acted emotion, which are in some respects ideal for the task because the spoken content is constrained to pre-selected utterances and thus manual transcription is not required. In addition, the lexical content for each emotion is identical, so no special adjustment for that confounding factor is needed in the acted corpora.

At the same time, it is important to validate these results on spontaneous, more natural exchanges, so we also present results on such a corpus of emotion in spontaneous speech. As the speech becomes more natural, it becomes harder to obtain large manual transcripts for a large portion of the data to carry out the studies that we present, so we also validate an alternative method for finding factors that influence the performance of commercial systems, relying on agreement between systems rather than manual transcripts. We present convincing evidence that the approach is a

16

Proceedings of the 2019 Conference of the North American Chapter of the Association for Computational Linguistics: Student Research Workshop, pages 16–21
Minneapolis, Minnesota, June 3 - 5, 2019. ©2017 Association for Computational Linguistics

reasonable approximation and it can be used for broader studies on factors influencing automatic speech recognition. Here, we apply the method to analyze data from a spontaneous emotional speech corpus.

2 Related Work

There has been much research in the field of emotion recognition from speech. However, relatively less research has been conducted on how emotion affects Automatic Speech Recognition (ASR).

(Polzin and Waibel, 1998) study the variation in word error rate with different emotions - NEUTRAL, ANGER, HAPINESS, AFRAID and SADNESS. They observed that SADNESS and AFRAID/FEAR perform worst while NEUTRAL and ANGER perform best. They integrate prosodic features into the model using Hidden Markov Models to first disambiguate the emotional state of the speaker, and then use emotion specific ASR models for transcription. They report a significant increase in ASR performance.

(Kostoulas et al., 2008) conduct a similar study over a much wider range of emotions (About 15 emotions) on the Wall Street Journal database with Sphinx III as the ASR system and report a large variance in the WER across emotions, ranging from about 6% for NEUTRAL to about 44% for HOT ANGER.

(Athanaselis et al., 2005) extract an emotionally *colored* subset of the British National Corpus (BNC) and append it multiple times to the BNC before training an emotionally-enhanced ASR system.

(Sheikhan et al., 2012) propose that the emotion in speech leads to changes in Mel-frequency cepstral coefficients (MFCC) and thus propose neutralizing MFCCs by *warping* the first three formant frequencies and conduct their experiments to analyze improvement in ASR performance for the emotions ANGER and HAPPINESS.

In this work, we analyze the performance of multiple modern commercial ASR systems on emotional speech. We further quantify the correlation between the Word Error Rate and emotion. We also compare the dependence of ASR performance on other factors - speaker identity and spoken content with the dependence on emotion.

3 Datasets and APIs

We use three acted Emotion datasets: CREMA-D (Cao et al., 2014), RAVDESS (Steven R. Livingstone1, 2018) and MSP-IMPROV (Busso et al., 2017). CREMA-D has 12 sentences recorded by 91 actors in 6 different emotions (Anger, Disgust, Fear, Happy, Neutral and Sad), for a total of 7,442 utterances in the dataset.[1]

RAVDESS has just two sentences, which are very similar to each other (*Kids are talking by the door* and *Dogs are sitting by the door*), recorded by 24 actors in 8 emotions with the addition of Surprised and Calm. RAVDESS has a total of 1,440 utterances, and each sentence is recorded in two intensities with two repetitions of each.

In addition to actors recording sentences in a pre-specified emotion, the MSP-IMPROV dataset contains 'improvised recordings', where actors converse to induce the desired emotion. In these interactions, there is at least one emotional rendition of the target utterance but other utterances may be emotionally neutral. MSP-IMPROV is comprised of 1,272 utterances distributed over 20 target sentences and four emotions (Neutral, Anger, Happy, Fear). We refer to this part of the corpus as *MSP-IMPROV Target*, where we only concern ourselves with recognizing the target sentence. We refer to the set of complete conversations as the *MSP-IMPROV Dialogue* Corpus. Manual transcripts are not available for this part. MSP-IMPROV has 1,085 complete conversations.

Commercial systems used for speech recognition are IBM Watson Speech-to-Text, Google Cloud Speech-to-Text and Amazon Transcribe. [2]. We will denote the APIs simply by IBM, GCP and AWS respectively.

4 Evaluation Metrics

We report two measures of automatic speech recognition performance: the Word Error Rate (WER) and the percentage of completely recognized sentences (CR). Minor semantic and grammatical errors are ignored by manually listing semantically equivalent sentences for computing CR. We report $1 - CR$ instead of CR to maintain consistency with WER interpretation, lower

---

[1] One of the sentences is recorded in three different intensities.

[2] **Websites:** https://www.ibm.com/watson/services/speech-to-text/, https://aws.amazon.com/transcribe/ and https://cloud.google.com/speech-to-text/ respectively

the better. We then perform an ANOVA analysis to determine the statistical significance of each factor in determining the WER.

The dialogues in the MSP-IMPROV corpus do not contain manual transcripts. We propose a metric to analyze the relative performance of different systems with varying emotions when manual transcripts are not available.

We calculate the performance of every system relative to other systems and then report the average of these cross-comparisons. This method accurately predicts the relative performance on emotional and neutral speech consistent with WER/CR results on the other corpora for which transcripts are available.

Dataset	Metric	IBM	AWS	GCP
CREMA-D	WER	**10.00**	13.09	18.80
	1-CR	**24.72**	39.20	41.78
RAVDESS	WER	**5.08**	13.31	6.19
	1-CR	**9.17**	56.38	15.49
MSP-IMPROV Target	WER	13.90	**9.21**	12.56
	1-CR	38.76	**35.72**	39.54

Table 1: Overall Performance of IBM, AWS and GCP

5 Observations

5.1 Variations across various factors

The overall performance of the APIs on the three datasets is given in Table 1. IBM performs best on 2 out of 3 datasets (CREMA-D and RAVDESS). AWS is, however, more consistent across datasets.

Figure 1 shows how WER varies with emotion. On CREMA-D, NEUTRAL speech is recognized more accurately than emotional speech, with ANGER most accurately recognized among the emotions, while SADNESS and FEAR are poorly recognized. Similarly on RAVDESS, FEAR has the worst WER. NEUTRAL and ANGER are recognized better than other emotions. On MSP-IMPROV Target, ANGER is recognized most accurately, followed by NEUTRAL speech. Overall NEUTRAL utterances for all datasets are more accurately recognized than the combined class of emotional speech. Further, there is a high variation in performance between different emotions. Improving performance while focusing on poorly performing emotions like sadness and fear, which have an extremely bad performance, will help improve speech recognition.

Corpus	Pearson	Spearman
CREMA-D	0.73	0.86
RAVDESS	0.82	0.93
MSP-IMPROV Target	0.74	0.84

Table 2: Spearman and Pearson Correlation between the cross-comparison WER and the observed WER

Performance varies largely with sentences—some show excellent performance while others do not. Performance also varies across APIs—sentences with good performance with one system may perform well with others.

RAVDESS has two similar sentences, and hence it does not make sense to look at performance variation with spoken content on RAVDESS. On MSP-IMPROV Target, the WER varies from lower than 5% for some sentences to above 30% for others. Similar variations are also observed with Speaker Identity.

Corpus	IBM AWS	IBM GCP	AWS GCP
CREMA-D	0.84	0.74	0.85
RAVDESS	0.84	0.63	0.84
MSP-IMPROV Target	0.67	0.69	0.65

Table 3: Spearman Correlation between two-system cross comparison WER and the observed WER

5.2 Evaluating Performance without Manual Transcripts

When manual transcripts are not available, we treat the output of one API as the reference and get WER for other APIs with respect to it. We refer to this as the *cross-comparison* WER. We then change the reference API and repeat the process. The performance is reported as the average of all cross-reference WERs. In our case, we use three API's. Thus the average cross-comparison WER is the average of 9 cross-comparison WERs.

We test our metric on CREMA-D, RAVDESS, and MSP-IMPROV Target by computing Spearman and Pearson's correlations between the true WER and the average of the nine cross-comparison WERs. The correlations, mentioned in Table 2, are high, all above 0.7, indicating that the approximation is not perfect but overall accurate.

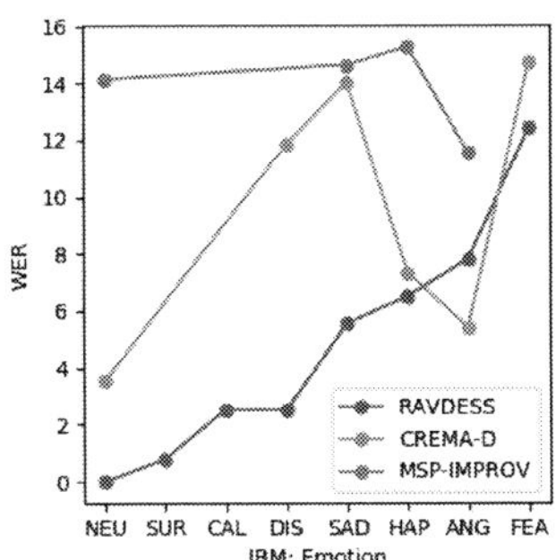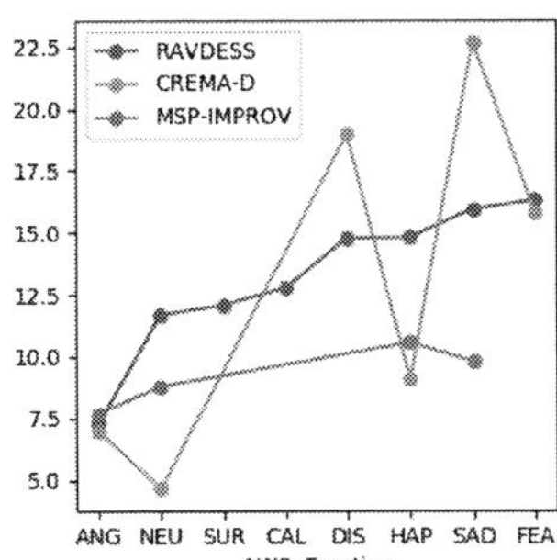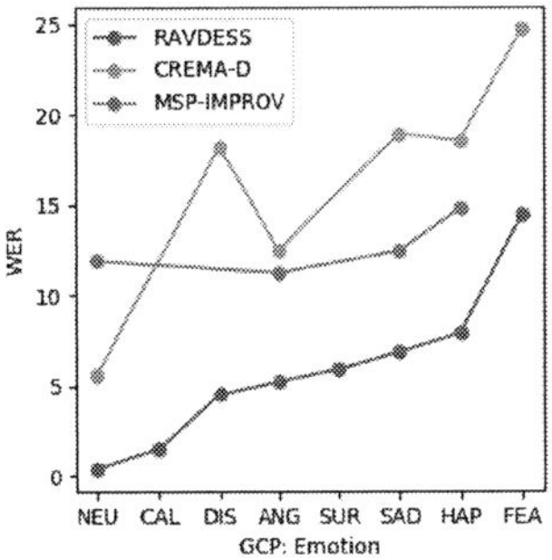

(a) IBM: WER on CREMA-D, RAVDESS and MSP-IMPROV Target   (b) AWS: WER on CREMA-D, RAVDESS and MSP-IMPROV Target   (c) GCP: WER on CREMA-D, RAVDESS and MSP-IMPROV Target

Figure 1: Performance based on emotion

Dataset	Improvisation	F-value/ P-value			Improvisation
		Sentence	Emotion	Actor	
CREMA-D		2163	56.6	5.73	
RAVDESS		0.02/0.87	12.96	12.54	
MSP-IMPROV Target	Complete	71.78	6.99	13.37	32.42
	Improvised	42.89	5.92	5.58	
	Unimprovised	48.37	2.78/0.04	18.75	
MSP-IMPROV Dialogue		0.11/0.73	0.81/0.48	2.43	

Table 4: Statistical significance of various factors on speech recognition performance. For entries where the P-value is not mentioned, it is almost zero.

We also conduct experiments to check whether the metric can be based on two systems instead of three. The Spearman Correlations are tabulated in Table 3. The two system cross-comparison metric is representative of the WER but the correlation is not as strong.

In Table 5, we report cross-comparison WER on the MSP-IMPROV Dialogue subcorpus which includes conversations used to evoke the desired emotion for the target sentence so that the required emotion sounds natural rather than acted. Each conversation is between a male and a female speaker. Emotions in natural speech are not as intense as they are in the acted versions. Also, only parts of the conversations contain emotional speech (neutral speech with parts of emotional speech) and it is natural to expect that the influence on recognition rates will be attenuated. It is however still present: ANGER and HAPPINESS have much worse recognition than NEUTRAL speech. Here however the best recognition is for SAD speech.

Emotion	Cross-Comparison WER
SAD	18.84
NEU	20.73
ANG	23.29
HAP	23.47
Overall	21.45

Table 5: Cross-comparison WER for MSP-IMRPOV Dialogue

6 Statistical Significance of Emotion, Speaker and Spoken Content

We now report the results of ANOVA analysis on each of the datasets, to compare the statistical significance of emotion, speaker and spoken content (sentence identity in our case) on performance. We compute the WER for each sentence separately. The F-values and P-values of the above-mentioned factors are listed in Table 4. As expected, spoken content has the highest impact on performance, other than RAVDESS which is expected to have low F-value for spoken-content. On CREMA-D and RAVDESS, Emotion impacts performance more than Speaker Identity.

On CREMA-D, the F-value for spoken content is about 40 times that of Emotion. Nevertheless, the Emotion and Actor Identity factors are statistically significant. Emotion has a much larger impact than actor identity. On RAVDESS, Emotion is slightly more impactful than Speaker Identity.

On MSP-IMPROV Target, the impact of Speaker Identity is more pronounced. However, on splitting the corpus based on whether the samples were improvised or not, on improvised speech, Emotion has a higher impact than actor identity. For non-improvised speech, Speaker Identity becomes important. Recognizing improvised speech, which is closer to natural speech, is more difficult. The impact of Actor Identity is thus lower (in improvised speech) than non-improvised speech. Note that the WER is higher for improvised speech (13.5%) compared to non-improvised speech (10.4%). Surprisingly, the impact of Emotion is higher in improvised speech.

For dialogues, Spoken Content has low significance, likely because factors are averaged out. Actor identity and gender of the interlocutor (together) impact recognition most.

7   Conclusions

We quantified the impact of Emotion on speech recognition performance. We developed a metric to analyze performance for audio samples where manual transcripts are unavailable and showed empirically that this metric works. In future work, we plan to analyze whether acoustic features are predictive of what sentences are likely to be misrecognized and the characteristic features per emotion.

References

Martine Adda-Decker and Lori Lamel. 2005. Do speech recognizers prefer female speakers? In *Ninth European Conference on Speech Communication and Technology*.

Theologos Athanaselis, Stelios Bakamidis, Ioannis Dologlou, Roddy Cowie, Ellen Douglas-Cowie, and Cate Cox. 2005. ASR for emotional speech: Clarifying the issues and enhancing performance. *Neural Networks*, 18(4):437–444.

Mohamed Benzeghiba, Renato de Mori, Olivier Deroo, Stéphane Dupont, Teodora Erbes, Denis Jouvet, Luciano Fissore, Pietro Laface, Alfred Mertins, Christophe Ris, Richard Rose, Vivek Tyagi, and Christian Wellekens. 2007. Automatic speech recognition and speech variability: A review. *Speech Communication*, 49(10-11):763–786.

Sahar E. Bou-Ghazale and John H. L. Hansen. 2000. A comparative study of traditional and newly proposed features for recognition of speech under stress. *IEEE Trans. Speech and Audio Processing*, 8(4):429–442.

Carlos Busso, Srinivas Parthasarathy, Alec Burmania, Mohammed Abdel-Wahab, Najmeh Sadoughi, and Emily Mower Provost. 2017. MSP-IMPROV: an acted corpus of dyadic interactions to study emotion perception. *IEEE Trans. Affective Computing*, 8(1):67–80.

William Byrne, David S. Doermann, Martin Franz, Samuel Gustman, Jan Hajic, Douglas W. Oard, Michael Picheny, Josef Psutka, Bhuvana Ramabhadran, Dagobert Soergel, Todd Ward, and Wei-Jing Zhu. 2004. Automatic recognition of spontaneous speech for access to multilingual oral history archives. *IEEE Trans. Speech and Audio Processing*, 12(4):420–435.

Houwei Cao, David G Cooper, Michael K Keutmann, Ruben C Gur, Ani Nenkova, and Ragini Verma. 2014. Crema-d: Crowd-sourced emotional multimodal actors dataset. *IEEE transactions on affective computing*, 5(4):377–390.

Stefania Druga, Randi Williams, Cynthia Breazeal, and Mitchel Resnick. 2017. "hey google is it ok if i eat you?": Initial explorations in child-agent interaction. In *Proceedings of the 2017 Conference on Interaction Design and Children*, IDC '17, pages 595–600. ACM.

Libby Ferland, Ziwei Li, Shridhar Sukhani, Joan Zheng, Luyang Zhao, and Maria Gini. 2018. Assistive ai for coping with memory loss.

Sharon Goldwater, Dan Jurafsky, and Christopher D Manning. 2010. Which words are hard to recognize? prosodic, lexical, and disfluency factors that increase speech recognition error rates. *Speech Communication*, 52(3):181–200.

John H. L. Hansen. 1996. Analysis and compensation of speech under stress and noise for environmental robustness in speech recognition. *Speech Communication*, 20(1-2):151–173.

John H. L. Hansen and Sanjay A. Patil. 2007. Speech under stress: Analysis, modeling and recognition. In *Speaker Classification*.

Yusuke Ijima, Makoto Tachibana, Takashi Nose, and Takao Kobayashi. 2009. Emotional speech recognition based on style estimation and adaptation with multiple-regression HMM. In *Proceedings of the IEEE International Conference on Acoustics, Speech, and Signal Processing, ICASSP 2009, 19-24 April 2009, Taipei, Taiwan*, pages 4157–4160.

Theodoros Kostoulas, Iosif Mporas, Todor Ganchev, and Nikos Fakotakis. 2008. The effect of emotional speech on a smart-home application. In *New Frontiers in Applied Artificial Intelligence, 21st International Conference on Industrial, Engineering and Other Applications of Applied Intelligent Systems, IEA/AIE 2008, Wroclaw, Poland, June 18-20, 2008, Proceedings*, pages 305–310.

Hong Meng, Johannes Pittermann, Angela Pittermann, and Wolfgang Minker. 2007. Combined speech-emotion recognition for spoken human-computer interfaces. In *2007 IEEE International Conference on Signal Processing and Communications*, pages 1179–1182. IEEE.

Masanobu Nakamura, Koji Iwano, and Sadaoki Furui. 2008. Differences between acoustic characteristics of spontaneous and read speech and their effects on speech recognition performance. *Computer Speech & Language*, 22(2):171–184.

YC Pan, MX Xu, LQ Liu, and PF Jia. 2006. Emotion-detecting based model selection for emotional speech recognition. In *The Proceedings of the Multiconference on" Computational Engineering in Systems Applications"*, volume 2, pages 2169–2172. IEEE.

Thomas S. Polzin and Er Waibel. 1998. Pronunciation variations in emotional speech. In *In: Proc. of the ESCA Workshop Modeling Pronunciation Variation for Automatic Speech Recognition*, pages 103–1008.

Arsénio Reis, Dennis Paulino, Hugo Paredes, and João Barroso. 2017. Using intelligent personal assistants to strengthen the elderlies social bonds. In *International Conference on Universal Access in Human-Computer Interaction*, pages 593–602. Springer.

Mansour Sheikhan, Davood Gharavian, and Farhad Ashoftedel. 2012. Using DTW neural-based MFCC warping to improve emotional speech recognition. *Neural Computing and Applications*, 21(7):1765–1773.

Matthew A Siegler and Richard M Stern. 1995. On the effects of speech rate in large vocabulary speech recognition systems. In *Acoustics, Speech, and Signal Processing, 1995. ICASSP-95., 1995 International Conference on*, volume 1, pages 612–615. IEEE.

Herman J. M. Steeneken and John H. L. Hansen. 1999. Speech under stress conditions: overview of the effect on speech production and on system performance. In *Proceedings of the 1999 IEEE International Conference on Acoustics, Speech, and Signal Processing, ICASSP '99, Phoenix, Arizona, USA, March 15-19, 1999*, pages 2079–2082.

Frank A. Russo Steven R. Livingstone1. 2018. The ryerson audio-visual database of emotional speech and song (ravdess): A dynamic, multimodal set of facial and vocal expressions in north american english. *PLoS ONE*, 13(5): e0196391.

Yanqing Sun, Yu Zhou, Qingwei Zhao, and Yonghong Yan. 2009. Acoustic feature optimization for emotion affected speech recognition. *2009 International Conference on Information Engineering and Computer Science*, pages 1–4.

Rachael Tatman. 2017. Gender and dialect bias in youtube's automatic captions. In *Proceedings of the First ACL Workshop on Ethics in Natural Language Processing*, pages 53–59.

David R. Traum, Kallirroi Georgila, Ron Artstein, and Anton Leuski. 2015. Evaluating spoken dialogue processing for time-offset interaction. In *Proceedings of the SIGDIAL 2015 Conference, The 16th Annual Meeting of the Special Interest Group on Discourse and Dialogue, 2-4 September 2015, Prague, Czech Republic*, pages 199–208.

The Strength of the Weakest Supervision:
Topic Classification Using Class Labels

Jiatong Li[1], Kai Zheng[2], Hua Xu[3], Qiaozhu Mei[4], Yue Wang[5]

[1]Department of Computer Science, Rutgers University
[2]Department of Informatics, University of California, Irvine
[3]School of Biomedical Informatics, The University of Texas Health Science Center at Houston
[4]School of Information, University of Michigan, Ann Arbor
[5]School of Information and Library Science, University of North Carolina at Chapel Hill

[1]`jiatong.li@rutgers.edu`, [2]`zhengkai@uci.edu`, [3]`hua.xu@uth.tmc.edu`,
[4]`qmei@umich.edu`, [5]`wangyue@email.unc.edu`

Abstract

When developing topic classifiers for real-world applications, we begin by defining a set of meaningful topic labels. Ideally, an intelligent classifier can understand these labels right away and start classifying documents. Indeed, a human can confidently tell if a news article is about science, politics, sports, or none of the above, after knowing just the class labels.

We study the problem of training an initial topic classifier using only class labels. We investigate existing techniques for solving this problem and propose a simple but effective approach. Experiments on a variety of topic classification data sets show that learning from class labels can save significant initial labeling effort, essentially providing a "free" warm start to the topic classifier.

1 Introduction

When developing topic classifiers for real-world tasks, such as news categorization, query intent detection, and user-generated content analysis, practitioners often begin by crafting a succinct definition, or a *class label*, to define each class. Unfortunately, these carefully written class labels are completely ignored by supervised topic classification models. Given a new task, these models typically require a significant amount of labeled documents to reach even a modest initial performance. In contrast, a human can readily understand new topic categories by reading the class definitions and making connections to prior knowledge. Labeling initial examples for every new task can be time-consuming and labor-intensive, especially in resource-constrained domains like medicine and law. Therefore it is desirable if a topic classifier can proactively interpret class labels before the training starts, giving itself a "warm start". An imperfect initial model can always be fine-tuned with more labeled documents.

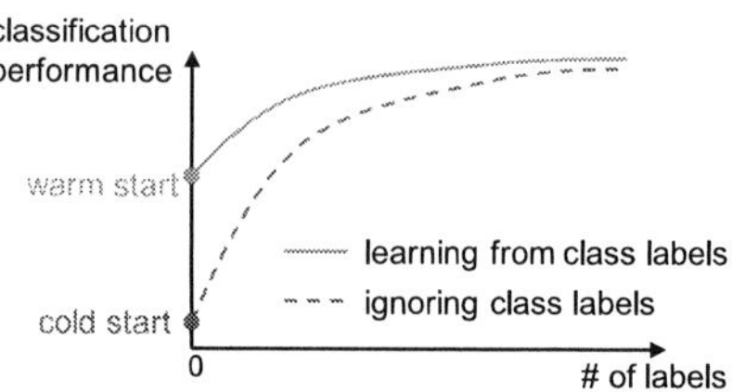

Figure 1: Learning from class labels can give "warm start" to a classifier, accelerating the learning process.

As conceptually shown in Figure 1, a warm start can reduce the total number of training labels for a classifier to reach certain performance level.

In this work, we study algorithms that can initialize a topic classifier using *class labels only*. Since class labels are the starting point of any topic classification task, they can be viewed as the earliest hence weakest supervision signal. We propose a simple and effective approach that combines word embedding and naive Bayes classification. On six topic classification data sets, we evaluate a suite of existing approaches and the proposed approach. Experimental results show that class labels can train a topic classifier that generalizes as well as a classifier trained on hundreds to thousands of labeled documents.

2 Related Work

Text retrieval. Classifying documents by short labels can be viewed as evaluating textual similarity between a document and a label. Baeza-Yates et al. (2011) called this approach "naive text classification". Treating labels as search queries, we can classify a document into a class if it best matches the label of that class. Well-studied text retrieval methods, such as vector space models and probabilistic models (Croft et al., 2010), can produce matching scores. To mitigate vocabulary mismatch, such a classifier can be further enhanced

Proceedings of the 2019 Conference of the North American Chapter of the Association for Computational Linguistics: Student Research Workshop, pages 22–28
Minneapolis, Minnesota, June 3 - 5, 2019. ©2017 Association for Computational Linguistics

by self-training: the classifier assigns pseudo labels to top-ranked documents as done in pseudo relevance feedback (Rocchio, 1965), and updates itself using those labels.

Semi-supervised learning. Our problem setting can be seen as an *extreme case* of weak supervision: we only use class labels as the (noisy) supervision signal, and nothing else. If we view class labels as "labeled documents", one from each class, and to-be-classified documents as unlabeled documents, then we cast the problem as semi-supervised learning (Zhu, 2006). Self-training is one such technique: a generative classifier is trained using only class labels, and then teaches itself using its own predictions on unlabeled data. If we view class labels as "labeled features", then we expect the classifier to predict a class when a document contains the class label words. For instance, Druck et al. (2008) proposed generalized expectation criteria that uses feature words (class labels) to train a discriminative classifier. Jagarlamudi et al. (2012) and Hingmire and Chakraborti (2014) proposed Seeded LDA to incorporate labeled words/topics into statistical topic modeling. The inferred document-topic mixture probabilities can be used to classify documents.

Zero-shot learning aims to classify visual objects from a new class using only word descriptions of that class (Socher et al., 2013). It first learns visual features and their correspondence with word descriptions, and then constructs a new classifier by composing learned features. Most research on zero-shot learning focuses on image classification, but the same principle applies to text classification as well (Pushp and Srivastava, 2017). Our proposed method constructs a new classifier by composing learned word embeddings in a probabilistic manner. Since the new classifier transfers semantic knowledge in word embedding to topic classification tasks, it is broadly related to **transfer learning** (Pan and Yang, 2010). The main difference is that in transfer learning the information about the new task is in the form of labeled data, not class definition words.

3 Proposed Method

Let a test document x be a sequence of words $(w_1, \cdots, w_j, \cdots)$, and a class topic description y be a sequence of words $d_y = (w_1, \cdots, w_y, \cdots)$. All words are in vocabulary V. We propose a generative approach, where the predictive probabil-

ity $p(y|x) \propto p(x|y)p(y)$. Generative approaches tends to perform well when training data is scarce, which is the case in our setting.

We assume there exists weak prior knowledge on which classes are popular and which are rare. We can then construct rough estimates $\hat{p}(y)$ using simple heuristics as described in (Schapire et al., 2002). It distributes probability mass q evenly among majority classes, and $1 - q$ evenly among minority classes. We treat the most frequent class as the majority class, the rest as minority classes, and $q = 0.7$ in our experiments.

By interpreting class topic description as words, we obtain $\hat{p}(x|y) = p(x|d_y)$. We assume that the d_y expresses a noisy-OR relation of the words it contains (Oniśko et al., 2001). Up to first-order approximation:

$$p(x|d_y) = 1 - \prod_{w_y \in d_y} (1 - p(x|w_y))$$
$$\approx \sum_{w_y \in d_y} p(x|w_y), \qquad (1)$$

where each w_y is a word in the class topic description d_y. Further, we assume that words in document x are conditionally independent given a label word w_y (naïve Bayes assumption):

$$p(x|w_y) = \prod_{w_j \in x} p(w_j|w_y). \qquad (2)$$

Combining (1) and (2), the document likelihood is

$$\hat{p}(x|y) = \sum_{w_y \in d_y} \prod_{w_j \in x} p(w_j|w_y). \qquad (3)$$

To this end, we need a word association model $p(w_1|w_2), \forall w_1, w_2 \in V$. It can be efficiently learned by word embedding algorithms. The skip-gram algorithm (Mikolov et al., 2013) learns vector representations of words, such that for words w_1, w_2, their vectors $\mathbf{u}_{w_1}, \mathbf{v}_{w_2}$ approximate the conditional probability[1]

$$p(w_1|w_2) = \frac{\exp\left(\mathbf{u}_{w_1}^\top \mathbf{v}_{w_2}\right)}{\sum_{w \in V} \exp\left(\mathbf{u}_w^\top \mathbf{v}_{w_2}\right)} . \qquad (4)$$

---

[1] The two sets of word vectors $\{\mathbf{u}_w : w \in V\}$ and $\{\mathbf{v}_w : w \in V\}$ produced by skip-gram correspond to the input and output parameters of a two-layer neural network. Typically, only the output parameters are used as the "learned word vectors". Here we need both input and output parameters to compute $p(w_1|w_2)$.

Combining (3) with (4), the document likelihood becomes

$$\hat{p}(x|y) = \sum_{w_y \in d_y} \exp\left(\sum_{w_j \in x}\left(\mathbf{u}_{w_j}^\top \mathbf{v}_{w_y} - C_{w_y}\right)\right),$$

where $C_{w_y} = \log \sum_{w \in V} \exp\left(\mathbf{u}_w^\top \mathbf{v}_{w_y}\right)$ is independent of document x and only related to label word w_y, therefore can be precomputed and stored to save computation.

Finally, we construct an generative classifier as $\hat{p}(y|x) \propto \hat{p}(x|y)\hat{p}(y)$. We call this method *word embedding naïve Bayes* (WENB).

3.1 Continued Training

The proposed method produces pseudo labels $\hat{p}(y|x_j)$ for unlabeled documents $\{x_j\}_{j=1}^m$. When true labels $\{(x_i, y_i)\}_{i=1}^n$ are available, we can train a new discriminative logistic regression classifier $p_\theta(y|x)$ using both true and pseudo labels (θ is the model parameter):

$$J(\theta) = \sum_{i=1}^n \sum_{y \in Y} -\mathbf{1}_{\{y_i=y\}} \log p_\theta(y|x_i) + \lambda \|\theta\|^2$$
$$+ \mu \sum_{j=1}^m \sum_{y \in Y} -\hat{p}(y|x_j) \log p_\theta(y|x_j). \quad (5)$$

To find the balance of pseudo vs. true labels in (5), we search the hyperparameter μ on a 5-point grid $\{10^{-2}, 10^{-1}, 0.4, 0.7, 1\}$. We expect pseudo labels to have comparable importance as true labels when n is small (fine granularity for $\mu \in [10^{-1}, 1]$), and their importance will diminish as n gets large ($\mu = 10^{-2}$). μ is automatically selected such that it gives the best 5-fold cross-validation accuracy on n true labels.

4 Experiments

We compare a variety of methods on six topic classification data sets. The goals are (1) to study the best classification performance achievable using class labels only, and (2) to estimate the equivalent amount of true labels needed to achieve the same warm-start performance.

4.1 Compared Methods

Retrieval-based methods. We use language modeling retrieval function with Dirichlet smoothing (Zhai and Lafferty, 2001) ($\mu = 2500$) to match a document to class labels (**IR**). The top 10 results are then used as pseudo-labeled documents to retrain three classifiers: **IR+Roc**: a Rocchio classifier ($\alpha = 1, \beta = 0.5, \gamma = 0$); **IR+NB**: a multinomial naive Bayes classifier (Laplace smoothing, $\alpha = 0.01$); **IR+LR** a logistic regression classifier (linear kernel, $C = 1$).

Semi-supervised methods. **ST-0**: the initial self-training classifier using class labels as "training documents" (multinomial naïve Bayes, Laplace smoothing $\alpha = 0.01$). **ST-1**: ST-0 retrained on 10 most confident documents predicted by itself. **GE**: a logistic regression classifier trained using generalized expectation criteria (Druck et al., 2008). Class labels are used as labeled features. **sLDA**: a supervised topic model trained using seeded LDA (Jagarlamudi et al., 2012). Besides k seeded topics (k is the number of classes), we use an extra topic to account for other content in the corpus.

Word embedding-based methods. **Cosine**: a centroid-based classifier, where class definitions and documents are represented as average of word vectors. **WENB**: The proposed method (Section 3). **WENB+LR**: a logistic regression classifier trained only on pseudo labels produced by WENB (Section 3.1, $n = 0$).

For general domain tasks, we take raw text from English Wikipedia, English news crawl (WMT, 2014), and 1 billion word news corpus (Chelba et al., 2013) to train word vectors. For medical domain tasks, we take raw text from MEDLINE abstracts (NLM, 2018) to train word vectors. We find 50-dimensional skip-gram word vectors perform reasonably well in the experiments.

4.2 Data Sets

We consider six topic classification data sets with different document lengths and application domains. Table 1 summarizes basic statistics of these data sets. Table 4 and 5 in the appendix show actual class labels used in each data set.

Data set	Avg word/doc	# classes	# docs
Wiki Titles	3.1 (1.1)	15	30,000
News Titles	6.7 (9.5)	4	422,937
Y Questions	5.0 (2.6)	10	1,460,000
20 News	101.6 (438.5)	20	18,846
Reuters	76.5 (117.3)	10	8,246
Med WSD	202.8 (46.6)	2/task	190/task

Table 1: Statistics of topic classification data sets. Numbers in column "Avg word/doc" are "mean (standard deviation)".

	Wiki Titles	News Titles	Y Questions	20 News	Reuters	Med WSD
Majority guess	.83	13.26	1.82	.48	6.47	34.20
IR	3.14 (.25)	14.20 (.06)	6.15 (.06)	19.57 (.95)	8.37 (.55)	52.99 (.64)
IR+Roc	2.93 (.24)	14.20 (.06)	8.35 (1.12)	25.09 (.93)	19.33 (1.87)	59.89 (.54)
IR+NB	5.44 (.53)	32.98 (2.13)	14.45 (.45)	30.45 (1.46)	**62.59 (2.43)**	**82.12 (.41)**
IR+LR	3.26 (.30)	13.44 (.10)	7.38 (2.08)	**34.76 (1.50)**	6.48 (.07)	68.35 (.38)
ST-0	3.16 (.32)	16.03 (.16)	6.15 (.02)	19.49 (.98)	6.79 (.17)	69.11 (.26)
ST-1	5.62 (.29)	24.34 (.36)	10.02 (.49)	22.91 (1.29)	**55.77 (1.62)**	**82.97 (.56)**
GE	9.55 (.90)	14.54 (.08)	31.72 (.05)	**48.71 (.41)**	21.65 (27.36)	62.63 (.37)
sLDA	7.07 (0.97)	51.16 (8.10)	40.98 (2.61)	24.80 (4.98)	30.61 (4.80)	69.81 (1.09)
Cosine	**27.67 (.59)**	33.49 (.11)	31.16 (.03)	26.19 (.75)	6.56 (.16)	32.65 (.19)
WENB	**26.70 (.48)**	**63.02 (.10)**	**44.89 (.06)**	32.23 (.48)	34.99 (1.99)	68.27 (.20)
WENB+LR	24.88 (.39)	**63.76 (.11)**	**45.69 (.09)**	30.57 (.71)	32.04 (1.44)	62.57 (.19)

Table 2: Macro-averaged F_1 (%) of compared methods on different data sets. The numbers are "mean (standard deviation)" of 5-fold cross validation. Top two numbers in each column are highlighted in **boldface**.

Data set	# of labels
Wiki Titles	1500
News Titles	200
Y Questions	1500-2000
20 News	100-200
Reuters	100-200
Med WSD	20/task $\times$ 198 tasks

Table 3: Number of true labels needed for a logistic regression classifier to achieve the same performance as "WENB+LR".

Three short text data sets are (1) **Wiki Titles**: Wikipedia article titles sampled from 15 main categories (Wikipedia Main Topic). (2) **News Titles**: The UCI news title data set (Lichman, 2013). (3) **Y Questions**: User-posted questions in Yahoo Answers (Yahoo Language Data, 2007).

Three long text data sets are (1) **20 News**: The well-known 20 newsgroup data set. (2) **Reuters**. The Reuters-21578 data set (Lewis). We take the articles from the 10 largest topics. (3) **Med WSD**: The MeSH word sense disambiguation (WSD) data set (Jimeno-Yepes et al., 2011).

Each WSD task aims to tell the sense (meaning) of an ambiguous term in a MEDLINE abstract. For instance, the term "cold" may refer to *Low Temperature, Common Cold*, or *Chronic Obstructive Lung Disease*, depending on its context. These senses are used as the class labels. We use 198 ambiguous words with at least 100 labeled abstracts in the data set, and report the average statistics over 198 independent classification tasks.

Although no true labels are used for training, some methods require unlabeled data for retrieval, pseudo-labeling, and re-training. We split unlabeled data into 5 folds, using 4 folds to "train" a classifier and 1 fold for test. We use macro-averaged F_1 as the performance metric because not all data sets have a balanced class distribution.

4.3 Results and Discussion

Label savings. Table 2 shows that overall, class labels can train text classifiers remarkably better than majority guess. This is no small feat considering that the classifier has not seen any labeled documents yet. Such performance gain essentially comes "for free", as any text classification task has to start by defining classes. In Table 3, we report the number of true labels needed for a logistic regression model to achieve the same performance as WENB+LR. The most significant savings happen on short documents: class labels are equivalent to hundreds to thousands of labeled documents at the beginning of the training process.

Effect of document length. On short documents (Wiki Titles, News Titles, Y Questions), leveraging unlabeled data does not help with most semi-supervised methods due to severe vocabulary mismatch. The proposed methods (WENB and WENB+LR) show robust performance, because pretrained word vectors can capture semantic similarity even without any word overlap between a class label and a document. This prior knowledge is essential when documents are short. On long documents (20 News, Reuters, Med WSD), leveraging unlabeled data helps, since long documents have richer content and are more likely to contain not only label words themselves, but also other topic-specific words. Retrieval-based and semi-supervised methods are able to learn these words by exploiting intra-document word co-occurrences.

Performance of other methods. Learning from class labels themselves provides very limited help (IR and ST-0). Using class labels as search queries and labeled documents are closely related: IR and ST-0 perform similarly; so do IR+NB and ST-1. When using class labels as search queries,

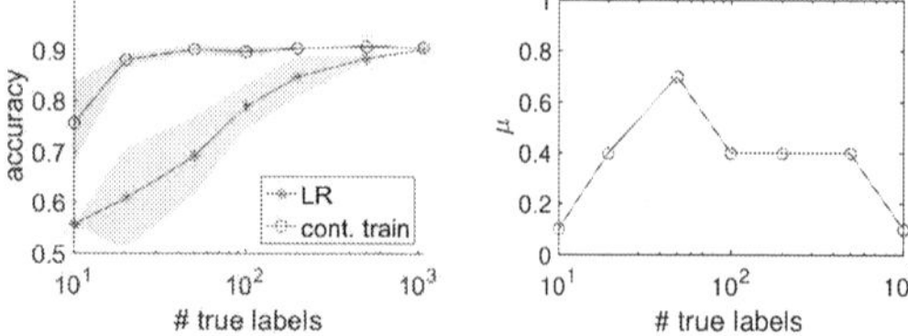

Figure 2: Continued training behavior: *Atheism* vs. *Autos*. Colored band: ±1 standard deviation.

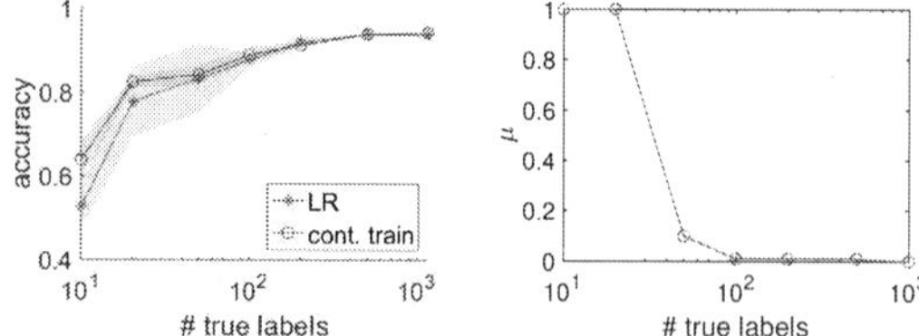

Figure 3: Continued training behavior: *Medical* vs. *Mideast*. Colored band: ±1 standard deviation.

re-ranking (IR+Roc) is less useful than training classifiers (IR+NB and IR+LR). After initial retrieval, training a naïve Bayes classifier is almost always better than a logistic regression classifier (IR+NB vs. IR+LR), demonstrating the power of generative models when supervision signal is sparse. Using class labels as labeled features (GE and sLDA) performs well occasionally (GE on 20 News; sLDA on Y Questions), but not consistently. The Cosine method performs well only on Wiki Titles, the shortest documents, because without supervision, representing a long document as an average of word vectors causes significant information loss. Finally, it is encouraging to see WENB+LR sometimes outperform WENB, as WENB+LR is much smaller than WENB+LR in terms of model size.

4.4 Continued Training and Error Analysis

Figure 2 and 3 compare logistic regression classifiers trained with and without pseudo labels generated by WENB. Note that the classifier trained with pseudo labels (cont. train) has a much lower performance variance than the logistic regression classifier trained only on true labels (LR).

The warm-started classifier can serve as a good starting point for further training. Figure 2 shows a salient warm-start effect on a balanced binary classification task in 20 News. The weight μ of pseudo labels increases when true labels are few (initial classifier as an informative prior). As expected, μ decreases when true labels become abundant.

Figure 3 shows another binary classification task in 20 News where the warm-start effect is limited. Correspondingly, μ quickly diminishes as more true labels are available. With 100 or more true labels, pseudo labels have a negligible weight ($\mu = 10^{-2}$). In machine learning terms, these pseudo labels specify an incorrect prior that the model should quickly forget, so that it will not hinder the overall learning process.

A closer investigation reveals that the word vector for *mideast* (the class label of one topic in Figure 3) is not well-trained. This is because in general text corpus, the word *mideast* is rather infrequent compared to commonly used alternatives, such as *middle_east*. The word vector of *mideast* is surrounded by other infrequent words or misspellings (such as *hizballah, jubeir, saudis, isreal*) as opposed to more frequent and relevant ones (such as *israel, israeli, saudi, arab*). Since WENB uses the semantic knowledge in word vectors to infer pseudo labels, the quality of class label word vectors will affect the pseudo label accuracy.

5 Conclusion and Future Directions

We studied the problem of training topic classifiers using only class labels. Experiments on six data sets show that class labels can save a significant amount of labeled examples in the beginning. Retrieval-based and semi-supervised methods tend to perform better on long documents, while the proposed method performs better on short documents.

This study opens up many interesting avenues for future work. First, we introduce a new perspective on text classification: can we build a text classifier by just providing a short description of each class? This is a more challenging (but more user-friendly) setup than standard supervised classification. Second, future work can investigate tasks such as sentiment and emotion classification, which are more challenging than topic classification tasks. Third, the two approaches – leveraging unlabeled data (retrieval-based and semi-supervised methods) and leveraging pretrained models (the proposed method) – could be combined to give robust performance on both short and long documents. Finally, we can invite users into the training loop: in addition to labeling documents, users can also revise the class definitions to improve the classifier.

Acknowledgments

We thank the anonymous reviewers for their helpful comments. This work was in part supported by the National Library of Medicine under grant number 2R01LM010681-05. Qiaozhu Mei's work was supported in part by the National Science Foundation under grant numbers 1633370 and 1620319. Yue Wang would like to thank the support of the Eleanor M. and Frederick G. Kilgour Research Grant Award by the UNC-CH School of Information and Library Science.

References

2014. WMT 2014 English News Crawl. `http://www.statmt.org/wmt14/training-monolingual-news-crawl`.

Ricardo Baeza-Yates, Berthier de Araújo Neto Ribeiro, et al. 2011. *8.3.2 Naive Text Classification*, chapter 8. New York: ACM Press; Harlow, England: Addison-Wesley,.

Ciprian Chelba, Tomas Mikolov, Mike Schuster, Qi Ge, Thorsten Brants, Phillipp Koehn, and Tony Robinson. 2013. One billion word benchmark for measuring progress in statistical language modeling. *arXiv preprint arXiv:1312.3005*.

W Bruce Croft, Donald Metzler, and Trevor Strohman. 2010. *Retrieval Models*, chapter 7. Addison-Wesley Reading.

Gregory Druck, Gideon Mann, and Andrew McCallum. 2008. Learning from labeled features using generalized expectation criteria. In *Proceedings of the 31st annual international ACM SIGIR conference on Research and development in information retrieval*, pages 595–602. ACM.

Swapnil Hingmire and Sutanu Chakraborti. 2014. Topic labeled text classification: a weakly supervised approach. In *Proceedings of the 37th international ACM SIGIR conference on Research & development in information retrieval*, pages 385–394. ACM.

Jagadeesh Jagarlamudi, Hal Daumé III, and Raghavendra Udupa. 2012. Incorporating lexical priors into topic models. In *Proceedings of the 13th Conference of the European Chapter of the Association for Computational Linguistics*, pages 204–213. Association for Computational Linguistics.

Antonio J Jimeno-Yepes, Bridget T McInnes, and Alan R Aronson. 2011. Exploiting mesh indexing in medline to generate a data set for word sense disambiguation. *BMC bioinformatics*, 12(1):223.

David D. Lewis. Reuters-21578. `http://www.daviddlewis.com/resources/testcollections/reuters21578`.

M Lichman. 2013. Uci machine learning repository [http://archive. ics. uci. edu/ml]. university of california, school of information and computer science. *Irvine, CA*.

Tomas Mikolov, Ilya Sutskever, Kai Chen, Greg S Corrado, and Jeff Dean. 2013. Distributed representations of words and phrases and their compositionality. In *Advances in neural information processing systems*, pages 3111–3119.

NLM. 2018. MEDLINE/PubMed Data. `ftp://ftp.ncbi.nlm.nih.gov/pubmed/baseline`.

Agnieszka Oniśko, Marek J Druzdzel, and Hanna Wasyluk. 2001. Learning bayesian network parameters from small data sets: Application of noisy-or gates. *International Journal of Approximate Reasoning*, 27(2):165–182.

Sinno Jialin Pan and Qiang Yang. 2010. A survey on transfer learning. *IEEE Transactions on knowledge and data engineering*, 22(10):1345–1359.

Pushpankar Kumar Pushp and Muktabh Mayank Srivastava. 2017. Train once, test anywhere: Zero-shot learning for text classification. *arXiv preprint arXiv:1712.05972*.

J. J. Rocchio. 1965. Relevance feedback in information retrieval, report no. *ISR-9 to the National Science Foundation, The Computation Laboratory of Harvard University, to appear August*.

Robert E Schapire, Marie Rochery, Mazin Rahim, and Narendra Gupta. 2002. Incorporating prior knowledge into boosting. In *ICML*, volume 2, pages 538–545.

Richard Socher, Milind Ganjoo, Christopher D Manning, and Andrew Ng. 2013. Zero-shot learning through cross-modal transfer. In *Advances in neural information processing systems*, pages 935–943.

Wikipedia Main Topic. Category:Main topic classifications. `https://en.wikipedia.org/wiki/Category:Main_topic_classifications`.

Yahoo Language Data. 2007. Yahoo! Answers Comprehensive Questions and Answers version 1.0 (multi part). `https://webscope.sandbox.yahoo.com/catalog.php?datatype=l`.

Chengxiang Zhai and John Lafferty. 2001. A study of smoothing methods for language models applied to ad hoc information retrieval. In *Proceedings of 24th International ACM SIGIR Conference on Research and Development in Information Retrieval*, pages 334–342.

Xiaojin Zhu. 2006. Semi-supervised learning literature survey. *Computer Science, University of Wisconsin-Madison*, 2(3):4.

A   Class Labels Used in Each Data Set

Data set	Class labels
Wiki Titles	*Arts, Games, Geography, Health, History, Industry, Law, Life, Mathematics, Matter, Nature, People, Religion, Science/Technology, Society*
News Titles	*Business, Technology, Entertainment, Health*
Y-Questions	*Society/Culture, Science/Mathematics, Health, Education/Reference, Computers/Internet, Sports, Business/Finance, Entertainment/Music, Family Relationships, Politics/Government*
20 News	*Atheism, Graphics, Microsoft, IBM, Mac,Windows, Sale, Autos, Baseball, Motorcycles, Hockey, Encrypt, Electronics, Medical, Space, Christian Guns, Mideast, Politics, Religion*
Reuters	*Earnings/Forecasts, Mergers/Acquisitions, Crude Oil, Trade, Foreign Exchange, Interest Rates, Money Supply, Shipping, Sugar, Coffee*

Table 4: Class labels in 5 topic classification data sets.

Task (ambiguous term)	Class labels (senses)
AA	*Amino Acids, Alcoholics Anonymous*
ADA	*Adenosine Deaminase, American Dental Association*
ADH	*Alcohol dehydrogenase, Argipressin*
ADP	*Adenosine Diphosphate, Automatic Data Processing*
Adrenal	*Adrenal Glands, Epinephrine*
Ala	*Alanine, Alpha-Linolenic Acid, Aminolevulinic Acid*
ALS	*Antilymphocyte Serum, Amyotrophic Lateral Sclerosis*
ANA	*American Nurses' Association, Antibodies, Antinuclear*
Arteriovenous Anastomoses	*Arteriovenous anastomosis procedure, Structure of anatomic-arteriovenous anastomosis*
Astragalus	*Talus, Astragalus Plant*
B-Cell Leukemia	*B-Cell Leukemia, Chronic Lymphocytic Leukemia*
BAT	*Chiroptera, Brown Fat*
BLM	*Bloom Syndrome, Bleomycin*
Borrelia	*Lyme Disease, Borrelia bacteria*
BPD	*Bronchopulmonary Dysplasia, Borderline Personality-Disorder*
BR	*Brazil, Bromides*
Brucella abortus	*Brucella abortus infection, Brucella abortus bacterium*
BSA	*Body Surface Area, Bovine Serum Albumin*
BSE	*Bovine Spongiform-Encephalopathy, Breast Self-Examination*
Ca	*Hippocampus (Brain), Calcium, California, Canada*

Table 5: The first 20 ambiguous terms/tasks in Med WSD data set.

Handling Noisy Labels for Robustly Learning from Self-Training Data for Low-Resource Sequence Labeling

Debjit Paul[*§]**, Mittul Singh**[†§]**, Michael A. Hedderich**[‡]**, Dietrich Klakow**[‡]

[*]Research Training Group AIPHES, Institute for Computational Linguistics,
Heidelberg University, Germany
[†]Department of Signal Processing and Acoustics, Aalto University, Finland
[‡]Spoken Language Systems (LSV), Saarland Informatics Campus,
Saarland University, Germany

`paul@cl.uni-heidelberg.de, mittul.singh@aalto.fi,`
`{mhedderich, dietrich.klakow}@lsv.uni-saarland.de`

Abstract

In this paper, we address the problem of effectively self-training neural networks in a low-resource setting. Self-training is frequently used to automatically increase the amount of training data. However, in a low-resource scenario, it is less effective due to unreliable annotations created using self-labeling of unlabeled data. We propose to combine self-training with noise handling on the self-labeled data. Directly estimating noise on the combined clean training set and self-labeled data can lead to corruption of the clean data and hence, performs worse. Thus, we propose the Clean and Noisy Label Neural Network which trains on clean and noisy self-labeled data simultaneously by explicitly modelling clean and noisy labels separately. In our experiments on Chunking and NER, this approach performs more robustly than the baselines. Complementary to this explicit approach, noise can also be handled implicitly with the help of an auxiliary learning task. To such a complementary approach, our method is more beneficial than other baseline methods and together provides the best performance overall.

1 Introduction

For many low-resource languages or domains, only small amounts of labeled data exist. Raw or unlabeled data, on the other hand, is usually available even in these scenarios. Automatic annotation or distant supervision techniques are an option to obtain labels for this raw data, but they often require additional external resources like human-generated lexica which might not be available in a low-resource context. Self-training is a popular technique to automatically label additional text. There, a classifier is trained on a small amount of labeled data and then used to obtain labels for

unlabeled instances. However, this can lead to unreliable or noisy labels on the additional data which impede the learning process (Pechenizkiy et al., 2006; Nettleton et al., 2010). In this paper, we focus on overcoming this slowdown of self-training. Hence, we propose to apply noise-reduction techniques during self-training to clean the self-labeled data and learn effectively in a low-resource scenario.

Inspired by the improvements shown by the Noisy Label Neural Network (*NLNN*, Bekker and Goldberger (2016)), we can directly apply *NLNN* to the combined set of the existing clean data and the noisy self-labeled data. However, such an application can be detrimental to the learning process (Section 6). Thus, we introduce the Clean and Noisy Label Neural Network (*CNLNN*) that treats the clean and noisy data separately while training on them simultaneously (Section 3).

This approach leads to two advantages over *NLNN* (Section 6 and 7) when evaluating on two sequence-labeling tasks, Chunking and Named Entity Recognition. **Firstly**, when adding noisy data, *CNLNN* is robust showing consistent improvements over the regular neural network, whereas *NLNN* can lead to degradation in performance. **Secondly**, when combining with an indirect-noise handling technique, i.e. with an auxiliary target in a multi-task fashion, *CNLNN* complements better than *NLNN* in the multi-task setup and overall leads to the best performance.

2 Related Work

Self-training has been applied to various NLP tasks, e.g. Steedman et al. (2003) and Sagae and Tsujii (2007). While McClosky et al. (2006) are able to leverage self-training for parsing, Charniak (1997) and Clark et al. (2003) obtain only minimal improvements at best on parsing and POS-tagging

---

§This work was started while the authors were at Saarland University.

Proceedings of the 2019 Conference of the North American Chapter of the Association for Computational Linguistics: Student Research Workshop, pages 29–34
Minneapolis, Minnesota, June 3 - 5, 2019. ©2017 Association for Computational Linguistics

respectively. In some cases, the results even deteriorate. Other successful approaches of automatically labeling data include using a different classifier trained on out-of-domain data (Petrov et al., 2010) or leveraging external knowledge (Dembowski et al., 2017).

A detailed review of learning in the presence of noisy labels is given in (Frénay and Verleysen, 2014). Recently, several approaches have been proposed for modeling the noise using a confusion matrix in a neural network context. Many works assume that all the data is noisy-labeled (Bekker and Goldberger, 2016; Goldberger and Ben-Reuven, 2017; Sukhbaatar et al., 2015). Hedderich and Klakow (2018) and Hendrycks et al. (2018) propose a setting where a mix of clean and unlabeled data is used. However, they require external knowledge sources for labeling the data or evaluate on synthetic noise. Alternatively, instances with incorrect labels might be filtered out, e.g. in the work by Guan et al. (2011) or Han et al. (2018), but this involves the risk of also filtering out difficult but correct instances. Another orthogonal approach is the use of noise-robust loss functions (Zhang and Sabuncu, 2018).

3 Clean and Noisy Label Neural Network

The Noisy Label Neural Network (*NLNN*, Bekker and Goldberger (2016)) assumes that all observed labels in the training set pass through a noise channel flipping some of them from a correct to an incorrect label (see left part of Figure 1). In our scenario, this means that both the human-annotated and the additional automatically-labeled (self-training) corpora are assumed to be noisy. In our experiments (Section 6 and 7), treating both corpora in this fashion degrades the overall performance. To remedy this effect, we propose to treat the human-annotated data as clean data and the self-training data as noisy.

We assume a similar setup as Bekker and Goldberger (2016), training a multi-class neural network soft-max classifier

$$p(y = i | x; w) = \frac{exp(u_i^T h)}{\sum_{j=1}^{k} exp(u_j^T h)}$$

where x is the feature vector, y is the label, w denotes the network weights, k is the number of possible labels, u are soft-max weights and $h = h(x)$ denotes the multi-layer neural network applied to x. In contrast to Bekker and Goldberger (2016), we assume that not all of the training data passes

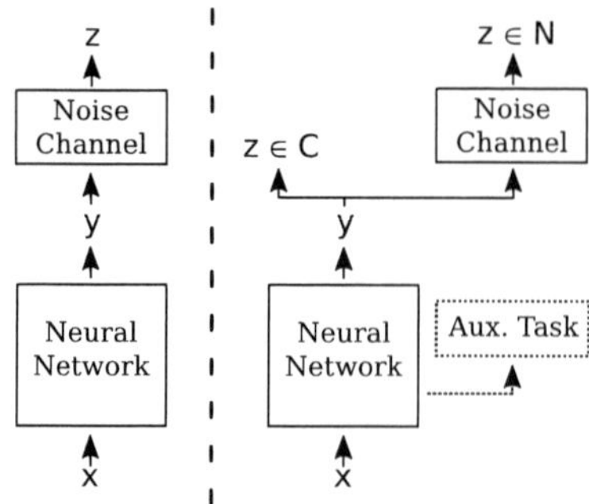

Figure 1: A representation of *NLNN* (left) compared to our proposed *CNLNN* model. The complementary multi-task component (aux. task) is dashed.

through a noisy channel changing the correct labels y to noisy ones ($z \in N$). A part of the training set remains clean ($z \in C$) such that $|C| + |N| = n$ where n is the total number of training examples. The clean labels are a copy of the corresponding correct labels. A schematic representation of this model is shown on the right side of Figure 1. The correct labels y and the noise distribution θ are hidden for the noisy labels.

We define the probability of observing a label z, which can either be noisy or clean and is, thus, dependent on the label's membership to C or N:

$$p(z = j | x, w, \theta) = \begin{cases} \sum_{i=1}^{k} p(z = j | y = i; \theta) p(y = i | x; w) \\ \qquad\qquad \text{if } z \in N \\ p(y = j | x; w) \quad \text{if } z \in C \text{ i.e. } z = y \end{cases}$$

Using this probability function and t to index training instances, the log-likelihood of the model parameters is defined as

$$L(w, \theta) = \sum_{z_t \in C} \log p(z_t | x_t, w) \\ + \sum_{z_t \in N} \log(\sum_{i=1}^{k} (p(z_t | y_t = i; \theta) \cdot p(y_t = i | x_t; w)))$$

As in Bekker and Goldberger (2016) the model parameters are computed using Expectation Maximization. In the E-step, θ and w are fixed and an estimate c of the true labels y is obtained for the noisy labels z:

$$c_{ti} = p(y_t = i | x_t, z_t; w, \theta) \\ = \frac{p(z_t | y_t = i, \theta) p(y_t = i | x_t; w)}{\sum_j p(z_t | y_t = j; \theta) p(y_t = j | x_t, w)} \quad \text{for } z_t \in N$$

Note that the estimate c is calculated only for the noisy labels whereas the clean labels remain unchanged. Similarly, the noise distribution θ is calculated only for the noisy labels. The initialization of θ and the θ's update step in M-step remain the same as in Bekker and Goldberger (2016), also

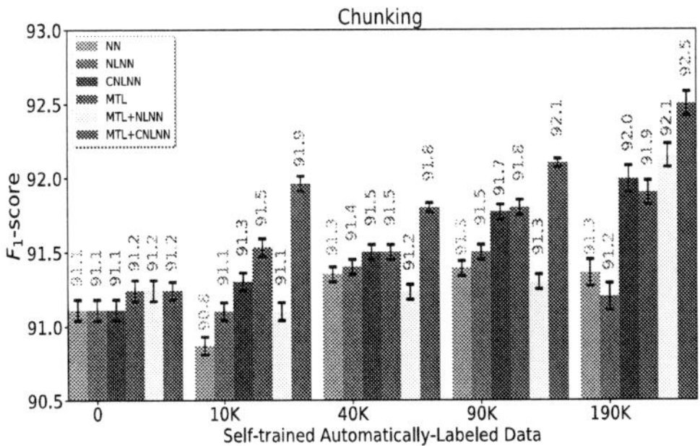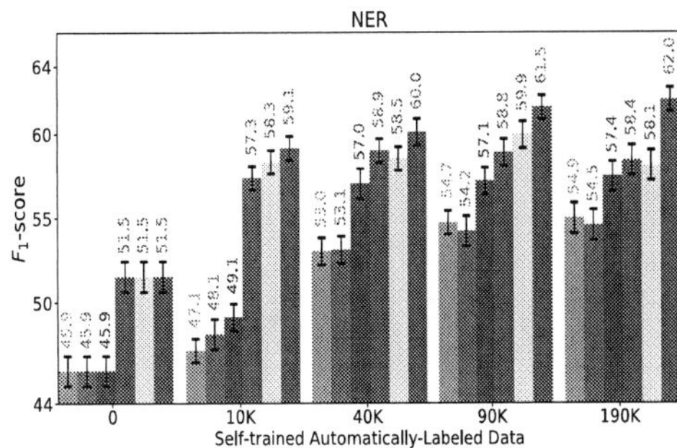

Figure 2: Micro-averaged F_1-scores (averaged over five runs) on English Penn Treebank's Chunking and English CoNLL 2003's NER tasks of models from Section 5 are plotted (with error bars) against the amount of automatically-labeled data. 0 on the x-axis represents models trained with only the clean training set (10k tokens).

shown below.

$$\theta(i,j) = \frac{\sum_t c_{ti} 1_{\{z_t = j\}}}{\sum_t c_{ti}} \qquad i,j \in \{1,...,k\}, z_t \in N$$

During the M-step, the neural network weights w are estimated as well. The loss function, however, changes compared to the original approach (Bekker and Goldberger, 2016) to (1) and thus, changing the calculation of the gradient to (2):

$$S(w) = \sum_{z_t \in C} \log p(z_t | x_t, w) + \sum_{z_t \in N} \sum_{i=1}^{k} c_{ti} \log p(y_t = i | x_t; w) \tag{1}$$

$$\frac{\partial S}{\partial u_i} = \sum_{z_t \in C} (1_{\{z_t = i\}} - p(z_t | x_t, w)) h(x_t)$$
$$+ \sum_{z_t \in N} (c_{ti} - p(y_t | x_t, w)) h(x_t) \tag{2}$$

Interestingly, the gradient calculation (2) is a summation of two parts: one to learn from the clean labels and another to learn from the noisy labels. We refer to this model as the Clean and Noisy Label Neural Network (*CNLNN*).

4 Training with Noisy Labels in a Multi-Task Setup

NLNN and *CNLNN* form explicit ways of handling noise as the noise distribution is calculated during training. In contrast, we can apply a Deep Multi-Task Learning (MTL) approach (Søgaard and Goldberg, 2016), which, unlike *NLNN* and *CNLNN*, does not estimate the noise directly and thus, is an implicit noise-cleaning approach. The MTL method leverages an auxiliary task that augments the data providing other reliable labels and hence, ignoring noisy labels (Ruder, 2017). In our experiments, we combine the implicit noise handling of Deep MTL with the explicit noise handling of *NLNN* and *CNLNN* to complement each other and obtain a more powerful noise handling model than the individual models. Schematic depiction of combining MTL and *CNLNN* is shown in Figure 1. MTL and *NLNN* can also be combined in a similar way.

5 Experimental Setup

We evaluate *CNLNN* and other methods on a Chunking and a Named Entity Recognition (NER) task with F_1-score as the metric in each case. For Chunking, we use the same data splits as (Søgaard and Goldberg, 2016) based on the English Penn Treebank dataset (Marcus et al., 1993). For NER, the data splits of the English CoNLL 2003 task are used (Sang and Buchholz, 2000). Note that in our NER setup, we evaluate using *BIO-2* labels, so F_1-scores reported below might not be comparable to prior work.

To mimic a low resource setting, we limit each training set to the first 10k tokens. The development sets are randomly chosen sentences from the original training set restricted to 1k tokens. The test sets remain unchanged. For the rest of the training data, the original labels are removed and the words are automatically labeled using the baseline model (*NN* described below). We add variable amounts of this automatically-annotated data for self-training in our experiments.

5.1 Models

We apply the following models to the above two tasks: **NN** (the simple baseline) is an architecture with bidirectional LSTMs (Hochreiter and Schmidhuber, 1997). For Chunking, we use three LSTM layers, for NER five. The *NN* model, only trained on the clean data, is used for automatically labeling the raw data (obtaining the noisy data). **NLNN** combines the *NN* with the original noise channel (Bekker and Goldberger, 2016), training it both on clean and noisy instances. **CNLNN** is our new approach of modeling noise, treating clean and noisy labels separately (section 3).

In contrast to the explicit noise handling of *NLNN* and *CNLNN*, we also apply **MTL** for implicit noise handling. Here, we use *NN* as the base architecture and POS-tagging as an auxiliary task. We hypothesise that this low-level task helps the model to generalise its representation and that the POS-tags are helpful because e.g. many named entities are proper nouns. The auxiliary task is trained jointly with the first LSTM layer of *NN* for Chunking and with the second LSTM layer for NER. In our low-resource setting, we use the first 10k tokens of section 0 of Penn Treebank for the auxiliary POS-tagging task for the MTL (Søgaard and Goldberg, 2016). This data is disjunct from the other datasets.

Additionally, we combine both the explicit and implicit noise handling. In the low-resource setting, in general, such a combination addresses the data scarcity better than the individual models. *NLNN* and *CNLNN* combinations with MTL are labeled as **MTL+NLNN** and **MTL+CNLNN** respectively.

5.2 Implementation Details

During training, we minimize the cross entropy loss which sums over the entire sentence. The networks are trained with Stochastic Gradient Descent (SGD). To determine the number of iterations for both the NN model and the EM algorithm we use the development data. All models are trained with word embeddings of dimensionality 64 that are initialized with pre-trained Polygot embeddings (Al-Rfou et al., 2013). We add Dropout (Srivastava et al., 2014) with p=0.1 in between the word embedding layer and the LSTM.

6 Results

In Figure 2, we present the F_1 scores of the models introduced in the previous section. We perform experiments on Chunking and NER with various amounts of added, automatically-labeled data. In general, adding additional, noisy data tends to improve the performance for all mod-

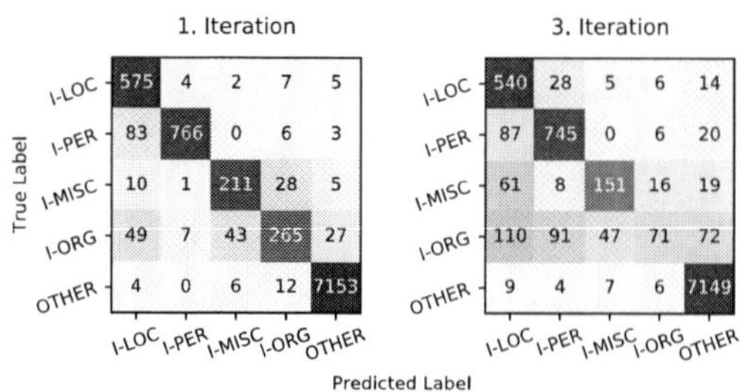

Figure 3: *NLNN* confusion matrices on Chunking's clean training set for 1. and 3. EM iteration. The colors correspond to row-normalized values.

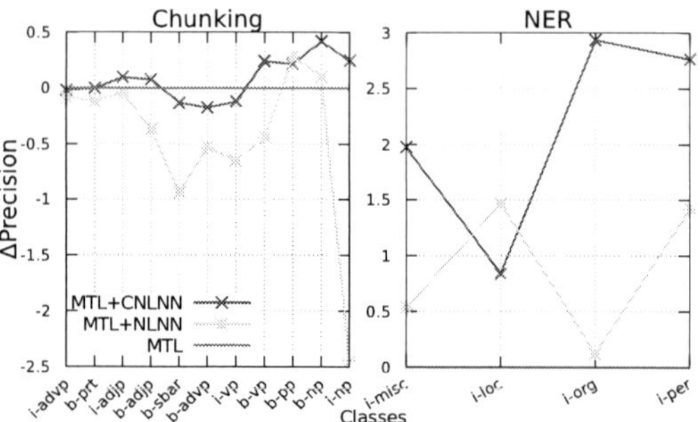

Figure 4: *MTL+CNLNN* vs *MTL+NLNN*: Difference in precision between the combined models and MTL for NER and Chunking test sets with 190K noisy data.

els. This includes the plain *NN*, showing that this model is somewhat robust to noise. Especially for the Chunking task, the possibility for improvement seems limited for *NN* as the performance converges after adding 40k noisy instances. In the Chunking 10k case, the negative effect of the noisy instances results in a score lower than if no data is added.

The original *NLNN* model performs similarly to the *NN* model without a noise-handling component. In some cases, the score is even lower. In contrast, *CNLNN* is able to consistently improve over these scores. This demonstrates the importance of our proposed *CNLNN* which treats clean and noisy data separately.

MTL is able to improve somewhat over *NN* even without adding automatically-annotated data thanks to the auxiliary task. Additionally, *MTL* performs even better when noisy data is added showing its implicit noise handling capabilities. On their own, both *CNLNN* and *MTL* are able to eliminate some of the negative effects of the noisy data and to leverage the additional data effectively.

Combining *MTL* with *NLNN* results in small improvements at best and can decrease performance, especially on Chunking. The best results are achieved with our combined *MTL+CNLNN* model as it outperforms all other models. Even when adding 19 times the amount of self-labeled data, the model is still able to cope with the noise and improve the performance.

7 Analysis

NLNN vs. CNLNN: In *NLNN*, we observed that clean training tokens were subverted to become noisy in subsequent EM iterations mostly due to the influence of noisy labels from self-labeled data and this effect leads to *NLNN*'s worse performance. Figure 3 presents one such case where the corruption of the confusion matrix from 1. iteration to 3. iteration is displayed. *CNLNN* treats clean and noise data separately and therefore avoids the corruption of clean labels.
MTL+CNLNN vs. MTL+NLNN: We noted that *MTL+CNLNN* consistently outperforms *MTL* and *MTL+NLNN*, whereas the *MTL+NLNN* combination can degrade *MTL*'s performance. For nearly all predicted labels the improvements in precision over *MTL* are higher for *MTL+CNLNN* when compared to *MTL+NLNN* (Figure 4). This shows that *CNLNN* complements *MTL* better than *NLNN*.

8 Concluding Remarks

In this paper, we apply self-training to neural networks for Chunking and NER in a low-resource setup. Adding automatically-labeled data, the performance of the classifier can wane or can even decline. We propose to mitigate this effect by applying noisy label handling techniques.

However, we found that directly applying an off-the-shelf noise-handling technique as NLNN leads to corruption of the clean training set and worse performance. Thus, we propose the Clean and Noisy Label Neural Network to work separately on the automatically-labeled data. Our model improves the performance faster for a lesser amount of additional data. Moreover, combing the training with auxiliary information can further help handle noise in a complementary fashion.

Meanwhile, more complex neural network architectures (Goldberger and Ben-Reuven, 2017; Luo et al., 2017; Veit et al., 2017) are available for handling noise and we look forward to working with these to upgrade our approach in the future.

9 Acknowledgements

This work has been supported by the German Research Foundation as part of the Research Training Group Adaptive Preparation of Information from Heterogeneous Sources (AIPHES) under grant No. GRK 1994/1. We also thank the anonymous reviewers whose comments helped improve this paper.

References

Rami Al-Rfou, Bryan Perozzi, and Steven Skiena. 2013. Polyglot: Distributed word representations for multilingual NLP. In *Proceedings of the Seventeenth Conference on Computational Natural Language Learning, CoNLL 2013, Sofia, Bulgaria, August 8-9, 2013*, pages 183–192.

Alan Joseph Bekker and Jacob Goldberger. 2016. Training deep neural-networks based on unreliable labels. In *Proceedings of the 2016 IEEE International Conference on Acoustics, Speech and Signal Processing*, pages 2682–2686.

Eugene Charniak. 1997. Statistical parsing with a context-free grammar and word statistics. In *Proceedings of the Fourteenth National Conference on Artificial Intelligence and Ninth Conference on Innovative Applications of Artificial Intelligence, AAAI'97/IAAI'97*, pages 598–603.

Stephen Clark, James R. Curran, and Miles Osborne. 2003. Bootstrapping pos taggers using unlabelled data. In *Proceedings of the Seventh Conference on Natural Language Learning at HLT-NAACL 2003 - Volume 4*, CONLL '03, pages 49–55.

Julia Dembowski, Michael Wiegand, and Dietrich Klakow. 2017. Language independent named entity recognition using distant supervision. In *Proceedings of Language and Technology Conference (LTC)*.

Benoît Frénay and Michel Verleysen. 2014. Classification in the presence of label noise: A survey. *IEEE Transactions on Neural Networks and Learning Systems*, 25(5):845–869.

Jacob Goldberger and Ehud Ben-Reuven. 2017. Training deep neural-networks using a noise adaptation layer. In *International Conference on Learning Representations (ICLR)*.

Donghai Guan, Weiwei Yuan, Young-Koo Lee, and Sungyoung Lee. 2011. Identifying mislabeled training data with the aid of unlabeled data. *Applied Intelligence*, 35(3):345–358.

Bo Han, Quanming Yao, Xingrui Yu, Gang Niu, Miao Xu, Weihua Hu, Ivor W. Tsang, and Masashi Sugiyama. 2018. Co-teaching: Robust training of deep neural networks with extremely noisy labels.

In *Advances in Neural Information Processing Systems 31: Annual Conference on Neural Information Processing Systems 2018, NeurIPS 2018, 3-8 December 2018, Montréal, Canada.*, pages 8536–8546.

Michael A. Hedderich and Dietrich Klakow. 2018. Training a neural network in a low-resource setting on automatically annotated noisy data. In *Proceedings of the Workshop on Deep Learning Approaches for Low-Resource NLP*, pages 12–18. Association for Computational Linguistics.

Dan Hendrycks, Mantas Mazeika, Duncan Wilson, and Kevin Gimpel. 2018. Using trusted data to train deep networks on labels corrupted by severe noise. In *Advances in Neural Information Processing Systems 31: Annual Conference on Neural Information Processing Systems 2018, NeurIPS 2018, 3-8 December 2018, Montréal, Canada.*, pages 10477–10486. Curran Associates, Inc.

Sepp Hochreiter and Jürgen Schmidhuber. 1997. Long short-term memory. *Neural computation*, 9(8):1735–1780.

Bingfeng Luo, Yansong Feng, Zheng Wang, Zhanxing Zhu, Songfang Huang, Rui Yan, and Dongyan Zhao. 2017. Learning with noise: Enhance distantly supervised relation extraction with dynamic transition matrix. In *Proceedings of the 55th Annual Meeting of the Association for Computational Linguistics (Volume 1: Long Papers)*.

Mitchell P. Marcus, Mary Ann Marcinkiewicz, and Beatrice Santorini. 1993. Building a large annotated corpus of english: The penn treebank. *Computational Linguistics*, 19(2):313–330.

David McClosky, Eugene Charniak, and Mark Johnson. 2006. Effective self-training for parsing. In *Proceedings of the main conference on human language technology conference of the North American Chapter of the Association of Computational Linguistics*, pages 152–159. Association for Computational Linguistics.

David F. Nettleton, Albert Orriols-Puig, and Albert Fornells. 2010. A study of the effect of different types of noise on the precision of supervised learning techniques. *Artificial Intelligence Review*, 33(4):275–306.

Mykola Pechenizkiy, Alexey Tsymbal, Seppo Puuronen, and Oleksandr Pechenizkiy. 2006. Class noise and supervised learning in medical domains: The effect of feature extraction. In *19th IEEE Symposium on Computer-Based Medical Systems*, pages 708–713.

Slav Petrov, Pi-Chuan Chang, Michael Ringgaard, and Hiyan Alshawi. 2010. Uptraining for accurate deterministic question parsing. In *Proceedings of the 2010 Conference on Empirical Methods in Natural Language Processing*, EMNLP '10, pages 705–713.

Sebastian Ruder. 2017. An overview of multi-task learning in deep neural networks. *arXiv e-prints*, page arXiv:1706.05098.

Kenji Sagae and Jun'ichi Tsujii. 2007. Dependency parsing and domain adaptation with lr models and parser ensembles. In *Proceedings of the 2007 Joint Conference on Empirical Methods in Natural Language Processing and Computational Natural Language Learning*.

Erik F. Tjong Kim Sang and Sabine Buchholz. 2000. Introduction to the conll-2000 shared task: Chunking. In *Proceedings of the 2nd workshop on Learning language in logic and the 4th conference on Computational natural language learning-Volume 7*, pages 127–132. Association for Computational Linguistics.

Anders Søgaard and Yoav Goldberg. 2016. Deep multi-task learning with low level tasks supervised at lower layers. In *Proceedings of the 54th Annual Meeting of the Association for Computational Linguistics (Volume 2: Short Papers)*.

Nitish Srivastava, Geoffrey Hinton, Alex Krizhevsky, Ilya Sutskever, and Ruslan Salakhutdinov. 2014. Dropout: A simple way to prevent neural networks from overfitting. *Journal of Machine Learning Research*, 15:1929–1958.

Mark Steedman, Miles Osborne, Anoop Sarkar, Stephen Clark, Rebecca Hwa, Julia Hockenmaier, Paul Ruhlen, Steven Baker, and Jeremiah Crim. 2003. Bootstrapping statistical parsers from small datasets. In *Proceedings of the Tenth Conference on European Chapter of the Association for Computational Linguistics - Volume 1*, EACL '03, pages 331–338.

Sainbayar Sukhbaatar, Joan Bruna, Manohar Paluri, Lubomir Bourdev, and Rob Fergus. 2015. Learning from noisy labels with deep neural networks. In *ICLR Workshop track*.

Andreas Veit, Neil Alldrin, Gal Chechik, Ivan Krasin, Abhinav Gupta, and Serge Belongie. 2017. Learning from noisy large-scale datasets with minimal supervision. In *Proceedings of the IEEE Conference on Computer Vision and Pattern Recognition*, pages 839–847.

Zhilu Zhang and Mert R. Sabuncu. 2018. Generalized cross entropy loss for training deep neural networks with noisy labels. In *Advances in Neural Information Processing Systems 31: Annual Conference on Neural Information Processing Systems 2018, NeurIPS 2018, 3-8 December 2018, Montréal, Canada.*, pages 8792–8802.

Opinion Mining with Deep Contextualized Embeddings

Wen-Bin Han
National Tsing Hua University
HsinChu, 30013, Taiwan, R.O.C.
`vincent.han@nlplab.cc`

Noriko Kando
National Institute of Informatics
Tokyo, 101-8430, JAPAN
`kando@nii.ac.jp`

Abstract

Detecting opinion expression is a potential and essential task in opinion mining that can be extended to advanced tasks. In this paper, we considered opinion expression detection as a sequence labeling task and exploited different deep contextualized embedders into the state-of-the-art architecture, composed of bidirectional long short-term memory (BiLSTM) and conditional random field (CRF). Our experimental results show that using different word embeddings can cause contrasting results, and the model can achieve remarkable scores with deep contextualized embeddings. Especially, using BERT embedder can significantly exceed using ELMo embedder.

1 Introduction

One of the crucial tasks in sentiment analysis field is opinion mining, which right now becomes more and more popular for survey. The purpose of opinion mining is to detect the emotional expression from a sentence or an entire document. To be more specific, those expressions usually contain human beings' emotions, interests, even attitudes via natural language.

Fine-grained opinion mining is not only fundamental but also important because bountiful Natural Language Processing (NLP) applications can benefit from it. For example, detecting opinion expression can be extended to identify opinion entity, such as Katiyar and Cardie (2016); Miwa and Bansal (2016); Katiyar and Cardie (2017), recognize stance (Somasundaran and Wiebe, 2010), and extract aspect (Xu et al., 2018; Wang et al., 2016).

Opinion expression detection can be viewed as a linguistic sequence labeling problem. Therefore, recognizing opinionated span from a sentence can be designed as a token-level sequence tagging problem. In this case, standard BIO encoding is usually applied in the same way in İrsoy

I	hope	you	are	going
O	B_DSE	O	O	O
to	see	more	of	an
O	O	B_ESE	I_ESE	I_ESE
effect	from	this	event	.
I_ESE	O	O	O	O

Table 1: An example with BIO labels for DSE and ESE.

and Cardie (2014); Choi et al. (2005). Thus, we used the dataset tagged with B, I, and O characters, which represent the beginning, inside, and outside respectively. The first token in each opinionated span is attached to B character, and then the rest of the span are assigned to I character. Table 1 is an example of BIO scheme.

Out of exactness, in this study, we chose the dataset MPQA 1.2 used in Xie (2017); İrsoy and Cardie (2014). To estimate the generalization of our model, we also took another opinion-oriented dataset MOAT from the organization NTCIR7 (Seki et al., 2008).

Opinion expression usually contains a speaker's emotion; hence, we assume that semantics contributes more than syntax. Even though pre-trained word embedding can improve the performance, it still doesn't fully utilize word meaning and its context. Therefore, generating word representations based on the contexts is critical. Owing to deep neural network, model can produce dynamic word representation, such as McCann et al. (2017); Peters et al. (2018); Akbik et al. (2018), on the contrary to fixed representation (Pennington et al., 2014; Mikolov et al., 2013). In this paper, we applied two state-of-the-art and innovative models, ELMo (Peters et al., 2018) and BERT (Devlin et al., 2018), to produce word representations and compared the performances. After obtaining the contextualized word representations,

Proceedings of the 2019 Conference of the North American Chapter of the Association for Computational Linguistics: Student Research Workshop, pages 35–42
Minneapolis, Minnesota, June 3 - 5, 2019. ©2017 Association for Computational Linguistics

we fed them into a robust neural network.

2 Related Work

Word Representation. In the past few years, distributed word representations, also known as word embeddings, have been broadly applied to NLP tasks because adding pre-trained one can improve the performance by 1 to 2 point.

Many researches are done with GloVe (Pennington et al., 2014) or Word2Vec (Mikolov et al., 2013). However, one vector can not represent all the meanings of a word. For the sake of deep neural networks, we can add contextual characteristic into word representation during converting. For instance, CoVe (McCann et al., 2017) learns contextualized word vectors via encoders in translation. ELMo (Peters et al., 2018) produces contextualized embeddings from language models computed on 2-layer BiLSTMs with character convolutions. Akbik et al. (2018) trained a character language model to produce contextual string embeddings.

Different from the models mentioned above, BERT (Devlin et al., 2018) extends Radford (2018), extracting features by Transformer (Vaswani et al., 2017), from uni-direction into bi-direction and outperforms impressively in many tasks. In this paper, we took BERT as our embedder because it can generate contextual features. In contrast, ELMo is selected as our baseline embedder.

According to Ruder and Howard (2018), pre-training on a large amount of unlabeled data do improve the model; thus, we used pre-trained BERT and ELMo model and then did fine-tuning with our data.

Neural Network. Recurrent Neural Network (RNN) (Jain and Medsker, 1999) handles variable length input and performs well on NLP tasks, in particular Long Short-Term Momory (LSTM) (Hochreiter and Schmidhuber, 1997). At present, state-of-the-art approaches for sequence labeling typically use bidirectional LSTMs (BiLSTMs) (Schuster and Paliwal, 1997), and a conditional random field (CRF) decoding layer. BiLSTMs can capture not only the previous information but also the following information.

Recently, RNNs have been generally utilized in sequential modeling, such as İrsoy and Cardie (2014), which stacked 3-layer bidirectional vanilla RNNs and the model outperformed the variants of CRF-based methods. Moreover, LSTM has multiple gates allowing the model to learn long-distance dependencies. For sequential labeling tasks, such as Name Entity Recognition (NER) and Part-of-speech (POS) tagging, BiLSTM can take both former and latter contexts into consideration without length limitation and perform better (e.g., Liu et al. (2015) resorted to LSTM with some linguistic features and Katiyar and Cardie (2016) applied deep BiLSTMs on detecting opinion entities and relations).

So far, there have been many variants of LSTM-based neural network models proposed to improve the model and achieve competitive performance against traditional models. Miwa and Bansal (2016) made use of dependency tree and fed it into tree-structured BiLSTM. Simpler and more ingenious, Katiyar and Cardie (2017) only employed attention-based BiLSTM for entity and relation without any manual features or dependency structure information.

Conditional random fields (CRFs) (Lafferty et al., 2001) have also been quite successful for sequence tasks. Thanks to CRF layer, the model can take advantage of sentence-level and neighbor tag information to predict current tag (Huang et al., 2015; Ma and Hovy, 2016).

Some researches combined CNN with RNN to gain the benefits from each other. They extracted character-level features via CNN and handled sentences via RNN, such as Chiu and Nichols (2016). BiLSTM-CNNs-CRF (Ma and Hovy, 2016) obtained features via CNN and stacks CRF on BiLSTM. Xie (2017) applied CNN with bi-direction Gated Recurrent Units (GRUs). Xu et al. (2018) applied CNN to extract features with dual embeddings.

Our study compared BiLSTM-CNNs-CRF (2016) with the model using ELMo as embedder (ELMo-BiLSTM-CRF) and then competed ELMo-BiLSTM-CRF with the one using BERT as embedder (BERT-BiLSTM-CRF). Afterwards, we compared the performance and the difference between two embedders.

Eventually, based on Katiyar and Cardie (2017); Vaswani et al. (2017), we employed attention mechanism in BERT-BiLSTM-CRF layer expected to improve the accuracy.

3 Model

The main focus of our research is to improve the performance by using the deep contextualized word representation and compare two kinds of word embedders. Therefore, rather than static word representations, we employed dynamic word embedders that create the word representation based on its context.

After transforming all tokens into continuous vector representations, we fed them into BiLSTM instead of feed-forward network because BiLSTM neural network is prevailing and dominant on NLP tasks and many opinion-related tasks are completed with it.

After finishing each epoch, we updated the parameters simultaneously via back-propagation through time (BPTT) (Werbos, 1990). Last, after our comparisons, we chose the better model and added attention mechanism on BiLSTM layer to strengthen the performance.

In the following subsections, we decompose our neural network architectures and describe the components (layers) in detail. Hence, we introduce the neural layers in our models one-by-one from bottom to top. Before describing the models, we first illustrate the annotation format of data, which is followed by the most important part, word embedders. Afterwards, the BiLSTM layers as well as CRF layer will be mentioned.

3.1 Data Scheme

Opinion expression detection can be viewed as a linguistic sequence labeling problem. In this case, BIO encoding is usually applied to identify the opinionated span in a sentence. Thus, in the dataset, each token is tagged with BIO.

3.2 Word Embedders

According to previous research, using pre-trained word embeddings in downstream tasks usually outperforms using randomly initialized vectors. Therefore, choosing a robust embedding way to transform tokens is influential in experiments. Nevertheless, although there have been abundant ways to convert words into dense distributions so far, we first did some experiments to discover how effective each approach is.

After observing the datasets, we found that opinion detection task concentrates more on semantics than syntax. Consequently, we used a deep neural network, BERT, to figure out this problem because it is flexible enough to produce the representation of each token based on its context, even more the whole sentence.

Moreover, the BERT model is so overwhelming that it works impressively on plenty of tasks. In order to examine the performance on different embedding in opinion mining, we used BERT model as the word embedder in our experiments. Besides, it is necessary to compare the main model with a baseline. Therefore, we took another contextualized embedding, ELMo, as word embedding, and regarded the results as our baseline.

3.3 Architecture

We stacked BiLSTM on top of embedders because of the following reasons. First of all, in our research, BERT and ELMo are only used as word embedders instead of the whole architecture. Second, many RNN-based neural network models are proposed to figure out the sequence labeling tasks, and also achieved competitive performance against traditional models (Ma and Hovy, 2016; Huang et al., 2015). Last but not least, we would like to compare the performances between different contextualized embeddings so we must fix the other parts of architecture.

In addition, we also added CRF (Lafferty et al., 2001) layer because it can consider the correlations between labels in neighborhoods to predict current tag. Thanks to CRF layer, the model took full advantage of sentence-level tag information and enhanced itself to decode the best chain of labels for a given input sentence. In summary, we combined BERT or ELMo embedders with BiLSTM and CRF layers (Bert-BiLSTM-CRF and ELMo-BiLSTM-CRF). Each model can efficiently benefit from the forward and backward input features through BiLSTM layer and sentence-level tag information via CRF layer.

3.4 Attention

Katiyar and Cardie (2017) displayed that attention mechanism can reinforce the model. Therefore, we extended the Bert-BiLSTM-CRF network with multi-head attention approach because it allows the model to jointly attend to information from different representation sub-spaces at different positions (Vaswani et al., 2017). More concretely, the hidden states from BiLSTM layers went through attention layer and then linear layer as well as CRF layer.

Dataset	Count
DSE	14492
ESE	14492
NTCIR7-MOAT	3376

Table 2: The number of sentences for each dataset.

4 Experiments

4.1 Data Sets

Due to the development of opinion mining, there are numerous existing datasets which are useful for us. For example, Multi-Perspective Question Answering (MPQA) offers the annotated dataset.

In this paper, we conducted the experiments on the processed dataset, MPQA 1.2, provided by İrsoy and Cardie (2014). It includes two types of opinion expression proposed by Wiebe et al. (2005) - direct subjective expressions(DSEs) and expressive subjective expressions (ESEs). DSEs represent both subjective speech events and explicitly mentioned private states, while ESEs consist of tokens that express emotion or sentiment in an indirect or implicit way. Table 1 is also an example of DSE and ESE.

In addition to MQPA 1.2, we have another dataset from MOAT task, which is also related to opinion expression and organized by NTCIR (Seki et al., 2008). Different datasets can confirm that our model is generalized enough. Table 2 depicts the number of sentences in each dataset.

In the research, we first used one tenth of the dataset as the development set, and the rest of the data are applied 10-fold in order to get a more balanced result.

4.2 Word Embeddings

This experiment contains the details of the comparison between ELMo and other embedding ways. Table 3 is the results from different notable embedding ways on DSEs, and the evaluation is token-based calculation.

we selected some pre-trained word embedding - Word2Vec (Mikolov et al., 2013), GloVe (Pennington et al., 2014), and dependency-based word embedding (Levy and Goldberg, 2014). Besides, we also tried BiLSTM-CNNs-CRF (Ma and Hovy, 2016), which extracted character features by CNN and concatenated GloVe.

All the architectures are identical except for the word representings and decoding ways. Each combination is composed of one type of embeddings and three BiLSTM layers with or without CRF layer.

According to the results, the model with CRF layer does defeat the model without CRF layer. It proves that adding CRF layer becomes more powerful. Moreover, all the scores are close except for ELMo one. BiLSTM-CNNs-CRF doesn't exceed the other models only with pre-trained word embedding. We assumed that opinion mining emphasizes more semantics than syntax. Therefore, character features do not boost the model much.

Subsequently, we compared BiLSTM-CNNs-CRF with the one using ELMo embedder (ELMo-BiLSTM-CRF), and it turned out that ELMo-BiLSTM-CRF surpasses BiLSTM-CNNs-CRF substantially. Therefore, we took it as our baseline in this paper.

4.3 Parameter Settings

We made use of pre-trained BERT and ELMo models and did the fine-tuning during training procedure guided by Devlin et al. (2018) in order to make the model learn the distribution of the dataset.

For ELMo model, we used ELMoForManyLangs [1] provided by HIT-SCIR (Che et al., 2018; Fares et al., 2017) and took the average of the hidden states from all the layers as token representation.

For BERT model, we used "BERT-Base, Multilingual Cased" provided by Google [2] (Devlin et al., 2018). Most of the hyper-parameters are instructed by the paper. Only the hidden state from the last layer is picked and regarded as token representation.

For the rest of shared properties, we stacked 3 layers of BiLSTM [3] based on İrsoy and Cardie (2014). Learning rate is 0.00005 advised by (Devlin et al., 2018). Dropout is set to 0.5 before fully connected layer. Optimizer uses Adam (Kingma and Ba, 2014).

4.4 Evaluation

In the evaluation, we calculated precision, recall, and F1-score. However, in order to evaluate our model comprehensively, we measured our model not only by token basis but also span basis. This

---

[1] https://github.com/HIT-SCIR/ELMoForManyLangs
[2] https://github.com/google-research/bert
[3] According to our experiments, the number of layers do not affect the result much.

Embedding	Non CRF		CRF	
	Dev	**Test**	**Dev**	**Test**
GloVe	0.5249	0.5483	0.5474	0.5546
Word2Vec	0.5363	0.5387	0.5347	0.5685
Dependency-based word embedding	0.5224	0.5407	0.5450	0.5630
CNN character embedding and Glove	0.5395	0.5339	0.5455	0.5686
ELMo	**0.5920**	**0.5928**	**0.6151**	**0.6293**

Table 3: The results of applying a variety of embeddings on DSEs. ELMo embedder outperforms others significantly. Besides, stacking a CRF layer as decoder can increase the performance slightly.

Model	Token basis			Binary Overlap			Proportional Overlap		
	Prec.	Rec.	F1	Prec.	Rec.	F1	Prec.	Rec.	F1
ELMo-BiLSTM-CRF	0.708	0.640	0.640	0.703	0.620	0.653	0.676	0.543	0.597
BERT-BiLSTM-CRF	0.735	0.753	0.720	0.738	0.766	0.750	0.702	0.705*	0.701
BERT-BiLSTM-Attn-CRF	**0.740**	**0.761**	**0.723**	**0.744**	**0.768**	**0.752**	**0.710**	0.705*	**0.703**

Table 4: Experimental evaluation of models for DSE.

Model	Token basis			Binary Overlap			Proportional Overlap		
	Prec.	Rec.	F1	Prec.	Rec.	F1	Prec.	Rec.	F1
ELMo-BiLSTM-CRF	0.637	0.518	0.552	0.644	0.510	0.560	0.586	0.391	0.460
BERT-BiLSTM-CRF	**0.672**	0.608	0.631	**0.686**	0.634	0.654	0.625	0.527	0.564
BERT-BiLSTM-Attn-CRF	0.665	**0.635**	**0.645**	0.654	**0.684**	**0.663**	0.598	**0.570**	**0.577**

Table 5: Experimental evaluation of models for ESE.

Model	Token basis			Binary Overlap			Proportional Overlap		
	Prec.	Rec.	F1	Prec.	Rec.	F1	Prec.	Rec.	F1
ELMo-BiLSTM-CRF	0.483	0.419	0.404	**0.465**	0.356	0.323	**0.426**	0.267	0.245
BERT-BiLSTM-CRF	0.468	0.428	0.430	0.426	0.432	**0.415**	0.387	0.354	0.359*
BERT-BiLSTM-Attn-CRF	**0.515**	**0.481**	**0.482**	0.360	**0.510**	0.407	0.337	**0.427**	0.359*

Table 6: Experimental evaluation of models for NTCIR-MOAT7. * means the same scores.

is because it is difficult to define the boundaries of expressions, even for human annotators. To put it another way, for token-based evaluation, F1-score pays attention to whether the individual tag is predicted correctly or not. In contrast, span-based evaluation cares about the count of overlap; hence, we used binary overlap along with proportional overlap. Binary overlap computes the number of matching overlaps between predicted sequence and ground-truth sequence. As long as predicted span overlaps ground-truth span, binary overlap views it as a correct prediction. To refine the evaluation, proportional overlap considers the length of overlap and imparts a partial correctness to each match, which is able to assess the model more accurate. We used these three evaluations to measure our models.

5 Results and Discussion

5.1 Results

Table 4, 5, and 6 display the results of the data sets individually. The scores show that using BERT embedder does achieve better performance than using ELMo embedder by dramatic difference, which implies that BERT is promising in opinion mining tasks. More interestingly, adding attention mechanism on BiLSTM can increase the performance slightly.

5.2 Discussion

According to the scores, it is easier to detect DSEs than ESEs because DSEs contain clear opinion-

DSE S1	My public affairs keepers [could]$_B$ [n't care less]$_I$.
ELMo-BiLSTM-CRF	My public affairs keepers could n't care less .
Bert-BiLSTM-CRF	My public affairs keepers [could]$_B$ [n't care]$_I$ less .
Bert-BiLSTM-Attn-CRF	My public affairs keepers [could]$_B$ [n't care less]$_I$.
ESE S1	By comparison , the al Qaedans [look]$_B$ [pretty fat , if not happy]$_I$.
ELMo-BiLSTM-CRF	By comparison , the al Qaedans look [pretty]$_B$ [fat]$_I$, [if]$_B$ [not happy]$_I$.
Bert-BiLSTM-CRF	[By]$_B$ comparison , the al Qaedans [look]$_B$ [pretty fat]$_I$, [if]$_B$ [not happy]$_I$.
Bert-BiLSTM-Attn-CRF	[By]$_B$ [comparison]$_I$, the al Qaedans [look]$_B$ [pretty fat]$_I$, [if]$_B$ [not happy]$_I$.
ESE S2	Their restroom arrangements [are]$_B$ [pretty spartan]$_I$.
ELMo-BiLSTM-CRF	Their restroom arrangements are [pretty]$_B$ [spartan]$_I$.
Bert-BiLSTM-CRF	Their restroom arrangements are [pretty]$_B$ [spartan]$_I$.
Bert-BiLSTM-Attn-CRF	Their restroom arrangements are [pretty]$_B$ [spartan]$_I$.
ESE S3	We can see for ourselves , [sort]$_B$ [of]$_I$.
ELMo-BiLSTM-CRF	We can see for ourselves , [sort]$_I$ of .
Bert-BiLSTM-CRF	We can [see]$_I$ for [ourselves]$_I$, [sort]$_B$ [of]$_I$.
Bert-BiLSTM-Attn-CRF	We can see for ourselves [,]$_B$ [sort]$_I$ [of]$_I$.
MOAT S1	[He]$_B$ [considers them as Indonesian as he is .]$_I$
ELMo-BiLSTM-CRF	He considers [them]$_I$ as [Indonesian]$_I$ as [he]$_I$ is .
Bert-BiLSTM-CRF	He considers them as [Indonesian]$_I$ as he is .
Bert-BiLSTM-Attn-CRF	[He]$_B$ [considers them as Indonesian as he is .]$_I$

Table 7: Output from our models for each dataset.

ated expression, which may be some adjectives. However, detecting ESEs requires understanding more implicit semantics, but BERT-BiLSTM-CRF works well on ESEs.

Adding attention mechanism does not improve much probably because BERT layer has already incorporated multi-head attention mechanism and caught well-represented information.

Moreover, the training epochs for ELMo-BiLSTM-CRF is 4 times more than that of BERT-BiLSTM-CRF to converge. In other words, applying BERT embedder can save much more time. To conclude, in our experiments, BERT embedder is much more efficient than other embeddings.

5.3 Error Analysis

In this section, we observed the predictions and analyzed the defect in our models. Table 7 is our several predictions from our model on each dataset. Many sentences are predicted approximately or even same; however, in some sentences ELMo-BiLSTM-CRF has lower recall.

BERT-BiLSTM-CRF can predict well, but some failures are caused by the inconsistency in dataset. For example, whether definite articles (e.g. "the") or punctuation should be included or not is one of the problems. Besides, the same verb, such as 'say', in similar contexts is not always annotated, either.

For ESEs, It is much more difficult to clearly identify implicit semantics because there are many fragmented predictions. Besides, although we have CRF layer to consider the entire sequence predictions, it still exists some wrong tagging, such as starting with I tag.

The opinionated spans in NTCIR7-MOAT data are usually too long, which is a little different from the other datasets. Besides, the number of sentences is not much; thus, the result does not meet the expectation.

Once the flaws in dataset are figured out, we can gain a better performance. Furthermore, adding another feature, such as GLoVe (Pennington et al., 2014) or linguistic characteristics, is also a way to enhance the model.

6 Conclusion

In this paper, we introduced contextualized embeddings into opinion mining task. Experimentally, our models have significant promotion for changing embedder and prove that deep contextualized embeddings perform well in opinion mining task. Specifically, our comparison shows that using BERT embedder dramatically surpasses using ELMo embedder.

In the future work, it would be better to supplement other word embedding (Pennington et al., 2014; Mikolov et al., 2013) as auxiliary, just like

Chiu and Nichols (2016); Xu et al. (2018). Even more, we can add contextual string embedding (Akbik et al., 2018) to support character-level features and apply it to advanced opinion mining tasks.

Acknowledgments

Thanks to the professor Noriko Kando to supervise me for the research and my friend for giving the advice for the paper. This work was supported by the International Internship Program of National Institute of Informatics, Japan, and JSPS KAKENHI Grant Numbers JP18H03338 and JP16H01756.

References

Alan Akbik, Duncan Blythe, and Roland Vollgraf. 2018. Contextual string embeddings for sequence labeling. In *COLING*.

Wanxiang Che, Yijia Liu, Yuxuan Wang, Bo Zheng, and Ting Liu. 2018. Towards better UD parsing: Deep contextualized word embeddings, ensemble, and treebank concatenation. In *Proceedings of the CoNLL 2018 Shared Task: Multilingual Parsing from Raw Text to Universal Dependencies*, pages 55–64, Brussels, Belgium. Association for Computational Linguistics.

Jason P. C. Chiu and Eric Nichols. 2016. Named entity recognition with bidirectional lstm-cnns. *Transactions of the Association for Computational Linguistics*, 4:357–370.

Yejin Choi, Claire Cardie, Ellen Riloff, and Siddharth Patwardhan. 2005. Identifying sources of opinions with conditional random fields and extraction patterns. In *HLT/EMNLP*.

Jacob Devlin, Ming-Wei Chang, Kenton Lee, and Kristina Toutanova. 2018. Bert: Pre-training of deep bidirectional transformers for language understanding. *CoRR*, abs/1810.04805.

Murhaf Fares, Andrey Kutuzov, Stephan Oepen, and Erik Velldal. 2017. Word vectors, reuse, and replicability: Towards a community repository of large-text resources. In *Proceedings of the 21st Nordic Conference on Computational Linguistics*, pages 271–276, Gothenburg, Sweden. Association for Computational Linguistics.

Sepp Hochreiter and Jürgen Schmidhuber. 1997. Long short-term memory. *Neural Comput.*, 9(8):1735–1780.

Zhiheng Huang, Wei Xu, and Kai Yu. 2015. Bidirectional lstm-crf models for sequence tagging. *CoRR*, abs/1508.01991.

Ozan İrsoy and Claire Cardie. 2014. Opinion mining with deep recurrent neural networks. In *Proceedings of the Conference on Empirical Methods in Natural Language Processing*, pages 720–728.

L. C. Jain and L. R. Medsker. 1999. *Recurrent Neural Networks: Design and Applications*, 1st edition. CRC Press, Inc., Boca Raton, FL, USA.

Arzoo Katiyar and Claire Cardie. 2016. Investigating lstms for joint extraction of opinion entities and relations. In *ACL*.

Arzoo Katiyar and Claire Cardie. 2017. Going out on a limb: Joint extraction of entity mentions and relations without dependency trees. In *ACL*.

Diederik P. Kingma and Jimmy Ba. 2014. Adam: A method for stochastic optimization. *CoRR*, abs/1412.6980.

John D. Lafferty, Andrew McCallum, and Fernando Pereira. 2001. Conditional random fields: Probabilistic models for segmenting and labeling sequence data. In *ICML*.

Omer Levy and Yoav Goldberg. 2014. Dependency-based word embeddings. In *ACL*.

Pengfei Liu, Shafiq R. Joty, and Helen M. Meng. 2015. Fine-grained opinion mining with recurrent neural networks and word embeddings. In *EMNLP*.

Xuezhe Ma and Eduard H. Hovy. 2016. End-to-end sequence labeling via bi-directional lstm-cnns-crf. *CoRR*, abs/1603.01354.

Bryan McCann, James Bradbury, Caiming Xiong, and Richard Socher. 2017. Learned in translation: Contextualized word vectors. In *NIPS*.

Tomas Mikolov, Ilya Sutskever, Kai Chen, Gregory S. Corrado, and Jeffrey Dean. 2013. Distributed representations of words and phrases and their compositionality. In *NIPS*.

Makoto Miwa and Mohit Bansal. 2016. End-to-end relation extraction using lstms on sequences and tree structures. *CoRR*, abs/1601.00770.

Jeffrey Pennington, Richard Socher, and Christopher D. Manning. 2014. Glove: Global vectors for word representation. In *EMNLP*.

Matthew E. Peters, Mark Neumann, Mohit Iyyer, Matt Gardner, Christopher Clark, Kenton Lee, and Luke S. Zettlemoyer. 2018. Deep contextualized word representations. In *NAACL 2018*.

Alec Radford. 2018. Improving language understanding by generative pre-training.

Sebastian Ruder and Jeremy Howard. 2018. Universal language model fine-tuning for text classification. In *ACL*.

M. Schuster and K.K. Paliwal. 1997. Bidirectional recurrent neural networks. *Trans. Sig. Proc.*, 45(11):2673–2681.

Yohei Seki, David Kirk Evans, Lun-Wei Ku, Le Sun, Hsin-Hsi Chen, and Noriko Kando. 2008. Overview of multilingual opinion analysis task at ntcir-7. *Proceedings of The IEEE - PIEEE*.

Swapna Somasundaran and Janyce Wiebe. 2010. Recognizing stances in ideological on-line debates.

Ashish Vaswani, Noam Shazeer, Niki Parmar, Jakob Uszkoreit, Llion Jones, Aidan N. Gomez, Lukasz Kaiser, and Illia Polosukhin. 2017. Attention is all you need. In *NIPS*.

Xin Wang, Yuanchao Liu, Chengjie Sun, Ming Liu, and Xiaolong Wang. 2016. Extended dependency-based word embeddings for aspect extraction. In *ICONIP*.

Janyce Wiebe, Theresa Wilson, and Claire Cardie. 2005. Annotating expressions of opinions and emotions in language. *Language Resources and Evaluation*, 39(2):165–210.

Xiaoxia Xie. 2017. Opinion expression detection via deep bidirectional c-grus. *2017 28th International Workshop on Database and Expert Systems Applications (DEXA)*, pages 118–122.

Hu Xu, Bing Liu, Lei Shu, and Philip S. Yu. 2018. Dual embeddings and cnn-based sequence labeling for aspect extraction. In *ACL 2018*.

A bag-of-concepts model improves relation extraction in a narrow knowledge domain with limited data

Jiyu Chen, Karin Verspoor and **Zenan Zhai**
School of Computing and Information Systems
The University of Melbourne, Australia
jiyuc@student.unimelb.edu.au, {karin.verspoor, zenan.zhai}@unimelb.edu.au

Abstract

This paper focuses on a traditional relation extraction task in the context of limited annotated data and a narrow knowledge domain. We explore this task with a clinical corpus consisting of 200 breast cancer follow-up treatment letters in which 16 distinct types of relations are annotated. We experiment with an approach to extracting typed relations called window-bounded co-occurrence (WBC), which uses an adjustable context window around entity mentions of a relevant type, and compare its performance with a more typical intra-sentential co-occurrence baseline. We further introduce a new bag-of-concepts (BoC) approach to feature engineering based on the state-of-the-art word embeddings and word synonyms. We demonstrate the competitiveness of BoC by comparing with methods of higher complexity, and explore its effectiveness on this small dataset.

1 Introduction

Applying automatic relation extraction on small data sets in a narrow knowledge domain is challenging. Here, we consider the specific context of a small clinical corpus, in which we have a variety of relation types of interest but limited examples of each. Transformation of clinical texts into structured sets of relations can facilitate the exploration of clinical research questions such as the potential risks of treatments for patients with certain characteristics, but large-scale annotation of these data sets is notoriously difficult due to the sensitivity of the data and the need for specialized clinical knowledge.

Rule-based methods (Abacha and Zweigenbaum, 2011; Verspoor et al., 2016) typically determine whether a particular type of relation exists in a given text by leveraging the context in which key clinical entities are mentioned. For instance,

if two entities with type TestName and TestResult, respectively, are observed in a given sentence, it is likely that a relation of type TestFinding exists between them. However, construction of high-precision rules defining relevant contexts is time-consuming and expensive, requiring extensive effort from domain experts.

The state-of-the-art machine learning algorithms such as neural network models (Nguyen and Grishman, 2016; Ammar et al., 2017; Huang and Wang, 2017) may over-fit in performing relation extraction in this context, due to a limited quantity of training instances.

In this work, we experiment with two automatic approaches to semantic relation extraction applied to a small corpus consisting of breast cancer follow-up treatment letters (Pitson et al., 2017), comparing a simple rule-based co-occurrence approach to machine learning classifiers.

The first approach, simple co-occurrence (Verspoor et al., 2016), is based on the assumption that most relevant relations are intra-sentential, that is, the relation between a pair of named entities is expressed within the scope of a single sentence. However, some relations may be expressed across sentence boundaries, and thus a single sentence may not be the ideal choice of scope, as shown in prior work that considers inter-sentential relations (also known as non-sentence or cross-sentence relations) (Panyam et al., 2016; Peng et al., 2017). We extend the co-occurrence approach to allow explicit adjustment of context window size, from one to two sentences, a method called Window-Bounded Co-occurrence (WBC). The best window size for a given relation is identified by choosing the one which produces the highest score under F_1-measure on a development set.

The second approach is based on supervised binary classification. We transform the multi-relation extraction task into several independent

43

Proceedings of the 2019 Conference of the North American Chapter of the Association for Computational Linguistics: Student Research Workshop, pages 43–52
Minneapolis, Minnesota, June 3 - 5, 2019. ©2017 Association for Computational Linguistics

binary tasks. We build on a bag-of-concepts (BoC) (Sahlgren and Cöster, 2004) approach which models the text in terms of phrases or pre-identified concepts, extending it with word embeddings and word synonyms. We compare two different pre-trained word embedding models, and a number of other model variations. We also explore grouping of synonyms into abstracted *concepts*.

We find that the intra-sentential rule-based approach outperforms the approach which allows for a larger context window. The supervised learning models outperforms rule-based approaches under F_1 measure, and their results show that models using BoC features outperform models with BoW, dependency parse, or sentence embedding features. We also show that SVM outperforms complex models such as a feed-forward ANN in our low resource scenario, with less tendency to over-fitting.

2   Background

At present, the two primary approaches to automatic relation extraction over biomedical corpora are rule-based approaches (Verspoor et al., 2016; Abacha and Zweigenbaum, 2011) and machine learning approaches based on learners such as logistic regression, support vector machines (SVM) (Panyam et al., 2016) and convolutional neural networks (CNN) (Nguyen and Verspoor, 2018) together with sophisticated feature engineering methods.

Verspoor et al. (2016) established a typical intra-sentential co-occurrence baseline with competitive performance comparing to a comprehensive machine learning-based system, PKDE4J (Song et al., 2015), on the extraction of relations between human genetic variants and disease on the Variome corpus (Verspoor et al., 2013). The sentential baseline is based on the assumption that the scope of relations is within one sentence, and further assumes that any pair of two entities mentioned in the same sentence and satisfying the type constraints of a given relation, expresses that relation. For example, if two entities with type TimeDescriptor and EndocrineTherapy respectively, the relation TherapyTiming will be extracted. The sentential co-occurrence baseline set a benchmark for relation extraction on Variome corpus.

Abacha and Zweigenbaum (2011) explored semantic rules for the extraction of relations between medical entities on PubMed Central (PMC) articles using linguistic patterns. They provide an example of implementing an end-to-end relation extraction system, applying named entity recognition in the first stage, then followed by the stage of relation extraction. They define several relation patterns based on medical knowledge, and leveraging the dependency parse tree of sentences in which entities occur. However, the linguistic patterns and rules developed for their corpus likely are not directly applicable to our semantically distinct context of clinical letters.

Machine learning methods vary based on the choice of models and the features considered. In model selection, the multi-type relation extraction task can be assigned to several independent binary classifiers, each making the decision of whether a certain type of relation exist or not. A basic binary classifier such as logistic regression with ridge regularization is capable of performing relation extraction in this scenario. Panyam et al. (2016) used support vector machines (SVM) with a dependency graph kernel to perform relation extraction on two biomedical relation extraction tasks, showing competitive results. Brown Clustering (Brown et al., 1992) is a hierarchical approach to clustering words into classes through maximizing mutual information of bi-grams; it showed competitive performances in many NLP tasks (Turian et al., 2010).Nguyen and Verspoor (2018) implemented a method using character-based word embeddings which can capture unknown words within the context, coupled with CNN and LSTM neural network models. This approach obtained state-of-the-art performance in extracting chemical-disease relations on the BioCreative-V CDR corpus (Li et al., 2016).

For feature engineering, text features can generally be divided into the two categories of lexical features and syntactic features. Typical features used in other relation extraction tasks are summarized here.

- **Bag-of-words (BoW) features** based on white-space delimited tokens, are used in many tasks as a starting point.

- **Bag-of-concepts (BoC) features** (Sahlgren and Cöster, 2004) represent the text in terms of concepts, that is, phrases in the text that correspond to meaningful units. The current methods for generating concepts are based on techniques such as mutual information (Sahlgren and Cöster, 2004), or through dictionary-based strategies (Funk et al., 2014). For clinical texts, the MetaMap tool (Aronson, 2001) is often used to recognize clinical concepts.

- **Syntactic features** take sentence structure into account. For example, RelEx (Fundel et al., 2006) uses dependency parse trees associated with small numbers of rules in extracting relations from MEDLINE abstract and reaches an overal 80% precision and recall. Approximate Sub-graph Matching (ASM) (Liu et al., 2013) enables sentences to be matched by considering the similarity of the structure of dependency parse subgraphs that connect relevant entities to subgraphs in the training data.

- **Word embeddings** aim to capture word semantics through lower-dimension projections of word contexts and can be used to find word synonyms by measuring cosine similarity between word vectors. There are two widely used approaches to train word embeddings, co-occurrence matrix based methods such as GloVe (Pennington et al., 2014), and learning-based methods using skip-grams (Mikolov et al., 2013b) and CBOW (Mikolov et al., 2013a).

3 Methods

We improve the approaches described above to achieve better efficiency in relation extraction in our context of a narrow knowledge domain with limited data, specific to cancer follow-up treatment.

3.1 Corpus

We consider a previously introduced corpus related to breast cancer follow-up treatment, randomly sampled and manually annotated by two physicians (Pitson et al., 2017). The corpus contains around 1000 sentences and 47,186 tokens. Despite its small size, the corpus is richly annotated with 16 medical named entity types and 16 types of semantic relations linking those entities with over 1,500 relation occurrences. Entities within the corpus are related to clinical therapies, temporal events, diseases, and so on. The annotation of clinical relations includes the associations between identified entities. For example, in the context "She remains on Arimidex tablets.", "remains on" is a TimeDescriptor, and "Arimidex" is a EndocrineTherapy. The relation TherapyTiming holds between these two entities in this context (e.g., TherapyTiming(TimeDescriptor, EndocrineTherapy)). For conciseness, we use abbreviations to refer to the entity types; hence we will use TD to represent the entity type of TimeDescriptor. While the dataset hasn't been published yet, the full terminology list of entity types can be found in Pitson et al. (2017). To focus exclusively on the relation extraction task, we decouple the named entity recognition task from the relation extraction task by utilizing the gold standard entity annotations from the corpus.

3.2 Method 1: Typed Sentential Co-occurrence

The simplest rule-based approach, given typed named entities, is to extract every pair of entities in a document that satisfies the type constraints of a relation. Such an approach yields high recall but poor precision, due to lack of use of context needed to ensure that a specific relation is expressed as holding between the entities. For example, in our data, only the semantic relation of Toxicity is defined as connecting a Therapy to a ClinicalFinding (expressing that a therapy was found to cause a specific toxic effect) and so it might seem reasonable to assume that a Toxicity event is being expressed in a document where both a Therapy and a ClinicalFinding are mentioned. However, the occurrence of these two entity types together in a document do not strictly indicate an occurrence of Toxicity relation between them; the entities may be connected to other mentioned entities via different relations. Hence assuming a Toxicity relation between them would result in a false positive.

We used intra-sentential constraints as described by (Verspoor et al., 2016) to improve precision by only considering that named entities that co-occur in the same sentence can have valid semantic relations. With this intra-sentential co-occurrence constraint, the relation extraction performance of the sentential baseline achieved strong recall and competitive precision, as well as reasonable overall F-score, on the Variome corpus (Verspoor et al., 2013).

We introduce the approach of Window-

Bounded Co-occurrence (WBC) to explore the impact of relaxing the constraint that the sentence boundary defines the scope of a relation. WBC defines a context window for a relation as the expansion to a base window of the sentence where an entity of the appropriate type occurs, and the adjustment of tokens beyond that sentence within which the related entity appears. We assume the occurrence of an inter-sentential relation relies on the distance of two entities, where distance is defined based on the number of tokens considered beyond the base sentence in which an entity occurs. We introduce a hyperparameter, ρ, to represent the distance of an entity pair in a context, namely the number of tokens allowed in exceeding the single base sentence. $\rho = 0$ denotes the entity pair is intra-sentential; $\rho = x$ denotes the second entity in a pair is x number of tokens away from the base window. If ρ is large than the length of the second context window, then the context window will set to the scope of two sentences by default.

Figure 1 shows an example when $\rho = 5$, WBC allows for the extraction of the semantic relation of TestToAssess across the base window containing the entity of ClinicalFinding, and into the expanded window encompassing the subsequent sentence and containing the TestName entity.

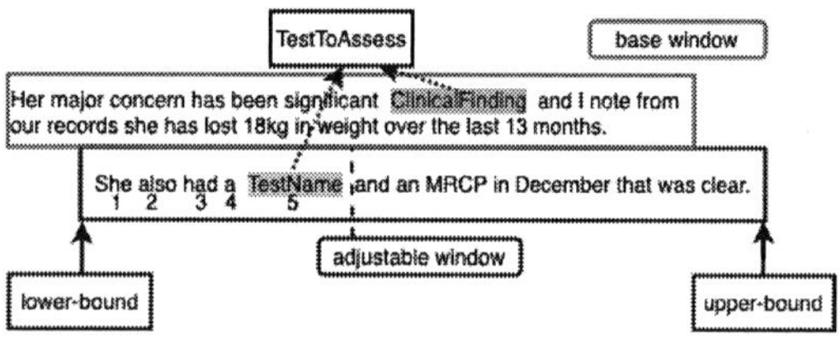

Figure 1: Example of length-awareness sliding window of WBC in TestToAssess relation case

3.3 Method 2: Supervised Binary Classification Approach

We adopt a traditional pipeline as the architecture of the relation extraction system. Each stage is introduced below.

3.3.1 Data Preparation

Considering the semantic variation in the texts, and the small number of examples, training several independent binary classifiers is more robust for mining individual type of semantic relation patterns. Therefore, we transform the original dataset into 16 independent subsets, by grouping instances by their relation type. An instance consists of a typed entity pair, one or two sentence(s) with the relevant named entities inside as context, a label as an indication of relation occurrence, and a treatment letter id for mapping its position in the original dataset. We remove four relation types with fewer than 10 annotated instances, specifically the relations Intervention, EffectOf, RecurLink and GetOpinion.

We apply context selection for generating instances during data transformation. One instance represents the occurrence of a single semantic relation, containing one relevant entity pair. The context for each instance is the entire raw text of the sentence where the entity pair appears. In cases where more than one entity pair occurs in the same text context, we generate an independent instance for each entity pair. Where cross-sentence relations occur, we concatenate the two sentences containing the relevant entities into a single sentence, structurally indicating that the two sentences are related. In each instance, we replace the two named entity phrases with their type. In the case of overlapping named entities, such as where one named entity partially or completely collides with another entity, both types are retained, adjacent to each other in the text. Other entities mentioned in the context not relevant for the specific relation are left in their original textual form.

We use NLTK (Bird et al., 2009) to perform tokenization and lemmatization to normalize the representation of the text, and strip punctuation. We use the Snowball English stopword list [1] to remove stopwords.

Further details are presented in the feature engineering section below.

3.3.2 Feature Engineering

We implement a set of traditional semantic features and three main feature sets based on ASM, BoC, and sentence embeddings in the sections below.

- **Traditional Semantic Features**
  The traditional semantic features includes bag-of-words (count-based), lemmas (base, uninflected form of a noun or verb), algebraic expressions, named entity type (derived from the

---

[1] http://anoncvs.postgresql.org/
cvsweb.cgi/pgsql/src/backend/snowball/
stopwords/

gold-standard), POS tags and dependency parse based on Stanford CoreNLP (Manning et al., 2014), and a transformation from dependency parse tree to graph using NetworkX (Hagberg et al., 2008) where edges are dependencies and nodes are tokens/labels.

- **ASM features**

The classical ASM measurement was developed by Liu et al. (2013), and was later extended to kernel method by Panyam et al. (2016). The ASM kernel was applied to the chemical induced disease (CID) task (Wei et al., 2015) and Seedev shared tasks (Chaix et al., 2016). The performance of ASM significantly depends on the result of POS-tagging and dependency tree parsing. All nodes are normalized to their lemmas. Here, Stanford CoreNLP (Manning et al., 2014) is used for POS tagging and dependency tree parsing of the text. The context is split into sentences before dependency parsing is applied on individual sentences.

We produce the ASM features following Panyam et al. (2016). Where the context includes two sentences, a dummy root node is introduced to connect the root nodes of two dependency parse trees. Figure 2 shows an example. After pre-processing, the dependency tree structure is transformed into a graph where nodes are lemmas with their POS tags, edges are dependencies across lemmas within sentence. Then, a shortest path algorithm is applied on the dependency graph to generate flat features. In cases where sentences are very long, processing time is unacceptable, and no ASM features are generated.

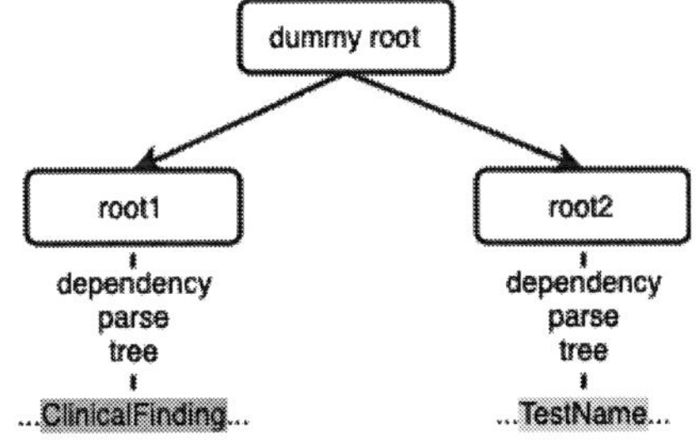

Figure 2: Illustration of concatenation of two sentence parsing results using dummy root in TestToAssess relation setting

- **Bag-of-Concepts features**

Word embeddings are used to capture word similarity based on shared surrounding context. The size of the surrounding context, known as window size control, varies the representation of word embeddings from more semantic (shorter window size) to more syntactic (longer window size). Synonyms can be identified by identifying two words with similar embeddings, based on cosine similarity measurement. Overfitting can occur for word embeddings, where a training corpus is not large enough or a corpus is limited to a narrow domain of knowledge. Therefore, instead of training word embeddings on our corpus, we use two publicly available pre-trained word embeddings, GloVe (Pennington et al., 2014) and a Wikipedia-PubMed-PMC embedding (Moen and Ananiadou, 2013) to capture more clinically relevant vocabulary. The vocabulary of word embeddings denotes the total number of words that are represented. In our experiment, only the top 20,000 most frequent lemmas are selected. Gensim (Rehurek and Sojka, 2010) is used to find the synonyms of a lemma from the vocabulary by measuring similarity between GloVe word vectors.

We then implement an algorithm for building BoC. Using a word2concept algorithm (see Equation 1), we map a lemma (key) to a concept (value) based on the embedding of the lemma expressed as $E(lemma)$ and the similarity threshold expressed as μ as a tunable hyperparameter.

$$CONCEPT = f(E(lemma), \mu) \quad (1)$$

The algorithm starts by extracting BoW features for each generated instance after data preparation process into a list L. Then, starting from the first lemma w_1 from L, we retrieve its embedding $x_{w_1} = E(w_1)$. We then retrieve a new lemma w_i and its embedding x_{w_i} from the vocabulary V, and calculate the similarity score $S = cos(x_{w_1}, x_{w_i})$. If $S >= \mu$, create mappings between $w_1 \rightarrow concept_1$ and $w_i \rightarrow concept_1$. If no w_i satisfies the condition of $S >= \mu$, then w_1 will be kept in its original form. Next, we move to the second word w_2 in L, check whether w_2 has already been mapped to a concept $concept_*$, and if so, directly create the mapping $w_2 \rightarrow concept_*$. Otherwise, we iterate.

Note that in this model, named entities will effectively be treated as out-of-vocabulary terms, since they have been mapped to and replaced with the names of the relevant entity types (e.g., "TestName" which is not a token that would be expected to be represented in any pre-trained word embedding model).

- **Sentence embedding features**
  Apart from being a tool for finding word synonyms and generating BoC data representation, word embeddings can also be used to obtain sentence embeddings through weighted average pooling. If S denotes a sentence, $E(S)$ denotes the embedding of sentence S. $E(w_1)$ denotes the embedding of the first word w_1 of sentence S, $Score(w_1)$ denotes the TF-IDF score of word w_1, the sentence embeddings based on weighted average pooling can be expressed as Equation 2. We calculate TF-IDF scores of each word using the original documents, as each instance has an index to its original document id. Out-of-vocabulary tokens and gold standard named entities will be ignored. However, entity information has been considered during that data preparation stage, because the generation of instances takes gold standard entities into account.

$$E(S) = \frac{1}{n} \sum_{i=1}^{n} E(w_i) \times Score(w_i) \quad (2)$$

3.4 Supervised Learning Models

We build individual binary classifiers for each relation type. We introduce the SVM classifiers and Feed-forward ANN models briefly here.

- **Support Vector Machine** We select the general SVM model (Hearst, 1998) and kernels provided by `scikit-learn` (Pedregosa et al., 2011). For SVM kernels, we integrate ASM kernel as part of feature engineering, to avoid colliding with the use of the linear kernel and the RBF (Radial Basis Function) kernel.

- **Feed-forward ANN** We use Keras (Chollet et al., 2015) to construct a simple feed-forward neural network model with two fully connected layers as shown in Figure 3.

The dimension of each input and the number of hidden units in each layer is the same as the dimension of feature vectors under each type of relation. The activation function for the first dense layer is ReLU, and for the second dense layer is softmax.

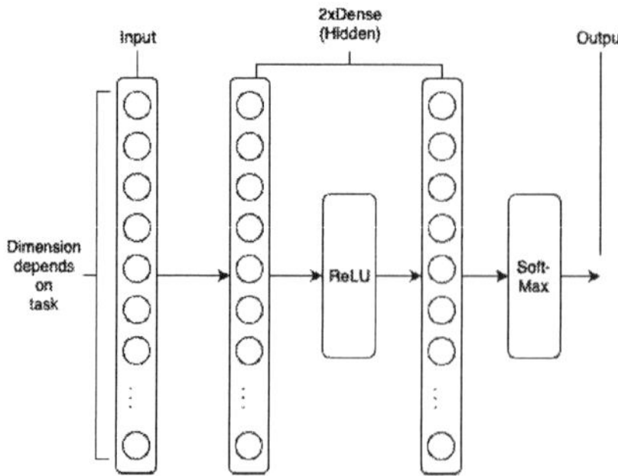

Figure 3: Architecture of FNN

3.5 Experiment Design

Considering the dataset is small, we split the transformed dataset into three independent combinations of training, development, and test sets with the ratio of 6:1:3.

In training stage, we train independent models for each specific relation type. We use cross-validation and grid search to tune the hyperparameters of the classifiers.

In prediction stage, the decision of applying sentence-bounded or window-bounded approach is made by setting the size of sliding window. Setting the window size to 0 will apply the sentence-bounded co-occurrence constraint. We choose window sizes of 0, 5, 10 to explore the value of additional context. In supervised binary classification approach, utilizing a similarity threshold of 1 leads to strict use of BoW (word) features, while relaxing the similarity threshold μ of 0.9, 0.8 will generate BoC (concepts). We compare the influence of different word embeddings in generating BoC based on their relation extraction performance on the test set.

Both rule-based approach and supervised binary classification approach will make predictions on the same test set, which allows empirical comparison between rule-based and machine learning approaches.

We compare the impact of increasing data size for BoW and BoC by sub-sampling the training set into nine instance-incremental and non-overlapping sub-sets (combining them into sets representing 10% to 90% of the original training set) and visualize the performance variation. We explore whether word embeddings as a medium for generating BoC are more effective than the direct use of sentence embeddings in cases where the dataset is small and knowledge domain is restricted to the specific domain of breast cancer treatment. We also explore the combination of BoC and sentence embeddings feature, in order to investigate how best to make integration of them

Finally, we explore the possibility of applying more complex models for analysis of our small and specific knowledge domain dataset. We start from simple linear models including logistic regression and lin-SVM, then apply rbf-SVM, feedforward ANN on Keras with 32 batch per time, and epochs of 2, 10, 100, and 500 for each relation type.

3.6 Evaluation

We evaluate both overall and per relation type performance. Evaluation of the two approaches is performed on the same test set derived from the data preparation stage. In addition, considering the dataset is small, we calculate the mean score from three independent combinations of training, development and test sets. We evaluate results using micro F_1-measure since the number of positives and negatives were highly imbalanced across all relation types. We finally evaluate the performance growth over nine sub-sampled training sets of increasing size.

4 Result and Discussion

We present experiment results with micro F_1 measurement. After experimenting with different similarity threshold values to generate BoC features, the best performance is achieved when the threshold is set to 0.9 (results not shown). Word embeddings derived from Wiki-PubMed-PMC outperform GloVe-based embeddings (Table 1). The models using BoC outperform models using BoW as well as ASM features.

As shown in Table 2, the intra-sentential co-occurrence baseline outperforms other approaches which allow boundary expansion. This is because a majority of relations in the corpus are intra-sentential.

A visualization of the growth in performance for both BoW and BoC-based models as training set size increases, over 12 relation types, based on micro F_1, is shown in Figure 4. The results of BoC in this figure is collected from lin-SVM$_{\text{Wiki-PubMed-PMC}, \mu = 0.9}$, and BoW is collected from lin-SVM. We find BoC tends to outperform BoW with only a small number of training instances, and also performs better than BoW with incremental training instance.

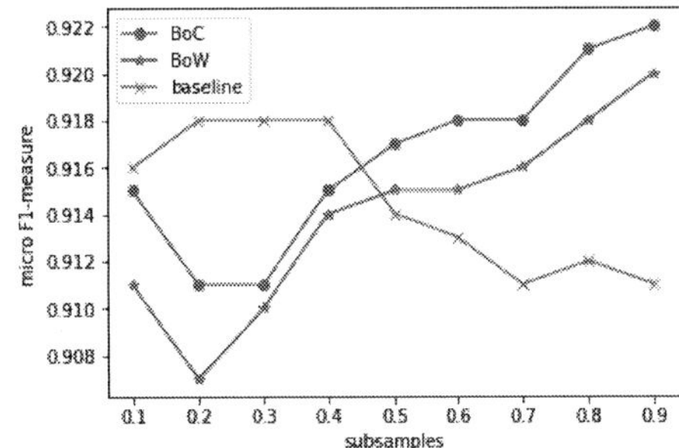

Figure 4: Performance variation of BoW and BoC($_{\text{Wiki-PubMed-PMC}, \mu = 0.9}$) with increasing data fractions, under linSVM, F_1 measure.

The reason that Wikipedia-PubMed-PMC embeddings (Moen and Ananiadou, 2013) outperforms GloVe (Mikolov et al., 2013a) in the extraction of most relation types (Table 1) is because its training corpus has a more similar domain and vocabulary as our dataset. Therefore, it leads to more relevant models of the distributional semantics of words. On the other hand, the GloVe embeddings are derived from a more general corpus; thus the semantics of domain specific terms in our dataset are not captured.

By observation, most lemmas that map into concepts are digits, time stamps, common verbs and medical terminologies. For example, in TimeStamp($_{\text{TD,TP}}$), drugs with similar effects such as "letrozole" and "anastrozole" map into "$CONCEPT_3$"; all single digits, ranges from 0-9 map into "$CONCEPT_{26}$; year tags such as "2011, 2009" map into "$CONCEPT_{56}$". We consider the cause of differences between the BoW and BoC representations. In the normalization process for BoW, stop-words collected from general knowledge domain are not well-suited to the knowledge domain for our specific task, while limited data does not allow the construction of an appropriate stop-words list from the data. In contrast, BoC models normalize the differences between individual words with shared meaning. While intuitively this should support an improvement over BoW models, we find BoW outperforms BoC when extracting certain relations such as TestTiming($_{\text{TN,TD}}$), TestToAssess($_{\text{TN,TR}}$) with gold standard named entities as arguments. The reason is that synonyms may express slightly different meanings; concept mapping discards such differences and leads to information loss, potentially causing more mis-classifications. The deci-

Feature	LR			SVM			ANN		
	P	R	F_1	P	R	F_1	P	R	F_1
+BoW	0.93	0.91	0.92	0.94	0.92	0.93	0.91	0.91	0.91
+BoC (Wiki-PubMed-PMC)	0.94	0.92	**0.93**	0.94	0.92	**0.93**	0.91	0.91	**0.91**
+BoC (GloVe)	0.93	0.92	0.92	0.94	0.92	0.93	0.91	0.91	0.91
+ASM	0.90	0.85	0.88	0.90	0.86	0.88	0.89	0.89	0.89
+Sentence Embeddings(SEs)	0.89	0.89	0.89	0.90	0.86	0.88	0.88	0.88	0.88
+BoC(Wiki-PubMed-PMC)+SEs	0.92	0.92	0.92	0.94	0.92	0.93	0.91	0.91	0.91

Table 1: Performance of supervised learning models with different features.

Relation type	Count	Intra-sentential co-occ.			BoC(Wiki-PubMed-PMC)		
		$\rho = 0$	$\rho = 5$	$\rho = 10$	LR	SVM	ANN
TherapyTiming($_{TP,TD}$)	428	**0.84**	0.59	0.47	0.78	0.81	0.78
NextReview($_{Followup,TP}$)	164	**0.90**	0.83	0.63	0.86	0.88	0.84
Toxicity($_{TP,CF/TR}$)	163	**0.91**	0.77	0.55	0.85	0.86	0.86
TestTiming($_{TN,TD/TP}$)	184	0.90	0.81	0.42	0.96	**0.97**	0.95
TestFinding($_{TN,TR}$)	136	0.76	0.60	0.44	**0.82**	0.79	0.78
Threat($_{O,CF/TR}$)	32	0.85	0.69	0.54	**0.95**	**0.95**	0.92
Intervention($_{TP,YR}$)	5	**0.88**	0.65	0.47	-	-	-
EffectOf($_{Com,CF}$)	3	**0.92**	0.62	0.23	-	-	-
Severity($_{CF,CS}$)	75	**0.61**	0.53	0.47	0.52	0.55	0.51
RecurLink($_{YR,YR/CF}$)	7	**1.0**	**1.0**	0.64	-	-	-
RecurInfer($_{NR/YR,TR}$)	51	0.97	0.69	0.43	**0.99**	**0.99**	0.98
GetOpinion($_{Referral,CF/other}$)	4	**0.75**	**0.75**	0.5	-	-	-
Context($_{Dis,DisCont}$)	40	**0.70**	0.63	0.53	0.60	0.41	0.57
TestToAssess($_{TN,CF/TR}$)	36	0.76	0.66	0.36	**0.92**	**0.92**	0.91
TimeStamp($_{TD,TP}$)	221	**0.88**	0.83	0.50	0.86	0.85	0.83
TimeLink($_{TP,TP}$)	20	**0.92**	0.85	0.45	0.91	**0.92**	0.90
Overall	1569	0.90	0.73	0.45	0.92	**0.93**	0.91

Table 2: F_1 score results per relation type of the best performing models.

sion of whether to use the BoC or BoW will depend on the characteristics of particular relation types.

Table 1 also shows the combination feature of BoC and sentence embeddings outperforms sentence embeddings alone, but do not exceed the upper boundary of BoC feature, in which again demonstrating the competitiveness of BoC feature.

Since this corpus is much smaller than other narrow knowledge domain corpus such as CID (Wei et al., 2015) and Seedev shared task (Chaix et al., 2016), the training instances are not enough for the learners to generalize well using syntactic representation. Therefore, the models using ASM kernel (Panyam et al., 2016) do not outperform the simple linear classifiers.

As the results of applying the co-occurrence baseline ($\rho = 0$) shows (Table 2), the semantic relations in this data are strongly concentrated within a sentence boundary, especially for the relation of RecurLink, with an F_1 of 1.0. The machine learning approaches based on BoC lexical features effectively complement the deficiency of cross-sentence relation extraction.

Lin-SVM outperforms other classifiers in extracting most relations. The feed-forward ANN displays significant over-fitting across all relation types, as the performance decreases when increasing the training epochs. Specifically, with only two training epochs, the performance of ANN is still slightly worse than lin-SVM. The result of lin-SVM present its robustness of avoiding over-fitting compares to feed-forward ANN with BoW, BoC, ASM flat features and sentence embeddings.

5 Conclusion and Future Work

We proposed two ways to perform relation extraction for a narrow knowledge domain, with only small available data set. We implemented a window-based context approach and experiment with determining the best context size for the relation extraction in the rule-based settings. The typical sentential co-occurrence baseline is competitive when most relations are intra-sentential. We implemented a BoC feature engineering method, by leveraging word embeddings as a tool for finding word synonyms and mapping them to concepts. BoC feature outperforms BoW, ASM syntactic feature and sentence embeddings derived by weighted average pooling across word embeddings in small dataset with respect to its significant improvements in micro F_1 score. In addition, it would be expected to show competitive results on other relation extraction tasks where it is useful to generalize specific tokens such as digits or time stamps.

We also explored the performance of models with different level of complexity, such as logistic regression, lin-SVM, rbf-SVM, and a simple feedforward ANN. The results highlight that strategies to avoid over-fitting must be considered since the number of training instances is limited.

In future work, we will explore a number of directions, including some unsupervised learning approaches. We will test the performance of BoC on other corpora, to explore BoC vs. BoW as a baseline data representation. We will address comparisons between BoC and other word clustering methods such as Brown Clustering (Brown et al., 1992). Finally, the integration of current named entity recognition tools and end-to-end relation extraction, to remove the reliance on gold standard named entity annotations, will also be explored.

References

Asma Ben Abacha and Pierre Zweigenbaum. 2011. Automatic extraction of semantic relations between medical entities: a rule based approach. *Journal of biomedical semantics*, 2(5):S4.

Waleed Ammar, Matthew Peters, Chandra Bhagavatula, and Russell Power. 2017. The AI2 system at SemEval-2017 Task 10 (ScienceIE): semi-supervised end-to-end entity and relation extraction. In *Proceedings of the 11th International Workshop on Semantic Evaluation (SemEval-2017)*, pages 592–596.

Alan R Aronson. 2001. Effective mapping of biomedical text to the UMLS Metathesaurus: the MetaMap program. In *Proceedings of the AMIA Symposium*, page 17. American Medical Informatics Association.

Steven Bird, Ewan Klein, and Edward Loper. 2009. *Natural language processing with Python: analyzing text with the natural language toolkit*. " O'Reilly Media, Inc.".

Peter F Brown, Peter V Desouza, Robert L Mercer, Vincent J Della Pietra, and Jenifer C Lai. 1992. Class-based n-gram models of natural language. *Computational linguistics*, 18(4):467–479.

Estelle Chaix, Bertrand Dubreucq, Abdelhak Fatihi, Dialekti Valsamou, Robert Bossy, Mouhamadou Ba, Louise Deléger, Pierre Zweigenbaum, Philippe Bessieres, Loic Lepiniec, et al. 2016. Overview of the Regulatory Network of Plant Seed Development (SeeDev) Task at the BioNLP Shared Task 2016. In *Proceedings of the 4th BioNLP Shared Task Workshop*, pages 1–11.

François Chollet et al. 2015. Keras. `https://keras.io`.

Katrin Fundel, Robert Küffner, and Ralf Zimmer. 2006. RelExRelation extraction using dependency parse trees. *Bioinformatics*, 23(3):365–371.

Christopher Funk, William Baumgartner, Benjamin Garcia, Christophe Roeder, Michael Bada, K Cohen, Lawrence Hunter, and Karin Verspoor. 2014. Large-scale biomedical concept recognition: an evaluation of current automatic annotators and their parameters. *BMC Bioinformatics*, 15(1):59.

Aric Hagberg, Pieter Swart, and Daniel S Chult. 2008. Exploring network structure, dynamics, and function using NetworkX. Technical report, Los Alamos National Lab.(LANL), Los Alamos, NM (United States).

Marti A. Hearst. 1998. Support Vector Machines. *IEEE Intelligent Systems*, 13(4):18–28.

Yi Yao Huang and William Yang Wang. 2017. Deep Residual Learning for Weakly-Supervised Relation Extraction. In *Proceedings of the 2017 Conference on Empirical Methods in Natural Language Processing, EMNLP 2017, Copenhagen, Denmark, September 9-11, 2017*, pages 1803–1807.

Jiao Li, Yueping Sun, Robin J Johnson, Daniela Sciaky, Chih-Hsuan Wei, Robert Leaman, Allan Peter Davis, Carolyn J Mattingly, Thomas C Wiegers, and Zhiyong Lu. 2016. Biocreative v cdr task corpus: a resource for chemical disease relation extraction. *Database*, 2016.

Haibin Liu, Lawrence Hunter, Vlado Kešelj, and Karin Verspoor. 2013. Approximate subgraph matching-based literature mining for biomedical events and relations. *PloS one*, 8(4):e60954.

Christopher Manning, Mihai Surdeanu, John Bauer, Jenny Finkel, Steven Bethard, and David McClosky. 2014. The Stanford CoreNLP natural language processing toolkit. In *Proceedings of 52nd annual meeting of the association for computational linguistics: system demonstrations*, pages 55–60.

Tomas Mikolov, Kai Chen, Greg Corrado, and Jeffrey Dean. 2013a. Efficient estimation of word representations in vector space. *CoRR*, abs/1301.3781.

Tomas Mikolov, Ilya Sutskever, Kai Chen, Greg S Corrado, and Jeff Dean. 2013b. Distributed representations of words and phrases and their compositionality. In *Advances in neural information processing systems*, pages 3111–3119.

SPFGH Moen and Tapio Salakoski2 Sophia Ananiadou. 2013. Distributional semantics resources for biomedical text processing. In *Proceedings of the 5th International Symposium on Languages in Biology and Medicine, Tokyo, Japan*, pages 39–43.

Dat Quoc Nguyen and Karin Verspoor. 2018. Convolutional neural networks for chemical-disease relation extraction are improved with character-based word embeddings. In *Proceedings of the BioNLP 2018 workshop*, pages 129–136. Association for Computational Linguistics.

Thien Huu Nguyen and Ralph Grishman. 2016. Combining Neural Networks and Log-linear Models to Improve Relation Extraction. In *Proceedings of IJ-CAI Workshop on Deep Learning for Artificial Intelligence (DLAI)*.

Nagesh C Panyam, Karin Verspoor, Trevor Cohn, and Rao Kotagiri. 2016. ASM Kernel: Graph Kernel using Approximate Subgraph Matching for Relation Extraction. In *Proceedings of the Australasian Language Technology Association Workshop 2016*, pages 65–73.

F. Pedregosa, G. Varoquaux, A. Gramfort, V. Michel, B. Thirion, O. Grisel, M. Blondel, P. Prettenhofer, R. Weiss, V. Dubourg, J. Vanderplas, A. Passos, D. Cournapeau, M. Brucher, M. Perrot, and E. Duchesnay. 2011. Scikit-learn: Machine learning in Python. *Journal of Machine Learning Research*, 12:2825–2830.

Nanyun Peng, Hoifung Poon, Chris Quirk, Kristina Toutanova, and Wen-tau Yih. 2017. Cross-Sentence N-ary Relation Extraction with Graph LSTMs. *Transactions of the Association of Computational Linguistics*, 5(1):101–115.

Jeffrey Pennington, Richard Socher, and Christopher Manning. 2014. Glove: Global vectors for word representation. In *Proceedings of the 2014 conference on empirical methods in natural language processing (EMNLP)*, pages 1532–1543.

Graham Pitson, Patricia Banks, Lawrence Cavedon, and Karin Verspoor. 2017. Developing a Manually Annotated Corpus of Clinical Letters for Breast Cancer Patients on Routine Follow-Up. *Studies in health technology and informatics*, 235:196–200.

Radim Rehurek and Petr Sojka. 2010. Software framework for topic modelling with large corpora. In *In Proceedings of the LREC 2010 Workshop on New Challenges for NLP Frameworks*. Citeseer.

Magnus Sahlgren and Rickard Cöster. 2004. Using bag-of-concepts to improve the performance of support vector machines in text categorization. In *Proceedings of the 20th international conference on Computational Linguistics*, page 487. Association for Computational Linguistics.

Min Song, Won Chul Kim, Dahee Lee, Go Eun Heo, and Keun Young Kang. 2015. PKDE4J: Entity and relation extraction for public knowledge discovery. *Journal of Biomedical Informatics*, 57:320 – 332.

Joseph Turian, Lev Ratinov, and Yoshua Bengio. 2010. Word representations: a simple and general method for semi-supervised learning. In *Proceedings of the 48th annual meeting of the association for computational linguistics*, pages 384–394. Association for Computational Linguistics.

Karin Verspoor, Antonio Jimeno Yepes, Lawrence Cavedon, Tara McIntosh, Asha Herten-Crabb, Zoë Thomas, and John-Paul Plazzer. 2013. Annotating the biomedical literature for the human variome. *Database*, 2013.

Karin M Verspoor, Go Eun Heo, Keun Young Kang, and Min Song. 2016. Establishing a baseline for literature mining human genetic variants and their relationships to disease cohorts. *BMC medical informatics and decision making*, 16(1):68.

Chih-Hsuan Wei, Yifan Peng, Robert Leaman, Allan Peter Davis, Carolyn J Mattingly, Jiao Li, Thomas C Wiegers, and Zhiyong Lu. 2015. Overview of the BioCreative V chemical disease relation (CDR) task. In *Proceedings of the fifth BioCreative challenge evaluation workshop*, pages 154–166.

Generating Text through Adversarial Training
using Skip-Thought Vectors

Afroz Ahamad

BITS Pilani Hyderabad Campus

`afroz.sahamad@gmail.com`

Abstract

GANs have been shown to perform exceedingly well on tasks pertaining to image generation and style transfer. In the field of language modelling, word embeddings such as GLoVe and word2vec are state-of-the-art methods for applying neural network models on textual data. Attempts have been made to utilize GANs with word embeddings for text generation. This study presents an approach to text generation using Skip-Thought sentence embeddings with GANs based on gradient penalty functions and f-measures. The proposed architecture aims to reproduce writing style in the generated text by modelling the way of expression at a sentence level across all the works of an author. Extensive experiments were run in different embedding settings on a variety of tasks including conditional text generation and language generation. The model outperforms baseline text generation networks across several automated evaluation metrics like BLEU-n, METEOR and ROUGE. Further, wide applicability and effectiveness in real life tasks are demonstrated through human judgement scores.

1 Introduction

Inducing a particular style in generated text is a promising development which can lead to producing acceptable responses in dialogue generation, image captioning and artificial chat bot systems. In unsupervised text generation, estimating the distribution of real text from a corpus is a challenging task. Recent approaches using adversarial training have addressed this issue by trying to overcome the exposure bias that models trained for maximum likelihood suffer from. This work proposes an approach for text generation using a Generative Adversarial Network (GAN) with Skip-Thought vectors (STGAN). GANs (Goodfellow et al., 2014) are a class of neural networks

that explicitly train a generator to produce high-quality samples by pitting the generator against an adversarial discriminative model. GANs output differentiable values and the task of discrete text generation is challenging because of the non-differentiable nature of generating discrete symbols. Hence, in the present work, the GANs are trained with sentence embedding vectors as a differentiable input. The sentence embeddings are produced using Skip-Thought (Kiros et al., 2015), a neural network model for learning fixed length representations of sentences.

People's way of expression and communication intention is more diverse across utterances than the vocabulary. To imitate this, the proposed STGAN architecture models the variability at the utterance level in a corpus rather than at word or character level. The effectiveness of this approach is evaluated on automated corpus-based metrics: BLEU-n (Papineni et al., 2002), METEOR (Banerjee and Lavie, 2005) and ROUGE (Lin, 2004) using different embeddings: Average GloVe (Pennington et al., 2014), Vector Extrema GloVe (Pennington et al., 2014) and Skip-Thought (Kiros et al., 2015). We perform an empirical study with human judgements to assess both the quality and the style reproduction in the generated text.

2 Related Works

Deep neural network architectures have demonstrated strong results on natural language generation tasks such as dialogue response generation and machine translation. Early techniques for generating text conditioned on some input information were template or rule-based engines (McRoy et al., 2000), or probabilistic models such as n-gram. In the recent past, state-of-the-art results on these tasks have been achieved by recurrent (Press et al., 2017; Mikolov et al., 2010) and con-

Proceedings of the 2019 Conference of the North American Chapter of the Association for Computational Linguistics: Student Research Workshop, pages 53–60

Minneapolis, Minnesota, June 3 - 5, 2019. ©2017 Association for Computational Linguistics

volutional neural network models trained for like-lihood maximization. Very recently, attempts have been made to generate text using purely generative adversarial training (Arjovsky et al., 2017).

Unsupervised learning with deep neural networks in the framework of encoder-decoder models has become the state-of-the-art methods for approaching NLP problems (Young et al., 2017). Recent text generation models have used a wide variety of GANs such as policy-gradient based sequence generation framework (Yu et al., 2016). Fedus et al. (2018) have used an actor-critic conditional GAN to fill in missing text conditioned on the surrounding text for natural language generation tasks. GANs have also been used for text style transfer by Yang et al. (2018) where language models act as the discriminator and by Chen et al. (2018) with the introduction of a new f-measure termed as feature-mover's distance.

Using adversaries of word and character level embeddings for text generation has been explored by Rajeswar et al. (2017). Models trained using generative adversarial networks or variational autoencoders have been shown to learn representations of continuous structures by leveraging deep latent variables such as text embeddings (Zhao et al., 2017). This work explores injecting sentence embeddings produced using the Skip Thought architecture (Kiros et al., 2015) into GANs in different setups.

3 Skip-Thought Generative Adversarial Network

In literature corpora such as fantasy and science fiction novels, the vocabulary does not vary significantly across the authors, but the manner of expression does, which is intuitively best captured at the level of sentences than words. The approach, hence, that this work takes in generating sentences with the writing style of one author is to make the adversarial model approximate the distribution of all sentences (rather than words or characters) in a latent space using skip-thought architecture. Previous attempts on text generation have used the character and word-level embeddings instead with GANs (Rajeswar et al., 2017).

This section introduces Skip-Thought Generative Adversarial Network with a background on neural network models that it is based on. The Skip-Thought model (Kiros et al., 2015) produces embedding vectors for sentences present in train-ing corpus. These vectors constitute the real distribution for the discriminator network. The generator network produces sentence vectors similar to those from the encoded real distribution. The generated vectors are sampled over the course of training and then decoded to produce sentences using a Skip-Thought decoder conditioned on the same text corpus.

3.1 Skip-Thought Vectors

Skip-Thought is an encoder-decoder framework with an unsupervised approach to train a generic, distributed sentence encoder. The encoder maps sentences sharing semantic and syntactic properties to similar vector representations and the decoder reconstructs the surrounding sentences of an encoded passage. The sentence encoding approach draws inspiration from the skip-gram model in producing vector representations using previous and next sentences.

The Skip-Thought model uses an RNN encoder with GRU activations (Chung et al., 2014) and an RNN decoder with conditional GRU. This combination is identical to the RNN encoder-decoder of Cho et al. (2014) used in neural machine translation.

Skip-Thought Architecture

For a given sentence tuple (s_{i-1}, s_i, s_{i+1}), let $\mathbf{w}_i^t$ denote the t-th word in sentence $\mathbf{s}_i$ and $\mathbf{x}_i^t$ denote its word embedding. The model is described as:

Encoder. Encoded vectors for a sentence s_i with N words w^i, w^{i+1},...,w^n are computed by iterating over the following sequence of equations:

$$\mathbf{r^t} = \sigma(\mathbf{W_r x^t} + \mathbf{U_r h^{t-1}})$$
$$\mathbf{z^t} = \sigma(\mathbf{W_z x^t} + \mathbf{U_z h^{t-1}})$$
$$\mathbf{\bar{h}^t} = \tanh(\mathbf{W x^t} + \mathbf{U}(\mathbf{r^t} \odot \mathbf{h^{t-1}}))$$
$$\mathbf{h^t} = (\mathbf{1} - \mathbf{z^t}) \odot \mathbf{h^{t-1}} + \mathbf{z^t} \odot \mathbf{\bar{h}^t}$$

where h_i^t is a hidden state at each time step and interpreted as a sequence of words $w_i^1,...,w_i^n$, $\mathbf{\bar{h}^t}$ is the proposed state update at time t, $\mathbf{z}^t$ is the update gate and $\mathbf{r}^t$ is the reset gate. Both update gates take values between zero and one.

Decoder. A neural language model conditioned on the encoder output h_i serves as the decoder. Bias matrices C_z, C_r, C are introduced for the update gate, reset gate and hidden state computation by the encoder. Two decoders are used in parallel,

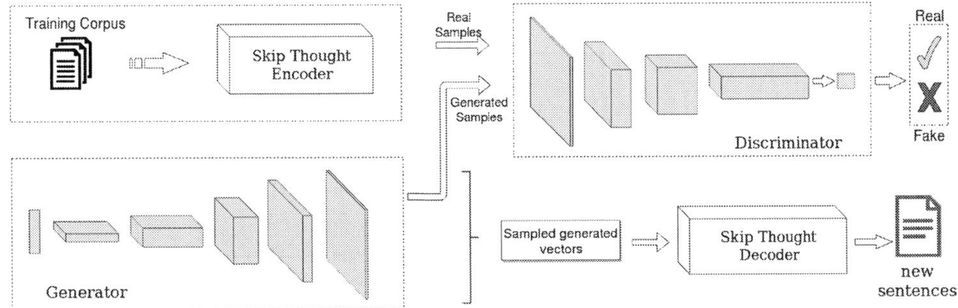

Figure 1: Skip-Thought Generative Adversarial Network model architecture

one each for sentences $\mathbf{s}_{i+1}$ and $\mathbf{s}_{i-1}$. The following equations are iterated over for decoding:

$$\mathbf{r^t} = \sigma(\mathbf{W_r^d x^{t-1}} + \mathbf{U_r^d h^{t-1}} + \mathbf{C_r h_i})$$

$$\mathbf{z^t} = \sigma(\mathbf{W_z^d x^{t-1}} + \mathbf{U_z^d h^{t-1}} + \mathbf{C_z h_i})$$

$$\mathbf{\bar{h}^t} = \tanh(\mathbf{W^d x^{t-1}} + \mathbf{U^d}(\mathbf{r^t} \odot \mathbf{h^{t-1}}) + \mathbf{C h_i})$$

$$\mathbf{h_{i+1}^t} = (\mathbf{1} - \mathbf{z^t}) \odot \mathbf{h^{t-1}} + \mathbf{z^t} \odot \mathbf{\bar{h}^t}$$

Objective. For the same tuple of sentences, objective function is the sum of log-probabilities for the forward and backward sentences conditioned on the encoder representation:

$$\sum_t log P(w_{i+1}^t | w_{i+1}^{<t}, h_i) +$$

$$\sum_t log P(w_{i-1}^t | w_{i-1}^{<t}, h_i)$$

3.2 Generative Adversarial Networks

Generative Adversarial Networks (Goodfellow et al., 2014) are deep neural net architectures comprised of two networks, contesting with each other in a zero-sum game framework. For a given data, GANs can mimic learning the underlying distribution and generate artificial data samples similar to those from the real distribution. Generative Adversarial Networks consists of two players: a Generator and a Discriminator. The generator G tries to produce data close to the real distribution $P(x)$ from some stochastic distribution $P(z)$ termed as noise. The discriminator D's objective is to differentiate between real and generated data $G(z)$.

The two networks - generator and discriminator compete against each other in a zero-sum game. The minimax strategy dictates that each network plays optimally with the assumption that the other network is optimal. This leads to Nash equilibrium which is the point of convergence for GAN model.

Objective. Goodfellow et al. (2014) have formulated the minimax game for a generator G, discriminator D adversarial network with value function $V(G, D)$ as:

$$\min_G \max_D V(D, G) = E_{x \sim p_{data}(x)}[log D(x)] +$$

$$E_{z \sim p_z(z)}[log(1 - D(G(z)))]$$

3.3 Model Architecture

The STGAN architecture (Figure 1) has two components: Skip Thought encoder-decoder and a generative adversarial network. The model uses a deep convolutional generative adversarial network, similar to the one used in DCGAN (Radford et al., 2015). During the training, the generator network is updated twice for each discriminator network update to prevent fast convergence of the discriminator network.

The Skip-Thought encoder for the model encodes sentences using 2400 GRU units (Chung et al., 2014) with a word vector dimensionality of 620. The encoder combines the sentence embeddings to produce 4800-dimensional combine-skip vectors with the first 2400 dimensions being uni-skip model and the last 2400 bi-skip model. This work uses the 4800-dimensional vectors as they have been found to be the best performing in experiments [1]. For training of the STGAN, the Skip-Thought encoder produces sentence embedding vectors which are labelled as real samples for GAN discriminator.

The decoder uses greedy decoding by taking the argmax over the softmax output distribution for a given time-step which also acts as input for next time-step. It reconstructs sentences conditioned on a sentence vector by randomly sampling

---

[1]`https://github.com/ryankiros/`
`skip-thoughts/`

from the predicted distributions with a preset beam width. A 620 dimensional RNN word embedding is used for the decoder with 1600 hidden GRU decoding units. All experiments are performed using the Adam optimizer (Kingma and Ba, 2014) with gradient clipping and a batch size of 16.

Each sentence is appended with a start token <s> and an end token </s> before encoding. During the process of training generator network with these embeddings, some generated vectors are randomly sampled. The sampled vectors are decoded using pretrained Skip-Thought decoder to produce a probability distribution over the vocabulary in order to reconstruct sentences. The decoding is terminated when the stop token </s> is encountered during reconstruction.

3.4 Improving Training and Loss

The training process of a GAN is notably difficult (Salimans et al., 2016) and several improvement techniques such as batch normalization, feature matching, historical averaging (Salimans et al., 2016) and unrolling GAN (Metz et al., 2016) have been suggested for making the training more stable. Training the Skip-Thought GAN often results in mode dropping (Arjovsky and Bottou, 2017; Srivastava et al., 2017) with a parameter setting where it outputs a very narrow distribution of points. To overcome this, it uses minibatch discrimination by looking at an entire batch of samples and modeling the distance between a given sample and all the other samples present in that batch.

The minimax formulation for an optimal discriminator in a vanilla GAN is Jensen-Shannon Distance between the generated distribution and the real distribution. Arjovsky et al. (2017) used Wasserstein distance or earth mover's distance to demonstrate how replacing distance measures can improve training loss for a GAN. Gulrajani et al. (2017) have incorporated a gradient penalty regularizer term in WGAN objective for discriminator's loss function. The experiments in this work use the above f-measures to improve performance of Skip-Thought GAN on text generation.

4 Results and Discussion

4.1 Conditional Generation of Sentences.

GANs can be conditioned on certain attributes to generate real valued data (Mirza and Osindero, 2014; Radford et al., 2015). In this experiment, both the generator and discriminator are conditioned on the Skip-Thought encoded vectors.

The data used for this setup consists of 250,000 sentences chosen from the BookCorpus dataset (Zhu et al., 2015) with a training/test/validation split of 5/1/1. All the sentences belong to one series of fantasy novels by a particular author of English language. This selection implies that the author's word choice, sentence structure, figurative language, and sentence arrangement are consistent and well-represented across the dataset. Conditioning on this high-level outline gives more robustness to the model in terms of generated samples.

The decoded sentences form the evaluation set for measuring performance of different models under corpus level BLEU-n (Papineni et al., 2002), METEOR (Banerjee and Lavie, 2005) and ROUGE(Lin, 2004) metrics. Table 1 compares these results for the proposed STGAN against standard LSTM and Attention Bidirectional LSTM models in two settings - using Skip Thought vectors and using tied GloVe (Pennington et al., 2014) embeddings. For this experiment, GloVe Average is obtained by averaging GloVe embeddings of all the words composing a given sentences while GloVe Extreme is computed by taking the most extreme value for each dimension across embeddings of all the words. All the three models used in the experiment: LSTM, Attention BiLSTM and Wasserstein GAN take the above three embeddings as input in separate runs and output vectors which are decoded to reconstruct sentences using the corresponding embedding's decoder.

Table 2 shows improvements in metric scores when using Wasserstein distance and gradient penalty regularizer as discussed in section 3.4. WGAN-GP gives the strongest across-the-board performance in both the GloVe and Skip-Thought settings, so we use this as the basis for the rest of our experiments. The METEOR scores are reportedly better for other models because though it does not rely on embeddings but it includes notions of synonymy and paraphrasing to compute alignment between hypothesis and reference sentences (Sharma et al., 2017).

4.2 Language Generation.

Language generation is performed on a dataset comprising simple English sentences referred to

MODEL	EMBEDDING	BLEU-1	BLEU-2	BLEU-3	BLEU-4	METEOR	ROUGE
LSTM	GLOVE AVERAGE	0.874	0.792	0.621	0.582	0.681	**0.692**
	GLOVE EXTREME	0.874	0.791	0.616	0.580	0.677	0.685
	SKIP THOUGHT	**0.885**	**0.807**	**0.633**	**0.585**	**0.683**	**0.692**
ATTENTION BiLSTM	GLOVE AVERAGE	**0.904**	**0.836**	0.645	0.583	**0.695**	0.698
	GLOVE EXTREME	0.886	0.827	0.643	0.581	0.689	0.696
	SKIP THOUGHT	0.900	0.827	**0.651**	**0.589**	0.692	**0.715**
WGAN -GP	GLOVE AVERAGE	0.879	0.807	0.668	0.585	**0.694**	0.702
	GLOVE EXTREME	0.853	0.799	0.666	0.579	0.689	0.697
	SKIP THOUGHT	**0.903**	**0.836**	**0.682**	**0.594**	0.692	**0.731**

Table 1: Evaluation of models on word-overlap based automated metrics when trained with different embeddings. Skip-Thought gives better results than GloVe for BLEU-n and ROUGE metrics, while the METEOR scores are comparable to that when using averaged GloVe embedding with Attention BiLSTM generator.

MODEL	BLEU-2		BLEU-3		METEOR		ROUGE	
	GLOVE	ST	GLOVE	ST	GLOVE	ST	GLOVE	ST
GAN	0.710	0.745	0.593	0.607	0.667	0.670	0.654	0.649
WGAN	0.786	0.833	0.645	0.669	0.681	0.681	0.681	0.675
WGAN-GP	0.807	0.836	0.668	0.682	0.694	0.692	0.702	0.731

Table 2: BLEU-2, BLEU-3 METEOR and ROUGE metric scores across GAN models with different f-measures. *GloVe: GLoVe Average, **ST**: Skip-Thought, **WGAN**: Wasserstein GAN, **GP**: Gradient Penalty*

as CMU-SE[2] (Rajeswar et al., 2017). The CMU-SE dataset consists of 44,016 sentences with a vocabulary of 3,122 words. The vectors are extracted in batches of same-lengthed sentences for encoding. The samples represent how mode collapse is manifested when using least-squares distance (Mao et al., 2016) f-measure without minibatch discrimination. Table 3(a) contains sentences generated from a vanilla STGAN which mode collapse is observed, while 3(b) contains examples wherein it is not observed when using minibatch discrimination. Table 3(c) shows generated samples from STGAN when using Wasserstein distance f-measure as WGAN (Arjovsky et al., 2017)) and 3(d) contains samples when using a gradient penalty regularizer term as WGAN-GP (Gulrajani et al., 2017). The two models generate longer human-like sentences and over a more diverse vocabulary.

4.3 Human Scores and Correlations

The performance of this approach to generate new sentences has been evaluated in reproducing writing style of a particular author. The participant group consisted of 14 individuals, who were familiar with writing style of the said author by having read all but a few of the literary works of the author. The setup prevents them from being certain whether a sentence in question has or has not appeared in any work of the author that they have already read. To form the evaluation set of sen-

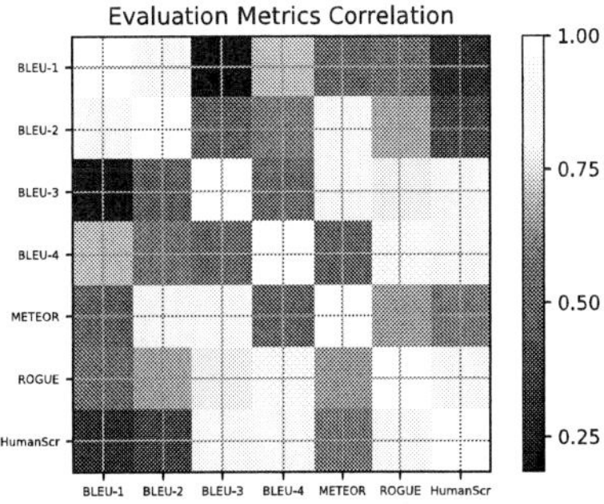

Figure 2: Pearson's correlation coefficient between automated computed metrics and human scores. Human scores correlate well with BLEU-3 and ROUGE scores.

Model	Generated Samples
a. **GAN (Mode collapse)**	1. it ?
	2. it ?
	3. it ?
	4. it ? how would it ?
	5. it ? how would it ?
b. **GAN (minibatch)**	1. it a bottle ?
	2. a glass bottle ?
	3. a glass bottle it ?
	4. it my hand a bottle ?
	5. the phone my hand it
c. **Skip Thought WGAN**	1. we have new year s holidays, always.
	2. here you can nt see your suitcase ,
	3. please show me how much is a transfer?
	4. i had a police take watch out of my wallet .
	5. here i collect my telephone card and telephone number
d. **Skip Thought WGAN-GP**	1. my passport and a letter card with my card , please
	2. here on my telephone, mr. kimuras registration cards address.
	3. i can nt see some shopping happened .
	4. get him my camera found a person s my watch .
	5. delta airlines flight six zero two from six p.m. to miami, please?

Table 3: Sentences sampled from STGAN when training on CMU-SE Dataset; mode collapse is overcome by using minibatch discrimination. Sample quality in terms of length and diversity further improved by using Wasserstein distance f-measure with gradient penalty regularizer. **WGAN**: *Wasserstein GAN*, **GP**: *Gradient Penalty*

	Real	Fake	% real	% fake
Real	30	**51**	37.04%	**62.96%**
Fake	**48**	75	**39.02%**	60.98%

Table 4: Weighted human scores for sentences. $|rating - 3|$ is weight given to each sentence's rating. 39.02% of the generated samples were marked as real.

tences, the generated samples were mixed with real sentences from the author's writing. 10 sentences from this mixed pool were chosen at random to be presented to each person. The participants were asked to mark on a scale of 1 to 5 if they thought that a sentence seemed to belong to the author's works or was generated from a model, with 1 being certainly from the author and 5 being certainly from a model. Table 4 shows the weighted scores computed as $|rating - 3|$ to account for the degree of uncertainty addressed by a participant when rating. The models performs well with 39.02% of the generated samples being marked as written by the author while a greater 62.96% of the actual sentences from author's writing being marked as fake generated ones. Figure 2 compiles Pearson's correlation coefficients between the obtained human scores and Skip-Thought GAN scores.

5 Conclusion

This work presents a simple and effective model for text generation based on adversarial training using sentence embeddings. It shows how the use of sentence-level embeddings allows modelling the way of expression of an author in generated text in a better way than when using word-level embeddings. A performance comparison across several metrics is made between different GAN architectures with improved training stability and attention augmented LSTM models. Finally, it discusses how the automated corpus-based evaluations correlate with human judgements. In future, this work aims to be applied for synthesizing images from text, exploring complementary architectures to projects like neural-storyteller[3] where skip-thought embeddings are already used to perform image captioning with story-style transfer.

---

[3] `https://github.com/ryankiros/neural-storyteller`

Acknowledgements

The author would like to thank Aruna Malapati for providing insights and access to an Nvidia Titan X GPU for the experiments; and Pranesh Bhargava, Greg Durrett and Yash Raj Jain for providing helpful feedback. The author also acknowledges the support of Microsoft Research India Travel Grant.

References

M. Arjovsky and L. Bottou. 2017. Towards Principled Methods for Training Generative Adversarial Networks. *ArXiv e-prints*.

M. Arjovsky, S. Chintala, and L. Bottou. 2017. Wasserstein GAN. *ArXiv e-prints*.

Satanjeev Banerjee and Alon Lavie. 2005. Meteor: An automatic metric for mt evaluation with improved correlation with human judgments. In *Proceedings of the ACL Workshop on Intrinsic and Extrinsic Evaluation Measures for Machine Translation and/or Summarization*, pages 65–72. Association for Computational Linguistics.

Liqun Chen, Shuyang Dai, Chenyang Tao, Dinghan Shen, Zhe Gan, Haichao Zhang, Yizhe Zhang, and Lawrence Carin. 2018. Adversarial text generation via feature-mover's distance. *CoRR*, abs/1809.06297.

Kyunghyun Cho, Bart van Merrienboer, Dzmitry Bahdanau, and Yoshua Bengio. 2014. On the properties of neural machine translation: Encoder–decoder approaches. In *Proceedings of SSST-8, Eighth Workshop on Syntax, Semantics and Structure in Statistical Translation*. Association for Computational Linguistics.

Junyoung Chung, Caglar Gulcehre, KyungHyun Cho, and Yoshua Bengio. 2014. Empirical evaluation of gated recurrent neural networks on sequence modeling. *arXiv preprint arXiv:1412.3555*.

W. Fedus, I. Goodfellow, and A. M. Dai. 2018. MaskGAN: Better Text Generation via Filling in the______. *ArXiv e-prints*.

Ian Goodfellow, Jean Pouget-Abadie, Mehdi Mirza, Bing Xu, David Warde-Farley, Sherjil Ozair, Aaron Courville, and Yoshua Bengio. 2014. Generative adversarial nets. In *Advances in Neural Information Processing Systems 27*, pages 2672–2680. Curran Associates, Inc.

Ishaan Gulrajani, Faruk Ahmed, Martin Arjovsky, Vincent Dumoulin, and Aaron C Courville. 2017. Improved training of wasserstein gans. In *Advances in Neural Information Processing Systems 30*, pages 5767–5777.

Diederik P. Kingma and Jimmy Ba. 2014. Adam: A method for stochastic optimization. *CoRR*, abs/1412.6980.

Ryan Kiros, Yukun Zhu, Ruslan Salakhutdinov, Richard S Zemel, Antonio Torralba, Raquel Urtasun, and Sanja Fidler. 2015. Skip-thought vectors. *arXiv preprint arXiv:1506.06726*.

Chin-Yew Lin. 2004. Rouge: A package for automatic evaluation of summaries. *Text Summarization Branches Out*.

Xudong Mao, Qing Li, Haoran Xie, Raymond Y. K. Lau, and Zhen Wang. 2016. Multi-class generative adversarial networks with the L2 loss function. *CoRR*.

Susan W McRoy, Songsak Channarukul, and Syed S Ali. 2000. Yag: A template-based generator for real-time systems. In *Proceedings of the first international conference on Natural language generation-Volume 14*, pages 264–267. Association for Computational Linguistics.

Luke Metz, Ben Poole, David Pfau, and Jascha Sohl-Dickstein. 2016. Unrolled generative adversarial networks. *CoRR*, abs/1611.02163.

Tomas Mikolov, Martin Karafiát, Lukás Burget, Jan Cernocký, and Sanjeev Khudanpur. 2010. Recurrent neural network based language model. In *INTERSPEECH*.

Mehdi Mirza and Simon Osindero. 2014. Conditional generative adversarial nets. *CoRR*, abs/1411.1784.

Kishore Papineni, Salim Roukos, Todd Ward, and Wei-Jing Zhu. 2002. Bleu: A method for automatic evaluation of machine translation. In *Proceedings of the 40th Annual Meeting on Association for Computational Linguistics*, ACL '02.

Jeffrey Pennington, Richard Socher, and Christopher Manning. 2014. Glove: Global vectors for word representation. In *Proceedings of the 2014 conference on empirical methods in natural language processing (EMNLP)*, pages 1532–1543.

Ofir Press, Amir Bar, Ben Bogin, Jonathan Berant, and Lior Wolf. 2017. Language generation with recurrent generative adversarial networks without pretraining. *CoRR*, abs/1706.01399.

Alec Radford, Luke Metz, and Soumith Chintala. 2015. Unsupervised representation learning with deep convolutional generative adversarial networks. *CoRR*, abs/1511.06434.

Sai Rajeswar, Sandeep Subramanian, Francis Dutil, Christopher Joseph Pal, and Aaron C. Courville. 2017. Adversarial generation of natural language. *CoRR*, abs/1705.10929.

Tim Salimans, Ian Goodfellow, Wojciech Zaremba, Vicki Cheung, Alec Radford, and Xi Chen. 2016. Improved techniques for training gans. In *Proceedings of the 30th International Conference on Neural Information Processing Systems*, NIPS'16.

Shikhar Sharma, Layla El Asri, Hannes Schulz, and Jeremie Zumer. 2017. Relevance of unsupervised metrics in task-oriented dialogue for evaluating natural language generation. *CoRR*, abs/1706.09799.

A. Srivastava, L. Valkov, C. Russell, M. U. Gutmann, and C. Sutton. 2017. VEEGAN: Reducing Mode Collapse in GANs using Implicit Variational Learning. *ArXiv e-prints*.

Zichao Yang, Zhiting Hu, Chris Dyer, Eric P. Xing, and Taylor Berg-Kirkpatrick. 2018. Unsupervised text style transfer using language models as discriminators. *CoRR*, abs/1805.11749.

Tom Young, Devamanyu Hazarika, Soujanya Poria, and Erik Cambria. 2017. Recent trends in deep learning based natural language processing. *CoRR*, abs/1708.02709.

Lantao Yu, Weinan Zhang, Jun Wang, and Yong Yu. 2016. Seqgan: Sequence generative adversarial nets with policy gradient. *CoRR*, abs/1609.05473.

J. Zhao, Y. Kim, K. Zhang, A. M. Rush, and Y. LeCun. 2017. Adversarially Regularized Autoencoders. *ArXiv e-prints*.

Yukun Zhu, Ryan Kiros, Richard S. Zemel, Ruslan Salakhutdinov, Raquel Urtasun, Antonio Torralba, and Sanja Fidler. 2015. Aligning books and movies: Towards story-like visual explanations by watching movies and reading books.

A Partially Rule-Based Approach to AMR Generation

Emma Manning
Department of Linguistics
Georgetown University
esm76@georgetown.edu

Abstract

This paper presents a new approach to generating English text from Abstract Meaning Representation (AMR). In contrast to the neural and statistical MT approaches used in other AMR generation systems, this one is largely rule-based, supplemented only by a language model and simple statistical linearization models, allowing for more control over the output. We also address the difficulties of automatically evaluating AMR generation systems and the problems with BLEU for this task. We compare automatic metrics to human evaluations and show that while METEOR and TER arguably reflect human judgments better than BLEU, further research into suitable evaluation metrics is needed.

1 Introduction

Abstract Meaning Representation, or AMR, is a representation of a sentence as a rooted, labeled graph. It provides a representation of the sentence's semantics while abstracting away from morphosyntactic details such as tense, number, word order, and part of speech (Banarescu et al., 2013).

Because of these abstractions, it can be very difficult to generate from an AMR back to a fluent English sentence which preserves the original meaning. It is also difficult to accurately evaluate the quality of generation results, since there is typically only one reference sentence available to compare results to, but one of the basic principles of AMR is the fact that the same AMR is used to represent many possible sentences; for example, "he described her as a genius", "his description of her: genius", and "she was a genius, according to his description" would all correspond to the same AMR (Banarescu et al., 2013).

The following represents an AMR graph for the sentence "A key European arms control treaty must be maintained.":

```
(o / obligate-01
  :ARG2 (m / maintain-01
    :ARG1 (t / treaty
      :ARG0-of (c2 / control-01
        :ARG1 (a / arms))
      :ARG1-of (k / key-02)
      :mod (c / continent
        :wiki "Europe"
        :name (n / name
          :op1 "Europe")))))
```

This example demonstrates several of the challenges faced by an AMR generation system. These include properly addressing constructions that do not correspond closely to the words in the reference, such as the use of the frame `obligate-01` to express 'must' and the specific construction used for named entities such as 'Europe', as well as word order and the passive construction 'be maintained'. In fact, this system successfully addresses some but not all of these challenges, producing the output "Must maintain Europe key arms control treaty ."

While most previous work in AMR generation has used statistical and neural techniques, the current work approaches the task with a combination of rules and statistical methods; the rules are intended to constrain possibilities, particularly the possible realizations of concepts and which information from the AMR is expressed. This allows for greater control over the output; even if the overall results do not score as well, on average, as those of other approaches, this approach has the potential to minimize the chances of significant adequacy errors such as omission of key information or addition of information not contained in the AMR, which are possible in machine-learning-based systems. Another advantage of a partially rule-based approach is that it can work without large amounts

Proceedings of the 2019 Conference of the North American Chapter of the Association for Computational Linguistics: Student Research Workshop, pages 61–70
Minneapolis, Minnesota, June 3 - 5, 2019. ©2017 Association for Computational Linguistics

of AMR-annotated data; it could thus be adapted to a new language or an altered AMR scheme in situations where there is insufficient data for a machine-learning-based system to achieve satisfactory performance.

2 Related Work

2.1 AMR Generation Systems

Flanigan et al. (2016) introduced the first AMR generator (JAMR), which transforms an AMR graph into a tree before using a weighted tree-to-string transducer to generate the string. While most of its rules are automatically extracted, these are supplemented with handwritten rules for some phenomena including dates, conjunctions, and some special concepts. An ablation experiment showed that these handwritten rules contributed significantly to the results.

AMR generation was included as a shared task at SemEval-2017 (May and Priyadarshi, 2017). The winner of the task, as determined by human judgments, was the RIGOTRIO system (Gruzitis et al., 2017), which uses handcrafted rules to convert AMRs to Abstract Syntax Trees, which are then realized as strings using existing Grammatical Framework resources. However, this approach has limited coverage, and is only used for about 12% of sentences, while the system defaults to using JAMR for other sentences.

Other submissions to the shared task included FORGe, which uses graph transducers (Mille et al., 2017); Sheffield, which treats AMR generation as an inverse of transition-based parsing, transforming the AMR graph into a syntactic dependency tree before realizing it as a sentence (Lampouras and Vlachos, 2017); and ISI, which uses phrase-based machine translation (PBMT) methods (Pourdamghani et al., 2016).

Beyond the shared task, other work in AMR generation has approached the task as a Traveling Salesman Problem (Song et al., 2016), with synchronous node replacement grammar (Song et al., 2017), and using a transition-based approach to transform the AMR into a syntactic dependency tree (Schick, 2017). Castro Ferreira et al. (2017) compare the effect of different types of preprocessing on the performance of AMR generation systems based on PBMT and NMT.

The best results to date have been obtained with neural methods, which excel when the small amount of manually-annotated training data is aug-mented with millions of unlabeled sentences which have been automatically parsed. Konstas et al. (2017) first used this approach to train a sequence-to-sequence model, and and Song et al. (2018) later adapted it to a graph-to-sequence model.

2.2 Evaluation

Most previous work in AMR generation has reported results exclusively using BLEU scores (Papineni et al., 2002), with the original sentence as the only reference. A notable exception is the five systems included in the SemEval-2017 shared task, which were additionally compared by human judgments. The human evaluations were shown not to correlate well with BLEU scores, raising questions about the suitability of the metric for this task (May and Priyadarshi, 2017). In particular, BLEU as used for AMR generation is intuitively inappropriate because it strictly measures similarity to one reference sentence, while by design, a single AMR can correspond to many different English sentences. Thus, BLEU is in practice more of a measure of how closely a system can replicate the exact wording used in the original sentence than of how adequately and fluently it expresses the meaning of the AMR.

Ideally, evaluation of AMR generation would be performed using human judgments or task-based evaluations; unfortunately, however, it is sometimes necessary to rely on the practicality of automatic metrics. We thus follow Castro Ferreira et al. (2017) in reporting two additional automatic metrics alongside BLEU, which may provide slightly more insight into system performance. The first is METEOR, which has been shown to correlate more strongly with human judgments of machine translation quality than BLEU does (Lavie and Agarwal, 2007; Denkowski and Lavie, 2014). It is a particularly appealing alternative to BLEU for AMR generation because, instead of only giving credit to exact word matches, METEOR also allows matching based on stems, synonyms, and paraphrases. This mitigates the issues associated with having a single reference sentence in AMR, because it does not penalize systems as harshly for not correctly guessing the forms of morphological and syntactic variants that are usually not specified within the AMR. The final evaluation metric used is Translation Edit Rate (TER), which has been shown to require only one reference sentence in order to correlate as well with human judgments for machine translation as BLEU does with four references (Snover et al., 2006). This robustness against lack of extra references makes it, too, likely to be better suited to the AMR generation task than BLEU is.

These metrics were all designed for evaluation of machine translation; it may also be useful in the future to explore evaluating AMR generation with metrics from other NLG-related tasks, such as referenceless measures developed for grammatical error correction (e.g. Napoles et al., 2016; Choshen and Abend, 2018).

3 Methods

The system introduced in this paper uses rules to generate realization hypotheses, which are ranked and combined by statistical methods.

We used the LDC2015E86 version of the AMR corpus for training the linearization models, tuning hyperparameters, and analyzing errors.

3.1 Algorithm

The system uses an algorithm based on cube pruning (Huang and Chiang, 2007). Hypotheses are generated by recursing down the AMR graph, ignoring subsequent mentions of variables that have already been processed (reentrancies) and therefore treating the AMR as a tree. The roles `:wiki` and `:mode` are also ignored: `:wiki` provides extra information about named entities that does not need to be expressed in the English realization. The `:mode` relation could be used in future versions of the system to generate particular sentence types such as questions and imperatives; however, this syntactic manipulation would require more complicated rules than are used in this algorithm, and so the relation is ignored for now.

At each node, a priority queue of scored hypotheses is generated.

In particular, at each leaf node, one or more hypotheses are created for the realization of the node, according to the process described in 3.2, and each of these partial hypotheses is scored by a language model.

At each non-terminal node, priority queues are recursively generated containing hypotheses for the realizations of each of the node's children, as well as one for the node itself. Each of these is prioritized by language model score. An additional priority queue represents possible linearizations of the current node and each of its children, scored as

discussed in 3.4. Thus, for a node with n children, a total of $n+2$ priority queues are created, simulating an $n+2$-dimensional hypercube. k nodes of the cube are then expanded and rescored by the language model.

When the root node of the AMR is reached, a period is added to the end and the k hypotheses are rescored by the language model, this time treated as a complete sentence. The realization associated with the best-scored hypothesis is postprocessed to capitalize the first letter, then returned.

3.2 Realization[1]

For each node, one or more possible strings are generated to realize the node's associated concept or constant and, in some cases, its relation. The system uses specific rules for some special cases, and more generalized rules for most nodes.

Special Cases: Special rules are used for a few constructions. In particular, the constructions for named entities and for people with relationships and roles in organizations (`have-rel-role-91` and `have-org-role-91`) are represented in AMR with some concepts that do not typically align with words in the text; rules prevent these and certain other AMR-specific concepts from being realized.

In addition, a '`-`' representing negative polarity is realized as 'not' or as one of several negative contractions; numbers in ordinal or month-name constructions are realized accordingly, and pronouns are realized as their possessive form in possessive constructions and may be realized as their subjective or objective forms otherwise. Finally, a handful of concepts whose names don't correspond to the English strings they typically represent are mapped to more likely English translations. These represent some conjunctions, modals, and other relationships that are associated with particular concepts in AMR; for example, `contrast-01` is realized as 'but' and `obligate-01` as 'can'.

Frames: Frames not dealt with in the special rules are likely to correspond to verbs, or occasionally adjectives, adverbs, and verb-derived nouns, and are treated as such. These are represented in English as they appear in the concept name, with frame numbers removed and words joined by spaces rather than hyphens. In addition to this base

---

[1] See the code, available at `https://github.com/esmanning/emmAMR`, for full details on the realization rules that could not be explained exhaustively due to space constraints.

concept name, several variations are generated, corresponding to different possible verbal, adjectival, and nominal forms. Verbal and adjectival forms are created by combining optional auxiliaries with verb forms such as those ending in '-ing', '-s', and '-ed', (with several variations depending on the base form, such as removing a final 'e' before adding an ending when appropriate). Nominal variants are similarly created with variations on the suffixes '-ment' and '-tion', and adverbs with '-ly'.

In many cases this generates forms that are implausible; this is not a problem because they are ranked by language model score, so forms that are unattested or very infrequent in the language model's training corpus receive poor scores and will be pruned out at a later stage. Nevertheless, this strategy inevitably misses some valid forms, such as those of many irregular verbs; this could be addressed in the future by integrating external resources that can produce inflections and derivations of a given word.

Non-Frame Concepts: Remaining non-frame concepts are given a treatment similar to the frames discussed above, except that they are assumed more likely to be nouns or elements of noun phrases (such as adjectives), and are given corresponding realizations. They may also represent other parts of speech, such as adverbs; in these cases, again, the language model can rule out any implausible forms that are spuriously generated.

The plain concept name is formed by simply replacing any hyphens in the original concept name with spaces, although concepts at this stage are usually already a single word. The hypotheses created are for the plain concept name, as well as variations which append 'the', 'a', or 'an' before the name or plural suffix 's' at its end, and a hypothesis which adds both 'the' and the plural 's'.

Relations: In addition to the variable realizations, a handful of relations are realized by strings attached before or after the realization of their associated variable. These are given in Table 1. Many of these represent prepositions, including the general `:prep-X` relation, which is realized as the given preposition.

3.3 Language Model

A 5-gram language model was created to score hypothesis strings. It was trained on the English Gigaword Fifth Edition Corpus (LDC2011T07) using KenLM (Heafield, 2011; Heafield et al., 2013). For

Concept	Realization	Type
:prep-X	X	prefix (+space)
:accompanier	with	prefix (+ space)
:destination	to	prefix (+ space)
:purpose	to	prefix (+ space)
:condition	if	prefix (+ space)
:compared-to	than	prefix (+ space)
:poss	's	suffix
	of	prefix (+space)
:domain	is	suffix (+ space)
:location	in	prefix (+ space)
	at	prefix (+ space)
	by	prefix (+ space)

Table 1: Realizations for relations.

time and space efficiency, the model was pruned: singleton 2-grams were removed, as well as 3-, 4-, and 5-grams that appear 3 or fewer times.

3.4 Linearization

The linearization model contains two components, the pair-order model and the coreness model. These may be used in combination, in which case the scores they assign are averaged, or either one may be used alone. There is also a simpler baseline, described below, which is used by default when both models are disabled. Each of the models is trained on the alignments provided with the training data.

When non-baseline linearization scoring is used, all permutations of a node and its children are scored, assuming the node has no more than 5 children (producing at most $6! = 720$ combinations to score). This covers the vast majority of cases, but on the occasion that a node has more children, only the three orderings generated by the baseline linearization are considered. Unlike baseline linearization, these three candidates are still scored by the model(s) rather than being assigned identical scores. This limiting of possibilities serves a practical purpose in limiting the maximum number of permutations that must be calculated and scored; however, it is likely that it does not hurt performance, since nodes with a large number of children often represent lists, where preserving the original order of the children is likely to match the original sentence.

Pair-Order Model: The pair-order model is designed to capture the intuition that particular relations are likely to be realized to either the left or the right of other particular relations, or of their parent, represented here as the special relation ROOT. For example, :ARG0, which usually represents an agent, occurs before its ROOT 77% of the time, while :ARG1, usually a patient, precedes its ROOT in only 25% of cases.

The model is trained by counting ordered pairs of relations when it can be determined that one is realized before the other based on the provided alignments. Counts are then normalized into the probability of a particular order for any pair of relations, using add-1 smoothing to avoid assigning probabilities of 0 to unattested orderings. The model scores a hypothesized ordering by combining the scores of each pair of relations in the ordering.

Focusing only on relations allows for a small, simple model and avoids data sparseness; however, there are situations where a lexicalized version of this model may provide useful information that is lost here, such as the fact that some frames are more likely than others to have `:ARG1` realized to their left. A version of this model that could capture such information is left for future work.

Coreness Model: The second component to the linearization model is the coreness model, which attempts to capture the intuition that in addition to the left-to-right ordering represented by the pair-order model, some relations are more 'core' and are more likely to be realized closer to their parent than others. For example, whether `:ARG1` appears before or after its parent, it is likely to be close to it, while a relation like `:time` or `:purpose` will usually appear farther away, either very early or very late in a sentence. Thus, the model stores a single score for each relation representing its average absolute distance from the root, as a proportional distance relative to other children. A hypothesis's score is penalized based on the difference between each child's observed and expected distance from the root.

Baseline Linearization: When neither of the statistical linearization models are available, only three orderings are considered. The children are kept in the order they appear in the penman representation of the AMR, with the parent inserted either initially, penultimately, or finally. The penultimate option is considered because this is typically the appropriate place when the parent is a conjunction like 'and'. This is particularly useful in cases where the baseline is used as a default due to a node having a large number of children, since these often represent a long list of conjuncts. These hypotheses are given equal scores, meaning that all will be combined with realization hypotheses to create new hypotheses, and only the language model determines which are best.

4 Experiments

4.1 System Evaluation

First, several variations on this system with different hyperparameters were tested on the 1368 AMRs in the dev data. As discussed in 3.4, the linearization model contains two separate components, each of which is optional, resulting in four different linearization configurations. The pruning parameter k was tested at values of 5, 10, and 100. In total, 12 different versions of the system were tested on dev data. Based on these results, an optimal version of the system was chosen, which was then evaluated quantitatively on test data with automatic metrics. This system's output on dev data was also evaluated qualitatively by reviewing a small sample of its sentences, and quantitatively by comparing the number of tokens and frequency of parts of speech to those of the references.

4.2 Evaluation Metrics for AMR Generation

As discussed in 2.2, AMR Generation is usually evaluated only with BLEU, but one shared task obtained human judgments of five systems which were shown not to correlate well with BLEU scores (May and Priyadarshi, 2017). We tested the system outputs from this task with BLEU[2] as well as METEOR[3] and TER[4] to determine whether these metrics would correspond more closely to human judgments; results are presented and discussed in 5.5.

5 Results

5.1 Intra-System Variation

Table 2 shows the performance of each variation of the system on the dev data.

Systems using the pair-order model for linearization always perform better than their counterparts without it. While the coreness model's results are more mixed, it seems overall to hurt more than it helps. Increasing the stack size k always improved BLEU and METEOR scores, and doesn't hurt TER scores except in the +P+C condition, where the

---

[2]Using the multi-bleu-detok.perl script provided with the MOSES toolkit (Koehn et al., 2007)

[3]Using version 1.5, downloaded from `http://www.cs.cmu.edu/~alavie/METEOR/`

[4]Downloaded from `http://www.cs.umd.edu/~snover/tercom/`

Model	BLEU	METEOR	TER
+P+C,k=5	7.51	27.9	76.1
+P+C,k=10	8.12	28.1	**75.9**
+P+C,k=100	8.8	28.3	76.1
+P-C,k=5	7.76	28.0	76.0
+P-C,k=10	8.13	28.1	76.0
+P-C,k=100	**9.03**	**28.4**	76.0
-P+C,k=5	6.18	26.9	81.4
-P+C,k=10	6.48	27.0	81.4
-P+C,k=100	7.70	27.7	80.4
-P-C,k=5	5.99	26.6	79.1
-P-C,k=10	6.87	27.0	78.3
-P-C,k=100	7.71	27.4	77.9

Table 2: System performance on dev data with various hyperparameter combinations. '+P' is used to designate systems using the pair-order model and '-P' to designate those without it; similarly, '+C' and '-C' are used to designate whether or not the coreness model was used. In the '-P-C' configuration, baseline linearization is used. The best score for each metric is shown in bold. The shaded row represents the configuration of the system selected for further evaluation.

k=10 condition achieves a slightly better TER score than either k=5 or k=100.

Because it performs best according to BLEU and METEOR, and achieves barely short of its best TER score, the system using only the pair-order linearization model and k=100 was selected as the best version. These are the hyperparameter values that are used for the following quantitative and qualitative analyses.

5.2 Comparison to Other Systems

Table 3 summarizes the best BLEU and (when available) METEOR and TER scores reported for this system and various others. This table excludes the results of participants in the SemEval shared task, which were evaluated on a separate test set and whose scores are given below in Table 6.

The best BLEU score of this system is substantially lower than that of others. However, the METEOR score does appear a little more competitive, outperforming Castro Ferreira et al.'s NMT system by a point, and it is currently unknown how most other system's METEOR and TER scores compare with this one.

While automatic metrics are not ideal for comparing systems, they do seem to indicate that this system is not currently competitive with state-of-the-art systems. While it could certainly be improved in many ways given more time, this may indicate that rules augmented only with limited statistical models are not as well-suited to this task as other approaches, particularly the state-of-the-art neural models (Konstas et al., 2017; Song et al.,

2018). Still, as discussed in Section 1, the partially rule-based approach has potential to be useful in situations where greater control over output is necessary or where training data is particularly limited.

5.3 Error Analysis

The system's output on a random sample of 25 sentences from the dev data was analyzed. Sentences were subjectively coded for quality into four categories: 'excellent', 'good', 'fair', and 'poor'. Descriptions, counts, and examples of each of these categories are given in Table 4. Crucially, unlike the automatic evaluations, this evaluation was based on how fluently and adequately the system output expresses the meaning of the AMR, not on how closely it matches the reference string. For example, a reference-based automatic metric would count 'Kinkel' in the third example as incorrect, because it does not match the misspelling 'Kinkerl' in the reference set; this evaluation, based on the AMR itself, recognizes the system's output of 'Kinkel' as correct.

Most sentences, especially those classified as fair and poor, include both linearization and realization errors. An example of a linearization error is in the fourth example in the table, where the linearization in the system output incorrectly implies that jcboy was the speaker, rather than the addressee. However, linearization that differs from the reference is not always considered incorrect: in the second example, the system places the 'even if...' clause before the main clause of the sentence, which is a valid ordering even though it differs from that of the reference.

Further insight into the limitations of this system can be gained by looking at the lengths of output sentences and the frequency of different parts of speech. To analyze these discrepancies, the system output and references were both automatically tagged, using the NLTK tagger (Bird et al., 2009) and part of speech tags from the Penn Treebank (Santorini, 1990). Table 5 summarizes the counts of each part-of-speech tag found in system output and in the references.

One striking finding is that the system output has noticeably fewer tokens in total than the reference. Part of this is due to punctuation: while the system output contains more periods than the references due to adding a period to every sentence, it has no rules to output other punctuation such as commas, colons, parentheses, and quotation marks.

LDC2014T12				LDC2015E86				LDC2016E25			
System	BLEU	METEOR	TER	System	BLEU	METEOR	TER	System	BLEU	METEOR	TER
Pourdamghani (2016)	26.9	-	-	Flanigan (2016)	22.1	-	-	Castro Ferreira (2017)[5]			
Schick (2017)	28.9	-	-	Song (2016)	22.4	-	-	-NMT	18.9	26.6	66.2
				Song (2017)	25.2	-	-	-PBMT	26.8	34.7	59.4
				Konstas (2017)	33.8	-	-				
				Konstas (2017)[6]	31.1	37.5	46.9				
				Song (2018)	33.0	-	-				
				This System	8.7	28.2	76.0	This System	8.6	28.0	76.2

Table 3: Comparison of test scores achieved by this system and others.

Further investigation into adding punctuation might not only improve scores from automatic metrics, but also increase readability of more complicated sentences if done correctly.

Beyond punctuation, the system under-produces many types of function words, particularly determiners (DT), existentials (EX), prepositions and subordinating conjunctions (IN), possessives (POS, PRP$), the word 'to' (TO), and all types of WH-words (WDT, WP, WP$, WRB). In the nominal domain, the system realizes too many nouns as singular rather than plural for both common and proper nouns, which is probably due to a combination of some irregular plurals being missed by the realization rules, and the language model perhaps preferring singular forms more than is appropriate for these reference sentences. In the verbal domain, the system outputs more '-ing' forms (VBG) than are found in the references, and under-produces all other verb types, especially base forms (VB). This last is somewhat surprising, since the base form should always be accurately generated as an option by the realization rules; it is likely that its probability is underestimated by the language model, perhaps because the infinitival 'to' is not usually generated in hypotheses.

5.4 Future Work

The prevalence of linearization errors in the output sampled indicates that improving the linearization models would substantially improve system performance. As mentioned in 3.4, a lexicalized version of the linearization model would likely improve performance, especially if the data sparseness is mitigated by using augmented training data, similar to the approaches used by Konstas et al. (2017) and Song et al. (2018). Additionally, it may help to base the linearization models on the alignments of Szubert et al. (2018), which provide more complete coverage of the AMRs.

Realization errors mostly arise from the fact that the restrictive realization rules do not allow for all valid possibilities; for example, there is no rule to allow relative clauses such as the 'the ones who...' construction used in the reference of the second example sentence. The analysis of part of speech and overall token frequency also shows the need for more realization options involving function words, such as prepositions, which are currently not produced in many situations where they should be. These problems can be improved by the addition of more realization options to the handcrafted rules, although this is a time-consuming process.

5.5 Evaluation Metrics

In the SemEval shared task, only BLEU scores were originally reported alongside measures of human rankings. To explore how well each of the three automatic metrics used in this paper correlate with human judgments, we tested the output of all the systems that participated in the task with each of these metrics. Table 6 shows these new results, alongside the results of the human rankings.

All four measures agree that RIGOTRIO and CMU are the best two systems out of the task participants, but METEOR and TER both agree with humans in rating RIGOTRIO highest, while CMU obtains a higher BLEU score. This provides some evidence for the claim that METEOR and TER may be better suited than BLEU to evaluating AMR generation, especially when it comes to distinguishing among stronger systems. However, none of the metrics fully match the ranking given by humans—in particular, while humans considered FORGe the third-best system, all of the automatic metrics rank it lower. Thus, while these alternatives may be an improvement over BLEU, more research is necessary to determine a more accurate way to auto-

---

[5]Castro Ferreira et al. report results for 8 versions of each of system (NMT and PBMT), using different combinations of preprocessing steps. For each system, we select the version that performs best according to two of the three metrics to represent here.

[6]Data provided to me by Konstas in personal communication; scores determined by the same tests used for my system's data.

Excellent (1): Human-like quality; fluently presents all meaning

```
(t / tool
  :mod (m / machine)
  :purpose (s / set-up-03
    :ARG1 (f2 / facility)
    :location-of (f / fabricate-01)))
```

REF: Machine Tools for setting up a fabrication facility.
SYS: Machine tools to set up fabrication facility .

Good (5): Adequately and intelligibly expresses all or nearly all meaning with minor disfluencies

```
(m / multi-sentence
  :snt1 (s / suffer-01
    :ARG0 (p / person
      :mod (o2 / ordinary)))
  :snt2 (f / fish
    :ARG1-of (s2 / salt-01)
    :mod (s3 / still)
    :domain f2
    :concession (e / even-if
      :op1 (t / turn-01
        :ARG1 (b / body
          :poss (f2 / fish
            :ARG1-of (s4 / salt-01)))
        :direction (o3 / over)))))
```

REF: the ones who are suffering are the ordinary people: even if the body of a salted fish is turned over, it is still a salted fish ...
SYS: An ordinary person suffer . salted fish is still salted fish even if the body turns over .

Fair (6): Meaning is partially intelligible

```
(s / say-01
  :ARG0 (p / person :wiki "Klaus_Kinkel"
    :name (n2 / name :op1 "Kinkel"))
  :ARG1 (a / and
    :op1 (c / correct-02
      :ARG1 (t / thing
        :ARG1-of (d / decide-01
          :ARG0 (m / military
            :wiki "NATO"
            :name (n3 / name
              :op1 "NATO")))))
    :op2 (n4 / need-01
      :ARG1 t)))
```

REF: Kinkerl said that NATO 's decision was " correct and necessary " .
SYS: Said Kinkel NATO decided things correctly and needs .

Poor (13): Meaning is barely or not at all intelligible

```
(s / say-01
  :ARG1 (c / correct-02
  :ARG1 (y / you))
    :ARG2 (p / person :wiki -
      :name (n / name :op1 "jcboy")))
```

REF: @jcboy, You are correct.
SYS: You correct jcboy said .

Table 4: Description and example for each of the four quality categories.

matically evaluate AMR generation. In particular, due to the limitations of reference-based evaluation, we plan to focus on developing referenceless automatic metrics in future work.

Tag	System	Ref	Tag	System	Ref
$	2	22	NNS	1847	2079
``	0	57	PDT	4	5
''	0	42	POS	253	71
(	0	106	PRP	345	541
)	0	105	PRP$	22	129
,	1	823	RB	887	876
.	1431	1230	RBR	53	28
:	0	255	RBS	25	2
CC	859	856	RP	81	63
CD	853	777	SYM	0	1
DT	820	2663	TO	155	663
EX	0	50	UH	3	9
FW	7	5	VB	451	910
IN	1425	3215	VBD	887	1029
JJ	1806	2144	VBG	838	521
JJR	73	84	VBN	427	656
JJS	38	55	VBP	431	508
LS	0	1	VBZ	430	569
MD	200	312	WDT	10	110
NN	4399	3883	WP	2	86
NNP	3131	2931	WP$	0	12
NNPS	65	83	WRB	30	80

Table 5: Comparison of counts of part-of-speech tags in system output vs. references.

System	Trueskill	BLEU[7]	METEOR	TER
RIGOTRIO	1.03	18.6	32.3	80.1
CMU	0.819	19.0	31.4	82.4
FORGe	0.458	2.8	20.0	92.0
ISI	-1.172	10.9	28.9	98.7
Sheffield	-2.132	1.2	20.0	87.5
This System	-	6.7	28.7	79.4

Table 6: Comparison of evaluation metrics to Trueskill (measure of human rankings) for shared task data and systems. This system's performance on the same data according to automatic metrics is provided for comparison.

6 Conclusion

Given that the relatively small amount of available data and the difficulty of the task have made it difficult for statistical and neural approaches to achieve truly satisfactory results in AMR generation, we hypothesized that a partially rule-based system, combined with some simple statistical methods, might be able to effectively harness human linguistic knowledge to achieve comparable results.

Judging by automatic metrics, this method does not seem able to compete well with state-of-the-art systems—although this system's scores could doubtless be improved somewhat with further development, especially if the primary goal were to optimize toward metrics like BLEU by providing more realization candidates that might better match the reference sentence's n-grams. However, we also argue that BLEU scores are a poor metric for

---

[7] These numbers differ slightly from the previously reported BLEU scores, presumably due to differences in BLEU configuration, but the ranking of systems is the same.

the AMR generation task. While METEOR and TER appear to do slightly better than BLEU at least at distinguishing among better-performing systems, none of these metrics fully reflect human rankings, making it difficult to fully determine how this system compares to others without human evaluation.

As research moves forward in AMR generation, it is essential to ensure that we are truly moving in a direction that will help us generate English realizations that both adequately and fluently express the meaning represented in an AMR. It is clear that the automatic metrics that have been used for this task fail to achieve these goals. More research is necessary to develop new metrics that are better suited to this task.

Acknowledgments

I would like to thank Nathan Schneider for his guidance, Ioannis Konstas and Jonathan May for sharing their data, and the anonymous reviewers for their comments and suggestions.

References

Laura Banarescu, Claire Bonial, Shu Cai, Madalina Georgescu, Kira Griffitt, Ulf Hermjakob, Kevin Knight, Philipp Koehn, Martha Palmer, and Nathan Schneider. 2013. Abstract Meaning Representation for Sembanking. In *Proceedings of the 7th Linguistic Annotation Workshop & Interoperability with Discourse*, pages 178–186, Sofia, Bulgaria.

Steven Bird, Edward Loper, and Ewan Klein. 2009. *Natural Language Processing with Python*. O'Reilly Media Inc.

Thiago Castro Ferreira, Iacer Calixto, Sander Wubben, and Emiel Krahmer. 2017. Linguistic realisation as machine translation: Comparing different MT models for AMR-to-text generation. In *Proceedings of the 10th International Conference on Natural Language Generation.*, pages 1–10, Santiago de Compostela, Spain. Association for Computational Linguistics.

Leshem Choshen and Omri Abend. 2018. Referenceless Measure of Faithfulness for Grammatical Error Correction. In *Proceedings of NAACL-HLT 2018*, pages 124–129, New Orleans, Louisiana. Association for Computational Linguistics.

Michael Denkowski and Alon Lavie. 2014. Meteor Universal: Language Specific Translation Evaluation for Any Target Language. In *Proceedings of the EACL 2014 Workshop on Statistical Machine Translation*, pages 376–380, Baltimore, Maryland.

Jeffrey Flanigan, Chris Dyer, Noah A Smith, and Jaime Carbonell. 2016. Generation from Abstract Meaning Representation using Tree Transducers. In *Proceedings of NAACL-HLT 2016*, pages 731–739, San Diego, California. Association for Computational Linguistics.

Normunds Gruzitis, Didzis Gosko, and Guntis Barzdins. 2017. RIGOTRIO at SemEval-2017 Task 9: Combining Machine Learning and Grammar Engineering for AMR Parsing and Generation. In *Proceedings of the 11th International Workshop on Semantic Evaluations (SemEval-2017)*, pages 924–928, Vancouver, Canada. Association for Computational Linguistics.

Kenneth Heafield. 2011. KenLM: Faster and Smaller Language Model Queries. In *Proceedings of the EMNLP 2011 Sixth Workshop on Statistical Machine Translation*, pages 187–197, Edinburgh, Scotland, United Kingdom.

Kenneth Heafield, Ivan Pouzyrevsky, Jonathan H Clark, and Philipp Koehn. 2013. Scalable Modified Kneser-Ney Language Model Estimation. In *Proceedings of the 51st Annual Meeting of the Association for Computational Linguistics*, pages 690–696, Sofia, Bulgaria.

Liang Huang and David Chiang. 2007. Forest Rescoring: Faster Decoding with Integrated Language Models. In *Proceedings of the 45th Annual Meeting of the Association of Computational Linguistics*, pages 144–151, Prague, Czech Republic.

Philipp Koehn, Hieu Hoang, Alexandra Birch, Chris Callison-Burch, Marcello Federico, Nicola Bertoldi Itc-Irst, Brooke Cowan, Wade Shen, Christine Moran Mit, Richard Zens, Rwth Aachen, Chris Dyer, Alexandra Constantin, Williams College, and Evan Herbst Cornell. 2007. Moses: Open Source Toolkit for Statistical Machine Translation. In *Proceedings of the 45th Annual Meeting of the Association of Computational Linguistics*, pages 177–180, Prague, Czech Republic.

Ioannis Konstas, Srinivasan Iyer, Mark Yatskar, Yejin Choi, Luke Zettlemoyer, and Paul G Allen. 2017. Neural AMR: Sequence-to-Sequence Models for Parsing and Generation. In *Proceedings of the 55th Annual Meeting of the Association for Computational Linguistics*, pages 146–157, Vancouver, Canada.

Gerasimos Lampouras and Andreas Vlachos. 2017. Sheffield at SemEval-2017 Task 9: Transition-based language generation from AMR. In *Proceedings of the 11th International Workshop on Semantic Evaluations (SemEval-2017)*, pages 586–591, Vancouver, Canada. Association for Computational Linguistics.

Alon Lavie and Abhaya Agarwal. 2007. Meteor: An Automatic Metric for MT Evaluation with High Levels of Correlation with Human Judgments. In *Proceedings of the Second Workshop on Statistical Machine Translation*, pages 228–231, Prague, Czech

Republic. Association for Computational Linguistics.

Jonathan May and Jay Priyadarshi. 2017. SemEval-2017 Task 9: Abstract Meaning Representation Parsing and Generation. In *Proceedings of the 11th International Workshop on Semantic Evaluations*, pages 536–545, Vancouver, Canada.

Simon Mille, Roberto Carlini, Alicia Burga, and Leo Wanner. 2017. FORGe at SemEval-2017 Task 9: Deep sentence generation based on a sequence of graph transducers. In *Proceedings of the 11th International Workshop on Semantic Evaluations (SemEval-2017)*, pages 920–923, Vancouver, Canada. Association for Computational Linguistics.

Courtney Napoles, Keisuke Sakaguchi, and Joel Tetreault. 2016. There's No Comparison: Reference-less Evaluation Metrics in Grammatical Error Correction. In *Proceedings of the 2016 Conference on Empirical Methods in Natural Language Processing*, pages 2109–2115, Austin, TX. Association for Computational Linguistics.

Kishore Papineni, Salim Roukos, Todd Ward, and Wei-Jing Zhu. 2002. BLEU: a Method for Automatic Evaluation of Machine Translation. In *Proceedings of the 40th Annual Meeting of the Association for Computational Linguistics*, pages 311–318, Philadelphia, Pennsylvania.

Nima Pourdamghani, Kevin Knight, and Ulf Hermjakob. 2016. Generating English from Abstract Meaning Representations. In *Proceedings of The 9th International Natural Language Generation conference*, pages 21–25, Edinburgh, UK.

Beatrice Santorini. 1990. Part-of-Speech Tagging Guidelines for the Penn Treebank Project (3rd Revision). Technical report, University of Pennsylvania.

Timo Schick. 2017. *Transition-Based Generation from Abstract Meaning Representations*. Ph.D. thesis, Technische Universität Dresden.

Matthew Snover, Bonnie Dorr, Richard Schwartz, Linnea Micciulla, and John Makhoul. 2006. A Study of Translation Edit Rate with Targeted Human Annotation. In *Proceedings of the 7th Conference of the Association for Machine Translation in the Americas*, pages 223–231, Cambridge.

Linfeng Song, Xiaochang Peng, Yue Zhang, Zhiguo Wang, and Daniel Gildea. 2017. AMR-to-text Generation with Synchronous Node Replacement Grammar. In *Proceedings of the 55th Annual Meeting of the Association for Computational Linguistics (Short Papers)*, pages 7–13, Vancouver, Canada. Association for Computational Linguistics.

Linfeng Song, Yue Zhang, Xiaochang Peng, Zhiguo Wang, and Daniel Gildea. 2016. AMR-to-text generation as a Traveling Salesman Problem. In *Proceedings of the 2016 Conference on Empirical Methods in Natural Language Processing*, pages 2084–2089, Austin, TX. Association for Computational Linguistics.

Linfeng Song, Yue Zhang, Zhiguo Wang, and Daniel Gildea. 2018. A Graph-to-Sequence Model for AMR-to-Text Generation. In *Proceedings of the 56th Annual Meeting of the Association for Computational Linguistics (Long Papers)*, pages 1616–1626, Melbourne, Australia. Association for Computational Linguistics.

Ida Szubert, Adam Lopez, and Nathan Schneider. 2018. A Structured Syntax-Semantics Interface for English-AMR Alignment. In *Proceedings of NAACL-HLT 2018*, pages 1169–1180, New Orleans, Louisiana. Association for Computational Linguistics.

Computational Investigations of Pragmatic Effects in Natural Language

Jad Kabbara

School of Computer Science, McGill Unviersity, Montreal, QC, Canada
Montreal Institute for Learning Algorithms (MILA), Montreal, QC, Canada
`jad@cs.mcgill.ca`

Abstract

Semantics and pragmatics are two complimentary and intertwined aspects of meaning in language. The former is concerned with the literal (context-free) meaning of words and sentences, the latter focuses on the intended meaning, one that is context-dependent. While NLP research has focused in the past mostly on semantics, the goal of this thesis is to develop computational models that leverage this pragmatic knowledge in language that is crucial to performing many NLP tasks correctly. In this proposal, we begin by reviewing the current progress in this thesis, namely, on the tasks of definiteness prediction and adverbial presupposition triggering. Then we discuss the proposed research for the remainder of the thesis which builds on this progress towards the goal of building better and more pragmatically-aware natural language generation and understanding systems.

1 Introduction

The past several years have seen growing trends in relying on intelligent systems to carry out day-to-day tasks. From interactions with your virtual personal assistant to carrying out a simple conversation with a chatbot to asking for directives or getting restaurant recommendations, the ability of said intelligent systems to properly understand its user is becoming increasingly important and crucial to their effective functioning.

For a proper *understanding*, these systems ought to rely on two different but complementary aspects of language: semantics and pragmatics. At a very high level, semantics is concerned with the literal meaning of words and sentences that is context-free, while pragmatics is concerned with the intended meaning, one that is context-dependent.

On the frontier of semantics, the past few years have witnessed a remarkable progress in language modeling and other tasks. Research on neural vector representations (word embeddings) has particularly exploded starting with the Word2vec model (Mikolov et al., 2013) and GloVe (Pennington et al., 2014). These neural models learn high-quality vector representations of words which are empirically shown to have state-of-the-art performance on semantic similarity tasks. Many variations have been proposed to account for varying textual structures (words vs sentences vs paragraphs vs documents), multiple languages (Luong et al., 2015), varying topics (Liu et al., 2015), etc.

Pragmatic reasoning, on the other hand, is arguably one of the major milestones on the road to general AI simply because for a machine to fully understand individuals, it has to understand the nuances and subtleties of the language that is being conveyed and which often goes beyond the literal meaning of the utterances being made. And while correctly performing pragmatic reasoning is at the core of many NLP tasks such as information extraction, automatic summarization, and machine translation, there has been not much focus on it in NLP research – at least not as much as its semantic counterpart.

The goal of this thesis is to develop computational models where pragmatics is a first-class citizen both in terms of natural language understanding and generation. We have already made progress toward this goal by (1) developing a neural model for definiteness prediction the task of determining whether a noun phrase should be definite or indefinite in contrast to prior work relying on heavily-engineered linguistic features and (2) by introducing the new task of adverbial presupposition triggering detection which focuses on detecting contexts where adverbs (e.g. "again") trigger presuppositions ("John came again" presupposes "he came before").

Moving forward, we propose to examine the

Proceedings of the 2019 Conference of the North American Chapter of the Association for Computational Linguistics: Student Research Workshop, pages 71–76
Minneapolis, Minnesota, June 3 - 5, 2019. ©2017 Association for Computational Linguistics

role of pragmatics, particularly presuppositions, in language understanding and generation. We will develop computational models and corpora that incorporate this understanding to improve: (1) summarization systems e.g. in a text rewriting step to learn how to appropriately allocate adverbs in generated sentences to make them more coherent, and (2) reading comprehension systems where pragmatic effects are crucial for the proper understanding of texts. By the end, this thesis would present the first study on presuppositional effects in language to enable pragmatically-empowered natural language understanding and generation systems.

In what follows, we will give a summary of our research effort thus far, briefly discussing the two tasks mentioned above and that can be seen as testbeds for pragmatic reasoning followed by exciting current and future research avenues for further exploration.

2 Definiteness Prediction

In (Kabbara et al., 2016), we focus on definiteness prediction, the task of determining whether a noun phrase should be definite or indefinite. In English, one instantiation of this task is to predict whether to use a definite article (the), indefinite article (a(n)), or no article at all. This task has applications in machine translation, and in L2 grammatical error detection and correction.

Definiteness prediction is an interesting testbed for pragmatic reasoning, because both contextual and local cues are crucial to determining the acceptability of a particular choice of article. Consider the following example: A/#the man entered the room. The/#a man turned on the TV. Factors such as discourse context, familiarity, and information status play a role in determining the choice of articles. Here, man is introduced into the discourse context by an indefinite article, then subsequently referred to by a definite article. On the other hand, non-context-dependent factors such as local syntactic and semantic restrictions may block the presence of an article. For example, demonstratives (e.g., this, that), certain quantifiers (e.g., no), and mass nouns (e.g., money) do not permit articles.

We present in this work a recurrent neural network model that employs an attention mechanism. The primary motivation for the use of an attention mechanism is to investigate whether LSTM models focus on certain parts of the sentence when making predictions, and if so, to gain more insight into what parts of the sentence affect the model's prediction.

Our model achieves state-of-the-art performance on definiteness prediction, outperforming a previous logistic regression classifier (De Felice, 2008) that uses 10 types of hand-crafted linguistic features. Our best model achieves 96.63% accuracy on the WSJ/PTB corpus, representing a relative error reduction of 51% compared to the previous state of the art. Each of the factors we examined (initializing with pre-trained vectors, giving more context, giving POS tags, attention) contributes to the performance of the model, though in different degrees. We perform a number of analyses to understand the behavior of the models, and show in particular how the attention mechanism can be useful for interpreting the model predictions.

The most interesting contribution of this work is highlighting the suitability of LSTMs for tackling complex cases of article usage where there is no obvious local cue for prediction. We find evidence that LSTMs given an extended context window can resolve cases of article usage that seem to require reasoning about coreferent entities involving synonymy. Our results suggest that recurrent neural network models such as LSTMs are a promising approach to capturing pragmatic knowledge.

3 Adverbial Presupposition Triggering

In (Cianflone, Feng, Kabbara et al., 2018), we introduce the task of predicting adverbial presupposition triggers such as also and again. Solving such a task requires detecting recurring or similar events in the discourse context, and has applications in natural language generation tasks such as summarization and dialogue systems.

Presuppositions have been extensively studied in linguistics and philosophy of language with the earliest work dating back to (Frege, 1892). They can be viewed as assumptions or beliefs in the common ground between discourse participants when an utterance is made. The importance of presuppositions is that they underlie spoken statements and written sentences and understanding them facilitates smooth communication. We refer to expressions that indicate the presence of presuppositions as presupposition triggers. These include, among others, definite descriptions, factive verbs and certain adverbs.

Our focus in this work is on adverbial presupposition triggers such as again, also and still. These triggers indicate the recurrence, continuation, or termination of an event in the discourse context, or the presence of a similar event, and are the most commonly occurring presupposition triggers after existential triggers (Khaleel, 2010).

As a first step towards language technology systems capable of understanding and using presuppositions, we propose to investigate the detection of contexts in which these triggers can be used. This task constitutes an interesting testing ground for pragmatic reasoning, because the cues that are indicative of contexts containing recurring or similar events are complex and often span more than one sentence. Moreover, such a task has immediate practical consequences. For example, in language generation applications such as summarization and dialogue systems, adding presuppositional triggers in contextually appropriate locations can improve the readability and coherence of the generated output.

We create two datasets for the task based on the Penn Treebank corpus (Marcus et al., 1993) and the English Gigaword corpus (Graff et al., 2007), extracting contexts that include presupposition triggers as well as other similar contexts that do not, in order to form a binary classification task. In creating our datasets, we consider a set of five target adverbs: *too, again, also, still,* and *yet*. We focus on these adverbs in our investigation because these triggers are well known in the existing linguistic literature and commonly triggering presuppositions. We control for a number of potential confounding factors, such as class balance, and the syntactic governor of the triggering adverb, so that models cannot exploit these correlating factors without any actual understanding of the presuppositional properties of the context.

In addition, we investigate the potential of attention-based deep learning models for detecting adverbial triggers and introduce a new weighted pooling attention mechanism designed for predicting adverbial presupposition triggers. Our attention mechanism allows for a weighted averaging of our RNN hidden states where the weights are informed by the inputs, as opposed to a simple unweighted averaging. Our model uses a form of self-attention (Paulus et al., 2018; Vaswani et al., 2017), where the input sequence acts as both the attention mechanism's query and key/value. Un-like other attention models, instead of simply averaging the scores to be weighted, our approach aggregates (learned) attention scores by learning a reweighting scheme of those scores through another level (dimension) of attention. Additionally, our mechanism does not introduce any new parameters when compared to our LSTM baseline, reducing its computational impact.

We compare our model using the novel attention mechanism against strong baseline classifiers, including a logistic regression model and RNN- and CNN-based deep learning models, in terms of prediction accuracy and show that it outperforms these baselines for most of the triggers on the two datasets without introducing additional parameters – achieving 82.42% accuracy on predicting the adverb "also" on the Gigaword dataset.

4 Proposed Research

The research work thus far in this thesis has explored two classes of function words, namely articles and adverbs, and investigated the suitability of deep learning models to pick up on complex contextual cues for handling pragmatic inferences in learning tasks involving these function words. The remainder of the research work to be carried in this thesis will build on this progress to explore how pragmatic effects in language such as presuppositional effects can be leveraged to improve natural language generation and understanding systems. Accordingly, the proposed research is divided among the following three main fronts:

1. Corpus construction

2. Language generation

3. Language understanding.

4.1 Corpus construction

Since our work is the first to explore presuppositional effects from a computational perspective, the research community currently lacks corpora that focus on these important pragmatic effects. For this reason, we are currently in the process of constructing a new corpus that focuses specifically on adverbial presuppositional effects in English. The goal of this corpus is to provide new resources that would push further the goal of understanding presuppositional effects in specific and research on computational pragmatics more generally. The corpus construction is motivated linguistically and will involve crowdsourcing data (e.g., through Amazon Mechanical Turk). Two approaches to the corpus construction are of interest:

1. One approach is to consider it from a generation problem perspective. Workers will be given sentences involving presuppositions and would be tasked with identifying the presupposition in context. For example, given the sentence "John went to the restaurant again", the worker would optimally provide a simple explanation describing that the presupposition is that "John went to the restaurant before". We envision the corpus to be useful in the context of language generation. Particularly, such corpus would be useful for designing learning models that can focus on contextual cues leading to pragmatic effects and accordingly generate what was presupposed in a sentence as a way of showing that it has a basic understanding of the relevant pragmatic effects in context.

2. The other approach is to consider it from the perspective of a presupposition-based entailment task which illustrates drawing conclusions from specific cues in text. Workers would be given a short passage involving a presupposition such as "John has been to the restaurant again". They would be asked something along the line of: "Is it true that John has been to the restaurant before?" to which the correct answer would be "yes". In this case, this would be an entailment setup where the presupposition is what leads to the correct conclusion.

It would be interesting to expand this to not just adverbs, but also to other kinds of presuppositions and possibly even implicature. A more general version of this crowdsourcing could involve, for example, asking the worker to qualify whether a certain statement seems to be true, or be suggested but not necessarily true or false.

We believe that such corpora are crucial for the development of learning models that can focus on the subtle pragmatic effects of language and will play an important role in improving language generation and language understanding systems.

4.2 Language Generation

Presuppositions are prevalent in language and they play a crucial role in shaping the conveyed meaning in a specific way. In summarization scenarios where information needs to be acquired from different parts of the text(s), this would be particularly more important.

Two pillars of effective summarization systems are (1) the ability to pinpoint key pieces of information and crucial parts of the text and (2) appropriately rewrite the original text in order to relay the information in those parts.

On the first front, we plan to investigate links between sentences that involve presuppositional effects and sentences occurring in the previous context. That is, if a sentence includes a presupposition trigger, it would be important – from a summarization point of view – to determine whether there is a specific sentence that occurred in the previous context and that plays a crucial role in how the meaning of that (*presuppositional*) sentence is understood. We believe investigating such links between sentences is crucial for designing better summarization systems.

On the latter front, we are interested in investigating how an understanding of presuppositional effects can lead to better summarization systems. Specifically, we will investigate how a learning model, in a text rewriting step, can make informed decisions on how to properly allocate adverbs with the goal of generating a more coherent output.

Framing the problem within a summarization setting enables to not have to rely on using the original document context but instead "manipulating" the summarized version. From that version, we can select groups of sentences and ask workers to add adverbs or to remove existing ones to create manipulated versions of summarized texts to be used for designing improved summarization systems. Indeed, oftentimes, missing one presupposition trigger such as an adverb while summarizing could lead to the presupposition context (and thus the overall meaning) not holding anymore. The goal in this case would be to design summarization systems that are also trained to fill/remove adverbs such that the final summarized version is more natural and more coherent. The idea would be for the summarization system to examine each relevant sentence in the summarized text and determine whether adding/removing a specific adverb would make the phrase more informative and so whether it should be included or not in the summarized version.

4.3 Language Understanding

Of interest to our pursuit is the task of machine/reading comprehension also referred to as text understanding or question answering (QA), where the goal is to determine if a learning system can answer basic questions about a passage in order to show some "comprehension" of the information in that passage.

Presuppositions play a crucial role in shaping the sentence meanings and extending what is explicitly conveyed by the semantics of the words making up the sentence. We believe that understanding their role and leveraging the pragmatic knowledge resulting from that role can improve text understanding systems.

The current QA datasets are not suitable however for the task of designing pragmatically-empowered QA systems. For example, among the popular datasets for this task, is the Stanford Question Answering Dataset (SQuAD) (Rajpurkar et al., 2016). SQuAD consists of questions posed by crowdworkers on a set of Wikipedia articles, with more than 100,000 question-answer pairs on 500 articles. A key feature of this dataset is that the answer to a question is always part of the context and also always appears as a continuous span of words. One simplified way to tackle the problem is then to find the start and end of the relevant span of words (in the given passage) that corresponds to the answer. Not only the answers in such datasets are explicitly present in the passage, they are typically of fact-based nature.

Our interest, on the other hand, is to design QA systems that can answer questions that tap implicit information in the text, one that is pragmatic in nature. The answers, unlike datasets like SQuAD, would not be explicitly stated in the text which makes the task more challenging. The constructed corpus that was discussed in Section 4.1 will be crucial to designing and testing such systems. A simple example would be a small passage with a sentence involving a presupposition such as "John has been to the restaurant yesterday". One possible question would be: "Is it true that John has been to the restaurant before?" and the answer should be true. There would be challenging *negative cases*, e.g., "Mary has been to the restaurant again, but John wants to go to the restaurant tomorrow. The answer to the same question above would be false in that case.

Answering effectively such questions would tap into the models abilities to pick up on complex contextual cues and would be a strong hint that the model can have a basic understanding of the pragmatic effects in language.

4.4 Leveraging Pragmatic Knowledge in Multi-Task Scenarios

Correctly performing the pragmatic reasoning explored in this proposal, i.e. that which deals with presuppositions, is at the core of many NLP tasks such as discourse parsing, discourse segmentation and coherence modeling.

We believe that by training a model to learn to produce simple explanations of the presupposition effect in context (in the fashion described in Section 4.1), we could leverage the learned representations to "supplement" the learning of other NLP tasks as the ones mentioned above and for which such pragmatic knowledge is essential.

5 Conclusion

We have presented in this proposal the research progress that was accomplished thus far in this thesis, exploring two classes of function words, namely articles and adverbs, and investigating the suitability of deep learning models to pick up on complex contextual cues for handling pragmatic inferences in learning tasks involving these function words, namely, the tasks of definiteness prediction and adverbial presupposition triggering. We also discussed current and future research directions that will guide the research for the remainder of this thesis mainly in the areas of natural language generation and understanding. We believe that the research in this thesis has the potential to open up exciting research directions that are unexplored in the NLP community and that are crucial for designing improved and nuanced language generation and understanding systems that bring us closer to the vision of truly intelligent systems.

Acknowledgments

This work was supported by the Centre de Recherche d'Informatique de Montréal (CRIM), the Fonds de Recherche du Québec Nature et Technologies (FRQNT) and the Natural Sciences and Engineering Research Council of Canada (NSERC).

References

Andre Cianflone, Yulan Feng, Jad Kabbara, and Jackie Chi Kit Cheung. 2018. Let's do it "again": A first computational approach to detecting adverbial presupposition triggers. In *Proceedings of the 56th Annual Meeting of the Association for Computational Linguistics (Volume 1: Long Papers)*, pages 2747–2755, Melbourne, Australia. Association for Computational Linguistics.

Rachele De Felice. 2008. *Automatic error detection in non-native English*. Ph.D. thesis, University of Oxford.

Gottlob Frege. 1892. Über sinn und bedeutung. *Zeitschrift für Philosophie und philosophische Kritik*, 100:25–50.

David Graff, Junbo Kong, Ke Chen, and Kazuaki Maeda. 2007. English gigaword third edition. Technical report, Linguistic Data Consortium.

Jad Kabbara, Yulan Feng, and Jackie Chi Kit Cheung. 2016. Capturing pragmatic knowledge in article usage prediction using lstms. In *COLING*, pages 2625–2634.

Layth Muthana Khaleel. 2010. An analysis of presupposition triggers in english journalistic texts. *Of College Of Education For Women*, 21(2):523–551.

Yang Liu, Zhiyuan Liu, Tat-Seng Chua, and Maosong Sun. 2015. Topical word embeddings. In *AAAI Conference on Artificial Intelligence*.

Thang Luong, Hieu Pham, and Christopher D Manning. 2015. Bilingual word representations with monolingual quality in mind. In *Proceedings of the 1st Workshop on Vector Space Modeling for Natural Language Processing*, pages 151–159.

Mitchell P. Marcus, Mary A. Marcinkiewicz, and Beatrice Santorini. 1993. Building a large annotated corpus of English: The Penn Treebank. *Computational Linguistics*, 19(2):313–330.

Tomas Mikolov, Ilya Sutskever, Kai Chen, Greg S Corrado, and Jeff Dean. 2013. Distributed representations of words and phrases and their compositionality. In *Advances in Neural Information Processing Systems*, pages 3111–3119.

Romain Paulus, Caiming Xiong, and Richard Socher. 2018. A deep reinforced model for abstractive summarization. In *International Conference on Learning Representations*, Vancouver, Canada.

Jeffrey Pennington, Richard Socher, and Christopher D Manning. 2014. Glove: Global vectors for word representation. In *EMNLP*, volume 14, pages 1532–1543.

Pranav Rajpurkar, Jian Zhang, Konstantin Lopyrev, and Percy Liang. 2016. Squad: 100,000+ questions for machine comprehension of text. In *Proceedings of the 2016 Conference on Empirical Methods in Natural Language Processing*, pages 2383–2392.

Ashish Vaswani, Noam Shazeer, Niki Parmar, Llion Jones, Jakob Uszkoreit, Aidan N Gomez, and Ł ukasz Kaiser. 2017. Attention is all you need. In *Advances in Neural Information Processing Systems 30*, pages 5994–6004.

SEDTWik: Segmentation-based Event Detection from Tweets using Wikipedia

Keval M. Morabia, Neti Lalita Bhanu Murthy, Aruna Malapati and **Surender S. Samant**
Birla Institute of Technology and Science (BITS), Pilani
Hyderabad, India
kevalmorabia97@gmail.com,
{bhanu, arunam, surender.samant}@hyderabad.bits-pilani.ac.in

Abstract

Event Detection has been one of the research areas in Text Mining that has attracted attention during this decade due to the widespread availability of social media data specifically twitter data. Twitter has become a major source for information about real-world events because of the use of hashtags and the small word limit of Twitter that ensures concise presentation of events. Previous works on event detection from tweets are either applicable to detect localized events or breaking news only or miss out on many important events. This paper presents the problems associated with event detection from tweets and a tweet-segmentation based system for event detection called SEDTWik, an extension to a previous work, that is able to detect newsworthy events occurring at different locations of the world from a wide range of categories. The main idea is to split each tweet and hash-tag into segments, extract bursty segments, cluster them, and summarize them. We evaluated our results on the well-known Events2012 corpus and achieved state-of-the-art results.

Keywords: Event detection, Twitter, Social Media, Microblogging, Tweet segmentation, Text Mining, Wikipedia, Hashtag.

1 Introduction

Microblogging, as a form of social media, is fast emerging in this decade. One of the best examples for this is Twitter which allows 280-character limit for a tweet. It is used not only to share and communicate with friends and family but also as a medium to share real-world events. An *event* according to the Topic Detection and Tracking (TDT) project (Allan et al., 1998), is "some unique thing that happens at some point in time". Becker et al. (2011) defines an event as "a real-world occurrence e with an associated time period T_e and

a time-ordered stream of Twitter messages M_e, of substantial volume, discussing the occurrence and published during time T_e". We borrow these definitions of an event in our work.

In Twitter, a user can not only publish about an event but can also propagate by *retweeting* the post by someone else. A user can also attach a *hashtag* with the tweet which can provide a significant amount of information about the event (e.g., **#RIP** to signify that the tweet is related to someone's death). But some hashtags can also be used to promote ideas known as *memes* (Kotsakos et al., 2014). Event detection from tweets also faces other challenges like noisy data, informal writing, grammatical errors, and a large volume of data coming at very high velocity. According to Internet Live Stats[1], on an average 6,000 tweets are published every second, which corresponds to nearly 500 million tweets per day. Moreover, nearly 40% of these tweets are just "pointless babbles"[2] which are insignificant to the task of event detection.

To tackle the above-mentioned challenges, we present SEDTWik - a tweet segmentation-based event detection system that utilizes an external knowledge base like Wikipedia. The rest of the paper is organized as follows. Section 2 describes the working of SEDTWik in detail. Section 3 presents our experimental results. Section 4 presents some related works in event detection. We conclude in section 5 along with future work to be done.

2 SEDTWik

In this section, we present SEDTWik, an extension of a previous work by Li et al. (2012a) called Twevent. SEDTWik is an event detection

---

[1] http://www.internetlivestats.com/twitter-statistics
[2] https://pearanalytics.com/blog/2009/twitter-study-reveals-interesting-results-40-percent-pointless-babble

Proceedings of the 2019 Conference of the North American Chapter of the Association for Computational Linguistics: Student Research Workshop, pages 77–85
Minneapolis, Minnesota, June 3 - 5, 2019. ©2017 Association for Computational Linguistics

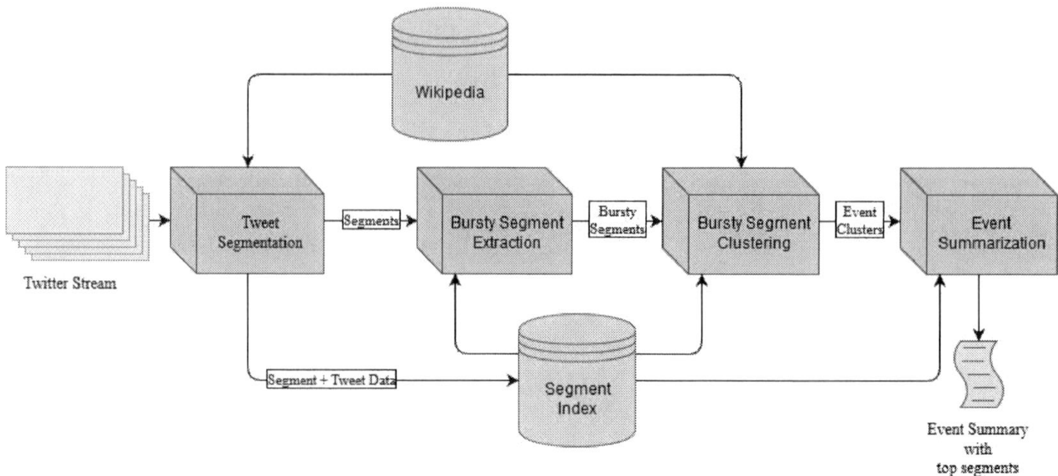

Figure 1: SEDTWik Architecture.

framework that consists of four components: *tweet segmentation, bursty segment extraction, bursty segment clustering,* and *event summarization.* Figure 1 shows the architecture of SEDTWik. Events are detected from a time window t of a fixed length during which all the tweets published are processed. In the tweet segmentation phase, all tweets coming from the Twitter stream within the current time window are segmented, and the segments along with the tweet details are indexed for use in next stages. Hashtags are given more weight as they contain more information. Based on the probability distribution of segments, retweet counts, user diversity, and user popularity, abnormally bursty segments are extracted and clustered in the next two stages. Finally, the clusters are summarized in the last step. In the rest of this section, we present all the four components in detail.

2.1 Tweet Segmentation

Tweet segmentation was introduced by Li et al. (2012b) and Li et al. (2015) for Named Entity Recognition (NER) in which they used a dynamic programming based approach to segment tweets based on a "stickiness" score of a segment. In this section, we present an alternative approach using Wikipedia Page Titles Dataset[3] for segmentation of tweets and hashtags.

The task of tweet segmentation is to split a given tweet into non-overlapping meaningful segments. A segment can be unigram (a word) or multi-gram

(a phrase). The reason why tweet segmentation is used is that a phrase contains much more specific information than the unigrams in it. So, a tweet segment makes the event more interpretable. For example, **[vice presidential debate]** is much more informative then **[vice], [presidential],** and **[debate]** separately that might be in any random order. While segmenting a tweet, we emphasize three components: *tweet text, name mentions,* and *hashtags.*

We consider *tweet text* as everything a user writes in a tweet except URL links, hashtags, and name mention. From tweet text, we only keep those segments that are present as a title of a Wikipedia page[3]. This ensures that only named entities (e.g., Barack Obama) or meaningful segments (e.g., new music) are kept from tweet text, and unnecessary words are removed that would otherwise increase noise in the event detection process.

Most Twitter users use a *name mention* in a tweet to mention a person by their username (e.g., **@iamsrk** for **Shah Rukh Khan**). So, we replace the username by their actual name and consider it as a segment.

The most important component in out event detection model is *hashtags.* Hashtags contain a lot of information in a concise form, and related tweets generally contain the same hashtag. Ozdikis et al. (2012a) used only hashtags for event detection as contrasted with Ozdikis et al. (2012b) and were able to get better results in the former. This motivated us to give more weight to hashtags in the segmentation process.

---

[3]http://dumps.wikimedia.org/enwiki/latest/enwiki-latest-all-titles-in-ns0.gz

We use $\mathcal{H}$ as *hashtag weight*, so an $\mathcal{H}$ value of 2 means that all hashtags are duplicated in the segmentation process, resulting in a twice weight that would allow hashtags to become more bursty in the next stage. This also ensures that if a segment is not previously seen in the Wikipedia page titles, then its use in hashtag would still make the segment bursty. Since hashtags do not contain whitespace or punctuations, we consider the capitalization of letters to segment a hashtag. For example, **#BreakingNews** will be segmented as **[breaking news]**. Hashtags that do not contain any capitalization of letters in them would be considered as a unigram when segmenting them.

2.2 Bursty Segment Extraction

Since there are hundreds of thousands of unique segments within a day, clustering all of them for detecting events would be a computationally expensive task. So, once the tweets are segmented, we find out abnormally bursty segments that might be related to an event and discard the remaining ones.

Let N_t denote the number of tweets within the current time window t and $f_{s,t}$ be the number of tweets containing segment s in t. The probability of observing s with a frequency $f_{s,t}$ can be considered as a Binomial distribution $B(N_t, p_s)$ where p_s is the expected probability of observing segment s in any random time window. Since N_t is very large in case of tweets, this probability distribution can be approximated to a Normal distribution with parameters $E[s|t] = N_t p_s$ and $\sigma[s|t] = \sqrt{N_t p_s(1 - p_s)}$.

If a segment has $f_{s,t} >= E[s|t]$, it will be called a bursty segment, while a segment with $f_{s,t} < E[s|t]$ will not be considered bursty and will be discarded. We use a formula for the *bursty probability* $P_b(s, t)$ for segment s in time window t defined by Li et al. (2012a) as given in (1) that transfers the frequency of a bursty segment to the range (0,1).

$$P_b(s, t) = S(10 \frac{f_{s,t} - (E[s|t] + \sigma[s|t])}{\sigma[s|t]}) \quad (1)$$

where $S(\bullet)$ is the sigmoid function, and since sigmoid function smooths well in the range [-10,10], the constant 10 is introduced.

Instead of depending entirely on tweet frequency, to incorporate user diversity, *user frequency* $u_{s,t}$ is also used which denotes the number of distinct users using segment s in time window t. A *retweet* is a copy of a tweet created by another user. According to Boyd et al. (2010), a retweet is "a conversational practice and can negotiate authorship, attribution, and communicative fidelity". We find that a tweet retweeted by many users might be related to an important event and can be used to provide more weight to segments in retweets. We define *segment retweet count* of a segment s in t as $src_{s,t}$ which is the sum of retweet counts of all tweets containing s in t. A tweet by someone who has millions of followers (e.g., a celebrity or a news page) might also be more important as compared with someone who has very few followers. Giving more weight to such tweets will ensure that spam or self-promoting tweets are filtered out and do not harm the accuracy of the event detection process. So, we define *segment follower count* of a segment s in t as $sfc_{s,t}$ which is the sum of follower count of all users using this segment in t. Combining all the above, the formula for *bursty weight* $w_b(s, t)$ for segment s in t is defined in (2).

$$w_b(s, t) = P_b(s, t)log(u_{s,t}) \times \\ log(src_{s,t})log(log(sfc_{s,t})) \quad (2)$$

Among all the segments, top $\mathcal{K}$ segments are selected as bursty segments based on their bursty weight. A small value of $\mathcal{K}$ would result in a very low recall of events detected, and a large value of $\mathcal{K}$ may bring in more noise leading to higher computational cost. Therefore, an optimal value of $\mathcal{K}$ is kept to be $\sqrt{N_t}$.

2.3 Bursty Segment Clustering

In this section, we cluster bursty segments and filter non-event clusters using the approach by Li et al. (2012a).

Since the topics in tweets are fast changing and extremely dynamic, the similarity of two segments is calculated from their temporal frequency and the contents of the tweets that contain the segment. Each time window is evenly split into $\mathcal{M}$ subwindows $t =< t_1, t_2, ..., t_M >$. Let $f_t(s, m)$ be the tweet frequency of segment s in the subwindow t_m and $T_t(s, m)$ be the concatenation of all the tweets in the subwindow t_m that contain segment s. The similarity $sim_t(s_a, s_b)$ between segments s_a and s_b in time window t is calculated based on formula (3).

$$sim_t(s_a, s_b) = \sum_{m=1}^{M} w_t(s_a, m) w_t(s_b, m) \times \\ sim(T_t(s_a, m), T_t(s_b, m)) \qquad (3)$$

where $w_t(s, m)$ is the fraction of frequency of segment s in the subwindow t_m as mentioned in (4) and $sim(T_1, T_2)$ is the tf-idf similarity of the set of tweets T_1 and T_2.

$$w_t(s, m) = \frac{f_t(s, m)}{f_{s,t}} \qquad (4)$$

Using the similarity measure given in (3), all the bursty segments are clustered using a variation of Jarvis-Patrick algorithm (Jarvis and Patrick, 1973). In this, all segments are considered as nodes and initially, all nodes are disconnected. An edge is added between segments s_a and s_b if k-Nearest neighbors of s_a contains s_b and vice versa. After adding all possible edges, all the connected components of the graph are considered as candidate event clusters. Those segments that do not have any edges are discarded from further processing.

After clustering the bursty segments, we found that some clusters were not related to any event. For example, one of the candidate event clusters detected from tweets of Sunday, October 14, 2012 had segments like **[sunday dinner]**, **[sunday night]**, **[every sunday]**, **[sunday funday]**, and **[next sunday]**. This kind of events have segments that are bursty on specific days of the week. Thus, some filtering has to be done to eliminate these events. So, use of external knowledge base like Wikipedia is made.

The newsworthiness $\mu(s)$ of a segment s, is defined as given in (5) which ensures that if a sub-phrase of a segment is an important phrase then the segment is also considered newsworthy.

$$\mu(s) = \begin{cases} e^{Q(s)} & s \text{ is a word} \\ \max_{l \in s} e^{Q(l)} - 1 & \text{otherwise} \end{cases} \qquad (5)$$

where l is any sub-phrase of segment s and $Q(l)$ is the probability of l appearing as anchor text in Wikipedia articles containing l.

The newsworthiness $\mu(e)$ of an event cluster e, is defined in (6) that considers the newsworthiness of its constituent segments and the weight of

edges of the event cluster in the form of segment similarity.

$$\mu(e) = \frac{\sum_{s \in e_s} \mu(s)}{|e_s|} \frac{\sum_{g \in E_e} sim(g)}{|e_s|} \qquad (6)$$

where e_s is the set of segments associated with event e, E_e is the set of edges between segments of the event e, and $sim(g)$ is the similarity between nodes of the edge g which is calculated from (3).

Candidate events that are not likely to be realistic events are observed to have very small newsworthiness as compared to real events. So, if an event e satisfies the condition $\frac{\mu_{max}}{\mu(e)} < \mathcal{T}$ then only it is kept as a realistic event otherwise discarded. Here μ_{max} is the highest newsworthiness among all candidate event clusters and $\mathcal{T}$ is a threshold.

2.4 Event Summarization

A list of segments associated with an event cluster might not provide all the information related to an event. So, we used the LexRank algorithm (Erkan and Radev, 2004) to summarize the event clusters obtained in the previous step. The LexRank algorithm takes as input multiple documents and provides a summary of it by combining the top-ranking sentences. To summarize an event, we use all the tweets in current time window t that contain the segments in the event cluster obtained from the segment index created in the tweet segmentation phase and apply the algorithm to provide a summary of the event.

3 Experimental Results

In this section, we will mention the dataset and evaluation metrics we used, the statistics about tweet segmentation, and our results. Our model outperforms Twevent (Li et al., 2012a) with better precision, a greater number of events, and less duplicate events.

3.1 Dataset and Experimental Setting

The Wikipedia page titles dataset used in subsection 2.1 was a dump from March 2018 which contains 8,007,358 page titles. We used the Wikipedia keyphraseness values $Q(s)$[4] used by Li et al. (2012a) which was based on a dump released on Jan 30, 2010, and contains 4,342,732 distinct entities that appeared as anchor text.

---

[4]https://www.ntu.edu.sg/home/axsun/datasets.html

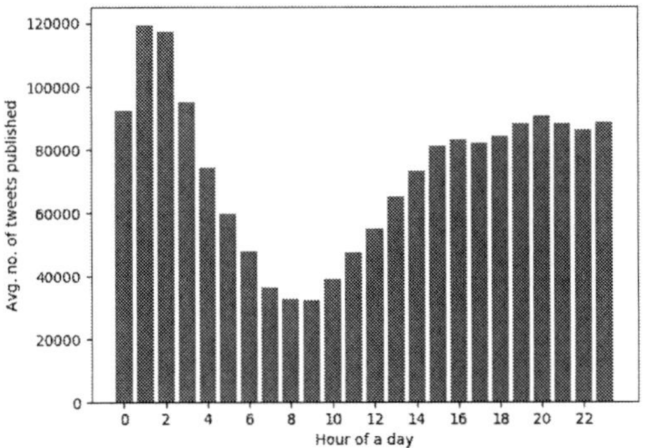

Figure 2: Tweet volume vs hour of day.

McMinn et al. (2013) created a Twitter corpus called Events2012 containing tweets from Oct 10 - Nov 7, 2012. They removed tweets containing more than 3 hashtags, 3 name mentions, or 2 URLs as they might be spam (Benevenuto et al., 2010). After all this filtering, the corpus contains over 120 million tweets. It also contains a list of 506 events detected in the corpus distributed among 8 categories. We used this corpus to estimate the segment probabilities p_s used in subsection 2.2 and to evaluate the performance of our model. Both Wikipedia Page Titles and the tweets in the corpus were preprocessed using using pyTweetCleaner[5]. Figure 2 shows a plot of average no. of tweets published within each hour of the day for this corpus.

There were several parameters that affect the performance of our model like time window size, number of subwindows $\mathcal{M}$, hashtag weight $\mathcal{H}$, number of neighbors k while clustering, and threshold $\mathcal{T}$. We set a time window to be of 24 hours which contains $\mathcal{M}$ = 12 subwindows of 2 hours each. We set $\mathcal{H}$ = 3, k = 3 neighbors and $\mathcal{T}$ = 4 in our work.

Allan et al. (1998) define **precision** as "the fraction of the detected events that are related to a realistic event". Moreover, Li et al. (2012a) defines another measure called **Duplicate Event Rate (DERate)** as "the percentage of events that have been duplicately detected among all realistic events detected". We use these definitions of *precision* and *DERate* in our evaluation. We did not use **recall** as a measure to evaluate the results found by our model because we find a lack of an exhaustive list of events in the Events2012

---

[5]https://github.com/kevalmorabia97/pyTweetCleaner

Date	Event Info
Oct 11	International Day of the Girl Child
Oct 12	Justin Bieber and Nicki Minaj's music video of Beauty and a beat released
Oct 13	National No Bra Day
Oct 14	Korean Grand Prix F-1 racing in which Sebastian Vettel won for the third consecutive year
Oct 15	Little Nemo in Slumberland by Winsor McCay anniversary (released on this day in 1905)
Oct 16	The Great British Bake Off 2012 finals
Oct 17	A live episode of the UK soap opera Emmerdale was broadcast, marking its 40th anniversary

Table 1: Some events not detected by McMinn et al. (2013) that were detected by SEDTWik during the period of Oct 11 - Oct 17, 2012.

dataset (McMinn et al., 2013). Although they have provided a list of 506 events detected by their model within the period of Oct 10 - Nov 7, 2012, our model SEDTWik finds 48 events within a period of Oct 11 - Oct 17, 2012, that were not reported by them. Their later work (McMinn and Jose, 2015) also agrees with this. Table 1 shows some of the events detected by SEDTWik that were not detected by McMinn et al. (2013). Note that the event info is manually written since the summary generated is a set of tweets that is quite large to fit in the table. Instead of *recall*, we use **No. of events**, which is the number of realistic events detected, as a measure to evaluate the performance of SEDTWik.

3.2 Tweet Segmentation Statistics

We segmented tweets from Oct 11 - Oct 17, 2012. After removing all the retweets, this period contained 11,705,978 tweets containing 3,653,039 distinct segments. Figure 3 shows the length of the segment along with their frequency within this period. We found that many of the bigrams were named entities (e.g., **[nicki minaj]**, **[mitt romney]**) or meaningful segments (e.g., **passed away**). Sample tweet segmentations with hashtag weight $\mathcal{H}$ = 3 are shown in Table 2. Notice that in the second row, the username **@ddlovato** corresponds to **Demi Lovato**, a pop singer. Thus,

Tweet	Segmentation
Joe Biden and Paul Ryan will be seated at the debate tonight **#VpDebate**	[joe biden], [paul ryan], [seated], [debate], [tonight], **[vp debate]**x3
My **#TeenChoice** for **#ChoiceSnapchatter** is *@ddlovato*	**[teen choice]**x3, **[choice snapchatter]**x3, *[demi lovato]*
Amanda Todd took her own life due to cyber bullying **#RipAmandaTodd #NoMoreBullying**	[amanda todd], [cyber bullying], **[rip amanda todd]**x3, **[no more bullying]**x3

Table 2: Sample tweet segmentations with $\mathcal{H} = 3$. Note that "x3" in the segmentation column signifies that the segment is present 3 times in the segmentation.

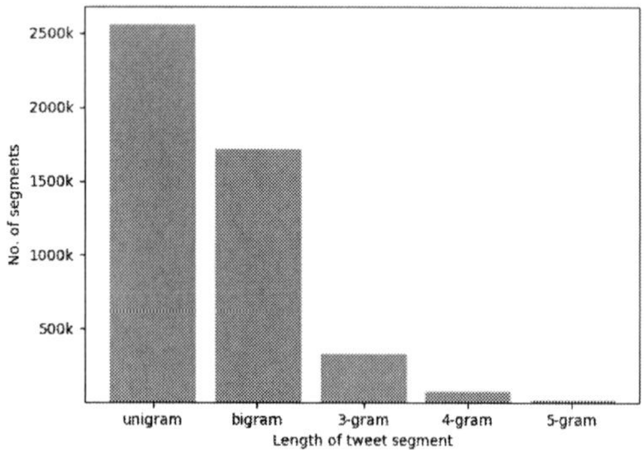

Figure 3: Segment length distribution during the period of Oct 11 - Oct 17, 2012.

Method	No. of events	Precision	DERate
SEDTWik	**79**	**88.12%**	**14.10%**
Twevent	42	80.32%	16.67%

Table 3: Comparison of SEDTWik (our method) with Twevent for events detected during the period of Oct 11 - Oct 17, 2012.

replacing username with the actual name makes the segment more interpretable.

3.3 Event Detection Results

Twevent (Li et al., 2012a) performs event detection from tweets using tweet segmentation and outperformed EDCoW (Weng and Lee, 2011) which was the state-of-the-art method that time, in terms of more no. of events, higher precision and recall, and less duplication rate. Since our model SEDTWik is an extension of Twevent, we set Twevent's results as a baseline for our model and compare both these models in this section.

Table 3 shows the comparison of SEDTWik

with Twevent in terms of *no. of events, precision, and DERate* for events detected in the period of Oct 11 - Oct 17, 2012. Recall that we are not calculating *recall* of our model because of lack of an exhaustive list of events within this period. Note that for calculating the results of Twevent, instead of Microsoft Web N-gram service, we used our estimates of probability which was also used in our model for the same task. The reason is that Microsoft has discontinued providing this Web-service. After the event clusters and summary are generated, we manually annotate the clusters as realistic or non-realistic event and calculate the precision on them.

As shown in Table 3, SEDTWik achieved a *precision* of 88.12% as compared to 80.32% by Twevent. The *no. of events* detected by SEDTWik were significantly more than that by Twevent (79 vs 42). In terms of *DERate*, SEDTWik performs slightly better than Twevent (14.10% vs 16.67%). Thus, our model SEDTWik outperforms Twevent in all the three metrics.

Edouard et al. (2017) and TwitterNews+ (Hasan et al., 2016) also evaluated their models on the same Events2012 dataset (McMinn et al., 2013) but on a different period of tweets and were able to get precision values of 75.0% and 78.0% only. Since we have to manually annotate the results, we did not re-evaluate the results of our model on these tweets but we believe our model would outperform both these models in terms of precision.

Table 4 shows some of the events detected by SEDTWik for each day in the period Oct 11 - Oct 17, 2012, along with top segments in the event cluster. Note that the event information is manually written since the summary consists of several tweets that is quite large to fit in the table.

SEDTWik code, the data used, and the entire

Date	Event
Oct 11	• [mo yan], [chinese writer], [nobel prize literature] $\rightarrow$ Chinese author Mo Yan wins the Nobel Prize in Literature. • [national coming out day], [national coming day], [lgbt], [coming day], [ncod] $\rightarrow$ National Coming Out Day celebrated on this day. • [steelers], [nfl], [titans], [tnf] $\rightarrow$ Pittsburgh Steelers vs. Tennessee Titans Thursday Night Football (TNF) game.
Oct 12	• [nobel peace prize], [nobel], [european union], [peace prize] $\rightarrow$ The European Union wins the 2012 Nobel Peace Prize. • [nlds], [st louis cardinals], [cardinal nation], [washington nationals] $\rightarrow$ St. Louis Cardinals win their National League Divisional Series (NLDS) against Washington Nationals.
Oct 13	• [xfactor], [x factor], [james arthur], [rylan clark] $\rightarrow$ X Factor UK finalists James Arthur and Rylan Clark give a live show in London. • [national no bra day], [no bra day], [th october] $\rightarrow$ National No Bra Day celebrated on 13th October.
Oct 14	• [arlen specter], [passed away], [sen arlen specter] $\rightarrow$ Former US Senator Arlen Specter, died at the age of 82. • [taylor swift], [xfactor], [the x factor] $\rightarrow$ Pop singer Taylor Swift performs live at the X Factor UK.
Oct 15	• [justin bieber], [baabworldrecord], [vevo] $\rightarrow$ Justin Bieber's music video Beauty and a Beat (BAAB) creates world record of most watched VEVO video in 24 hrs. • [breast cancer awareness month], [breast cancer awareness], [cure cancer] $\rightarrow$ Every year, October is celebrated as Breast Cancer Awareness Month.
Oct 16	• [debate], [barack obama], [presidential debate] $\rightarrow$ 2nd US presidential debate between Barack Obama and Mitt Romney. • [hilary mantel], [man booker prize], [booker prize] $\rightarrow$ Hilary Mantel wins the 2012 Man Booker Prize for her novel.
Oct 17	• [lance armstrong], [endorsement deal], [nike] $\rightarrow$ Nike ended the promotional agreements they had with Lance Armstrong when he was accused of using performance enhancing drugs. • [emmerdale live], [emmerdalelive], [live love] $\rightarrow$ A live episode of the UK soap opera Emmerdale was broadcast, marking its 40th anniversary.

Table 4: Some of the events detected by SEDTWik for each day in the period Oct 11 - Oct 17, 2012, along with top segments in the event cluster.

list of events detected can be found here[6].

3.4 Impact of $\mathcal{H}$ and $\mathcal{T}$

Recall that while performing tweet segmentation in subsection 2.1, we used $\mathcal{H}$ as hashtag weight which signifies by how many times, the frequency of a hashtag is multiplied. As most users associate a hashtag with any important tweet and that hashtag is common among similar tweets, giving more weight to hashtags seems intuitive. A lower value of $\mathcal{H}$ would cause noisy segments from tweet text to dominate and harm the accuracy of the event detection model. Similarly, a higher value of $\mathcal{H}$ would not allow other frequently used segments in the tweet text to become bursty and again reduce the accuracy. We experimented with $\mathcal{H}$ values 1,2,3, and 4, and found the best results at $\mathcal{H} = 3$.

The threshold $\mathcal{T}$ was used in deciding if a candidate event cluster is a realistic event or not in subsection 2.3. We observed that on increasing $\mathcal{T}$, more event would be considered realistic that would increase the number of events detected, but reduce the precision of the model. On experimenting with different values of $\mathcal{T}$ from 2,3,4, and 5, we found optimal results at $\mathcal{T} = 4$.

[6]https://github.com/kevalmorabia97/SEDTWik-Event-Detection-from-Tweets

4   Related Work

Event detection from tweets is not a new topic of research, but rather an area on which extensive research has been done over this decade. In this section, we will present some of the related works in event detection from tweets that have motivated us to research in this field.

Panagiotou et al. (2016), Weiler et al. (2016) and Farzindar and Khreich (2015) presented a survey of many approaches that have been used over the past few years for event detection from Twitter. They had also mentioned several open challenges for event detection from tweets. Our work has tried to address some of these challenges in this paper.

TwInsight (Valkanas and Gunopulos, 2013) identified events by monitoring surges in 6 emotional states (anger, fear, disgust, happiness, sadness, and surprise) and gave information about the location, timestamp, emotion, and description of the event.

EvenTweet (Abdelhaq et al., 2013) used a fixed historical usage of words for finding those that have a burstiness degree two standard deviation above mean and then clustered them. Their method was used to find localized events only. EventRadar (Boettcher and Lee, 2012) also used Twitter to detect local events like parties and art exhibitions.

McMinn et al. (2013) created a pool of events using Locality Sensitive Hashing (LSH), Cluster Summarization, and Wikipedia, and clustered them using category, temporal, and content-based features and found events distributed among 8 categories (e.g., Sports, Science & Technology, etc.). But as shown in Table 1, there were many events that were not detected by their model.

Phuvipadawat and Murata (2010) used features like hashtags, usernames, follower count, retweet count, and proper noun terms to cluster and rank breaking news detected from Twitter.

Twevent (Li et al., 2012a) used a segmentation-based event detection from tweets method. In this method, tweets were segmented using a "stickiness" score of segments, and bursty segments were selected based on the prior probability distribution of segments, and user diversity, and were clustered into events. Our work SEDTWik is extension of Twevent so we have compared these two methods in subsection 3.3.

Recently, ArmaTweet (Tonon et al., 2017) used semantic event detection on Tweets to detect events such as 'politician dying' and 'militia terror act'.

5   Conclusion And Future Work

Twitter has experienced an explosive increase in both users and the volume of information in the recent time which has attracted great interests from both industry and academia. Tweets being short and containing noisy data in large volume poses challenges on event detection task. In this paper, we presented SEDTWik - a tweet segmentation-based event detection system in which hashtags, retweet count, user popularity, and follower count were key features. Giving more weight to hashtags significantly improved the model's performance. Our model achieved outstanding results on event detection from tweets using Wikipedia. As part of future work, we will explore ways to improve the segmentation process and use URL links in the event detection process. We will try to find more efficient ways to estimate segment probabilities considering the days and months in which specific segments are observed. We also plan to apply more sophisticated methods for event summarization that also leverage the segment and cluster information instead of just using the them to find tweets to use for summarization.

Acknowledgments

We thank Dr. Aixin Sun, Associate Professor at Nanyang Technological University (NTU), Singapore for providing the Wikipedia keyphraseness values Q(s) that was used in calculating segment newsworthiness in subsection 2.3. We would also like to thank Mr. Siddhant Shenoy and Mr. Nitish Ravishankar for providing their valuable feedbacks on our earlier drafts.

References

Hamed Abdelhaq, Christian Sengstock, and Michael Gertz. 2013. Eventweet: Online localized event detection from twitter. *Proc. VLDB Endow.*, 6(12):1326–1329.

James Allan, Jaime Carbonell, George Doddington, Jonathan Yamron, et al. 1998. Topic detection and tracking pilot study: Final report.

Hila Becker, Mor Naaman, and Luis Gravano. 2011. Beyond trending topics: Real-world event identification on twitter. In *Proceedings of the Fifth International Conference on Weblogs and Social Media, Barcelona, Catalonia, Spain, July 17-21, 2011*.

Fabrcio Benevenuto, Gabriel Magno, Tiago Rodrigues, and Virglio Almeida. 2010. Detecting spammers on twitter. In *In Collaboration, Electronic messaging, Anti-Abuse and Spam Conference (CEAS)*.

Alexander Boettcher and Dongman Lee. 2012. Eventradar: A real-time local event detection scheme using twitter stream. In *2012 IEEE International Conference on Green Computing and Communications*, pages 358–367.

Danah Boyd, Scott Golder, and Gilad Lotan. 2010. Tweet, tweet, retweet: Conversational aspects of retweeting on twitter. In *2010 43rd Hawaii International Conference on System Sciences*, pages 1–10.

Amosse Edouard, Elena Cabrio, Sara Tonelli, and Nhan Le Thanh. 2017. Graph-based event extraction from twitter. In *RANLP*.

Günes Erkan and Dragomir R. Radev. 2004. Lexrank: Graph-based lexical centrality as salience in text summarization. *J. Artif. Int. Res.*, 22(1):457–479.

Atefeh Farzindar and Wael Khreich. 2015. A survey of techniques for event detection in twitter. *Computational Intelligence*, 31:132–164.

Mahmud Hasan, Mehmet A. Orgun, and Rolf Schwitter. 2016. Twitternews+: A framework for real time event detection from the twitter data stream. In *Social Informatics*, pages 224–239, Cham. Springer International Publishing.

Raymond A. Jarvis and Edward A. Patrick. 1973. Clustering using a similarity measure based on shared near neighbors. *IEEE Transactions on Computers*, C-22(11):1025–1034.

Dimitrios Kotsakos, Panos Sakkos, Ioannis Katakis, and Dimitrios Gunopulos. 2014. #tag: Meme or event? In *Proceedings of the 2014 IEEE/ACM International Conference on Advances in Social Networks Analysis and Mining*, ASONAM '14, pages 391–394, Piscataway, NJ, USA. IEEE Press.

Chenliang Li, Aixin Sun, and Anwitaman Datta. 2012a. Twevent: Segment-based event detection from tweets. In *Proceedings of the 21st ACM International Conference on Information and Knowledge Management*, CIKM '12, pages 155–164, New York, NY, USA. ACM.

Chenliang Li, Aixin Sun, Jianshu Weng, and Qi He. 2015. Tweet segmentation and its application to named entity recognition. *IEEE Transactions on Knowledge and Data Engineering*, 27:558–570.

Chenliang Li, Jianshu Weng, Qi He, Yuxia Yao, Anwitaman Datta, Aixin Sun, and Bu-Sung Lee. 2012b. Twiner: Named entity recognition in targeted twitter stream. In *Proceedings of the 35th International ACM SIGIR Conference on Research and Development in Information Retrieval*, SIGIR '12, pages 721–730, New York, NY, USA. ACM.

Andrew J. McMinn, Yashar Moshfeghi, and Joemon M. Jose. 2013. Building a large-scale corpus for evaluating event detection on twitter. In *Proceedings of the 22Nd ACM International Conference on Information & Knowledge Management*, CIKM '13, pages 409–418, New York, NY, USA. ACM.

Andrew James McMinn and Joemon M. Jose. 2015. Real-time entity-based event detection for twitter.

Ozer Ozdikis, Pinar Senkul, and Halit Oguztuzun. 2012a. Semantic expansion of hashtags for enhanced event detection in twitter. In *Proceedings of the 1st International Workshop on Online Social Systems*.

Ozer Ozdikis, Pinar Senkul, and Halit Oguztuzun. 2012b. Semantic expansion of tweet contents for enhanced event detection in twitter. In *Proceedings of the 2012 International Conference on Advances in Social Networks Analysis and Mining (ASONAM 2012)*, ASONAM '12, pages 20–24, Washington, DC, USA. IEEE Computer Society.

Nikolaos Panagiotou, Ioannis Katakis, and Dimitrios Gunopulos. 2016. Detecting events in online social networks: Definitions, trends and challenges. In *Solving Large Scale Learning Tasks. Challenges and Algorithms*, volume 9580, pages 42–84. Springer.

Swit Phuvipadawat and Tsuyoshi Murata. 2010. Breaking news detection and tracking in twitter. In *Proceedings of the 2010 IEEE/WIC/ACM International Conference on Web Intelligence and Intelligent Agent Technology - Volume 03*, WI-IAT '10, pages 120–123, Washington, DC, USA. IEEE Computer Society.

Alberto Tonon, Philippe Cudré-Mauroux, Albert Blarer, Vincent Lenders, and Boris Motik. 2017. Armatweet: Detecting events by semantic tweet analysis. In *ESWC*.

George Valkanas and Dimitrios Gunopulos. 2013. Event detection from social media data. *IEEE Data Eng. Bull.*, 36(3):51–58.

Andreas Weiler, Michael Grossniklaus, and Marc H. Scholl. 2016. Survey and Experimental Analysis of Event Detection Techniques for Twitter. *The Computer Journal*, 60(3):329–346.

Jianshu Weng and Bu-Sung Lee. 2011. Event detection in twitter. In *ICWSM*.

Multimodal Machine Translation with Embedding Prediction

Tosho Hirasawa and **Hayahide Yamagishi** and **Yukio Matsumura** and **Mamoru Komachi**
Tokyo Metropolitan University
{tosho.hirasawa@, yamagishi-hayahide@ed., matsumura-yukio@ed.,
komachi@}tmu.ac.jp

Abstract

Multimodal machine translation is an attractive application of neural machine translation (NMT). It helps computers to deeply understand visual objects and their relations with natural languages. However, multimodal NMT systems suffer from a shortage of available training data, resulting in poor performance for translating rare words. In NMT, pretrained word embeddings have been shown to improve NMT of low-resource domains, and a search-based approach is proposed to address the rare word problem. In this study, we effectively combine these two approaches in the context of multimodal NMT and explore how we can take full advantage of pretrained word embeddings to better translate rare words. We report overall performance improvements of 1.24 METEOR and 2.49 BLEU and achieve an improvement of 7.67 F-score for rare word translation.

1 Introduction

In **multimodal machine translation**, a target sentence is translated from a source sentence together with related nonlinguistic information such as visual information. Recently, neural machine translation (NMT) has superseded traditional statistical machine translation owing to the introduction of the attentional encoder-decoder model, in which machine translation is treated as a sequence-to-sequence learning problem and is trained to pay attention to the source sentence while decoding (Bahdanau et al., 2015).

Most previous studies on multimodal machine translation are classified into two categories: visual feature adaptation and data augmentation. In visual feature adaptation, multitask learning (Elliott and Kádár, 2017) and feature integration architecture (Caglayan et al., 2017a; Calixto et al., 2017) are proposed to improve neural network models. Data augmentation aims to deal with the fact that the size of available datasets for multimodal translation is quite small. To alleviate this problem, parallel corpora without a visual source (Elliott and Kádár, 2017; Grönroos et al., 2018) and pseudo-parallel corpora obtained using back-translation (Helcl et al., 2018) are used as additional learning resources.

Due to the availability of parallel corpora for NMT, Qi et al. (2018) suggested that initializing the encoder with pretrained word embedding improves the translation performance in low-resource language pairs. Recently, Kumar and Tsvetkov (2019) proposed an NMT model that predicts the embedding of output words and searches for the output word instead of calculating the probability using the softmax function. This model performed as well as conventional NMT, and it significantly improved the translation accuracy for rare words.

In this study, we introduce an NMT model with embedding prediction for multimodal machine translation that fully uses pretrained embeddings to improve the translation accuracy for rare words.

The main contributions of this study are as follows:

1. We propose a novel multimodal machine translation model with embedding prediction and explore various settings to take full advantage of word embeddings.

2. We show that pretrained word embeddings improve the model performance, especially when translating rare words.

2 Multimodal Machine Translation with Embedding Prediction

We integrate an embedding prediction framework (Kumar and Tsvetkov, 2019) with the multimodal

Proceedings of the 2019 Conference of the North American Chapter of the Association for Computational Linguistics: Student Research Workshop, pages 86–91
Minneapolis, Minnesota, June 3 - 5, 2019. ©2017 Association for Computational Linguistics

machine translation model and take advantage of pretrained word embeddings. To highlight the effect of pretrained word embeddings and embedding prediction architecture, we adopt IMAGINATION (Elliott and Kádár, 2017) as a simple multimodal baseline.

IMAGINATION jointly learns machine translation and visual latent space models. It is based on a conventional NMT model for a machine translation task. In latent space learning, a source sentence and the paired image are mapped closely in the latent space. We use the latent space learning model as it is, except for the preprocessing of images. The models for each task share the same textual encoder in a multitask scenario.

The loss function for multitask learning is the linear interpolation of loss functions for each task.

$$J = \lambda J_\mathrm{T}(\theta, \phi_\mathrm{T}) + (1 - \lambda) J_\mathrm{V}(\theta, \phi_\mathrm{V}) \quad (1)$$

where θ is the parameter of the shared encoder; ϕ_T and ϕ_V are parameters of the machine translation model and latent space model, respectively; and λ is the interpolation coefficient[1].

2.1 Neural Machine Translation with Embedding Prediction

The machine translation part in our proposed model is an extension of Bahdanau et al. (2015). However, instead of using the probability of each word in the decoder, it searches for output words based on their similarity with word embeddings. Once the model predicts a word embedding, its nearest neighbor in the pretrained word embeddings is selected as the system output.

$$\hat{e}_j = \tanh(W_o s_j + b_o) \quad (2)$$
$$\hat{y}_j = \underset{w \in \mathcal{V}}{\operatorname{argmin}}\{d(\hat{e}_j, \mathbf{e}(w))\} \quad (3)$$

where s_j, $\hat{e}_j$, and $\hat{y}_j$ are the hidden state of the decoder, predicted embedding, and system output, respectively, for each timestep j in the decoding process. $\mathbf{e}(w)$ is the pretrained word embedding for a target word w. d is a distance function that is used to calculate the word similarity. W_o and b_o are parameters of the output layer.

We adopt margin-based ranking loss (Lazaridou et al., 2015) as the loss function

of the machine translation model.

$$J_\mathrm{T}(\theta, \phi_\mathrm{T}) = \sum_j^M \max\{0, \gamma + d(\hat{e}_j, \mathbf{e}(w_j^-)) \\ - d(\hat{e}_j, \mathbf{e}(y_j))\} \quad (4)$$

$$w_j^- = \underset{w \in \mathcal{V}}{\operatorname{argmax}}\{d(\hat{e}_j, \mathbf{e}(w)) - d(\hat{e}_j, \mathbf{e}(y_j))\} \quad (5)$$

where M is the length of a target sentence and γ is the margin[2]. w_j^- is a negative sample that is close to the predicted embedding and far from the gold embedding as measuring using d.

Pretrained word embeddings are also used to initialize the embedding layers of the encoder and decoder, and the output layer of the decoder. The embedding layer of the encoder is updated during training, and the embedding layer of the decoder is fixed to the initial value.

2.2 Visual Latent Space Learning

The decoder of this model calculates the average vector over the hidden states h_i in the encoder and maps it to the final vector $\hat{v}$ in the latent space.

$$\hat{v} = \tanh(W_\mathrm{v} \cdot \frac{1}{N} \sum_i^N h_i) \quad (6)$$

where N is the length of an input sentence and $W_\mathrm{v} \in \mathbb{R}^{N*M}$ is learned parameter of the model.

We use max margin loss as the loss function; it learns to make corresponding latent vectors of a source sentence and the paired image closer.

$$J_\mathrm{V}(\theta, \phi_\mathrm{V}) = \sum_{v' \neq v} \max\{0, \alpha + d(\hat{v}, v') - d(\hat{v}, v)\} \quad (7)$$

where v is the latent vector of the paired image; v', the image vector for other examples; and α, the margin that adjusts the sparseness of each vector in the latent space[3].

3 Experiment

3.1 Dataset

We train, validate, and test our model with the Multi30k (Elliott et al., 2016) dataset published in the WMT17 Shared Task.

We choose French as the source language and English as the target one. The vocabulary size of both the source and the target languages is 10,000.

---

[1] We use $\lambda = 0.01$ in the experiment.

[2] We use $\gamma = 0.5$ in the experiment.
[3] We use $\alpha = 0.1$ in our experiment.

Following Kumar and Tsvetkov (2019), byte pair encoding (Sennrich et al., 2016) is not applied. The source and target sentences are preprocessed with lower-casing, tokenizing and normalizing the punctuation.

Visual features are extracted using pretrained ResNet (He et al., 2016). Specifically, we encode all images in Multi30k with ResNet-50 and pick out the hidden state in the pool5 layer as a 2,048-dimension visual feature. We calculate the centroid of visual features in the training dataset as the bias vector and subtract the bias vector from all visual features in the training, validation and test datasets.

3.2 Model

The model is implemented using nmtpytorch toolkit v3.0.0[4] (Caglayan et al., 2017b).

The shared encoder has 256 hidden dimensions, and therefore the bidirectional GRU has 512 dimensions. The decoder in NMT model has 256 hidden dimension. The input word embedding size and output vector size is 300 each. The latent space vector size is 2,048.

We used the Adam optimizer with learning rate of 0.0004. The gradient norm is clipped to 1.0. The dropout rate is 0.3.

BLEU (Papineni et al., 2002) and METEOR (Denkowski and Lavie, 2014) are used as performance metrics. We also evaluated the models using the F-score of each word; this shows how accurately each word is translated into target sentences, as was proposed in Kumar and Tsvetkov (2019). The F-score is calculated as the harmonic mean of the precision (fraction of produced sentences with a word that is in the references sentences) and the recall (fraction of reference sentences with a word that is in model outputs). We ran the experiment three times with different random seeds and obtained the mean and variance for each model.

To clarify the effect of pretrained embeddings on machine translation, we also initialized the encoder and decoder of our models with random values instead of pretrained embeddings, and investigated the effect of fixing decoder embeddings.

3.3 Word Embedding

We use publicly available pretrained Fast-Text (Bojanowski et al., 2017) embeddings (Grave et al., 2018). These word embeddings are

[4]https://github.com/toshohirasawa/nmtpytorch-emb-pred

Model	val BLEU	test BLEU	METEOR
NMT	50.83	51.00±.37	42.65±.12
+ pretrained	52.05	52.33±.66	43.42±.13
IMAG+	51.03	51.18±.16	42.80±.19
+ pretrained	52.40	52.75±.25	43.56±.04
Ours	**53.14**	**53.49±.20**	**43.89±.14**

Table 1: Results on Multi30k validation and test dataset. NMT denotes the text-only conventional NMT model (Bahdanau et al., 2015) and IMAG+ denotes our reimplementation of the IMAGINATION (Elliott and Kádár, 2017) model. "+ pretrained" models are initialized with pretrained embeddings.

trained on Wikipedia and Common Crawl using the CBOW algorithm, and the dimension is 300.

The embedding for unknown words is calculated as the average embedding over words that are a part of pretrained embeddings but are not included in the vocabularies. Both the target and the source embeddings are preprocessed according to Mu and Viswanath (2018), in which all embeddings are debiased to make the average embedding into a zero vector and the top five principal components are subtracted for each embedding.

4 Results

Table 1 shows the overall performance of the proposed and baseline models. Compared with randomly initialized models, our model outperforms the text-only baseline by +2.49 BLEU and +1.24 METEOR, and the multimodal baseline by +2.31 BLEU and +1.09 METEOR, respectively. While pretrained embeddings improve NMT/IMAGINATION models as well, the improved models are still beyond our model.

Table 2 shows the results of ablation experiments of the initialization and fine-tuning methods. The pretrained embedding models outperform other models by up to +2.77 BLEU and +1.37 METEOR.

5 Discussion

Rare Words Our model shows a great improvement for low-frequency words. Figure 1 shows a variety of F-score according to the word frequency in the training corpus. Whereas IMAGINATION improves the translation accuracy uniformly, our model shows substantial improvement

Encoder	Decoder	Fixed	BLEU	METEOR
fasttext	fasttext	Yes	**53.49**	**43.89**
random	fasttext	Yes	53.22	43.83
fasttext	random	No	51.53	43.07
random	random	No	51.42	42.77
fasttext	fasttext	No	51.42	42.88
random	fasttext	No	50.72	42.52

Table 2: Results on test dataset with variations of model initialization and fine-tuning in decoder.

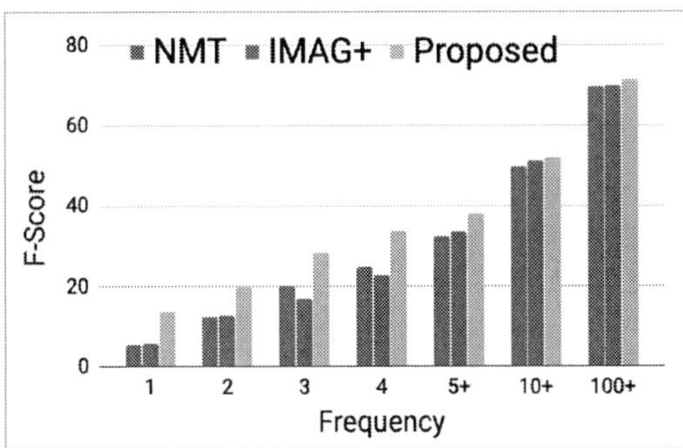

Figure 1: F-score of word prediction per frequency breakdown in training corpus.

for rare words.

Word Embeddings Furthermore, we found that decoder embeddings must be fixed to improve multimodal machine translation with embedding prediction. When we allow fine-tuning on the embedding layer, the performance drops below the baseline. It seems that fine-tuning embeddings in NMT with embedding prediction makes the model search for common words more than expected, thus preventing it from predicting rare words.

More interestingly, using pretrained FastText embeddings on the decoder rather than the encoder improves performance. This finding is different from Qi et al. (2018), in which only the encoder benefits from pretrained embeddings. Compared with the model initialized with a random value, initializing the decoder with the embedding results in an increase of +1.80 BLEU; in contrast, initializing the encoder results in an increase of only +0.11 BLEU. This is caused by the multitask learning model that trains the encoder with images and takes it away from what the embedding prediction model wants to learn from the sentences.

Model	val BLEU	test BLEU	METEOR
Ours	**53.14**	**53.49**	43.89
− Debias	52.65	53.27	**43.91**
− Images	52.97	53.25	**43.91**

Table 3: Ablation experiments of visual features. "− Debias" denotes the result without subtracting the bias vector. "− Images" shows the result of text-only NMT with embedding prediction.

Visual Feature We also investigated the effect of images and its preprocessing in NMT with embedding prediction (Table 3). The interesting result is that multitask learning with raw images would not help the predictive model. Debiasing images is an essential preprocessing for NMT with embedding prediction to use images effectively in multitask learning scenario.

Translation Examples In Table 4, we show French-English translations generated by different models. In the left example, our proposed model correctly translates "voûte" into "archway" (occurs five times in the training set), Although the baseline model translates it to its synonym having higher frequency (nine times for "arch" and 12 times for "monument"). At the same time, our outputs tend to be less fluent for long sentences. The right example shows that our model translates some words ("patterned" and "carpet") more concisely; however, it generates a less fluent sentence than the baseline.

6 Related Works

Most studies on multimodal machine translation are divided into two categories: visual feature adaptation and data augmentation.

First, in visual feature adaptation, visual features are extracted using image processing techniques and then integrated into a machine translation model. In contrast, most multitask learning models use latent space learning as their auxiliary task. Elliott and Kádár (2017) proposed the IMAGINATION model that learns to construct the corresponding visual feature from the textual hidden states of a source sentence. The visual model shares its encoder with the machine translation model; this helps in improving the textual encoder.

Second, in data augmentation, parallel corpora without images are widely used as additional train-

Image		
Source	un homme en vélo pédale devant une **voûte** .	quatre hommes , dont trois portent des kippas , sont assis sur un **tapis** à **motifs** bleu et vert olive .
Reference	a man on a bicycle pedals through an **archway** .	four men , three of whom are wearing prayer caps , are sitting on a blue and olive green **patterned mat** .
NMT	a man on a bicycle pedal past an **arch** .	four men , three of whom are wearing aprons , are sitting on a blue and green **speedo carpet** .
IMAG+	a man on a bicycle pedals outside a **monument** .	four men , three of them are wearing alaska , are sitting on a blue **patterned carpet** and green green seating .
Ours	a man on a bicycle pedals in front of a **archway** .	four men , three are wearing these are wearing these are sitting on a blue and green **patterned mat** .

Table 4: French to English translation examples in the Multi30k test set.

ing data. Grönroos et al. (2018) trained their multimodal model with parallel corpora and achieved state-of-the-art performance in the WMT 2018. However, the use of monolingual corpora has seldom been studied in multimodal machine translation. Our study proposes using word embeddings that are pretrained on monolingual corpora.

7 Conclusion

We have proposed a multimodal machine translation model with embedding prediction and showed that pretrained word embeddings improve the performance in multimodal translation tasks, especially when translating rare words.

In the future, we will tailor the training corpora for embedding learning, especially for handling the embedding for unknown words in the context of multimodal machine translation. We will also incorporate visual features into contextualized word embeddings.

References

Dzmitry Bahdanau, Kyunghyun Cho, and Yoshua Bengio. 2015. Neural machine translation by jointly learning to align and translate. In *ICLR*.

Piotr Bojanowski, Edouard Grave, Armand Joulin, and Tomas Mikolov. 2017. Enriching word vectors with subword information. In *TACL*, volume 5, pages 135–146.

Ozan Caglayan, Walid Aransa, Adrien Bardet, Mercedes García-Martínez, Fethi Bougares, Loïc Barrault, Marc Masana, Luis Herranz, and Joost van de Weijer. 2017a. LIUM-CVC submissions for WMT17 multimodal translation task. In *WMT*, pages 432–439.

Ozan Caglayan, Mercedes García-Martínez, Adrien Bardet, Walid Aransa, Fethi Bougares, and Loïc Barrault. 2017b. NMTPY: A flexible toolkit for advanced neural machine translation systems. *Prague Bull. Math. Linguistics*, 109:15–28.

Iacer Calixto, Qun Liu, and Nick Campbell. 2017. Doubly-attentive decoder for multi-modal neural machine translation. In *ACL*, pages 1913–1924.

Michael Denkowski and Alon Lavie. 2014. Meteor universal: Language specific translation evaluation for any target language. In *WMT*, pages 376–380.

Desmond Elliott, Stella Frank, Khalil Sima'an, and Lucia Specia. 2016. Multi30k: Multilingual English-German image descriptions. In *Proceedings of the 5th Workshop on Vision and Language*, pages 70–74.

Desmond Elliott and Àkos Kádár. 2017. Imagination improves multimodal translation. In *IJCNLP*, volume 1, pages 130–141.

Edouard Grave, Piotr Bojanowski, Prakhar Gupta, Armand Joulin, and Tomas Mikolov. 2018. Learning word vectors for 157 languages. In *LREC*, pages 3483–3487.

Stig-Arne Grönroos, Benoit Huet, Mikko Kurimo, Jorma Laaksonen, Bernard Merialdo, Phu Pham, Mats Sjöberg, Umut Sulubacak, Jörg Tiedemann, Raphael Troncy, and Raúl Vázquez. 2018. The MeMAD submission to the WMT18 multimodal translation task. In *WMT*, pages 603–611.

Kaiming He, Xiangyu Zhang, Shaoqing Ren, and Jian Sun. 2016. Deep residual learning for image recognition. In *CVPR*, pages 770–778.

Jindřich Helcl, Jindřich Libovický, and Dusan Varis. 2018. CUNI system for the WMT18 multimodal translation task. In *WMT*, pages 616–623.

Sachin Kumar and Yulia Tsvetkov. 2019. Von Mises-Fisher loss for training sequence to sequence models with continuous outputs. In *ICLR*.

Angeliki Lazaridou, Georgiana Dinu, and Marco Baroni. 2015. Hubness and pollution: Delving into cross-space mapping for zero-shot learning. In *ACL-IJCNLP*, pages 270–280.

Jiaqi Mu and Pramod Viswanath. 2018. All-but-the-Top: Simple and effective postprocessing for word representations. In *ICLR*.

Kishore Papineni, Salim Roukos, Todd Ward, and Wei-Jing Zhu. 2002. BLEU: a method for automatic evaluation of machine translation. In *ACL*, pages 311–318.

Ye Qi, Devendra Sachan, Matthieu Felix, Sarguna Padmanabhan, and Graham Neubig. 2018. When and why are pre-trained word embeddings useful for neural machine translation? In *NAACL*, pages 529–535.

Rico Sennrich, Barry Haddow, and Alexandra Birch. 2016. Neural machine translation of rare words with subword units. In *ACL*, pages 1715–1725.

Deep Learning and Sociophonetics:
Automatic Coding of Rhoticity Using Neural Networks

Sarah Gupta
Dartmouth College
sarah.gupta.19@dartmouth.edu

Anthony DiPadova
Dartmouth College
anthony.f.dipadova.iii.19@dartmouth.edu

Abstract

Automated extraction methods are widely available for vowels (Rosenfelder et al., 2014), but automated methods for coding rhoticity have lagged far behind. R-fulness versus r-lessness (in words like park, store, etc.) is a classic and frequently cited variable (Labov, 1966), but it is still commonly coded by human analysts rather than automated methods. Human-coding requires extensive resources and lacks replicability, making it difficult to compare large datasets across research groups (Yaeger-Dror et al., 2008; Heselwood et al., 2008). Can reliable automated methods be developed to aid in coding rhoticity? In this study, we use Neural Networks/Deep Learning, training our model on 208 Boston-area speakers.

1 Introduction

Despite advances in automation for phonetic alignment and extraction of vowel formants, there is still no reliable automated method for classifying r-dropping, that is, whether a given word is pronounced with an /r/ in words like *park (pahk)*, *start (staht)*, and so on. R-dropping, also known as non-rhotic speech, is an important sociolinguistic variable in modern dialect research. But unfortunately most researchers continue to depend on human judgments (Nagy and Irwin, 2010; Becker, 2009; Nagy and Roberts, 2004), which is an inconsistent and time-consuming method that lacks replicability. Turning to the field of machine learning, our deep learning approach investigates a new way to distinguish rhotic versus non-rhotic pronunciations in recorded data. This is the first study to use neural networks to classify rhotic versus non-rhotic speech.

Although human-coding requires extensive resources and lacks consistency and replicability (Yaeger-Dror et al., 2008; Heselwood et al., 2008),

making it difficult to compare large datasets across different research groups, it is the only method we have right now. How soon will computers be able to quickly and reliably code rhoticity up to this standard? In terms of other machine learning approaches, McLarty, Jones, and Hall work on this challenge using Support Vector Machines (SVMs) (Mclarty et al., 2018). The present study uses Neural Networks/Deep Learning, one of the most effective and fastest-growing approaches in machine-learning. To our knowledge, this is the first attempt to use neural networks for automatic coding of any sociophonetic variable.

This new method was developed using audio recordings from over 200 New England speakers from Boston, Maine, and central New Hampshire (Stanford, forthcoming), and is here compared to other work on rhoticity (Heselwood et al., 2008; Mclarty et al., 2018). In what ways can neural networks be effective tools in assisting the coding of rhoticity? To what level can they perform compared to traditional coding methods and other approaches?

2 Background

The phoneme /r/ has been particularly difficult to pin down because it may be articulated in different ways, yet still produce the same acoustic signal. As most phoneticians have come to agree, F3 is one of the primary acoustic correlates of rhoticity (Espy-Wilson et al., 2000; Hagiwara, 1995; Thomas, 2011). The general consensus is that the F3 measurement for /r/ is lower than that of other non-rhotic vowels, but reliable standards for coding rhoticity are lacking.

In this paper, rhoticity will refer to post-vocalic realizations of the phoneme /r/ which do not occur before other vowels. For example, rhotic tokens of interest would include *park* and *father* but not

Proceedings of the 2019 Conference of the North American Chapter of the Association for Computational Linguistics: Student Research Workshop, pages 92–96
Minneapolis, Minnesota, June 3 - 5, 2019. ©2017 Association for Computational Linguistics

marry. British phonetician John Wells used the term "rhotic", which has been subsequently considered in the field as one of the most defining traits of varieties of English (Wells, 1982).

Rhotic and non-rhotic dialects have been widely studied as they relate to sociolinguistic features of location, age, gender, and socioeconomic status. However, we are still reliant on human analysts to make judgements of rhotic vs. non-rhotic speech, which can require a lot of time and money. Despite advances in many areas of computational linguistics, there is still not an accurate way to determine rhoticity based on acoustic components alone; a human must judge for themselves whether or not an /r/ has been dropped. As expected, this is not highly replicable as different speakers may perceive things differently especially when it comes to dialects that are not so clear-cut (Yaeger-Dror et al., 2008). For this reason, an automated way to determine rhotic/non-rhotic tokens would be especially helpful in these contexts.

3   Other work

3.1   Heselwood, Plug, and Tickle

Heselwood et al. (2008) extracted formant data from the spectrograms on the Bark scale – usually, formant data F2/F3 is reported on the Hertz scale. The Bark scale more closely correlates to human perception of sounds, that is, on a logarithmic scale rather than absolute. After conversion, F2 was labeled Z2 and F3 was labeled Z3, and a series of perceptual experiments were performed to ascertain rhoticity thresholds. Note that it was conducted for the purposes of perceptual research rather than coding applications.

3.2   McLarty, Jones, and Hall

Mclarty et al. (2018) trained a Support Vector Machine (SVM) on pre-vocalic /r/ and vowels, and their approach did quite well in classifying prevocalic /r/s. They then took this pre-trained model and applied it to classifying postvocalic /r/ tokens, which classified 84% as vowels, and 15% as /r/. As they describe, this is likely because all postvocalic segments still contain vowel-like properties; furthermore, their training set excluded postvocalic /r/ so the accuracy is expected to decrease.

However, their method did not perform as well in comparison to humans. On tokens where there was no ground truth, humans only agreed with the SVM classification about 55% of the time.

4   Methods

In this initial study, we used Boston-area field recordings of 208 speakers, 100 tokens per speaker (107 women/101 men, born 1915-1997). These on-the-street interviews (15-20 minutes each) are typical sociolinguistic recordings in terms of speech styles (word-list, sentences, reading passage, free speech) and occasional background noise. We chose to omit free speech because its token variability between speakers would present another challenging factor, leaving us with recordings where participants were reading (word-list, sentences, passage). Given word transcriptions, we used the Montreal Forced Aligner (McAuliffe et al., 2017) and modified Praat scripts (DiCanio, 2014; Koops, 2013) to align and extract vowel+(r) sequences, e.g., park, short. However, note that because non-rhotic dialects are less common, and some of our recordings had background noise, it could be possible that alignments were not perfect for all of our tokens.

Two human analysts listened to recordings and judged each vowel+(r) token as r-ful or r-less. The human analysts agreed on 89.9% of the tokens, similar to human agreement elsewhere (Nagy and Irwin, 2010). Like other studies, we omitted tokens when the human analysts disagreed (10%). So overall, 1700 tokens were discarded because of speaker disagreement, and 6500 rhotic tokens and 5300 non-rhotic tokens remained for analysis.

4.1   Preliminary Investigations

In early testing, we attempted classification into r-ful, r-less, and unknown, but this did not provide strong results so we simplified to a binary classification. From the beginning of this project, we knew we wanted to use a machine learning approach, so before using neural networks we tried some easier classifiers. However, we did not get encouraging results. For example, our Random Forest Classifier only gave about 54% accuracy. When we tried simpler neural networks, these gave much more promising results to we chose to pursue this method.

4.2   Data Extraction and Model Specifications

Following standard methods of Automatic Speech Recognition, we converted the audio to 12 Mel-Frequency-Cepstral-Coefficients (MFCCs). We used the 12 MFCCs, similar to Mclarty et al.. For each vowel+(r) sequence, we normalized across the length to extract 100 time-points per token, as shown in figure 1. In the training, MFCCs were

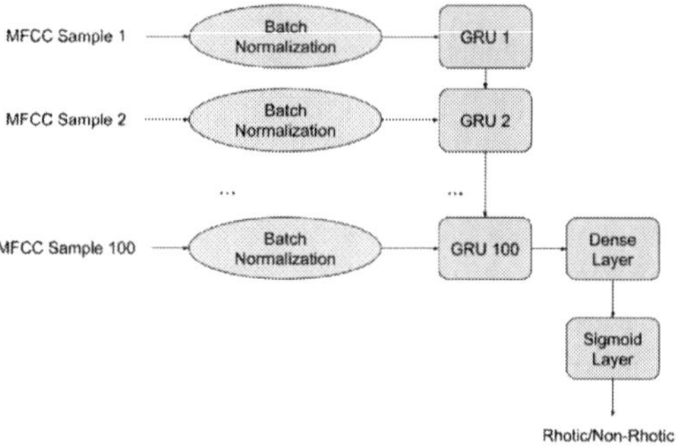

Figure 1: Model architecture.

more effective than traditional sociophonetic /r/ correlates F2 and F3 (Thomas, 2011). These samples were used in the model architecture as shown in figure 1, where there are 100 samples for each vowel + /r/ sequence. The Gated Recurrent Unit is shown in more detail in figure 2, where we can see the input from the previous timestep and layer, and how this is filtered through gates using *tanh* and *sigmoid* activation functions.

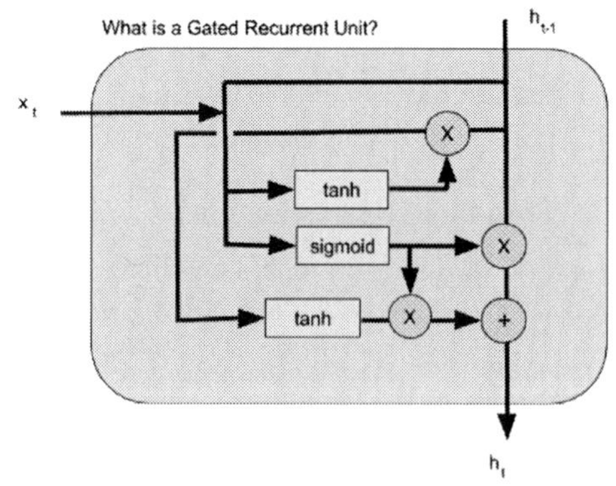

Figure 2: Gated Recurrent Unit (GRU) architecture.

Importantly, no work on coding rhoticity has made use of Recurrent Neural Networks, and we believe our methods are a promising step. We used Gated Recurrent Units (Cho et al., 2014; Chung et al., 2014) to train our system to classify vowel+(r) tokens as r-ful or r-less. Following standard methods in machine-learning, we split the data in order to train with 80% of the data and test with 20%.

We chose hyperparameters based on a grid search using 3-fold cross validation (only 3 due to the small dataset). We saved the test set to validate results. The hidden layer size was 50 nodes, and dense layer size was 200 nodes. For regularization we used a kernel L2 regularization for the dense layer and we used both activation L2 and Recurrent L2 for the GRU layer. All of the alphas for this regularization are 0.01. The optimization method was RMSprop, and the learning rate was 0.001.

5 Results

In figure 3, we see the Normalized Confusion Matrix, which summarizes our results by lining up true labels and predicted labels for our rhotic and non-rhotic tokens. We consider this binary classification either rhotic (positive) or non-rhotic (negative). In this way we can see the proportion of true positives (predicted to be rhotic and indeed truly rhotic), false positive (predicted to be rhotic but actually non-rhotic), true negative (predicted to be non-rhotic and actually non-rhotic), and false negative (predicted to be non-rhotic and actually rhotic). In deciding which model to use, we tried a

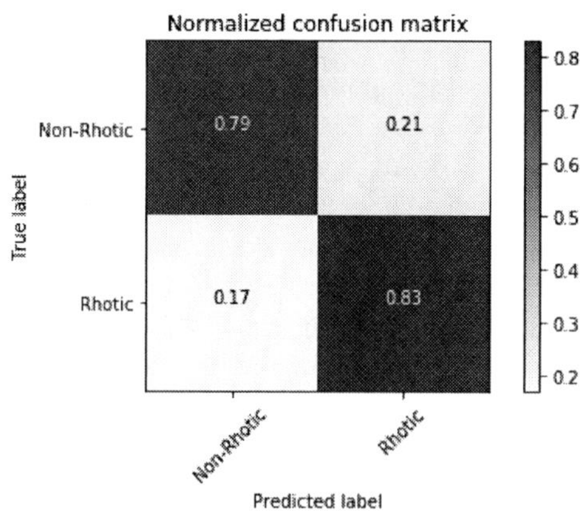

Figure 3: Normalized Confusion Matrix.

few different configurations. We used the sampled MFCCs (as described earlier, figure 1) as well as Bark measurements that were extracted also at 100 time-points across the vowel. Because our MFCC data is multi-dimensional and time-dependent, we wanted to see how a Convolutional Neural Network would perform (table 1), but it turned out not to be as high in performance as our earlier model.

Figure 4 shows the Receiver Operating Characteristic (ROC) for our model (created using scikit-learn), which is fairly good by machine learning standards. The Area Under the Curve (AUC, as noted in Table 1) is 0.892, and as evident from the graph, is much closer to 1. Our system had 81.1%

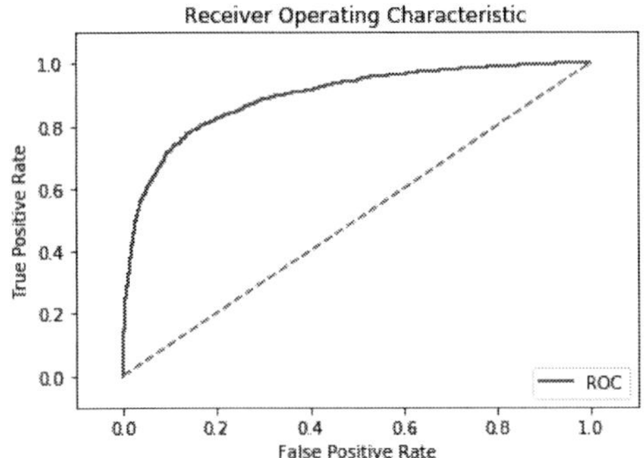

Figure 4: Receiver Operating Characteristic.

accuracy with the human analysts in judging tokens as r-less or r-ful, scoring 0.829 for F-measure.

	Accuracy	Precision	Recall	F1	AUC
GRU-MFCC	0.811	0.829	0.830	0.829	0.892
GRU-Bark	0.806	0.844	0.856	0.850	0.869
CNN-MFCC	0.746	0.796	0.815	0.805	0.808

Table 1: Metrics showing the performance of different models – our top performing model was using GRUs with MFCCs as input (as described previously).

We also used the Heselwood et al. approach (section 3.1) of classifying front or back vowels to see how accurately it would perform on the same test dataset. This classification gave an average speaker accuracy of 63.3% and an average token accuracy of 62.1% (Table 2), much lower than our best model's overall accuracy (i.e. average across all tokens) of 81.1% (Table 1).

Average Speaker Accuracy	63.3%
Average Token Accuracy	62.1%

Table 2: Heselwood et al. approach on test dataset (using Bark thresholds Z2 and Z3)

6   Discussion

The initial results of this study are promising. Our results are quite strong, as shown by the metrics in Table 1. When testing the Heselwood et al. approach (Table 2), it only predicted correctly approximately 60% of the time; our model performs significantly better, at an accuracy of 81.1% (Table 1). It seems that we are also slightly better at predicting rhotic tokens than non-rhotic (Figure 3),

which likely has to do with the fact that we have more rhotic tokens in total.

We aimed to reach human levels – considering that analyst agreement is 89.9% for our dataset (as mentioned above), our accuracy of 81.1% is quite good. However, these numbers are not strictly comparable as we discarded tokens that proved difficult for human analysts.

In future development of this method, we want to consider any sources of error on our part. For example, some audio and text files could be misaligned so we might consider hand-correcting these alignments. However, the nature of the neural network could correct for this in that it learns to forget irrelevant or noisy data. By gathering more data, we would expect that our accuracy would improve and eventually reach a plateau where additional speakers would not affect anything.

Additionally, a study that involves cross-corpus analysis could provide greater insight into how this model might be applicable on a larger scale, and how well our model actually performs. Furthermore, if we had 3 analysts rather than 2, we could have used a majority vote for classifying tokens, and would not have to discard tokens where rhoticity was ambiguous.

A shortcoming of this study is that it only involves speech that is elicited through reading – ideally future studies would involve free speech in order to use more natural speech.

R-dropping is a crucial sociolinguistic variable for English dialect research in the US Northeast, Great Britain, Australia, New Zealand, Singapore, and other locations. Our neural network model takes a significant step toward automation of this key variable. In the future, we will continue optimizing and improving our model. Other groups have studied automated methods for coding sociolinguistic variables (Yuan and Liberman, 2011; Bailey, 2016), and there are great ideas to be found in these works. When automated methods for rhoticity reach the accuracy level of humans, along with consistency and full replicability, this will open the floodgates to large amounts of /r/ data and greatly expand sociolinguistic knowledge of dialect variation around the world, efficiently allowing studies to be replicated across research groups.

References

George Bailey. 2016. Automatic Detection of Sociolinguistic Variation Using Forced Alignment. *University of Pennsylvania Working Papers in Linguistics:*, 22(3).

Kara Becker. 2009. /r/ and the construction of place identity on New York City's Lower East Side. *Journal of Sociolinguistics*, 13(5):634 – 658.

Kyunghyun Cho, Bart Van Merrienboer, Caglar Gulcehre, Dzmitry Bahdanau, Fethi Bougares, Holger Schwenk, and Yoshua Bengio. 2014. Learning Phrase Representations using RNN EncoderDecoder for Statistical Machine Translation. *Proceedings of the 2014 Conference on Empirical Methods in Natural Language Processing (EMNLP)*.

Junyoung Chung, Caglar Gulcehre, KyungHyun Cho, and Yoshua Bengio. 2014. Empirical evaluation of Gated Recurrent Neural Networks on sequence modeling. *Neural Information Processing Systems 2014, Deep Learning and Representation Learning Workshop*.

Christian DiCanio. 2014. Combine intervals.praat.

Carol Y. Espy-Wilson, Suzanne E. Boyce, Michel Jackson, Shrikanth Narayanan, and Abeer Alwan. 2000. Acoustic modeling of American English /r/. *The Journal of the Acoustical Society of America*, 108(1):343 – 356.

Robert Hagiwara. 1995. Acoustic Realizations of American /r/ as Produced by Women and Men.

Barry Heselwood, Leendert Plug, and Alison Tickle. 2008. Assessing rhoticity using auditory, acoustic and psychoacoustic methods. *Proceedings of the 13th Methods in Dialectology.*, pages 331 – 340.

Chris Koops. 2013. Praat script for extracting vowel formants.

William Labov. 1966. The Social Stratification of English in New York City. *CAL*, pages 380 – 403.

Michael McAuliffe, Michaela Socolof, Sarah Mihuc, Michael Wagner, and Morgan Sonderegger. 2017. Montreal Forced Aligner: Trainable Text-Speech Alignment Using Kaldi. *Proceedings of the 18th Conference of the International Speech Communication Association*.

Jason Mclarty, Taylor Jones, and Christopher Hall. 2018. Corpus-Based Sociophonetic Approaches to Postvocalic R-lessness in African American Language. *American Speech*, pages 1 – 18.

Naomi Nagy and Patricia Irwin. 2010. Boston (r): Neighbo(r)s nea(r) and fa(r). *Language Variation and Change*, 22(02):241 – 278.

Naomi Nagy and Julie Roberts. 2004. *New England: Phonology*, pages 270 – 281. De Gruyter Mouton.

Ingrid Rosenfelder, Josef Fruehwald, Keelan Evanini, Scott Seyfarth, Kyle Gorman, Hilary Prichard, and Jiahong Yuan. 2014. FAVE (Forced Alignment and Vowel Extraction).

James N Stanford. forthcoming. *New England English: Large-scale acoustic sociophonetics and dialectology.* Oxford University Press.

Erik Thomas. 2011. *Sociophonetics: An introduction.* Palgrave Macmillan.

J. C. Wells. 1982. *Accents of English.* Cambridge University Press.

Malcah Yaeger-Dror, Tyler Kendall, Paul Foulkes, Dominic Watt, Jillian Eddie, Philip Harrison, and Colleen Kavenagh. 2008. *NWAV 37*.

Jiahong Yuan and Mark Liberman. 2011. Automatic detection of g-dropping in American English using forced alignment.

Data Augmentation by Data Noising for Open-vocabulary Slots
in Spoken Language Understanding

Hwa-Yeon Kim[1,2], Yoon-Hyung Roh[2], Young-Kil Kim[1,2]
University of Science and Technology[1]
Electronics and Telecommunications Research Institute[2]
`hy.kim.aai@gmail.com,{yhroh, kimyk}@etri.re.kr`

Abstract

One of the main challenges in Spoken Language Understanding (SLU) is dealing with 'open-vocabulary' slots. Recently, SLU models based on neural network were proposed, but it is still difficult to recognize the slots of unknown words or 'open-vocabulary' slots because of the high cost of creating a manually tagged SLU dataset. This paper proposes data noising, which reflects the characteristics of the 'open-vocabulary' slots, for data augmentation. We applied it to an attention based bi-directional recurrent neural network (Liu and Lane, 2016) and experimented with three datasets: Airline Travel Information System (ATIS), Snips, and MIT-Restaurant. We achieved performance improvements of up to 0.57% and 3.25 in intent prediction (accuracy) and slot filling (f1-score), respectively. Our method is advantageous because it does not require additional memory and it can be applied simultaneously with the training process of the model.

1 Introduction

Dialog processing enables dialogue between humans and voice assistants such as 'Siri' and 'Alexa'. In dialogue processing, spoken language understanding (SLU) is aimed at understanding and generating the user intention from an utterance. The user intention consists of an intent and slots, which are semantic entities, and it is generally defined variously according to the domain.

Neural networks (NNs) have been actively studied and applied to SLU. Xu and Sarikaya (2013) and Vu (2016) proposed models for SLU using Convolutional Neural Networks and many other researchers used recurrent neural networks (RNNs). Liu and Lane (2016) used bi-directional RNN models and applied the attention mechanism. They showed good results by using a joint learning method for both slot filling and intent

prediction tasks. For considering the relationship between the two tasks, Wang et al. (2018) constructed two models for each task and Goo et al. (2018) used a 'slot-gate'.

Training an SLU model using an NN requires a large amount of training data labeled with slots and intents, which is expensive to build. In particular, plenty of corpora or dictionaries are required to recognize the value of an 'open-vocabulary' slot, such as a song title. In addition, it is difficult to predict the slot type of words used in the 'open-vocabulary' slot because there is neither a semantic restriction nor a length limit.

Kim et al. (2018) presented the features and examples of 'open-vocabulary' slot and proposed a new model that could effectively predict this type of slot. They exploited a long-term aware attention structure and positional encoding with multi-task learning of a character-based language model and intent detection model to focus more on relatively global information within a sentence.

The objective is to recognize slots, including 'open-vocabulary' slots, and predict the intent effectively by data augmentation. We propose a data noising method that reflects the characteristics of the 'open-vocabulary' slots. This method is advantageous in that it does not require additional memory. Moreover, it is performed simultaneously with the training of the model.

2 Related works

2.1 Data noising as a form of data augmentation

Data augmentation is a technique to avoid overfitting by increasing the size of the training datasets. This technique is widely used in many machine learning tasks. A typical method in natural language processing (NLP) is generating a sentence/corpus by replacing its words with their

Proceedings of the 2019 Conference of the North American Chapter of the Association for Computational Linguistics: Student Research Workshop, pages 97–102
Minneapolis, Minnesota, June 3 - 5, 2019. ©2017 Association for Computational Linguistics

synonyms based on rules, dictionaries, or ontology constructed by a person. In recent years, Kobayashi (2018) proposed a method of modifying sentences by the analogy of words to be replaced using an NN-based language model to achieve data augmentation.

One of the methods of data augmentation is data noising. Data noising is an effective technique for normalizing a neural network, and has been widely applied in fields such as computer vision and speech recognition. Its application in the field of NLP is relatively limited because NLP is based on discrete values like words and the quality of the data generated is not guaranteed. Several studies have used data noising for data augmentation. Iyyer et al. (2015); Bowman et al. (2015); Kumar et al. (2016) used a method for randomly dropping input word embedding. Xie et al. (2017) improved the performance by replacing a word with another word sampled from the unigram distribution or by blanking out as interpolation in language modeling. Cheng et al. (2018) improved the robustness of neural machine translation models against noisy inputs by randomly adding Gaussian noise to the word embedding and maintaining consistent behavior of the encoder to normal and perturbed inputs through adversarial learning. They showed that data noising is effective in normalizing sequence models based on neural networks.

2.2 Data augmentation for SLU

The NN model for SLU requires numerous labeled training corpora; therefore, some studies have attempted to improve SLU performance by data augmentation. Kurata et al. (2016) proposed a method of using encoder-decoder long short-term memory (LSTM) to generate labeled data. Hou et al. (2018) generated diverse utterances of existing training data through a data augmentation framework based on sequence-to-sequence generation. Yoo et al. (2018) proposed a data augmentation method that sampled similar words using a variational autoencoder. These methods have shown good performance improvements with data augmentation, but they require new models or consume additional memory.

3 Proposed Method

3.1 Motivation

First, we would like to cite an example of an utterance in the Snips dataset as the motive for the

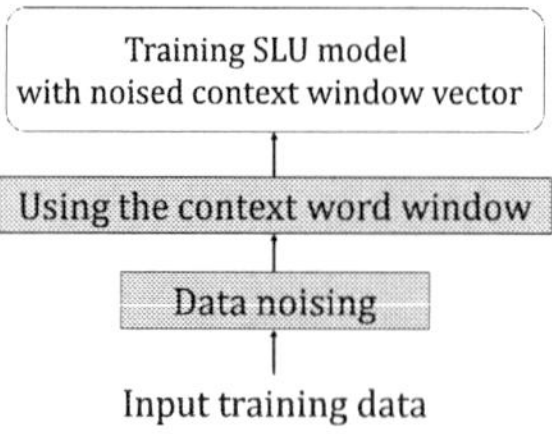

Figure 1: Proposed data augmentation method

proposed method. Consider the sentence 'i d like a table for midday at the unseen bean'; 'the unseen bean' is the value of the 'restaurant_name' slot. Even when people read 'the unseen bean,' it is difficult to recognize it as the name of a restaurant without prior knowledge. However, people can infer the slot type from the context (i.e., 'i d like a table at').

'Open-vocabulary' slots, such as the name of a restaurant or the title of a song, have no restriction on the length or the specific patterns of content in the slot. Therefore, it is hard to recognize the slot type from only the words in the slots, but it is possible to predict them based on the surrounding words or the context.

Considering these linguistic features, the purpose of this study is to augment the data by transforming them into utterances with the same context/surrounding words but various slot values. It has the effect of creating utterance patterns.

3.2 Data noising for SLU

The flow of our proposed method is shown in Figure 1. It consists of two steps: data noising and using the context word window. When the training data are input, they become noised embedding vectors after data noising. Then, we use a context word window as the input to a layer of the neural network. These steps are performed per batch and the model trains with different noised data in each step. Because data augmentation is performed in the same embedding space, it does not need additional memory and is included in the training process.

Data noising: We propose a data noising method for SLU, which augments the training data by replacing the slot values with a random value while maintaining the surrounding context. The augmented data are used to train the NN for an utterance pattern. This method is shown in Figure 2 and follows the procedure described below.

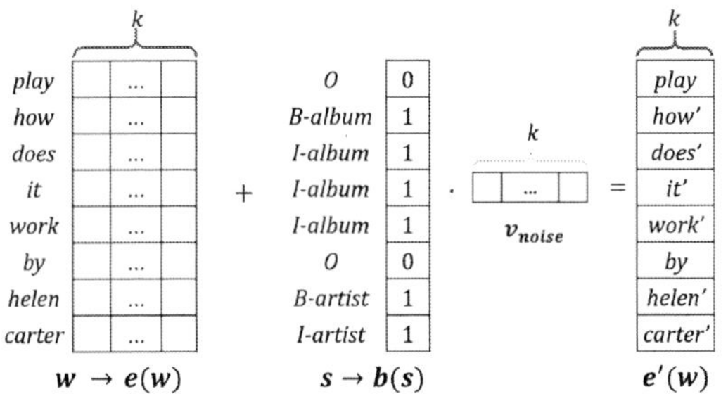

Figure 2: An example of data noising

1) Express an utterance $w = \{w_1, ..., w_T\}$ as an embedding vector $e(w) \in \mathbb{R}^{T \times k}$. T is the length of the word sequence and k is the size of the word embedding vector.

2) Extract the binary vector $b(s) = \{b_0, ..., b_T\}$ for the slot sequence $s = \{s_0, ..., s_T\}$ in the utterance w. The value of b_i is set to 1 when the i-th word w_i is the slot value (e.g., s_i is 'B-album'), and to 0 when it is not the slot value (e.g., s_i is 'O').

3) Multiply the binary vector $b(s)$ by the randomly sampled vector $v_{noise} \in \mathbb{R}^k$. Next, the noise is added only to the slot values, as shown in equation (1). This is to maintain unchanged the surrounding context of the slot value.

$$e'(w) = e(w) + b(s) \cdot v_{noise}, e'(w) \in \mathbb{R}^{T \times k} \quad (1)$$

The noised embedding vector $e'(w_i)$ is located somewhere in the same embedding space as w_i. Because 'open-vocabulary' slots can contain *any* word, we do not need to know the words that are replaced. Therefore, we augment the training data by replacing the words in the 'open-vocabulary' slots with the embedding vector of *any* unknown word, through data noising.

Noised context word window: Mesnil et al. (2015) and Zhang and Wang (2016) used a context word window to improve the performance of the RNNs in slot filling. This can reflect the context information well by examining the surrounding words together. We also use the d-context word window as an input to the recurrent layer to reflect the contextual information. In this study, the noised context word window c_i^d is the result of the concatenation of the noised embedding vector $e'^k(w_i)$ of the center word w_i and the noised embedding vectors of the d previous words and d next words, as shown in equation (2).

$$c_i^d = [e'^k(w_{i-d}), .., e'^k(w_i), .., e'^k(w_{i+d})] \quad (2)$$

4 Experiments and Results

4.1 Data

We experimented with three datasets: Airline Travel Information System (ATIS) (Hemphill et al., 1990), Snips[1], and MIT-restaurant (MR)[2]. The statistics of each dataset are shown in Table 1. We calculated the length of each slot and identified the maximum slot length. This was to numerically confirm whether each dataset had the characteristic of an 'open-vocabulary' slot, namely, there was no limit on the length of the slot value.

	ATIS	Snips	MR
Train set	4,978	13,084	6,894
Evaluation set	-	700	766
Test set	893	700	1,521
Max. slot length	5	20	10

Table 1: Statistics of ATIS, Snips, and MR datasets.

- **ATIS**: It is used in many SLU researches (Liu and Lane, 2016; Wang et al., 2018; Kim et al., 2018), including those on utterances for flight reservations. The training set is from ATIS-2 and ATIS-3 corpora, and the testing set is from ATIS-3, NOV93, and DEC94 datasets.

- **Snips**: It is an open-sourced NLU dataset of custom-intent-engines by Snips. It is used in SLU studies (Goo et al., 2018; Yoo et al., 2018). The Snips dataset contains user utterances from various domains, such as playing music or searching a movie schedule. It has 'open-vocabulary' slots, such as movie title.

- **MR**: It is a single-domain dataset, which is associated with restaurant reservations. MR contains 'open-vocabulary' slots, such as restaurant names.

4.2 Baseline and details of experiments

We set the attention based bi-directional LSTM model (Liu and Lane, 2016) without the label dependency as the baseline for the experiment. We

---

[1]https://github.com/snipsco/nlu-benchmark/tree/master/2017-06-custom-intent-engines
[2]https://groups.csail.mit.edu/sls/downloads/restaurant/

applied our data augmentation method to the baseline and evaluated the following two cases: *Just add noise* (+Noise) , *Add noise and use context window* (+Noise, cw).

We followed the set-up in Liu and Lane (2016). We set the number of LSTM cells to 128, the batch size was 16, and the dropout rate was 0.5. We considered one layer and used the Adam optimizer (Kingma and Ba, 2015) for parameter optimization. The word embeddings were randomly initialized and then fine-tuned and their size was 128 for experiments with ATIS and MR, and 64 for experiments with Snips, for comparison with previous studies.

The noise vector was created with probability p and it defined the number of augmented data. In this paper, because we performed the data augmentation in batches during the training, the number of augmented utterances was defined as $(the\_number\_of\_step \times batch\_size) \times p$. The probability was set to 0.25, 0.5, 0.75, or 1.0. The noise vector was sampled randomly from the normal distribution or uniform distribution and its size was equal to the word embedding size. We set the mean of the normal distribution to 0.0, and the σ value to 0.1, 0.2, or 0.3. The range of the uniform distribution was set to [-0.2, 0.2] or [-0.5, 0.5].

As in previous SLU studies, we used the F1-score and the accuracy to evaluate the performance of the slot filling (SF) and the intent prediction(IP), respectively.

4.3 Performances of intent prediction and slot filling

Table 2 shows the performance improvements achieved by the proposed method versus the baseline. The proposed method showed clear improvements for the Snips and MR datasets. It is considered that the proposed method is effective in the two datasets because they have larger length of slots (as shown in Table 1) and more 'open-vocabulary' slots. Experimental results show that our approach improves slot filling of an unknown word or 'open-vocabulary' slots by learning the patterns of utterances. Examples illustrating the results can be found in Table 4. They show that the proposed method improves the slot filling of unknown words and 'open-vocabulary' slots by learning the utterance patterns.

Additionally, the proposed method is more ef-

| Method | ATIS | | Snips | | MR |
	Intent	Slot	Intent	Slot	Slot
Baseline	98.10	95.88	97.86	89.68	72.56
+Noise	98.32	95.80	98.57	92.58	74.60
+Noise, cw	**98.43**	**96.20**	**98.43**	**92.93**	**75.21**

Table 2: Performance of the proposed method with ATIS, Snips, and MR datasets.

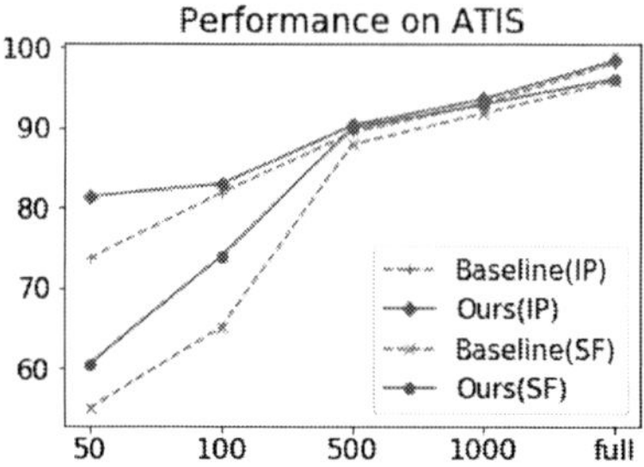

Figure 3: Performance of the proposed method with ATIS data of different sizes. The X-axis of each graph is the size of the training data. The Y-axis is the Accuracy (%) for Intent Prediction (IP) and F1-score for Slot Filling (SF).

Dataset	Model	Intent Prediction	Slot Filling
ATIS	Liu and Lane (2016)	98.21	95.98
	Kim et al. (2018)	98.54	95.93
	Wang et al. (2018)	**98.99**	**96.89**
	Ours	98.43	96.20
Snips	Goo et al. (2018)	97.00	88.80
	Yoo et al. (2018)	97.30	89.30
	Ours	**98.43**	**92.93**
MR	Yoo et al. (2018)	-	73.00
	Ours	-	**75.21**

Table 3: Comparison of the results for each dataset.

fective when the size of the training data is small. Figure 3 shows the performance according to the training data size with ATIS.

4.4 Comparison with previous studies

Table 3 shows the comparison of the performance of previous studies with each data set. In the case of the ATIS dataset, our method shows better performance than the 'Baseline' study (Liu and Lane, 2016) and a study targeting 'open-vocabulary' slots (Kim et al., 2018), but it is not state-of-the-art. However, we achieve the best performance among studies using the Snips and MR datasets.

Input	what s the weather in <u>low</u> *moor*
Baseline Pred.	O O O O O <u>O</u> I-timeRange
Proposed Pred.	O O O O O **B-city I-city**
Input	what is the *niceville* forecast in fm
Baseline Pred.	O O O <u>O</u> O O B-state
Proposed Pred.	O O O **B-city** O O B-state
Input	how can i view the show *corpus:* <u>a</u> <u>home</u> <u>movie</u> about <u>selena</u>
Baseline Pred.	O O O O O B-obj_type <u>O</u> <u>O</u> I-obj_nm B-obj_type I-obj_nm B-obj_nm
Proposed Pred.	O O O O O B-obj_type **B-obj_nm I-obj_nm I-obj_nm I-obj_nm I-obj_nm I-obj_nm**
Input	add the song <u>don</u> t *drink* <u>the</u> <u>water</u> to my playlist
Baseline Pred.	O O B-music_item B-artist I-entity_nm I-entity_nm I-playlist I-playlist O B-playlist_owner O
Proposed Pred.	O O B-music_item **B-playlist I-playlist I-playlist I-playlist I-playlist** O B-playlist_owner O
Input	book a restaurant close by <u>my</u> daughters <u>s</u> <u>work</u> <u>location</u> with burrito three years from now
Baseline Pred.	O O B-rest_type B-spatial_relation I-spatial_relation <u>O</u> <u>O</u> I-poi <u>O</u> I-poi O B-served_dish B-timeR I-timeR I-timeR I-timeR
Proposed Pred.	O O B-rest_type B-spatial_relation I-spatial_relation **B-poi I-poi I-poi I-poi I-poi** O B-served_dish B-timeR I-timeR I-timeR I-timeR

Unknown word, <u>Slot filling error</u>, **Correct slot filling (Ground Truth)**

Abbreviation 'object': 'obj', '_name' : '_nm', 'restaurant' : 'rest', 'timeRange' : 'timeR'

Table 4: Examples of slot filling with the Snips dataset. 'Input' is the input utterance, and 'Baseline Pred.' is the slot filling result of the baseline model. 'Proposed pred.' is the result of applying the proposed method and is the ground truth. Unknown words are represented as italicized text. The slot filling errors are marked with underline and instances of correct slot filling are represented in bold text.

5   Conclusion

This paper focuses on data augmentation by reflecting the characteristics of 'open-vocabulary' slot in order to achieve better SLU. The experiments show that the proposed method outperforms the baseline, especially with datasets that include more 'open-vocabulary' slots. The proposed method has the following three advantages. Data augmentation can be performed during training. It does not need additional memory because it utilizes the input embedding space. It is straightforward and intuitive; hence, it can be easily applied to any model. In this paper, we added noise in all slots without classifying types of slots, i.e., without determining whether they were open-vocabulary slots. In our future work, we will perform additional experiments by classifying the types of slots and adding noise depending on the types. In addition, we plan to apply this method to Named Entity Recognition because it also has the problem of 'open-vocabulary' tags.

Acknowledgments

This work was supported by Institute of Information & Communications Technology Planning & Evaluation(IITP) grant funded by the Korea government(MSIT) (2019-0-0004, Development of semi-supervised learning language intelligence technology and Korean tutoring service for foreigners).

References

Samuel R Bowman, Luke Vilnis, Oriol Vinyals, Andrew M Dai, Rafal Jozefowicz, and Samy Bengio. 2015. Generating sentences from a continuous space. In *Proceedings of the 20th SIGNLL Conference on Computational Natural Language Learning (CoNLL)*, pages 10–21.

Yong Cheng, Zhaopeng Tu, Fandong Meng, Junjie Zhai, and Yang Liu. 2018. Towards robust neural machine translation. In *Proceedings of the 56th Annual Meeting of the Association for Computational Linguistics (ACL)*, pages 1756–1766.

Chih-Wen Goo, Guang Gao, Yun-Kai Hsu, and Chih-Li Huo. 2018. Slot-gated modeling for joint slot filling and intent prediction. In *Proceedings of the 2018 Conference of the North American Chapter of the Association for Computational Linguistics: Human Language Technologies (NAACL-HLT)*, pages 753–757.

Charles T Hemphill, John J Godfrey, and George R Doddington. 1990. The atis spoken language systems pilot corpus. In *Proceedings of the DARPA speech and natural language workshop*, pages 96–101.

Yutai Hou, Yijia Liu, Wanxiang Che, and Ting Liu. 2018. Sequence-to-sequence data augmentation for dialogue language understanding. In *Proceedings of the 27th International Conference on Computational Linguistics (COLING)*, page 1234–1245.

Mohit Iyyer, Varun Manjunatha, Jordan Boyd-Graber, and Hal Daumé III. 2015. Deep unordered composition rivals syntactic methods for text classification. In *Proceedings of the 53rd Annual Meeting of the Association for Computational Linguistics (ACL) and the 7th International Joint Conference on Natural Language Processing (IJCNLP)*, pages 1681–1691.

Jun-Seong Kim, Junghoe Kim, SeungUn Park, Kwangyong Lee, and Yoonju Lee. 2018. Modeling with recurrent neural networks for open vocabulary slots. In *Proceedings of the 27th International Conference on Computational Linguistics (COLING)*, pages 2778–2790.

Diederik P Kingma and Jimmy Ba. 2015. Adam: A method for stochastic optimization. In *Proceedings of International Conference on Learning Representations (ICLR)*.

Sosuke Kobayashi. 2018. Contextual augmentation: Data augmentation by words with paradigmatic relations. In *Proceedings of the 2018 Conference of the North American Chapter of the Association for Computational Linguistics: Human Language Technologies (NAACL-HLT)*, pages 452–457.

Ankit Kumar, Ozan Irsoy, Peter Ondruska, Mohit Iyyer, James Bradbury, Ishaan Gulrajani, Victor Zhong, Romain Paulus, and Richard Socher. 2016. Ask me anything: Dynamic memory networks for natural language processing. In *Proceedings of the 33rd International Conference on Machine Learning (ICML)*, pages 1378–1387.

Gakuto Kurata, Bing Xiang, and Bowen Zhou. 2016. Labeled data generation with encoder-decoder lstm for semantic slot filling. In *Proceedings of INTER-SPEECH 2016*, pages 725–729.

Bing Liu and Ian Lane. 2016. Attention-based recurrent neural network models for joint intent detection and slot filling. In *Proceedings of INTERSPEECH 2016*, pages 685–689.

Grégoire Mesnil, Yann Dauphin, Kaisheng Yao, Yoshua Bengio, Li Deng, Dilek Hakkani-Tur, Xiaodong He, Larry Heck, Gokhan Tur, Dong Yu, et al. 2015. Using recurrent neural networks for slot filling in spoken language understanding. *IEEE/ACM Transactions on Audio, Speech, and Language Processing*, pages 530–539.

Ngoc Thang Vu. 2016. Sequential convolutional neural networks for slot filling in spoken language understanding. In *Proceedings of INTERSPEECH 2016*, pages 3250–3254.

Yu Wang, Yilin Shen, and Hongxia Jin. 2018. A bi-model based rnn semantic frame parsing model for intent detection and slot filling. In *Proceedings of the 2018 Conference of the North American Chapter of the Association for Computational Linguistics: Human Language Technologies (NAACL-HLT)*, pages 309–314.

Ziang Xie, Sida I Wang, Jiwei Li, Daniel Lévy, Aiming Nie, Dan Jurafsky, and Andrew Y Ng. 2017. Data noising as smoothing in neural network language models. In *Proceedings of International Conference on Learning Representations (ICLR)*.

Puyang Xu and Ruhi Sarikaya. 2013. Convolutional neural network based triangular crf for joint intent detection and slot filling. In *Proceedings of 2013 IEEE Workshop on Automatic Speech Recognition and Understanding (ASRU)*, pages 78–83.

Kang Min Yoo, Youhyun Shin, and Sang-goo Lee. 2018. Data augmentation for spoken language understanding via joint variational generation. In *arXiv preprint arXiv:1809.02305*.

Xiaodong Zhang and Houfeng Wang. 2016. A joint model of intent determination and slot filling for spoken language understanding. In *Proceedings of the 25th International Joint Conference on Artificial Intelligence (IJCAI)*, pages 2993–2999.

Expectation and Locality Effects in the Prediction of Disfluent Fillers and Repairs in English Speech

Samvit Dammalapati
IIT Delhi
samvit1998@gmail.com

Rajakrishnan Rajkumar
IISER Bhopal
rajak@iiserb.ac.in

Sumeet Agarwal
IIT Delhi
sumeet@iitd.ac.in

Abstract

This study examines the role of three influential theories of language processing, *viz.*, Surprisal Theory, Uniform Information Density (UID) hypothesis and Dependency Locality Theory (DLT), in predicting disfluencies in speech production. To this end, we incorporate features based on lexical surprisal, word duration and DLT integration and storage costs into logistic regression classifiers aimed to predict disfluencies in the Switchboard corpus of English conversational speech. We find that disfluencies occur in the face of upcoming difficulties and speakers tend to handle this by lessening cognitive load before disfluencies occur. Further, we see that reparandums behave differently from disfluent fillers possibly due to the lessening of the cognitive load also happening in the word choice of the reparandum, i.e., in the disfluency itself. While the UID hypothesis does not seem to play a significant role in disfluency prediction, lexical surprisal and DLT costs do give promising results in explaining language production. Further, we also find that as a means to lessen cognitive load for upcoming difficulties speakers take more time on words preceding disfluencies, making duration a key element in understanding disfluencies.

1 Introduction

In contrast to written text which can be rewritten or edited, speech happens spontaneously making it more prone to mistakes. Speakers tend not to speak fluently and take pauses or even repeat words. Such errors where speakers interrupt their flow of speech are known as disfluencies. One of the primary reasons for speech disfluencies is difficulties in language production (Tree and Clark, 1997; Clark and Wasow, 1998). In this study, we aim to understand the role of disfluencies and classify disfluencies into two categories namely, disfluent fillers and reparandums. Disfluent fillers are utterances like *uh*, *um* which break fluency by interjecting and creating an interruption between words. For example, suppose a speaker says "thinking about the *uh* day when I". Here, there is a break of fluency between the words *the* and *day* due to the interjection of the filler *uh*. Reparandums involve cases where speakers break fluency by making corrections in their speech. For example, when a speaker says "Go *to the righ-* to the left". Here, the speaker makes a correction to *to the righ-* by restarting with the intended (corrected) speech *to the left*. We call the words to be corrected as the reparandum (*to the righ-*) and the correction the speaker follows with as the repair (*to the left*).

In order to study disfluencies, we use transcribed data from the Switchboard corpus (Godfrey et al., 1992), a corpus of fully spontaneous speech of American English. We focus on testing the role of three influential linguistic theories, *viz.*, Surprisal Theory (Levy, 2008; Hale, 2001), Uniform Information Density (UID) hypothesis (Jaeger and Levy, 2007) and Dependency Locality Theory (Gibson, 2000) in accounting for disfluencies. Surprisal Theory defines an information-theoretic measure of comprehension difficulty *viz.*, surprisal. Recently, Demberg et al. (2012) showed that syntactic surprisal is a significant predictor of word duration in spontaneous speech even amidst the presence of competing controls like lexical frequency. Thus surprisal can be used to model language production as well, with words with high surprisal associated with speech disfluencies *i.e.*, fillers and repairs. The UID hypothesis predicts that in language production, speakers prefer to minimize variation of information density (mathematically same as surprisal) across the speech signal. Thus based on the UID hypothesis, it is plausible to assume that disfluencies are associated with higher informa-

Proceedings of the 2019 Conference of the North American Chapter of the Association for Computational Linguistics: Student Research Workshop, pages 103–109
Minneapolis, Minnesota, June 3 - 5, 2019. ©2017 Association for Computational Linguistics

tion density variation. Finally, DLT posits integration and storage costs as measures of comprehension difficulty. Scontras et al. (2015) showed that for English relative clause production, locality results in greater speech disfluencies and starting time for object relatives compared to subject relatives. Thus, we conceive higher values of integration and storage costs leading to disfluencies in language production.

We predict disfluencies in the Switchboard corpus using a one-vs-all logistic regression classifier containing features based on lexical surprisal, UID, DLT-inspired costs and duration. Further, by looking into the classifier's regression weights and accuracies, we get an insight behind how these theories affect disfluencies in speech. Our results do not uncover evidence to indicate UID hypothesis plays a significant role in disfluency prediction; however, lexical surprisal and DLT costs do give promising results in explaining language production. The latter two theories indicate that disfluencies tend to be followed with upcoming difficulties and speakers lower cognitive load on words preceding these disfluencies to ease this difficulty. Apart from these three theories, we look into how duration behaves in disfluent contexts and find that speakers take more time in words preceding disfluencies which we explain as a means to lower cognitive load for upcoming difficulties by buying more processing time. Further, we see that reparandums do not occur prior to words with lower surprisal like in the case of disfluent fillers. This effect may be due to the lessening of the cognitive load also happening in the word choice of the reparandum, i.e., in the disfluency itself.

2   Background

In the context of disfluency detection, disfluent fillers tend to be easier to identify as they mostly consist of a closed set of fixed utterances (e.g. *um*, *uh*). Reparandums on the other hand are more difficult to identify because they tend to resemble fluent words a lot more. One of the effective feature types for detecting these reparandums are distance and pattern matching based features that look into the similarity of words and POS tags with their neighbours (Honnibal and Johnson, 2014; Zayats et al., 2014, 2016; Wang et al., 2017). The reason for their effectiveness could stem from how the repair that follows the reparandum is usually a "rough copy" of the reparandum, i.e., it incorpo-

rates the same or very similar words in roughly the same word order as the reparandum. Apart from this, disfluency detection has also been shown to be effective with other features like language models and lexical features (Zwarts and Johnson, 2011; Zayats et al., 2016); prosody (Shriberg et al., 1997; Kahn et al., 2005; Tran et al., 2017) and dependency based features (Honnibal and Johnson, 2014).

Seeing how disfluency detection in the past has collected features from lexical language models, dependency grammar and prosody, we are motivated to test influential linguistic theories in these domains and study whether disfluencies can be explained by these theories, *viz.*, Surprisal Theory (Levy, 2008), the UID hypothesis (Jaeger and Levy, 2007) and DLT (Gibson, 2000). Further, to examine the effects of prosody we look into duration as a feature to explain disfluencies.

Building on Shannon's (1948) definition of information, it has been shown in recent work formalized as Surprisal Theory (Hale, 2001; Levy, 2008) that the information content of a word is a measure of human sentence comprehension difficulty. The surprisal of a word is defined as the negative log of its conditional probability in a given context (either lexical or syntactic). The second theory we examine, the Uniform Information Density (henceforth UID) hypothesis also relates to information density and states that language production exhibits a preference for distributing information uniformly across a linguistic signal. Our third theory is the Dependency Locality Theory (henceforth DLT) proposed by Gibson (2000). This theory defines processing costs that have successfully accounted for the comprehension difficulty associated with many constructions (subject and object relative clauses for example).

3   Experiments and Results

Our study focuses on 3 classes of words in the Switchboard corpus: reparandum, disfluent filler and fluent word. We use the corpus provided by the switchboard NXT project (Calhoun et al., 2010) and base our features for machine learning from the fluent words that immediately follow or precede these disfluencies (for reparandum based disfluencies, these are taken as the words that immediately follow repair and precede the reparandum), this was done out of uniformity as disfluencies such as a disfluent filler *uh* do not posses the

Features	Accuracy	Fluent	Filler	Repar.
Baseline	37.18%			
Preceding surprisal**	38.12%	0.014	-0.0664	0.0525
Following surprisal**	38.78%	-0.1204	0.0915	0.0389
Both surprisals**	40.02%			

Table 1: Accuracy and weights for lexical surprisal. Here * denotes p-value < 0.05 and ** denotes p-value < 0.01 for McNemar's test relative to the baseline.

same linguistic features as fluent words. All the cases where the surrounding words have unclear POS tags or non-aligned duration have been excluded from this dataset. This results in a total of 14923 cases of reparandum, 12183 cases of disfluent filler and 558361 cases of a fluent word. For uniformity in classes we randomly sample 12183 cases from each class. We setup a one-vs-all logistic regression classifier to classify between our 3 categories. To set up a baseline performance for this multi-classification, we train the classifier on features pertaining to the speaker and listener particularly the gender, age and rate of speech. The change in accuracy relative to the baseline on adding features, *viz.*, lexical surprisal, UID, DLT costs and duration, tells us whether these theories explain the presence of disfluent contexts. Further, using the regression weights we look at whether the correlations are indeed as the theory expects. The next three subsections will describe these results in depth.

3.1 Lexical Surprisal

We deploy lexical surprisal as measure of predicting disfluencies. We use the definition proposed by Hale (2001) which states that the lexical surprisal of the kth word w_k in a sentence is $S_k = -logP(w_k \mid w_{k-1}, w_{k-2})$. Where $P(w_k \mid w_{k-1}, w_{k-2})$ refers to the conditional probability of kth word in the sentence given the previous two words. We calculate lexical surprisal of each word in our corpus by training a simple trigram model over words on the Open American National Corpus (Ide and Suderman, 2004) using the SRILM toolkit (Stolcke, 2002). The lexical surprisal feature of the surrounding words turns out to be significant with a p-value < 0.05 and we can note from Table 1 that these classifiers with surprisal give a significant improvement from baseline (McNemar's test). Further, using surprisal of the word following the disfluency gives a 1.6% boost in accuracy and the regression coefficients from Table 1 indicate that the words that follow disfluencies (this would be the word following the repair in

the case of reparandums) show a higher surprisal, suggesting that disfluencies occur in the presence of an upcoming difficulty. Previous studies have shown similar results that disfluencies occur in the presence of production difficulties due to new information (Arnold et al., 2000; Barr, 2001; Arnold et al., 2003; Heller et al., 2015). Examples from the corpus illustrated such a behaviour where disfluent sentences such as *"for the **uh** scud missiles"* or *"imagine **thats a - thats a** pillsbury plant?"* have high surprisal difficulties like scud or pillsbury following the disfluency.

We also note that lexical surprisal of the word preceding the disfluency leads to an accuracy increase of 0.94%. There is a low surprisal of the preceding words in the case of disfluent fillers, as seen from Table 1, suggestive that speakers use easier words (lesser cognitive load due to low surprisal) to handle the production problems better. However, the other type of disfluency, reparandum shows a higher preceding surprisal which might be attributed to the fact that unlike fillers, reparandums consist of words in themselves and these words may be the ones that hold the low surprisal rather than the preceding word to the reparandum.

3.2 Uniform Information Density (UID)

In order to quantify the uniformity in information density spread, we use two types of UID measures proposed in previous works by Collins (2014) and Jain et al. (2018). The two measures are as follows:

- $UIDglob = \frac{-1}{N} \sum_{i=1}^{N} (id_i - \mu)^2$

- $UIDglobNorm = \frac{-1}{N} \sum_{i=1}^{N} (\frac{id_i}{\mu} - 1)^2$

Here, N is the number of words in the sentence, id_i refers to the information density, i.e., lexical surprisal of ith word and μ is the average information density of the sentence. We note from the equation above that the uniformity measure, UIDglob is defined as the negative of variance of lexical surprisal. Further, our second measure UIDglobNorm is nothing but the normalized version of the first measure UIDglob.

We calculate the UID measures for the surrounding words, i.e., the immediate preceding and following words to the class, and the UID measures for that sentence. From the accuracies that are listed in Table 2, we can see that the best accuracy is an increase of 0.42% from UIDglob of the

Features	Accuracy
Baseline	37.18%
UIDglob surrounding	37.22%
UIDglob sentence*	37.60%
UIDglob both*	37.49%
UIDglobNorm surrounding	37.31%
UIDglobNorm sentence*	36.94%
UIDglobNorm both*	37.28%

Table 2: Accuracy for UID measures.

Features	Accuracy	Fluent	Filler	Repar.
Baseline	37.18%			
Preceding IC**	37.65%	0.0042	-0.0069	0.0027
Following IC**	39.06%	-0.0334	-0.0375	0.0709
Preceding SC**	39.48%	0.2895	-0.0575	-0.232
Following SC**	37.56%	-0.1731	0.0098	0.1633
Both ICs**	39.18%			
Both SCs**	41.61%			
Both ICs and SCs**	48.57%			

Table 3: Accuracy and weights for DLT costs.

sentence. However, this UIDglob measure for sentence when normalized (UIDglobNorm) shows a net decrease in accuracy. Though these UID measures on the sentence are significant features with a p-value < 0.05, the UID measures on the surrounding words are not. Further, these improvements in accuracy upon using sentence level UID features are significant (McNemar's test) only with p-value 0.05 but not with 0.01. We see that the UID measure for the surrounding words causes an increase of 0.13% which is far less compared to the increase in preceding (0.94%) and following (1.6%) surprisal noted earlier. The UID hypothesis we've examined has hence failed to bring about any notable improvements in our model in comparison to competing explanations like surprisal theory. It may also be possible that the UID hypothesis is limited only to syntactic reduction in English (Jaeger and Levy, 2007). Previous work by Jain et al. (2018) in Hindi word order choices has shown that the UID measures does not outperform lexical surprisal.

3.3 DLT: Integration and Storage Costs

The central notion of DLT revolves around two costs: integration cost (IC) and storage cost (SC) as proposed by Gibson (2000). We compute DLT costs as follows: For a word to be integrated into the structure built so far, its integration cost, a backward-looking cost, would be the sum of the dependency lengths of all dependencies that include the word to be integrated and its previously encountered head/dependent word (grammatical link provided by dependency grammar). In contrast, the storage cost is a forward-looking cost and corresponds to the number of incomplete dependencies in our integrated structure thus far. To calculate these costs, the dependency relations for our corpus were extracted by removing disfluencies from the constituency-based parse trees and converting these trees into dependency graphs using the Stanford parser (De Marneffe et al.). Our theory of DLT makes use of these dependency

parses and in this way is inspired from the original DLT that makes use of constituency parsing. We see from the McNemar's test (Table 3) that the increase in accuracy for DLT costs are all significant improvements w.r.t baseline. The integration costs and storage costs, all significant features with p-value < 0.05, give an increase of 2% and 4.43% individually (from Table 3). Further, combining all these four features gives a far larger increase of 11.39% from the baseline. This can indeed be explained as the two costs serve complementary functions (can be seen from their negative correlation of -0.26) as forward and backing looking costs, and a combination would possess greater information on the whole. We see that DLT seems to perform well for our disfluency prediction task and so we will proceed to examining the correlations of the DLT costs in disfluent contexts.

From Table 3 we see that following integration cost is expectantly high for reparandum based disfluencies but contrarily is lower in the context of disfluent fillers which goes against the expectation of an upcoming difficulty in the case of disfluencies. Recent work by Demberg and Keller (2008) has shown integration cost to behave anomalous and act in the expected direction only for high values of dependency length. With preceding word's integration cost getting lowered in the context of disfluent fillers and higher in the context of reparandums, we can see that apart from the anomalous result for following integration cost in fillers, integration cost functions gets explained similar to lexical surprisal. We also see that disfluencies, i.e., both disfluent fillers and reparandums have a lower preceding storage cost and higher following storage cost. This makes sense as a lower preceding storage cost lowers the cognitive load and helps process the upcoming difficulty better (indicated by high following storage cost).

3.4 Duration

Looking into how duration affects disfluencies, from Table 4, we can note that the duration of the preceding word gives a huge accuracy increase of

Features	Accuracy	Fluent	Filler	Repar.
Baseline	37.18%			
Preceding duration**	46.82%	-2.9315	2.7944	0.1371
Following duration**	37.71%	-0.4512	0.0046	0.4466
Both durations**	46.89%			

Table 4: Accuracy and weights for duration features.

9.64% from baseline. From McNemar's test it is indicated that the increase in accuracy from using duration features w.r.t baseline are all significant. The duration features are also significant features with p-value < 0.05 and are higher in the context of disfluencies as can be seen from the regression weights in Table 4. These results are in concert with Bell et al's (2003) study of duration in disfluent contexts. The higher duration of words preceding disfluencies suggests that speakers try to buy time in order to better process for the upcoming production difficulties that follow these disfluencies.

3.5 Correlations between features

We observe that the maximum correlation from the feature correlations is between duration and surprisal. This positive correlation of 0.49 between surprisal and duration can be expected as higher information density for a word would take the speaker a longer duration to process. Given the performance of duration in disfluency prediction, this correlation could also explain the significant performance of disfluency prediction with surprisal. Further, recent work by Demberg et al. (2012) has shown how syntactic surprisal is a significant predictor of word duration. This is suggestive of the fact that surprisal can possibly be used to model language production, despite being an information-theoretic measure of comprehension difficulty. For further correlation values between features refer to Table 1 in Appendix A.

4 Discussion

Our results indicate that disfluencies occur when speaker has upcoming difficulties, as evinced from high storage cost and lexical surprisal at words following disfluencies. Speakers also seem to want to lower their cognitive load before disfluencies to help in planning, as suggested by low values of duration, storage cost, surprisal and integration cost on the preceding word. Ease of production is often

attributed to ease of retrieval of words from memory. More accessible words (more salience, more predictability) are known to be easier to retrieve compared words with low accessibility. Since surprisal quantifies contextual predictability, the low surprisal prior to fillers indicate the ease of retrievability of words prior to fillers. Though words preceding reparandums do not show a lowering in surprisal and integration cost, it could be attributed to the fact that reparandums in itself consists of words, which may be the ones that hold low surprisal or integration costs, rather than the word preceding to the reparandum. This difference in the context of fillers and reparandums indicates the presence of distinct memory operations in language production.

DLT-based costs hitherto used to explain language comprehension gave the best increase in accuracy to 48.57%, showing it has promise in explaining language production too. We did however note that the integration costs behaved in contrary directions, and so further detailed research is needed. The anomalous DLT effects need to be investigated more thoroughly in future work. In the comprehension literature Vasishth and Lewis (2006) proffer a unified explanation for both locality and anti-locality effects in Hindi verb-final constructions by resorting to either decay or interference (on account of similar intervening words) at a verbal head while integrating a previously encountered argument head. In a survey of dependency distance, Liu et al. (2017) state that long dependencies might not be difficult to process due to the presence of mitigating factors like frequency, contextual familiarity and positional salience.

Given that DLT costs bring about a large increase in accuracy, incorporating other syntax-based features like syntactic surprisal and UID (based on syntactic surprisal) might confer further insights on the role of syntax in disfluency prediction and language production. Despite seeing how DLT, duration and lexical surprisal behave individually, we have not as such compared these features against each other and studied if they account for explaining same parts of the data. We leave these steps for future work. Our modelling presupposes linear dependence between individual predictors. In future inquiries we plan to use other non-linear classifiers like decision trees and KNN models.

[0]We thank the anonymous reviewers, Micha Elsner and Sidharth Ranjan for insightful comments and feedback.

References

Jennifer E Arnold, Maria Fagnano, and Michael K Tanenhaus. 2003. Disfluencies signal theee, um, new information. *Journal of psycholinguistic research*, 32(1):25–36.

Jennifer E Arnold, Anthony Losongco, Thomas Wasow, and Ryan Ginstrom. 2000. Heaviness vs. newness: The effects of structural complexity and discourse status on constituent ordering. *Language*, 76(1):28–55.

Dale J Barr. 2001. Trouble in mind: Paralinguistic indices of effort and uncertainty in communication. *Oralité et gestualité: Interactions et comportements multimodaux dans la communication*, pages 597–600.

Alan Bell, Daniel Jurafsky, Eric Fosler-Lussier, Cynthia Girand, Michelle Gregory, and Daniel Gildea. 2003. Effects of disfluencies, predictability, and utterance position on word form variation in english conversation. *The Journal of the Acoustical Society of America*, 113(2):1001–1024.

Sasha Calhoun, Jean Carletta, Jason M Brenier, Neil Mayo, Dan Jurafsky, Mark Steedman, and David Beaver. 2010. The nxt-format switchboard corpus: a rich resource for investigating the syntax, semantics, pragmatics and prosody of dialogue. *Language resources and evaluation*, 44(4):387–419.

Herbert H Clark and Thomas Wasow. 1998. Repeating words in spontaneous speech. *Cognitive psychology*, 37(3):201–242.

Michael Xavier Collins. 2014. Information density and dependency length as complementary cognitive models. *Journal of psycholinguistic research*, 43(5):651–681.

Marie-Catherine De Marneffe, Bill MacCartney, Christopher D Manning, et al. Generating typed dependency parses from phrase structure parses.

Vera Demberg and Frank Keller. 2008. Data from eye-tracking corpora as evidence for theories of syntactic processing complexity. *Cognition*, 109(2):193–210.

Vera Demberg, Asad B. Sayeed, Philip J. Gorinski, and Nikolaos Engonopoulos. 2012. Syntactic surprisal affects spoken word duration in conversational contexts. In *Proceedings of the 2012 Joint Conference on Empirical Methods in Natural Language Processing and Computational Natural Language Learning*, EMNLP-CoNLL '12, pages 356–367, Stroudsburg, PA, USA. Association for Computational Linguistics.

Edward Gibson. 2000. The dependency locality theory: A distance-based theory of linguistic complexity. *Image, language, brain*, pages 95–126.

J. J. Godfrey, E. C. Holliman, and J. McDaniel. 1992. Switchboard: telephone speech corpus for research and development. In *[Proceedings] ICASSP-92: 1992 IEEE International Conference on Acoustics, Speech, and Signal Processing*, volume 1, pages 517–520 vol.1.

John Hale. 2001. A probabilistic earley parser as a psycholinguistic model. In *Proceedings of the second meeting of the North American Chapter of the Association for Computational Linguistics on Language technologies*, pages 1–8. Association for Computational Linguistics.

Daphna Heller, Jennifer E Arnold, Natalie Klein, and Michael K Tanenhaus. 2015. Inferring difficulty: Flexibility in the real-time processing of disfluency. *Language and speech*, 58(2):190–203.

Matthew Honnibal and Mark Johnson. 2014. Joint incremental disfluency detection and dependency parsing. *Transactions of the Association for Computational Linguistics*, 2:131–142.

Nancy Ide and Keith Suderman. 2004. The american national corpus first release. In *LREC*.

T Florian Jaeger and Roger P Levy. 2007. Speakers optimize information density through syntactic reduction. In *Advances in neural information processing systems*, pages 849–856.

Ayush Jain, Vishal Singh, Sidharth Ranjan, Rajakrishnan Rajkumar, and Sumeet Agarwal. 2018. Uniform information density effects on syntactic choice in hindi. In *Proceedings of the Workshop on Linguistic Complexity and Natural Language Processing*, pages 38–48.

Jeremy G Kahn, Matthew Lease, Eugene Charniak, Mark Johnson, and Mari Ostendorf. 2005. Effective use of prosody in parsing conversational speech. In *Proceedings of the conference on human language technology and empirical methods in natural language processing*, pages 233–240. Association for Computational Linguistics.

Roger Levy. 2008. Expectation-based syntactic comprehension. *Cognition*, 106(3):1126–1177.

Haitao Liu, Chunshan Xu, and Junying Liang. 2017. Dependency distance: A new perspective on syntactic patterns in natural languages. *Physics of Life Reviews*, 21:171 – 193.

Gregory Scontras, William Badecker, Lisa Shank, Eunice Lim, and Evelina Fedorenko. 2015. Syntactic complexity effects in sentence production. *Cognitive Science*, 39(3):559–583.

Claude Elwood Shannon. 1948. A mathematical theory of communication. *Bell system technical journal*, 27(3):379–423.

Elizabeth Shriberg, Rebecca Bates, and Andreas Stolcke. 1997. A prosody only decision-tree model for disfluency detection. In *Fifth European Conference on Speech Communication and Technology*.

Andreas Stolcke. 2002. Srilm-an extensible language modeling toolkit. In *Seventh international conference on spoken language processing*.

Trang Tran, Shubham Toshniwal, Mohit Bansal, Kevin Gimpel, Karen Livescu, and Mari Ostendorf. 2017. Parsing speech: a neural approach to integrating lexical and acoustic-prosodic information. *arXiv preprint arXiv:1704.07287*.

Jean E Fox Tree and Herbert H Clark. 1997. Pronouncing the as thee to signal problems in speaking. *Cognition*, 62(2):151–167.

Shravan Vasishth and Richard L. Lewis. 2006. Argument-head distance and processing complexity: Explaining both locality and antilocality effects. *Language*, 82(4):767–794.

Shaolei Wang, Wanxiang Che, Yue Zhang, Meishan Zhang, and Ting Liu. 2017. Transition-based disfluency detection using lstms. In *Proceedings of the 2017 Conference on Empirical Methods in Natural Language Processing*, pages 2785–2794.

Vicky Zayats, Mari Ostendorf, and Hannaneh Hajishirzi. 2016. Disfluency detection using a bidirectional lstm. *arXiv preprint arXiv:1604.03209*.

Victoria Zayats, Mari Ostendorf, and Hannaneh Hajishirzi. 2014. Multi-domain disfluency and repair detection. In *Fifteenth Annual Conference of the International Speech Communication Association*.

Simon Zwarts and Mark Johnson. 2011. The impact of language models and loss functions on repair disfluency detection. In *Proceedings of the 49th Annual Meeting of the Association for Computational Linguistics: Human Language Technologies-Volume 1*, pages 703–711. Association for Computational Linguistics.

Gating Mechanisms for Combining Character and Word-level Word Representations: An Empirical Study

Jorge A. Balazs and **Yutaka Matsuo**
Graduate School of Engineering
The University of Tokyo
{jorge, matsuo}@weblab.t.u-tokyo.ac.jp

Abstract

In this paper we study how different ways of combining character and word-level representations affect the quality of both final word and sentence representations. We provide strong empirical evidence that modeling characters improves the learned representations at the word and sentence levels, and that doing so is particularly useful when representing less frequent words. We further show that a feature-wise sigmoid gating mechanism is a robust method for creating representations that encode semantic similarity, as it performed reasonably well in several word similarity datasets. Finally, our findings suggest that properly capturing semantic similarity at the word level does not consistently yield improved performance in downstream sentence-level tasks. Our code is available at `https://github.com/jabalazs/gating`.

1 Introduction

Incorporating sub-word structures like substrings, morphemes and characters to the creation of word representations significantly increases their quality as reflected both by intrinsic metrics and performance in a wide range of downstream tasks (Bojanowski et al., 2017; Luong and Manning, 2016; Wu et al., 2016; Ling et al., 2015).

The reason for this improvement is related to sub-word structures containing information that is usually ignored by standard word-level models. Indeed, when representing words as vectors extracted from a lookup table, semantically related words resulting from inflectional processes such as *surf*, *surfing*, and *surfed*, are treated as being independent from one another[1]. Further, word-level embeddings do not account for derivational

processes resulting in syntactically-similar words with different meanings such as *break*, *breakable*, and *unbreakable*. This causes derived words, which are usually less frequent, to have lower-quality (or no) vector representations.

Previous works have successfully combined character-level and word-level word representations, obtaining overall better results than using only word-level representations. For example Luong and Manning (2016) achieved state-of-the-art results in a machine translation task by representing unknown words as a composition of their characters. Botha and Blunsom (2014) created word representations by adding the vector representations of the words' surface forms and their morphemes ($\overrightarrow{perfectly} = \overrightarrow{perfectly} + \overrightarrow{perfect} + \overrightarrow{ly}$), obtaining significant improvements on intrinsic evaluation tasks, word similarity and machine translation. Lample et al. (2016) concatenated character-level and word-level representations for creating word representations, and then used them as input to their models for obtaining state-of-the-art results in Named Entity Recognition on several languages.

What these works have in common is that the models they describe first learn how to represent subword information, at character (Luong and Manning, 2016), morpheme (Botha and Blunsom, 2014), or substring (Bojanowski et al., 2017) levels, and then combine these learned representations at the word level. The incorporation of information at a finer-grained hierarchy results in higher-quality modeling of rare words, morphological processes, and semantics (Avraham and Goldberg, 2017).

There is no consensus, however, on which combination method works better in which case, or how the choice of a combination method affects downstream performance, either measured intrinsically at the word level, or extrinsically at the sen-

---

[1] Unless using pre-trained embeddings with a notion of subword information such as `fastText` (Bojanowski et al., 2017)

Proceedings of the 2019 Conference of the North American Chapter of the Association for Computational Linguistics: Student Research Workshop, pages 110–124
Minneapolis, Minnesota, June 3 - 5, 2019. ©2017 Association for Computational Linguistics

tence level.

In this paper we aim to provide some intuitions about how the choice of mechanism for combining character-level with word-level representations influences the quality of the final word representations, and the subsequent effect these have in the performance of downstream tasks. Our contributions are as follows:

- We show that a feature-wise sigmoidal gating mechanism is the best at combining representations at the character and word-level hierarchies, as measured by word similarity tasks.

- We provide evidence that this mechanism learns that to properly model increasingly infrequent words, it has to increasingly rely on character-level information.

- We finally show that despite the increased expressivity of word representations it offers, it has no clear effect in sentence representations, as measured by sentence evaluation tasks.

2 Background

We are interested in studying different ways of combining word representations, obtained from different hierarchies, into a single word representation. Specifically, we want to study how combining word representations (1) taken directly from a word embedding lookup table, and (2) obtained from a function over the characters composing them, affects the quality of the final word representations.

Let $\mathcal{W}$ be a set, or vocabulary, of words with $|\mathcal{W}|$ elements, and $\mathcal{C}$ a vocabulary of characters with $|\mathcal{C}|$ elements. Further, let $x = w_1, \ldots, w_n; \; w_i \in \mathcal{W}$ be a sequence of words, and $c^i = c^i_1, \ldots, c^i_m; \; c^i_j \in \mathcal{C}$ be the sequence of characters composing w_i. Each token w_i can be represented as a vector $v^{(w)}_i \in \mathbb{R}^d$ extracted directly from an embedding lookup table $E^{(w)} \in \mathbb{R}^{|\mathcal{W}| \times d}$, pre-trained or otherwise, and as a vector $v^{(c)}_i \in \mathbb{R}^d$ built from the characters that compose it; in other words, $v^{(c)}_i = f(c^i)$, where f is a function that maps a sequence of characters to a vector.

The methods for combining word and character-level representations we study, are of the form $G(v^{(w)}_i, v^{(c)}_i) = v_i$ where v_i is the final word representation.

2.1 Mapping Characters to Character-level Word Representations

The function f is composed of an *embedding* layer, an optional *context* function, and an *aggregation* function.

The **embedding layer** transforms each character c^i_j into a vector r^i_j of dimension d_r, by directly taking it from a trainable embedding lookup table $E^{(c)} \in \mathbb{R}^{|\mathcal{C}| \times d_r}$. We define the *matrix* representation of word w_i as $C^i = [r^i_1, \ldots, r^i_m], \; C^i \in \mathbb{R}^{m \times d_r}$.

The **context function** takes C^i as input and returns a context-enriched matrix representation $H^i = [h^i_1, \ldots, h^i_m], \; H^i \in \mathbb{R}^{m \times d_h}$, in which each h^i_j contains a measure of information about its context, and interactions with its neighbors. In particular, we chose to do this by feeding C^i to a Bidirectional LSTM (BiLSTM) (Graves and Schmidhuber, 2005; Graves et al., 2013)[2].

Informally, we can think of a Long Short-Term Memory Network (LSTM) (Hochreiter and Schmidhuber, 1997) as a function $\mathbb{R}^{m \times d_r} \rightarrow \mathbb{R}^{m \times d_h}$ that takes a matrix $C = [r_1, \ldots, r_m]$ as input and returns a context-enriched matrix representation $H = [h_1, \ldots, h_m]$, where each h_j encodes information about the previous elements $h_1, \ldots, h_{j-1}$[3].

A BiLSTM is simply composed of 2 LSTMs, one that reads the input from left to right (forward), and another that does so from right to left (backward). The output of the forward and backward LSTMs are $\overrightarrow{H} = [\overrightarrow{h}_1, \ldots, \overrightarrow{h}_m]$ and $\overleftarrow{H} = [\overleftarrow{h}_1, \ldots, \overleftarrow{h}_m]$ respectively. In the backward case the LSTM reads r_m first and r_1 last, therefore $\overleftarrow{h}_j$ will encode the context from $\overleftarrow{h}_{j+1}, \ldots, \overleftarrow{h}_m$.

The **aggregation function** takes the context-enriched matrix representation of word w_i for both directions, $\overrightarrow{H^i}$ and $\overleftarrow{H^i}$, and returns a single vector $v^{(c)}_i \in \mathbb{R}^{d_h}$. To do so we followed Miyamoto and Cho (2016), and defined the character-level representation $v^{(c)}_i$ of word w_i as the linear combination of the forward and backward last hidden states re-

---

[2]Other methods for encoding the characters' context, such as CNNs (Kim et al., 2016), could also be used.

[3]In terms of implementation, the LSTM is applied iteratively to each element of the input sequence regardless of dimension m, which means it accepts inputs of variable length, but we will use this notation for the sake of simplicity.

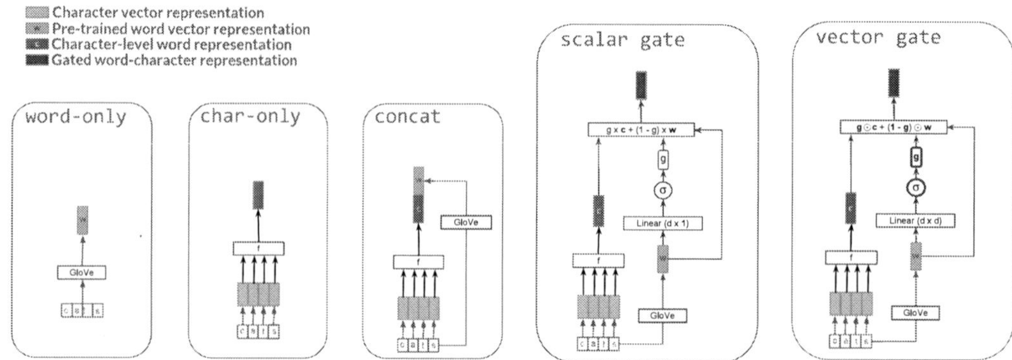

Figure 1: Character and Word-level combination methods.

turned by the context function:

$$v_i^{(c)} = W^{(c)}[\overrightarrow{h^i}_m; \overleftarrow{h^i}_1] + b^{(c)} \qquad (1)$$

where $W^{(c)} \in \mathbb{R}^{d_h \times 2d_h}$ and $b^{(c)} \in \mathbb{R}^{d_h}$ are trainable parameters, and $[\circ; \circ]$ represents the concatenation operation between two vectors.

2.2 Combining Character and Word-level Representations

We tested three different methods for combining $v_i^{(c)}$ with $v_i^{(w)}$: simple concatenation, a learned scalar gate (Miyamoto and Cho, 2016), and a learned vector gate (also referred to as feature-wise sigmoidal gate). Additionally, we compared these methods to two baselines: using pre-trained word vectors only, and using character-only features for representing words. See fig. 1 for a visual description of the proposed methods.

word-only (w) considers only $v_i^{(w)}$ and ignores $v_i^{(c)}$:

$$v_i = v_i^{(w)} \qquad (2)$$

char-only (c) considers only $v_i^{(c)}$ and ignores $v_i^{(w)}$:

$$v_i = v_i^{(c)} \qquad (3)$$

concat (cat) concatenates both word and character-level representations:

$$v_i = [v_i^{(c)}; v_i^{(w)}] \qquad (4)$$

scalar gate (sg) implements the scalar gating mechanism described by Miyamoto and Cho (2016):

$$g_i = \sigma(w^\top v_i^{(w)} + b) \qquad (5)$$

$$v_i = g_i v_i^{(c)} + (1 - g_i)v_i^{(w)} \qquad (6)$$

where $w \in \mathbb{R}^d$ and $b \in \mathbb{R}$ are trainable parameters, $g_i \in (0, 1)$, and σ is the sigmoid function.

vector gate (vg):

$$g_i = \sigma(W v_i^{(w)} + b) \qquad (7)$$

$$v_i = g_i \odot v_i^{(c)} + (1 - g_i) \odot v_i^{(w)} \qquad (8)$$

where $W \in \mathbb{R}^{d \times d}$ and $b \in \mathbb{R}^d$ are trainable parameters, $g_i \in (0, 1)^d$, σ is the element-wise sigmoid function, $\odot$ is the element-wise product for vectors, and $1 \in \mathbb{R}^d$ is a vector of ones.

The vector gate is inspired by Miyamoto and Cho (2016) and Yang et al. (2017), but is different to the former in that the gating mechanism acts upon each dimension of the word and character-level vectors, and different to the latter in that it does not rely on external sources of information for calculating the gating mechanism.

Finally, note that word only and char only are special cases of both gating mechanisms: $g_i = 0$ (scalar gate) and $g_i = 0$ (vector gate) correspond to word only; $g_i = 1$ and $g_i = 1$ correspond to char only.

2.3 Obtaining Sentence Representations

To enable sentence-level classification we need to obtain a sentence representation from the word vectors v_i. We achieved this by using a BiLSTM with max pooling, which was shown to be a good universal sentence encoding mechanism (Conneau et al., 2017).

Let $x = w_1, \ldots, w_n$, be an input sentence and $V = [v_1, \ldots, v_n]$ its matrix representation, where each v_i was obtained by one of the methods described in section 2.2. $S = [s_1, \ldots, s_n]$ is the context-enriched matrix representation of x obtained by feeding V to a BiLSTM of output dimension d_s[4]. Lastly, $s \in \mathbb{R}^{d_s}$ is the final sentence representation of x obtained by max-pooling S along the sequence dimension.

Finally, we initialized the word representations $v_i^{(w)}$ using GloVe embeddings (Pennington et al., 2014), and fine-tuned them during training. Refer to appendix A for details on the other hyperparameters we used.

3 Experiments

3.1 Experimental Setup

We trained our models for solving the Natural Language Inference (NLI) task in two datasets, SNLI (Bowman et al., 2015) and MultiNLI (Williams et al., 2018), and validated them in each corresponding development set (including the matched and mismatched development sets of MultiNLI).

For each dataset-method combination we trained 7 models initialized with different random seeds, and saved each when it reached its best validation accuracy[5]. We then evaluated the quality of each trained model's word representations v_i in 10 word similarity tasks, using the system created by Jastrzebski et al. (2017)[6].

Finally, we fed these obtained word vectors to a BiLSTM with max-pooling and evaluated the final sentence representations in 11 downstream transfer tasks (Conneau et al., 2017; Subramanian et al., 2018).

3.2 Datasets

Word-level Semantic Similarity A desirable property of vector representations of words is that semantically similar words should have similar vector representations. Assessing whether a set of word representations possesses this quality is referred to as the semantic similarity task. This is the most widely-used evaluation method for evaluating word representations, despite its shortcomings (Faruqui et al., 2016).

This task consists of comparing the similarity between word vectors measured by a distance metric (usually cosine distance), with a similarity score obtained from human judgements. High correlation between these similarities is an indicator of good performance.

A problem with this formulation though, is that the definition of "similarity" often confounds the meaning of both *similarity* and *relatedness*. For example, *cup* and *tea* are related but dissimilar words, and this type of distinction is not always clear (Agirre et al., 2009; Hill et al., 2015).

To face the previous problem, we tested our methods in a wide variety of datasets, including some that explicitly model relatedness (WS353R), some that explicitly consider similarity (WS353S, SimLex999, SimVerb3500), and some where the distinction is not clear (MEN, MTurk287, MTurk771, RG, WS353). We also included the RareWords (RW) dataset for evaluating the quality of rare word representations. See appendix B for a more complete description of the datasets we used.

Sentence-level Evaluation Tasks Unlike word-level representations, there is no consensus on the desirable properties sentence representations should have. In response to this, Conneau et al. (2017) created SentEval[7], a sentence representation evaluation benchmark designed for assessing how well sentence representations perform in various downstream tasks (Conneau and Kiela, 2018).

Some of the datasets included in SentEval correspond to sentiment classification (CR, MPQA, MR, SST2, and SST5), subjectivity classification (SUBJ), question-type classification (TREC), recognizing textual entailment (SICK E), estimating semantic relatedness (SICK R), and measuring textual semantic similarity (STS16, STSB). The datasets are described by Conneau et al. (2017), and we provide pointers to their original sources in the appendix table B.2.

To evaluate these sentence representations SentEval trained a linear model on top of them, and evaluated their performance in the validation sets accompanying each dataset. The only exception was the STS16 task, in which our representations were evaluated directly.

4 Word-level Evaluation

4.1 Word Similarity

Table 1 shows the quality of word representations in terms of the correlation between word similarity

---

[4] $s_i = [\overrightarrow{s_i}; \overleftarrow{s_i}]$ for each i, and both $\overrightarrow{s_i}$ and $\overleftarrow{s_i} \in \mathbb{R}^{\frac{d_s}{2}}$.

[5] We found that models validated on the matched development set of MultiNLI, rather than the mismatched, yielded best results, although the differences were not statistically significant.

[6] https://github.com/kudkudak/word-embeddings-benchmarks/tree/8fd0489

[7] https://github.com/facebookresearch/SentEval/tree/906b34a

		MEN	MTurk287	MTurk771	RG65	RW	SimLex999	SimVerb3500	WS353	WS353R	WS353S
SNLI	w	71.78	35.40	49.05	61.80	18.43	19.17	10.32	39.27	28.01	53.42
	c	9.85	-5.65	0.82	-5.28	17.81	0.86	2.76	-2.20	0.20	-3.87
	cat	71.91	**35.52**	48.84	62.12	18.46	19.10	10.21	39.35	28.16	53.40
	sg	70.49	34.49	46.15	59.75	18.24	17.20	8.73	35.86	23.48	50.83
	vg	<u>**80.00**</u>	32.54	**62.09**	**68.90**	**20.76**	**37.70**	**20.45**	**54.72**	**47.24**	**65.60**
MNLI	w	68.76	50.15	68.81	65.83	18.43	42.21	25.18	61.10	58.21	70.17
	c	4.84	0.06	1.95	-0.06	12.18	3.01	1.52	-4.68	-3.63	-3.65
	cat	68.77	50.40	68.77	65.92	18.35	42.22	25.12	61.15	58.26	70.21
	sg	67.66	49.58	68.29	64.84	18.36	41.81	24.57	60.13	57.09	69.41
	vg	**76.69**	<u>**56.06**</u>	<u>**70.13**</u>	<u>**69.00**</u>	<u>**25.35**</u>	<u>**48.40**</u>	<u>**35.12**</u>	**68.91**	<u>**64.70**</u>	<u>**77.23**</u>

Table 1: Word-level evaluation results. Each value corresponds to average Pearson correlation of 7 identical models initialized with different random seeds. Correlations were scaled to the $[-100; 100]$ range for easier reading. **Bold** values represent the best method per training dataset, per task; <u>underlined</u> values represent the best-performing method per task, independent of training dataset. For each task and dataset, every best-performing method was significantly different to other methods ($p < 0.05$), except for w trained in SNLI at the MTurk287 task. Statistical significance was obtained with a two-sided Welch's t-test for two independent samples without assuming equal variance (Welch, 1947).

scores obtained by the proposed models and word similarity scores defined by humans.

First, we can see that for each task, `character only` models had significantly worse performance than every other model trained on the same dataset. The most likely explanation for this is that these models are the only ones that need to learn word representations from scratch, since they have no access to the global semantic knowledge encoded by the GloVe embeddings.

Further, **bold** results show the overall trend that `vector gates` outperformed the other methods regardless of training dataset. This implies that learning how to combine character and word-level representations at the dimension level produces word vector representations that capture a notion of word similarity and relatedness that is closer to that of humans.

Additionally, results from the MNLI row in general, and <u>underlined</u> results in particular, show that training on MultiNLI produces word representations better at capturing word similarity. This is probably due to MultiNLI data being richer than that of SNLI. Indeed, MultiNLI data was gathered from various sources (novels, reports, letters, and telephone conversations, among others), rather than the single image captions dataset from which SNLI was created.

Exceptions to the previous rule are models evaluated in MEN and RW. The former case can be explained by the MEN dataset[8] containing only words that appear as image labels in the ESP-Game[9] and MIRFLICKR-1M[10] image datasets (Bruni et al., 2014), and therefore having data that is more closely distributed to SNLI than to MultiNLI.

More notably, in the RareWords dataset (Luong et al., 2013), the `word only`, `concat`, and `scalar gate` methods performed equally, despite having been trained in different datasets ($p > 0.1$), and the `char only` method performed significantly worse when trained in MultiNLI. The `vector gate`, however, performed significantly better than its counterpart trained in SNLI. These facts provide evidence that this method is capable of capturing linguistic phenomena that the other methods are unable to model.

4.2 Word Frequencies and Gating Values

Figure 2 shows that for more common words the `vector gate` mechanism tends to favor only a few dimensions while keeping a low average gating value across dimensions. On the other hand, values are greater and more homogeneous across dimensions in rarer words. Further, fig. 3 shows this mechanism assigns, on average, a greater gating value to less frequent words, confirming the findings by Miyamoto and Cho (2016), and Yang et al. (2017).

In other words, the less frequent the word, the more this mechanism allows the character-level representation to influence the final word representation, as shown by eq. (8). A possible interpretation of this result is that exploiting charac-

<hr>

[8] https://staff.fni.uva.nl/e.bruni/MEN

[9] http://www.cs.cmu.edu/~biglou/resources/

[10] http://press.liacs.nl/mirflickr/

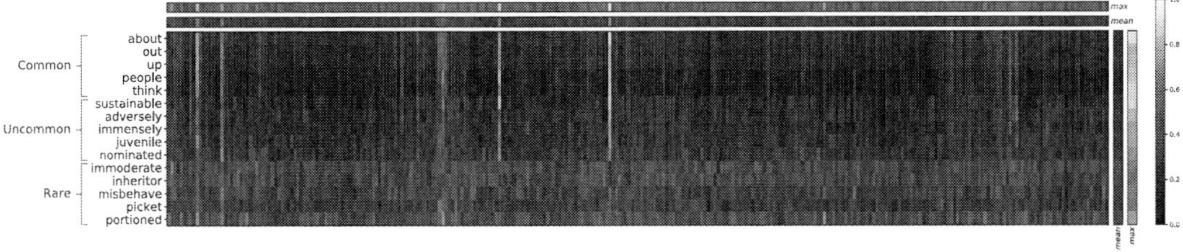

Figure 2: Visualization of gating values for 5 common words (freq. ~ 20000), 5 uncommon words (freq. ~ 60), and 5 rare words (freq. ~ 2), appearing in both the RW and MultiNLI datasets.

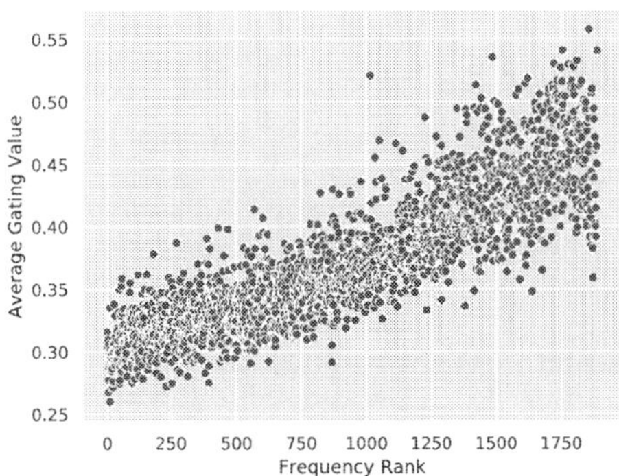

Figure 3: Average gating values for words appearing in both RW and MultiNLI. Words are sorted by decreasing frequency in MultiNLI.

ter information becomes increasingly necessary as word-level representations' quality decrease.

Another observable trend in both figures is that gating values tend to be low on average. Indeed, it is possible to see in fig. 3 that the average gating values range from 0.26 to 0.56. This result corroborates the findings by Miyamoto and Cho (2016), stating that setting $g = 0.25$ in eq. (6), was better than setting it to higher values.

In summary, the gating mechanisms learn how to compensate the lack of expressivity of under-represented words by selectively combining their representations with those of characters.

5 Sentence-level Evaluation

Table 2 shows the impact that different methods for combining character and word-level word representations have in the quality of the sentence representations produced by our models.

We can observe the same trend mentioned in section 4.1, and highlighted by the difference between **bold** values, that models trained in MultiNLI performed better than those trained in

SNLI at a statistically significant level, confirming the findings of Conneau et al. (2017). In other words, training sentence encoders on MultiNLI yields more general sentence representations than doing so on SNLI.

The two exceptions to the previous trend, SICKE and SICKR, benefited more from models trained on SNLI. We hypothesize this is again due to both SNLI and SICK (Marelli et al., 2014) having similar data distributions[11].

Additionally, there was no method that significantly outperformed the `word only` baseline in classification tasks. This means that the added expressivity offered by explicitly modeling characters, be it through concatenation or gating, was not significantly better than simply fine-tuning the pre-trained GloVe embeddings for this type of task. We hypothesize this is due to the conflation of two effects. First, the fact that morphological processes might not encode important information for solving these tasks; and second, that SNLI and MultiNLI belong to domains that are too dissimilar to the domains in which the sentence representations are being tested.

On the other hand, the `vector gate` significantly outperformed every other method in the STSB task when trained in both datasets, and in the STS16 task when trained in SNLI. This again hints at this method being capable of modeling phenomena at the word level, resulting in improved semantic representations at the sentence level.

6 Relationship Between Word- and Sentence-level Evaluation Tasks

It is clear that the better performance the `vector gate` had in word similarity tasks did not trans-

---

[11]SICK was created from Flickr-8k (Rashtchian et al., 2010), and SNLI from its expanded version: Flickr30k (Young et al., 2014).

		Classification							Entailment	Relatedness	Semantic Textual Similarity	
		CR	MPQA	MR	SST2	SST5	SUBJ	TREC	SICKE	SICKR†	STS16†	STSB†
SNLI	w	80.50	84.59	74.18	78.86	42.33	**90.38**	**86.83**	86.37	88.52	59.90*	71.29*
	c	74.90*	78.86*	65.93*	69.42*	35.56*	82.97*	83.31*	84.13*	83.89*	59.33*	67.20*
	cat	80.44	84.66	74.31	78.37	41.34*	90.28	85.80*	<u>**86.40**</u>	88.44	59.90*	71.24*
	sg	**80.59**	84.60	**74.49**	**79.04**	41.63*	90.16	86.00	86.10*	<u>**88.57**</u>	60.05*	71.34*
	vg	80.42	**84.66**	74.26	78.87	**42.38**	90.07	85.97	85.67	88.31*	**60.92**	**71.99**
MNLI	w	83.80	<u>**89.13**</u>	79.05	83.38	45.21	91.79	89.23	84.92	86.33	66.08	71.96*
	c	70.23*	72.19*	62.83*	64.55*	32.47*	79.49*	74.74*	81.53*	75.92*	51.47*	61.74*
	cat	<u>**83.96**</u>	89.12	<u>**79.23**</u>	83.70	45.08*	**91.92**	<u>**90.03**</u>	**85.06**	86.45	<u>**66.17**</u>	71.82*
	sg	83.88	89.06	79.22	83.71	45.26	91.66*	88.83*	84.96	86.40	65.49*	71.87*
	vg	83.45*	89.05	79.13	<u>**83.87**</u>	<u>**45.88**</u>	91.55*	89.49	84.82	**86.50**	65.75	<u>**72.82**</u>

Table 2: Experimental results. Each value shown in the table is the average result of 7 identical models initialized with different random seeds. Values represent accuracy (%) unless indicated by †, in which case they represent Pearson correlation scaled to the range $[-100, 100]$ for easier reading. **Bold** values represent the best method per training dataset, per task; <u>**underlined**</u> values represent the best-performing method per task, independent of training dataset. Values marked with an asterisk (*) are significantly different to the average performance of the best model trained on the same dataset ($p < 0.05$). Results for every best-performing method trained on one dataset are significantly different to the best-performing method trained on the other. Statistical significance was obtained in the same way as described in table 1.

late into overall better performance in downstream tasks. This confirms previous findings indicating that intrinsic word evaluation metrics are not good predictors of downstream performance (Tsvetkov et al., 2015; Chiu et al., 2016; Faruqui et al., 2016; Gladkova and Drozd, 2016).

Figure 4(b) shows that the word representations created by the `vector gate` trained in MultiNLI had positively-correlated results within several word-similarity tasks. This hints at the generality of the word representations created by this method when modeling similarity and relatedness.

However, the same cannot be said about sentence-level evaluation performance; there is no clear correlation between word similarity tasks and sentence-evaluation tasks. This is clearly illustrated by performance in the STSBenchmark, the only in which the `vector gate` was significantly superior, not being correlated with performance in any word-similarity dataset. This can be interpreted simply as word-level representations capturing word-similarity not being a sufficient condition for good performance in sentence-level tasks.

In general, fig. 4 shows that there are no general correlation effects spanning both training datasets and combination mechanisms. For example, fig. 4(a) shows that, for both `word-only` and `concat` models trained in SNLI, performance in word similarity tasks correlates positively with performance in most sentence evaluation tasks, however, this does not happen as clearly for the

same models trained in MultiNLI (fig. 4(b)).

7   Related Work

7.1   Gating Mechanisms for Combining Characters and Word Representations

To the best of our knowledge, there are only two recent works that specifically study how to combine word and subword-level vector representations.

Miyamoto and Cho (2016) propose to use a trainable scalar gating mechanism capable of learning a weighting scheme for combining character-level and word-level representations. They compared their proposed method to manually weighting both levels; using characters only; words only; or their concatenation. They found that in some datasets a specific manual weighting scheme performed better, while in others the learned scalar gate did.

Yang et al. (2017) further expand the gating concept by making the mechanism work at a finer-grained level, learning how to weight each vector's dimensions independently, conditioned on external word-level features such as part-of-speech and named-entity tags. Similarly, they compared their proposed mechanism to using words only, characters only, and a concatenation of both, with and without external features. They found that their vector gate performed better than the other methods in all the reported tasks, and beat the state of the art in two reading comprehension tasks.

Both works showed that the gating mechanisms assigned greater importance to character-level rep-

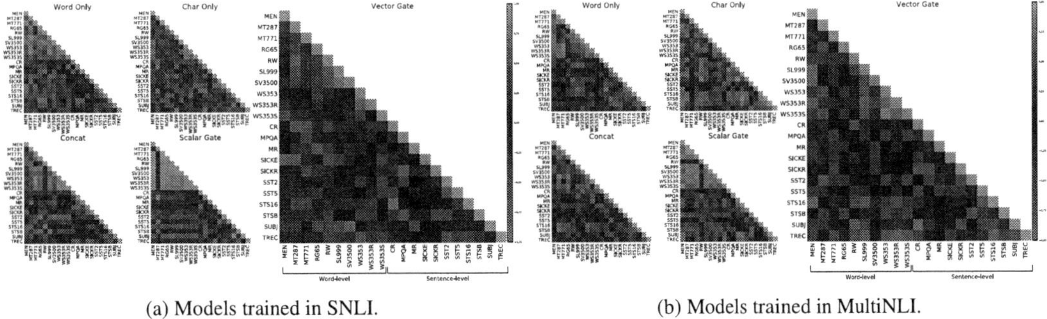

(a) Models trained in SNLI.   (b) Models trained in MultiNLI.

Figure 4: Spearman correlation between performances in word and sentence level evaluation tasks.

resentations in rare words, and to word-level representations in common ones, reaffirming the previous findings that subword structures in general, and characters in particular, are beneficial for modeling uncommon words.

7.2 Sentence Representation Learning

The problem of representing sentences as fixed-length vectors has been widely studied.

Zhao et al. (2015) suggested a self-adaptive hierarchical model that gradually composes words into intermediate phrase representations, and adaptively selects specific hierarchical levels for specific tasks. Kiros et al. (2015) proposed an encoder-decoder model trained by attempting to reconstruct the surrounding sentences of an encoded passage, in a fashion similar to Skip-gram (Mikolov et al., 2013). Hill et al. (2016) overcame the previous model's need for ordered training sentences by using autoencoders for creating the sentence representations. Jernite et al. (2017) implemented a model simpler and faster to train than the previous two, while having competitive performance. Similar to Kiros et al. (2015), Gan et al. (2017) suggested predicting future sentences with a hierarchical CNN-LSTM encoder.

Conneau et al. (2017) trained several sentence encoding architectures on a combination of the SNLI and MultiNLI datasets, and showed that a BiLSTM with max-pooling was the best at producing highly transferable sentence representations. More recently, Subramanian et al. (2018) empirically showed that sentence representations created in a multi-task setting (Collobert and Weston, 2008), performed increasingly better the more tasks they were trained in. Zhang et al. (2018) proposed using an autoencoder that relies on multi-head self-attention over the concatenation of the max and mean pooled encoder outputs

for producing sentence representations. Finally, Wieting and Kiela (2019) show that modern sentence embedding methods are not vastly superior to random methods.

The works mentioned so far usually evaluate the quality of the produced sentence representations in sentence-level downstream tasks. Common benchmarks grouping these kind of tasks include SentEval (Conneau and Kiela, 2018), and GLUE (Wang et al., 2019). Another trend, however, is to *probe* sentence representations to understand what linguistic phenomena they encode (Linzen et al., 2016; Adi et al., 2017; Conneau et al., 2018; Perone et al., 2018; Zhu et al., 2018).

7.3 General Feature-wise Transformations

Dumoulin et al. (2018) provide a review on feature-wise transformation methods, of which the mechanisms presented in this paper form a part of. In a few words, the g parameter, in both `scalar gate` and `vector gate` mechanisms, can be understood as a *scaling parameter* limited to the $(0, 1)$ range and conditioned on word representations, whereas adding the scaled $v_i^{(c)}$ and $v_i^{(w)}$ representations can be seen as *biasing* word representations conditioned on character representations.

The previous review extends the work by Perez et al. (2018), which describes the Feature-wise Linear Modulation (FiLM) framework as a generalization of Conditional Normalization methods, and apply it in visual reasoning tasks. Some of the reported findings are that, in general, scaling has greater impact than biasing, and that in a setting similar to the `scalar gate`, limiting the scaling parameter to $(0, 1)$ hurt performance. Future decisions involving the design of mechanisms for combining character and word-level representations should be informed by these insights.

117

8 Conclusions

We presented an empirical study showing the effect that different ways of combining character and word representations has in word-level and sentence-level evaluation tasks.

We showed that a vector gate performed consistently better across a variety of word similarity and relatedness tasks. Additionally, despite showing inconsistent results in sentence evaluation tasks, it performed significantly better than the other methods in semantic similarity tasks.

We further showed through this mechanism, that learning character-level representations is always beneficial, and becomes increasingly so with less common words.

In the future it would be interesting to study how the choice of mechanism for combining subword and word representations affects the more recent language-model-based pretraining methods such as ELMo (Peters et al., 2018), GPT (Radford et al., 2018, 2019) and BERT (Devlin et al., 2018).

Acknowledgements

Thanks to Edison Marrese-Taylor and Pablo Loyola for their feedback on early versions of this manuscript. We also gratefully acknowledge the support of the NVIDIA Corporation with the donation of one of the GPUs used for this research. Jorge A. Balazs is partially supported by the Japanese Government MEXT Scholarship.

References

Yossi Adi, Einat Kermany, Yonatan Belinkov, Ofer Lavi, and Yoav Goldberg. 2017. Fine-grained Analysis of Sentence Embeddings Using Auxiliary Prediction Tasks. In *Proceedings of the 5th International Conference on Learning Representations (ICLR)*, Toulon, France.

Eneko Agirre, Enrique Alfonseca, Keith Hall, Jana Kravalova, Marius Pasca, and Aitor Soroa. 2009. A Study on Similarity and Relatedness Using Distributional and WordNet-based Approaches. In *Proceedings of Human Language Technologies: The 2009 Annual Conference of the North American Chapter of the Association for Computational Linguistics*, pages 19–27, Boulder, Colorado. Association for Computational Linguistics.

Eneko Agirre, Carmen Banea, Daniel Cer, Mona Diab, Aitor Gonzalez-Agirre, Rada Mihalcea, German Rigau, and Janyce Wiebe. 2016. SemEval-2016 Task 1: Semantic Textual Similarity, Monolingual and Cross-Lingual Evaluation. In *Proceedings of the 10th International Workshop on Semantic Evaluation (SemEval-2016)*, pages 497–511, San Diego, California. Association for Computational Linguistics.

Sanjeev Arora, Yingyu Liang, and Tengyu Ma. 2017. A Simple but Tough-to-Beat Baseline for Sentence Embeddings. In *International Conference on Learning Representations*.

Oded Avraham and Yoav Goldberg. 2017. The Interplay of Semantics and Morphology in Word Embeddings. *arXiv preprint arXiv:1704.01938*.

Piotr Bojanowski, Edouard Grave, Armand Joulin, and Tomas Mikolov. 2017. Enriching Word Vectors with Subword Information. *Transactions of the Association for Computational Linguistics*, 5:135–146.

Jan Botha and Phil Blunsom. 2014. Compositional Morphology for Word Representations and Language Modelling. In *Proceedings of the 31st International Conference on Machine Learning*, volume 32 of *Proceedings of Machine Learning Research*, pages 1899–1907, Bejing, China. PMLR.

Samuel R. Bowman, Gabor Angeli, Christopher Potts, and Christopher D. Manning. 2015. A Large Annotated Corpus for Learning Natural Language Inference. In *Proceedings of the 2015 Conference on Empirical Methods in Natural Language Processing*, pages 632–642, Lisbon, Portugal. Association for Computational Linguistics.

Elia Bruni, Nam-Khanh Tran, and Marco Baroni. 2014. Multimodal Distributional Semantics. *Journal of Artificial Intelligence Research*, 49:1–47.

Daniel Cer, Mona Diab, Eneko Agirre, Inigo Lopez-Gazpio, and Lucia Specia. 2017. SemEval-2017 Task 1: Semantic Textual Similarity Multilingual and Crosslingual Focused Evaluation. In *Proceedings of the 11th International Workshop on Semantic Evaluation (SemEval-2017)*, pages 1–14, Vancouver, Canada. Association for Computational Linguistics.

Billy Chiu, Anna Korhonen, and Sampo Pyysalo. 2016. Intrinsic Evaluation of Word Vectors Fails to Predict Extrinsic Performance. In *Proceedings of the 1st Workshop on Evaluating Vector-Space Representations for NLP*, pages 1–6, Berlin, Germany. Association for Computational Linguistics.

Ronan Collobert and Jason Weston. 2008. A Unified Architecture for Natural Language Processing: Deep Neural Networks with Multitask Learning. In *Proceedings of the 25th Annual International Conference on Machine Learning (ICML 2008)*, pages 160–167, Helsinki, Finland.

Alexis Conneau and Douwe Kiela. 2018. SentEval: An Evaluation Toolkit for Universal Sentence Representations. In *Proceedings of the Eleventh International Conference on Language Resources and Evaluation (LREC-2018)*, Miyazaki, Japan. European Language Resource Association.

Alexis Conneau, Douwe Kiela, Holger Schwenk, Loïc Barrault, and Antoine Bordes. 2017. Supervised Learning of Universal Sentence Representations from Natural Language Inference Data. In *Proceedings of the 2017 Conference on Empirical Methods in Natural Language Processing*, pages 670–680, Copenhagen, Denmark. Association for Computational Linguistics.

Alexis Conneau, Germán Kruszewski, Guillaume Lample, Loïc Barrault, and Marco Baroni. 2018. What you can cram into a single $&!#* vector: Probing sentence embeddings for linguistic properties. In *Proceedings of the 56th Annual Meeting of the Association for Computational Linguistics (Volume 1: Long Papers)*, pages 2126–2136, Melbourne, Australia. Association for Computational Linguistics.

Jacob Devlin, Ming-Wei Chang, Kenton Lee, and Kristina Toutanova. 2018. BERT: Pre-training of Deep Bidirectional Transformers for Language Understanding. *CoRR*, abs/1810.04805.

Vincent Dumoulin, Ethan Perez, Nathan Schucher, Florian Strub, Harm de Vries, Aaron Courville, and Yoshua Bengio. 2018. Feature-wise transformations. *Distill*.

Manaal Faruqui, Yulia Tsvetkov, Pushpendre Rastogi, and Chris Dyer. 2016. Problems With Evaluation of Word Embeddings Using Word Similarity Tasks. In *Proceedings of the 1st Workshop on Evaluating Vector-Space Representations for NLP*, pages 30–35, Berlin, Germany. Association for Computational Linguistics.

Christiane Fellbaum, editor. 1998. *WordNet: an Electronic Lexical Database*. MIT Press.

Lev Finkelstein, Evgeniy Gabrilovich, Yossi Matias, Ehud Rivlin, Zach Solan, Gadi Wolfman, and Eytan Ruppin. 2002. Placing Search in Context: The Concept Revisited. *ACM Transactions on Information Systems*, 20(1):116–131.

Zhe Gan, Yunchen Pu, Ricardo Henao, Chunyuan Li, Xiaodong He, and Lawrence Carin. 2017. Learning Generic Sentence Representations Using Convolutional Neural Networks. In *Proceedings of the 2017 Conference on Empirical Methods in Natural Language Processing*, pages 2390–2400, Copenhagen, Denmark. Association for Computational Linguistics.

Daniela Gerz, Ivan Vulić, Felix Hill, Roi Reichart, and Anna Korhonen. 2016. SimVerb-3500: A Large-Scale Evaluation Set of Verb Similarity. In *Proceedings of the 2016 Conference on Empirical Methods in Natural Language Processing*, pages 2173–2182, Austin, Texas. Association for Computational Linguistics.

Anna Gladkova and Aleksandr Drozd. 2016. Intrinsic Evaluations of Word Embeddings: What Can We Do Better? In *Proceedings of the 1st Workshop on Evaluating Vector-Space Representations for NLP*, pages 36–42, Berlin, Germany. Association for Computational Linguistics.

Alex Graves, Abdel-rahman Mohamed, and Geoffrey Hinton. 2013. Speech Recognition with Deep Recurrent Neural Networks. In *Proceedings of the 2013 International Conference on Acoustics, Speech and Signal Processing (ICASSP)*, pages 6645–6649, Vancouver, Canada. IEEE.

Alex Graves and Jürgen Schmidhuber. 2005. Framewise Phoneme Classification with Bidirectional LSTM and Other Neural Network Architectures. *Neural Networks*, 18(5-6):602–610.

Guy Halawi, Gideon Dror, Evgeniy Gabrilovich, and Yehuda Koren. 2012. Large-scale Learning of Word Relatedness with Constraints. In *Proceedings of the 18th ACM SIGKDD International Conference on Knowledge Discovery and Data Mining*, KDD '12, pages 1406–1414, Beijing, China. ACM.

Felix Hill, Kyunghyun Cho, and Anna Korhonen. 2016. Learning Distributed Representations of Sentences from Unlabelled Data. In *Proceedings of the 2016 Conference of the North American Chapter of the Association for Computational Linguistics: Human Language Technologies*, pages 1367–1377, San Diego, California. Association for Computational Linguistics.

Felix Hill, Roi Reichart, and Anna Korhonen. 2015. SimLex-999: Evaluating Semantic Models With (Genuine) Similarity Estimation. *Computational Linguistics*, 41(4):665–695.

Sepp Hochreiter and Jürgen Schmidhuber. 1997. Long Short-Term Memory. *Neural Computation*, 9(8):1735–1780.

Minqing Hu and Bing Liu. 2004. Mining and Summarizing Customer Reviews. In *Proceedings of the Tenth ACM SIGKDD International Conference on Knowledge Discovery and Data Mining*, KDD '04, pages 168–177, Seattle, Washington. ACM.

Stanisław Jastrzebski, Damian Leśniak, and Wojciech Marian Czarnecki. 2017. How to evaluate word embeddings? on importance of data efficiency and simple supervised tasks. *arXiv preprint arXiv:1702.02170*.

Yacine Jernite, Samuel R. Bowman, and David Sontag. 2017. Discourse-Based Objectives for Fast Unsupervised Sentence Representation Learning. *CoRR*, abs/1705.00557.

John D. Hunter. 2007. Matplotlib: A 2D Graphics Environment. *Computing in Science & Engineering*, 9(3):90–95.

Eric Jones, Travis Oliphant, Pearu Peterson, et al. 2001–. SciPy: Open source scientific tools for Python.

Yoon Kim, Yacine Jernite, David Sontag, and Alexander Rush. 2016. Character-Aware Neural Language Models. In *Proceedings of the 30th AAAI Conference on Artificial Intelligence*, pages 2741–2749, Phoenix, Arizona.

Karin Kipper, Anna Korhonen, Neville Ryant, and Martha Palmer. 2008. A large-scale classification of English verbs. *Language Resources and Evaluation*, 42(1):21–40.

Ryan Kiros, Yukun Zhu, Ruslan R Salakhutdinov, Richard Zemel, Raquel Urtasun, Antonio Torralba, and Sanja Fidler. 2015. Skip-Thought Vectors. In C. Cortes, N. D. Lawrence, D. D. Lee, M. Sugiyama, and R. Garnett, editors, *Advances in Neural Information Processing Systems 28*, pages 3294–3302. Curran Associates, Inc.

Guillaume Lample, Miguel Ballesteros, Sandeep Subramanian, Kazuya Kawakami, and Chris Dyer. 2016. Neural Architectures for Named Entity Recognition. In *Proceedings of the 2016 Conference of the North American Chapter of the Association for Computational Linguistics: Human Language Technologies*, pages 260–270, San Diego, California. Association for Computational Linguistics.

Xin Li and Dan Roth. 2002. Learning Question Classifiers. In *COLING 2002: The 19th International Conference on Computational Linguistics*.

Wang Ling, Chris Dyer, Alan W Black, Isabel Trancoso, Ramon Fermandez, Silvio Amir, Luis Marujo, and Tiago Luis. 2015. Finding Function in Form: Compositional Character Models for Open Vocabulary Word Representation. In *Proceedings of the 2015 Conference on Empirical Methods in Natural Language Processing*, pages 1520–1530, Lisbon, Portugal. Association for Computational Linguistics.

Tal Linzen, Emmanuel Dupoux, and Yoav Goldberg. 2016. Assessing the Ability of LSTMs to Learn Syntax-Sensitive Dependencies. *Transactions of the Association for Computational Linguistics*, 4(1):521–535.

Minh-Thang Luong and Christopher D. Manning. 2016. Achieving Open Vocabulary Neural Machine Translation with Hybrid Word-Character Models. In *Proceedings of the 54th Annual Meeting of the Association for Computational Linguistics (Volume 1: Long Papers)*, pages 1054–1063, Berlin, Germany. Association for Computational Linguistics.

Thang Luong, Richard Socher, and Christopher D. Manning. 2013. Better Word Representations with Recursive Neural Networks for Morphology. In *Proceedings of the Seventeenth Conference on Computational Natural Language Learning*, pages 104–113, Sofia, Bulgaria. Association for Computational Linguistics.

Marco Marelli, Stefano Menini, Marco Baroni, Luisa Bentivogli, Raffaella bernardi, and Roberto Zamparelli. 2014. A SICK cure for the evaluation of compositional distributional semantic models. In *Proceedings of the Ninth International Conference on Language Resources and Evaluation (LREC-2014)*, Reykjavik, Iceland. European Language Resources Association (ELRA).

Wes McKinney. 2010. Data Structures for Statistical Computing in Python. In *Proceedings of the 9th Python in Science Conference*, pages 51 – 56.

Tomas Mikolov, Ilya Sutskever, Kai Chen, Greg S Corrado, and Jeff Dean. 2013. Distributed Representations of Words and Phrases and their Compositionality. In C. J. C. Burges, L. Bottou, M. Welling, Z. Ghahramani, and K. Q. Weinberger, editors, *Advances in Neural Information Processing Systems 26*, pages 3111–3119. Curran Associates, Inc.

Yasumasa Miyamoto and Kyunghyun Cho. 2016. Gated Word-Character Recurrent Language Model. In *Proceedings of the 2016 Conference on Empirical Methods in Natural Language Processing*, pages 1992–1997, Austin, Texas. Association for Computational Linguistics.

Douglas L. Nelson, Cathy L. McEvoy, and Thomas A. Schreiber. 2004. The University of South Florida free association, rhyme, and word fragment norms. *Behavior Research Methods, Instruments, & Computers*, 36(3):402–407.

Travis E. Oliphant. 2015. *Guide to NumPy*, 2nd edition. CreateSpace Independent Publishing Platform, USA.

Bo Pang and Lillian Lee. 2004. A Sentimental Education: Sentiment Analysis Using Subjectivity Summarization Based on Minimum Cuts. In *Proceedings of the 42nd Annual Meeting of the Association for Computational Linguistics (ACL-04)*.

Bo Pang and Lillian Lee. 2005. Seeing Stars: Exploiting Class Relationships for Sentiment Categorization with Respect to Rating Scales. In *Proceedings of the 43rd Annual Meeting of the Association for Computational Linguistics (ACL'05)*, pages 115–124, Ann Arbor, Michigan. Association for Computational Linguistics.

Adam Paszke, Sam Gross, Soumith Chintala, Gregory Chanan, Edward Yang, Zachary DeVito, Zeming Lin, Alban Desmaison, Luca Antiga, and Adam Lerer. 2017. Automatic differentiation in PyTorch. In *NeurIPS Autodiff Workshop*, Long Beach, California.

Jeffrey Pennington, Richard Socher, and Christopher Manning. 2014. Glove: Global Vectors for Word Representation. In *Proceedings of the 2014 Conference on Empirical Methods in Natural Language Processing (EMNLP)*, pages 1532–1543, Doha, Qatar. Association for Computational Linguistics.

Ethan Perez, Florian Strub, Harm de Vries, Vincent Dumoulin, and Aaron Courville. 2018. FiLM: Visual Reasoning with a General Conditioning Layer. In *AAAI Conference on Artificial Intelligence*, New Orleans, Louisiana.

Christian S. Perone, Roberto Silveira, and Thomas S. Paula. 2018. Evaluation of sentence embeddings in downstream and linguistic probing tasks. *CoRR*, abs/1806.06259.

Matthew Peters, Mark Neumann, Mohit Iyyer, Matt Gardner, Christopher Clark, Kenton Lee, and Luke Zettlemoyer. 2018. Deep contextualized word representations. In *Proceedings of the 2018 Conference of the North American Chapter of the Association for Computational Linguistics: Human Language Technologies, Volume 1 (Long Papers)*, pages 2227–2237, New Orleans, Louisiana. Association for Computational Linguistics.

Alec Radford, Karthik Narasimhan, Tim Salimans, and Ilya Sutskever. 2018. Improving Language Understanding by Generative Pre-Training. Technical report, OpenAI.

Alec Radford, Jeffrey Wu, Rewon Child, David Luan, Dario Amodei, and Ilya Sutskever. 2019. Language Models are Unsupervised Multitask Learners. Technical report, OpenAI.

Kira Radinsky, Eugene Agichtein, Evgeniy Gabrilovich, and Shaul Markovitch. 2011. A Word at a Time: Computing Word Relatedness Using Temporal Semantic Analysis. In *Proceedings of the 20th International Conference on World Wide Web*, WWW '11, pages 337–346, Hyderabad, India.

Cyrus Rashtchian, Peter Young, Micah Hodosh, and Julia Hockenmaier. 2010. Collecting Image Annotations Using Amazon's Mechanical Turk. In *Proceedings of the NAACL HLT 2010 Workshop on Creating Speech and Language Data with Amazon's Mechanical Turk*, pages 139–147, Los Angeles, California. Association for Computational Linguistics.

Guido van Rossum. 1995. Python Tutorial. Technical Report CS-R9526, Department of Computer Science, CWI, Amsterdam, The Netherlands.

Herbert Rubenstein and John B. Goodenough. 1965. Contextual Correlates of Synonymy. *Communications of the ACM*, 8(10):627–633.

Richard Socher, Alex Perelygin, Jean Wu, Jason Chuang, Christopher D. Manning, Andrew Ng, and Christopher Potts. 2013. Recursive Deep Models for Semantic Compositionality Over a Sentiment Treebank. In *Proceedings of the 2013 Conference on Empirical Methods in Natural Language Processing*, pages 1631–1642, Seattle, Washington. Association for Computational Linguistics.

Sandeep Subramanian, Adam Trischler, Yoshua Bengio, and Christopher J Pal. 2018. Learning General Purpose Distributed Sentence Representations via Large Scale Multi-task Learning. In *International Conference on Learning Representations*.

Yulia Tsvetkov, Manaal Faruqui, Wang Ling, Guillaume Lample, and Chris Dyer. 2015. Evaluation of Word Vector Representations by Subspace Alignment. In *Proceedings of the 2015 Conference on Empirical Methods in Natural Language Processing*, pages 2049–2054, Lisbon, Portugal. Association for Computational Linguistics.

Alex Wang, Amanpreet Singh, Julian Michael, Felix Hill, Omer Levy, and Samuel R. Bowman. 2019. GLUE: A Multi-Task Benchmark and Analysis Platform for Natural Language Understanding. In *Proceedings of the 7th International Conference on Learning Representations (ICLR)*, New Orleans, Louisiana.

Sida Wang and Christopher Manning. 2012. Baselines and Bigrams: Simple, Good Sentiment and Topic Classification. In *Proceedings of the 50th Annual Meeting of the Association for Computational Linguistics (Volume 2: Short Papers)*, pages 90–94, Jeju Island, Korea. Association for Computational Linguistics.

Michael Waskom, Olga Botvinnik, Drew O'Kane, Paul Hobson, Joel Ostblom, Saulius Lukauskas, David C Gemperline, Tom Augspurger, Yaroslav Halchenko, John B. Cole, Jordi Warmenhoven, Julian de Ruiter, Cameron Pye, Stephan Hoyer, Jake Vanderplas, Santi Villalba, Gero Kunter, Eric Quintero, Pete Bachant, Marcel Martin, Kyle Meyer, Alistair Miles, Yoav Ram, Thomas Brunner, Tal Yarkoni, Mike Lee Williams, Constantine Evans, Clark Fitzgerald, Brian, and Adel Qalieh. 2018. mwaskom/seaborn: v0.9.0 (july 2018).

Bernard Lewis Welch. 1947. The Generalization of "Student's" Problem When Several Different Population Variances are Involved. *Biometrika*, 34(1-2):28–35.

Janyce Wiebe, Theresa Wilson, and Claire Cardie. 2005. Annotating Expressions of Opinions and Emotions in Language. *Language Resources and Evaluation*, 39(2):165–210.

John Wieting and Douwe Kiela. 2019. No Training Required: Exploring Random Encoders for Sentence Classification. In *Proceedings of the 7th International Conference on Learning Representations (ICLR)*, New Orleans, Louisiana.

Adina Williams, Nikita Nangia, and Samuel Bowman. 2018. A Broad-Coverage Challenge Corpus for Sentence Understanding through Inference. In *Proceedings of the 2018 Conference of the North American Chapter of the Association for Computational Linguistics: Human Language Technologies, Volume 1 (Long Papers)*, pages 1112–1122, New Orleans, Louisiana. Association for Computational Linguistics.

Yonghui Wu, Mike Schuster, Zhifeng Chen, Quoc V. Le, Mohammad Norouzi, Wolfgang Macherey, Maxim Krikun, Yuan Cao, Qin Gao, Klaus Macherey, Jeff Klingner, Apurva Shah, Melvin Johnson, Xiaobing Liu, Lukasz Kaiser, Stephan Gouws, Yoshikiyo Kato, Taku Kudo, Hideto Kazawa, Keith Stevens, George Kurian, Nishant Patil, Wei Wang, Cliff Young, Jason Smith, Jason Riesa, Alex Rudnick, Oriol Vinyals, Greg Corrado, Macduff Hughes, and Jeffrey Dean. 2016. Google's Neural Machine Translation System: Bridging the Gap between Human and Machine Translation. *arXiv preprint arXiv:1609.08144*.

Zhilin Yang, Bhuwan Dhingra, Ye Yuan, Junjie Hu, William W. Cohen, and Ruslan Salakhutdinov. 2017. Words or Characters? Fine-grained Gating for Reading Comprehension. In *Proceedings of the 5th International Conference on Learning Representations (ICLR)*, Toulon, France.

Peter Young, Alice Lai, Micah Hodosh, and Julia Hockenmaier. 2014. From image descriptions to visual denotations. *Transactions of the Association for Computational Linguistics*, 2:67–78.

Minghua Zhang, Yunfang Wu, Weikang Li, and Wei Li. 2018. Learning Universal Sentence Representations with Mean-Max Attention Autoencoder. In *Proceedings of the 2018 Conference on Empirical Methods in Natural Language Processing*, pages 4514–4523, Brussels, Belgium. Association for Computational Linguistics.

Han Zhao, Zhengdong Lu, and Pascal Poupart. 2015. Self-Adaptive Hierarchical Sentence Model. In *Proceedings of the 24th International Joint Conference on Artificial Intelligence*, pages 4069–4076, Buenos Aires, Argentina. AAAI Press.

Xunjie Zhu, Tingfeng Li, and Gerard de Melo. 2018. Exploring Semantic Properties of Sentence Embeddings. In *Proceedings of the 56th Annual Meeting of the Association for Computational Linguistics (Volume 2: Short Papers)*, pages 632–637, Melbourne, Australia. Association for Computational Linguistics.

A Hyperparameters

We only considered words that appear at least twice, for each dataset. Those that appeared only once were considered UNK. We used the Treebank Word Tokenizer as implemented in NLTK[12] for tokenizing the training and development datasets.

In the same fashion as Conneau et al. (2017), we used a batch size of 64, an SGD optmizer with an initial learning rate of 0.1, and at each epoch divided the learning rate by 5 if the validation accuracy decreased. We also used gradient clipping when gradients where > 5.

We defined character vector representations as 50-dimensional vectors randomly initialized by sampling from the uniform distribution in the $(-0.05; 0.05)$ range.

The output dimension of the character-level BiLSTM was 300 per direction, and remained of such size after combining forward and backward representations as depicted in eq. 1.

Word vector representations where initialized from the 300-dimensional GloVe vectors (Pennington et al., 2014), trained in 840B tokens from the Common Crawl[13], and finetuned during training. Words not present in the GloVe vocabulary where randomly initialized by sampling from the uniform distribution in the $(-0.05; 0.05)$ range.

The input size of the word-level LSTM was 300 for every method except `concat` in which it was 600, and its output was always 2048 per direction, resulting in a 4096-dimensional sentence representation.

B Datasets

B.1 Word Similarity

Table B.1 lists the word-similarity datasets and their corresponding reference. As mentioned in section 3.2, all the word-similarity datasets contain pairs of words annotated with similarity or relatedness scores, although this difference is not always explicit. Below we provide some details for each.

MEN contains 3000 annotated word pairs with integer scores ranging from 0 to 50. Words correspond to image labels appearing in the ESP-Game[14] and MIRFLICKR-1M[15] image datasets.

MTurk287 contains 287 annotated pairs with scores ranging from 1.0 to 5.0. It was created from words appearing in both DBpedia and in news articles from The New York Times.

---

[12] https://www.nltk.org/
[13] https://nlp.stanford.edu/projects/glove/
[14] http://www.cs.cmu.edu/~biglou/resources/
[15] http://press.liacs.nl/mirflickr/

Dataset	Reference	URL
MEN	Bruni et al. (2014)	https://staff.fnwi.uva.nl/e.bruni/MEN
MTurk287	Radinsky et al. (2011)	https://git.io/fhQA8 (Unofficial)
MTurk771	Halawi et al. (2012)	http://www2.mta.ac.il/~gideon/mturk771.html
RG	Rubenstein and Goodenough (1965)	https://git.io/fhQAB (Unofficial)
RareWords (RW)	Luong et al. (2013)	https://nlp.stanford.edu/~lmthang/morphoNLM/
SimLex999	Hill et al. (2015)	https://fh295.github.io/simlex.html
SimVerb3500	Gerz et al. (2016)	http://people.ds.cam.ac.uk/dsg40/simverb.html
WS353	Finkelstein et al. (2002)	http://www.cs.technion.ac.il/~gabr/resources/data/wordsim353/
WS353R	Agirre et al. (2009)	http://alfonseca.org/eng/research/wordsim353.html
WS353S	Agirre et al. (2009)	http://alfonseca.org/eng/research/wordsim353.html

Table B.1: Word similarity and relatedness datasets.

MTurk771 contains 771 annotated pairs with scores ranging from 1.0 to 5.0, with words having synonymy, holonymy or meronymy relationships sampled from WordNet (Fellbaum, 1998).

RG contains 65 annotated pairs with scores ranging from 0.0 to 4.0 representing "similarity of meaning".

RW contains 2034 pairs of words annotated with similarity scores in a scale from 0 to 10. The words included in this dataset were obtained from Wikipedia based on their frequency, and later filtered depending on their WordNet synsets, including synonymy, hyperonymy, hyponymy, holonymy and meronymy. This dataset was created with the purpose of testing how well models can represent rare and complex words.

SimLex999 contains 999 word pairs annotated with similarity scores ranging from 0 to 10. In this case the authors explicitly considered similarity and not relatedness, addressing the shortcomings of datasets that do not, such as MEN and WS353. Words include nouns, adjectives and verbs.

SimVerb3500 contains 3500 verb pairs annotated with similarity scores ranging from 0 to 10. Verbs were obtained from the USF free association database (Nelson et al., 2004), and VerbNet (Kipper et al., 2008). This dataset was created to address the lack of representativity of verbs in SimLex999, and the fact that, at the time of creation, the best performing models had already surpassed inter-annotator agreement in verb similarity evaluation resources. Like SimLex999, this dataset also explicitly considers similarity as opposed to relatedness.

WS353 contains 353 word pairs annotated with similarity scores from 0 to 10.

WS353R is a subset of WS353 containing 252 word pairs annotated with relatedness scores. This dataset was created by asking humans to classify each WS353 word pair into one of the following classes: synonyms, antonyms, identical, hyperonym-hyponym, hyponym-hyperonym, holonym-meronym, meronym-holonym, and none-of-the-above. These annotations were later used to group the pairs into: *similar* pairs (synonyms, antonyms, identical, hyperonym-hyponym, and hyponym-hyperonym), *related* pairs (holonym-meronym, meronym-holonym, and none-of-the-above with a human similarity score greater than 5), and *unrelated* pairs (classified as none-of-the-above with a similarity score less than or equal to 5). This dataset is composed by the union of related and unrelated pairs.

WS353S is another subset of WS353 containing 203 word pairs annotated with similarity scores. This dataset is composed by the union of similar and unrelated pairs, as described previously.

B.2 Sentence Evaluation Datasets

Table B.2 lists the sentence-level evaluation datasets used in this paper. The provided URLs correspond to the original sources, and not necessarily to the URLs where SentEval[16] got the data from[17].

The version of the CR, MPQA, MR, and SUBJ datasets used in this paper were the ones preprocessed by Wang and Manning (2012)[18]. Both SST2 and SST5 correspond to preprocessed versions of the Stanford Sentiment Treebank (SST) dataset by Socher et al. (2013)[19]. SST2 corresponds to a subset of SST used by Arora et al. (2017) containing flat representations of sentences annotated with binary sentiment labels, and SST5 to another subset annotated with more fine-grained sentiment labels (very negative, negative, neutral, positive, very positive).

---

[16] https://github.com/facebookresearch/SentEval/tree/906b34a

[17] A list of the data used by SentEval can be found in its data setup script: https://git.io/fhQpq

[18] https://nlp.stanford.edu/~sidaw/home/projects:nbsvm

[19] https://nlp.stanford.edu/sentiment/

Dataset	Reference	URL
CR	Hu and Liu (2004)	`https://www.cs.uic.edu/~liub/FBS/sentiment-analysis.html#datasets`
MPQA	Wiebe et al. (2005)	`https://mpqa.cs.pitt.edu/corpora/mpqa_corpus/`
MR	Pang and Lee (2005)	`http://www.cs.cornell.edu/people/pabo/movie-review-data/`
SST2	Arora et al. (2017)	`https://github.com/PrincetonML/SIF/tree/master/data`
SST5	See caption.	`https://git.io/fhQAV`
SUBJ	Pang and Lee (2004)	`http://www.cs.cornell.edu/people/pabo/movie-review-data/`
TREC	Li and Roth (2002)	`http://cogcomp.org/Data/QA/QC/`
SICKE	Marelli et al. (2014)	`http://clic.cimec.unitn.it/composes/sick.html`
SICKR	Marelli et al. (2014)	`http://clic.cimec.unitn.it/composes/sick.html`
STS16	Agirre et al. (2016)	`http://ixa2.si.ehu.es/stswiki/index.php/Main_Page`
STSB	Cer et al. (2017)	`http://ixa2.si.ehu.es/stswiki/index.php/STSbenchmark`

Table B.2: Sentence representation evaluation datasets. SST5 was obtained from a GitHub repository with no associated peer-reviewed work.

A Pregroup Representation of Word Order Alternation using Hindi Syntax

Alok Debnath and **Manish Shrivastava**
Language Technologies Research Center (LTRC)
Kohli Center on Intelligent Systems
International Institute of Information Technology, Hyderabad
`alok.debnath@research.iiit.ac.in`
`m.shrivastava@iiit.ac.in`

Abstract

Pregroup calculus has been used for the representation of free word order languages (Sanskrit and Hungarian), using a construction called precyclicity. However, restricted word order alternation has not been handled before. This paper aims at introducing and formally expressing three methods of representing word order alternation in the pregroup representation of any language. This paper describes the word order alternation patterns of Hindi, and creates a basic pregroup representation for the language. In doing so, the shortcoming of correct reductions for ungrammatical sentences due to the current apparatus is highlighted, and the aforementioned methods are invoked for a grammatically accurate representation of restricted word order alternation. The replicability of these methods is explained in the representation of adverbs and prepositional phrases in English.

1 Introduction

Categorial grammars are one of the frameworks for the representation of syntactic structures of languages (Oehrle et al., 2012). A foundational problem in such formalisms, including the well established lexical formalism combinatory categorial grammars (CCG), is the representation of free word order in light of syntactic or semantic constraints presented by the language. Extensive resources following the different formalisms, such as CCG Banks (Hockenmaier and Steedman, 2007), have been developed. Development in pregroup calculus, however, has been more focused on developing formal constraints in the calculus for the representation of syntactic phenomena. In that vein, this paper aims at presenting the problem of restricted word alternation (constituent scrambling) by using the example of Hindi syntax, and uses that to develop three formal approaches to represent word alternation in the pregroup calculus framework.

Pregroups are mathematical structures which were developed initially by Lambek and can be used to analyze sentences in English algebraically (Lambek, 1997). Pregroup calculus was a revision of Lambek's previous categorial grammar called Syntactic Calculus (Lambek, 1958). Various languages have since adopted the use of pregroup calculus as the formal representation of syntax of a fragment or a particular property of the language, including Arabic (Bargelli and Lambek, 2001b), French (Bargelli and Lambek, 2001a), German (Lambek, 2000), Japanese (Cardinal, 2002), Persian (Sadrzadeh, 2007), Polish (Kislak-Malinowska, 2008), and Sanskrit (Casadio and Sadrzadeh, 2014), among others. Coecke et al. (2010)'s compositional distributional model of meaning also uses pregroup calculus as the compositional theory for grammatical types.

In the study of free word order languages (or languages with clitics), such as Italian (Casadio, 2010), Latin (Casadio and Lambek, 2005) and Hungarian (Sadrzadeh, 2011), a transformation was introduced, knows as the precyclic transformation (section 3.1). This transformation was also used for Sanskrit (Casadio and Sadrzadeh, 2014), where generation of ungrammatical sentences was restricted by disallowing certain transformations.

In this paper, we first establish a preliminary pregroup grammar of Hindi and highlight the syntactic constraints of the language. We then show the shortcomings of the current word order alternation mechanism. We also formally define the

Proceedings of the 2019 Conference of the North American Chapter of the Association for Computational Linguistics: Student Research Workshop, pages 125–135
Minneapolis, Minnesota, June 3 - 5, 2019. ©2017 Association for Computational Linguistics

karaka	vibhakti	Equivalent Case
karta	ϕ	Nominative
	ne	Ergative
karam	ko	Accusative
		Dative
karan	se	Instrumental
sampradan	ko, ke liye	Purpose/Reason
apadaan	se	Source
adhikaran	me, par	Locative

Table 1: Case/Role Marking in Hindi

aforementioned restrictions presented for Sanskrit, and present two other novel methods for representing restricted word order alternation, which can be applied to other languages as well, evidenced by the examples of prepositional phrases in English.

2 Properties of Hindi Syntax

This section details the syntactic properties of Hindi, which include postpositional case marking (*karaka* and *sambandha* markers) in noun phrases, lexicalized tense and aspect markers in verb phrases, and the default word order and constituent scrambling. These properties are essential to developing a pregroup representation of Hindi syntax. Section 2.1 highlights the word order movement properties of Hindi.

In the Paninian linguistic tradition, noun phrases in Hindi have a system of case marking known as the *karaka* system. *karaka* is analogous to a case, which is marked by a *vibhakti* (case marker). The *karaka* is a syntacto-semantic system which distinctly identifies the role of a noun to a verb (Pedersen et al., 2004). Table 1 shows the *karakas*, their respective markers and their analogous cases.

The genitive case (called *sambandh*) in Hindi is not a *karaka*, as it shows the relationship of one noun to another noun. These are gender marked, to reflect the gender of the following noun. For instance the phrase "Neha's ball" will be translated as *Neha kI gend*.

The verb phrase consists of either a single verb or a conjunct verb, complex verb or a light verb complex, which usually follows the construction "noun/adjective/verb + verbalizer" (Ahmed et al., 2012). The tense markers and aspect markers are separate lexical items, while the future marker is a suffix on the trailing verb or verbalizer. The verbalizer interactions can be further classified based

on their behavior with aspect markers such as infinitive + forms of *lagnaa* (to begin) (Spencer et al., 2005; Chakrabarti et al., 2008).

2.1 Restricted Word Order Alternation

Hindi follows a general SOV word order (more specifically, S-IO-DO-V) (Seddah et al., 2010).[1] In the default word order, Hindi is a head-final with a relatively free word order (Patil et al., 2008). However, constituents are often "mixed up", which may be done for focus or emphasis, but this is not always the case (Butt and King, 1996; Kidwai, 2000).

We take an example of the sentence:

raam   ne   sitaa   ko   kitaab   dii
Ram   erg.   Sita   dat.   book   gave-fem.

"Ram gave the book to Sita" to explain the possible word orders (Ambati et al., 2010).

- Default word order (S-IO-DO-V) used above

- S-DO-IO-V: *raam ne kitaab sitaa ko dii*

- IO-S-DO-V: *sitaa ko raam ne kitaab dii*

- IO-DO-S-V: *sitaa ko raam ne kitaab dii*

- DO-S-IO-V: *kitaab raam ne sitaa ko dii*

- DO-IO-S-V: *kitaab sitaa ko raam ne dii*

Note that due to its isolating nature, the word order in the constituents remains intact, which is difficult to represent. The pregroup representation should allow only for valid constituent alternation while keeping the word order in the constituents in agreement with the grammar. The example provided in Section 4.3 explains this in detail.

3 Pregroup Calculus and Precyclicity

In this section, we define pregroups and pregroup grammars. We also explore the mathematical apparatus required to define word order change, based upon the concept of precyclicity.

A pregroup is a partially ordered monoid [2] $(P, \cdot, 1, \rightarrow, (-)^l, (-)^r)$, which has two unary operators, the left and the right adjoint such that $\forall x \in P$:

$$x^l \cdot x \rightarrow 1 \rightarrow x \cdot x^r$$

---

[1] S = subject, O = object, IO = indirect object, DO = direct object, V = verb

[2] A monoid is a set closed under an associative binary operation. Partial order indicates that the binary relation has to be reflexive, anti0symmetric and transitive.

where 1 is the identity element, the $\cdot$ operator is a concatenation operator (usually not explicitly mentioned) and the $\to$ operator indicates partial order.

Some other properties of pregroups include:

$$1^l = 1 = 1^r$$

$$(a \cdot b)^l = b^l \cdot a^l \quad (a \cdot b)^r = b^r \cdot a^r$$

$$(a^l)^l = a^{ll} \quad (a^r)^r = a^{rr}$$

$$a^{rl} = a = a^{lr}$$

Adjoints are switching in nature, which means that:

$$a \to b \implies b^l \to a^l \quad a \to b \implies b^r \to a^r$$

The operations $x^l \cdot x \to 1$ and $x \cdot x^r \to 1$ are called contractions and the operations $1 \to x \cdot x^l$ and $1 \to x^r \cdot x$ are called expansions. The monoids used for pregroup grammars are called free pregroups, which have the property that without loss of generality, contractions precede expansions. This is called the *switching lemma* (Lambek, 1999).

Pregroup calculus defines a basic type as an element $a \in P$. A simple type can be obtained by basic types as:

$$a^{lll}, a^{ll}, a^l, a, a^r, a^{rr}, a^{rrr}$$

A compound type is a concatenation of simple types. Pregroup grammars, much like other categorial grammars, assigns compound types to words in a sentence. A sentence is considered grammatical if it reduces (by concatenation with adjoints) to the simple type of the main verb in the sentence.

Therefore, in English a simple transitive verb will be represented as follows:

$$\text{subject} \quad \text{verb} \quad \text{object}$$
$$\underbrace{n} \quad \underbrace{n^r \, s \, o^l \quad o} \quad \to s$$

The reductions are shown by the arcs, and the sentence reduces to type s, the type of the main verb.

A pregroup grammar is a quintuple $G = (\Sigma, P, \to, s, I)$ such that Σ is a nonempty, finite alphabet, $(P, \to)$ is a finite poset, $s \in P$, and I is a finite relation between symbols from Σ and non-empty types (on P) (Buszkowski, 2001). Contemporary literature symbolizes the set of all basic types as $\mathcal{B}$, and the set of all compound types as $T(\mathcal{B})$. $\mathcal{B}$ is a partially ordered set, while $T(\mathcal{B})$ is a free, proper pregroup over the set $\mathcal{B}$.

3.1 Precyclicity in Pregroups

A detailed understanding of cyclic properties of a pregroup can be derived from Lambek's syntactic calculus, and using a translation between residuated monoids (the structure used in syntactic calculus) and pregroups (Casadio and Lambek, 2002). Since pregroups used for language formalism are free, proper pregroups (Buszkowski, 2001), the classical definition of cyclicity $a \cdot b \to c \implies b \cdot a \to c$ does not hold. However, a weak form of cyclicity, called precyclicity, is admitted, which has the following properties (Yetter, 1990):

$$pq \to r \implies q \to p^r r \tag{1}$$
$$q \to rp \implies qp^r \to r \tag{2}$$
$$pq \to r \implies q \to rp^l \tag{3}$$
$$q \to pr \implies p^l q \to r \tag{4}$$

Due to this, we obtain the following rules for precyclicity with double adjoints (Abrusci, 1991):

$$1 \to ab \stackrel{ll}{\Rightarrow} 1 \to ba^{ll} \tag{5}$$
$$1 \to ab \stackrel{rr}{\Rightarrow} 1 \to b^{rr}a \tag{6}$$

Here, ba^{ll} and $b^{rr}a$ are known as the precyclic permutations of ab. Given these precyclic permutations, for $A, B, C \in P$, the following precyclic transformations are defined:

$$(ll) - transformation$$
$$A \to B(ab)C \rightsquigarrow^{ll} A \to B(ba^{ll})C \tag{7}$$
$$(rr) - transformation$$
$$A \to B(ab)C \rightsquigarrow^{rr} A \to B(b^{rr}a)C \tag{8}$$

These precyclic transformations provide the following two equations,

$$p^r q \leq qp^l \tag{9}$$
$$qp^l \leq p^r q \tag{10}$$

which can be seen to be empirically derived in clitic movement patterns in other languages, explored in Casadio and Sadrzadeh (2009).

4 A Preliminary Pregroup Grammar for Hindi

This section identifies the basic types and compound types used in Hindi. The basic types are pregroup pregroup represnenations of syntactic features discussed in Section 2.

4.1 Basic Types

The basic types will be similar to the set of basic types chosen for English, $\{\pi, o, p, n, s\}$, which are personal pronouns, the direct object of a transitive verb, simple predicate, noun phrase, and sentence respectively (Lambek, 2004). The basic types for the lexicalized case markers as well as the tense and aspect markers have to be included, explained below.

The basic type κ_i and ρ represent *karaka* and *sambandh* markers (for the genitive case) respectively. The subscript on κ denotes the case of the noun that precedes it (refer Table 2). A simple example of the genitive case interaction, for the noun phrase "Ram's brother" (*raam kaa bhai*), is as:

$$(n)(n^r \rho)(\rho^r n) \to n$$

The type assignment seems to imply that in the genitive case marker is the headword of the noun phrase *raam kaa*, which is not the case. Genitives in Hindi are gender marked, and they agree with the gender of the following noun phrase, which is preserved by the current type assignment. The type assignment is reflective of the Paninian framework of modifier-modified relationship, in which the genitive case marker reflects the modification of the following noun phrase (Bharati and Sangal, 1993).

The VP consists of a verb, an optional auxiliary (denoted by α) and a tense marker (denoted by τ), in that order of occurrence. Verb transitivity does affect the verb typing, but only in the sentence. All statement verbs are given the type s. Verbs in Hindi are unique for their tense marking system, which include a gender-marked past tense marker, a gender-neutral present tense marker, and a suffixed future tense marker.

Given the semantic nature of *karaka* markers in Hindi, verb transitivity raises ambiguous cases. For example, the sentence *Ram ne seb **ko** khaaya* and *Ram ne seb khaaya* both translate to "Ram ate an apple". In this analysis, there are three distinct cases of the use of *karaka* intransitive verbs are: (1) no case markers, (2) ergative case marker on the subject and (3) ergative case marker on the

subject and accusative case marker on the direct object (Palmer et al., 2009).

4.2 Examples of Hindi Sentences

Given the set of basic types $\{\pi, s, p, o, n, \kappa_i, \rho, \alpha, \tau\}$, simple sentences can be typed in Hindi as follows. The toy examples chosen here are similar in to a few of the simple sentences of the Hindi treebank (Bhatt et al., 2009).

1. I go to school.

mein	*skool*	*jaataa*	*hun*
I	school	go-perf.-masc.	am
π	o	$o^r \pi^r s \tau^l$	τ

$$(\pi)(o)(o^r \pi^r s \tau^l)(\tau) \to s$$

2. Tina sang a song.

tinaaa	*ne*	*gaanaa*	*gaayaa*
Tina	erg.	song	sang-masc.
$n\kappa_1^l$	κ_1	o	$o^r n^r s$

$$(n\,\kappa_1^l)(\kappa_1)(o)(o^r n^r s) \to s$$

3. Ram had hit the ball with a bat.

raam	*ne*	*gend*	*ko*
Ram	erg.	ball	acc.
$n\kappa_1^l$	κ_1	$o\kappa_2^l$	κ_2

balle	*se*	*maaraa*	*thaa*
bat	with	hit-masc.	was-masc.
$p\kappa_3^l$	κ_3	$p^r o^r n^r s \tau^l$	τ

$$(n\kappa_1^l)(\kappa_1)(o\kappa_2^l)(\kappa_2)(p\kappa_3^l)(\kappa_3)(p^r o^r n^r$$
$$s\,\tau^l)(\tau) \to s$$

κ_i	*karaka*
κ_1	*karta*
κ_2	*karma*
κ_3	*karan*
κ_4	*sampradan*
κ_5	*apaadan*
κ_6	*adhikaran*

Table 2: Type given to *karaka*

4.3 Consequences of Restricted Word Order Alternation

In order to apply precyclicity rules,[3] the example chosen is a simple transitive verb from the sentence "Tina sang a song", which has been typed above in section 4.2. As above, the arcs denote a reduction, while the underline shows the arguments of the precyclic transformation.

4.

gaanaa	*tina*	*ne*	*gaayaa*
song	Tina	erg.	sang-masc.

$$(o)(n\kappa_1{}^l)(\kappa_1)(o^r n^r s)$$
$$\rightarrow (o)(n)(o^r n^r s)$$
$$\leadsto^{ll} (o)(n)(n^r o^l s)$$
$$\rightarrow (o)(o^l s)$$
$$\leadsto^{rr} (o^l s)^{rr}(o)$$
$$\rightarrow (o^r s^{rr})(o)$$
$$\leadsto^{ll} (s^{rr} o^l)(o)$$
$$\rightarrow s^{rr}$$
$$\leadsto^{ll} s$$

An example of a sentence with two movements is as follows, for the sentence "Ram had hit the ball with a bat".

5.

balle	*se*	*gend*	*ko*
bat	with	ball	acc.

raam	*ne*	*maaraa*	*thaa*
Ram	erg.	hit-masc.	was-masc.

$$(p\kappa_3{}^l)(\kappa_3)(o\kappa_2{}^l)(\kappa_2)(n\kappa_1{}^l)(\kappa_1)(p^r o^r n^r s \tau^l)(\tau)$$
$$\rightarrow (p)(o)(n)(p^r o^r n^r s)$$
$$\leadsto^{ll} (p)(o)(n)(p^r n^r o^l s)$$
$$\leadsto^{ll} (p)(o)(n)(n^r p^l o^l s)$$
$$\rightarrow (p)(o)(p^l o^l s)$$
$$\leadsto^{rr} (p)(o)(o^r p^l s)$$
$$\rightarrow (p)(p^l s)$$
$$\leadsto^{rr} (p^l s)^{rr}(p)$$
$$\rightarrow (p^r s^{rr})(p)$$
$$\leadsto^{ll} (s^{rr} p^l)(p)$$
$$\rightarrow s^{rr}$$
$$\leadsto^{ll} s$$

Note that in the first example, the movement was *gaanaa* and *tinaa ne*, and not just *tinaa*; similarly, in the second sentence, the constituents being shuffled are *balle se* and *gend ko*. Hindi allows

only constituent scrambling, the pregroup grammar has to account for this restriction. For example, the following construction should **NOT** be allowed:

6. *

tinaa	*gaanaa*	*ne*	*gaayaa*
Tina	song	erg.	sang
$n\kappa_1{}^l$	o	κ_1	$o^r n^r s$

$$(n\kappa_1{}^l)(o)(\kappa_1)(o^r n^r s)$$
$$\leadsto^{ll} (n\kappa_1{}^l)(\kappa_1)(o^{ll})(o^r n^r s)$$
$$\rightarrow (n)(o^{ll})(o^r n^r s)$$
$$\leadsto^{rr} (o)(n)(o^r n^r s)$$
$$\leadsto^{ll} (o)(n)(n^r o^l s)$$
$$\rightarrow (o)(o^l s)$$
$$\leadsto^{rr} (o^l s)^{rr}(o)$$
$$\rightarrow (o^r s^{rr})(o)$$
$$\leadsto^{ll} (s^{rr} o^l)(o)$$
$$\rightarrow s^{rr}$$
$$\leadsto^{ll} s$$

5 Restricting Word Movement

As seen in section 4, the current pregroup grammar rules allow for the reduction of sentences which are disallowed by the grammar. This section explains the methods taken to restrict word movement, in order to allow only constituent scrambling, keeping the order of the words within a constituent constant.

5.1 Pregroup Grammar Rules

Pregroup grammar rules for restricting word order movement have been briefly discussed in (Casadio, 2004) and (Casadio and Sadrzadeh, 2014). Here, instead of treating restrictive rules as an exception, we treat it as a part of the pregroup framework, by creating a formal representation of these restrictions.

For example, a word order rule in Hindi syntax is "The alternation of ANY phrase with a *karaka* marker is disallowed" (Bopche et al., 2012), it may be represented in the following way:

$$\forall x \in \mathcal{B}$$
$$(x)(\kappa_i) \not\leadsto^{ll} (\kappa_i)(x^{ll})$$
$$(x)(\kappa_i) \not\leadsto^{rr} (\kappa_i^{rr})(x)$$

where, as discussed in Section 3, $\mathcal{B}$ is the set of all basic types in the language. A similar set of

---

rules can be created for alternation in verb constituents, where no word order alternation is allowed between a verb and its aspect marker, and between the aspect and the tense marker, mirroring the rules of the language.

$$(s)(\tau) \not\leadsto^{ll} (\tau)(s^{ll}) \qquad (s)(\tau) \not\leadsto^{rr} (\tau^{rr})(s)$$
$$(\tau)(\alpha) \not\leadsto^{ll} (\alpha)(\tau^{ll}) \qquad (\tau)(\alpha) \not\leadsto^{rr} (\alpha^{rr})(\tau)$$
$$(s)(\alpha) \not\leadsto^{ll} (\alpha)(s^{ll}) \qquad (s)(\alpha) \not\leadsto^{rr} (\alpha^{rr})(s)$$

Therefore, in the example *tinaa gaanaa ne gaayaa* (Tina song erg. sang) presented above, we have:

$$(n\kappa_1^l)(o)(\kappa_1)(o^r n^r s)$$
$$\not\leadsto^{ll} (n\kappa_1{}^l)(\kappa_1)(o^{ll})(o^r n^r s)$$

Thus the sentence will not reduce to s as it is deemed ungrammatical.

5.2 Selective Transformation

Selective transformation is a procedure that disallows the precyclic transformation of a step in the reduction, provided that some elements of the pregroup representation belong to a set that does not allow precyclic transformation, hence allowing only a selective application of the precyclic conversion rules.

As discussed in section 3, $\mathcal{B}$ is the set of all basic types in the language, and $T(\mathcal{B})$ is the free pregroup over that set. In order to apply selective transformation, two sets The sets $\mathcal{B}_T$ and $\mathcal{B}_{NT}$ are defined, such that the set of all basic types $\mathcal{B} = \mathcal{B}_T \cup \mathcal{B}_{NT}$, where $T(\mathcal{B}_{NT})$ is a free, proper, non-precyclic pregroup, while $T(\mathcal{B}_T)$ is a proper, free, precyclic pregroup. The union of a precyclic and a non-precyclic pregroup is a non-precyclic pregroup, and no other properties of the pregroup are affected (Refer to the Appendix for the proof).

Within the examples seen above, the basic types of the *karaka* marker and *sambandh* marker in the noun phrase, and the tense and aspect marker in the verb phrase should not ll- or rr-transformed, while the personal pronoun, sentence, predicate, noun phrase, and direct object types are allowed to transform. Therefore, $\{\kappa_i, \rho, \alpha, \tau\} \in \mathcal{B}_{NT}$ and $\{\pi, s, p, o, n\} \in \mathcal{B}_T$. Therefore, to apply transformation rules, only the types in the sentence should be those belonging in $\mathcal{B}_T$. Therefore, in the example *tinaa ne gaanaa gaayaa* (Tina erg. song sang), we have:

$$(o)(n\kappa_1{}^l)(\kappa_1)(o^r n^r s)$$
$$\rightarrow (o)(n)(o^r n^r s)$$

where all the elements in the second line belong to $\mathcal{B}_T$, which allows the transformations and reductions:

$$\leadsto^{ll} (o)(n)(n^r o^l s)$$
$$\rightarrow (o)(o^l s)$$
$$\leadsto^{rr} (o^l s)^{rr}(o)$$
$$\rightarrow (o^r s^{rr})(o)$$
$$\leadsto^{ll} (s^{rr} o^l)(o)$$
$$\rightarrow s^{rr}$$
$$\leadsto^{ll} s$$

while in the example of the construction *tinaa gaanaa ne gaayaa* (Tina song erg. sang) presented above, we have:

$$(n\kappa_1^l)(o)(\kappa_1)(o^r n^r s)$$

which is not reducible as the transformations cannot be applied. Therefore ungrammatical reductions are disallowed.[4]

5.3 Two-Step Reduction

As mentioned above, Hindi allows constituent scrambling as opposed to word order scrambling. Therefore the reduction of a sentence can be deconstructed into two steps, the reduction of constituents, followed by reduction of the sentence. This process guarantees that ungrammatical reductions will not take place.

For the two-step reductions, first the "constituent profile" has to be defined. A constituent profile is a general construction to which constituents in Hindi can be mapped. Each constituent profile has a reduction which can be applied to a sentence. A constituent profile is specific to the type of phrase expected. A sequence of words which does not follow any constituent profile cannot be reduced. This will disallow the reduction of ungrammatical sentences.

Table 3 shows the constituent profiles for the examples provided above. The $[x]^+$ represents one or more elements of the basic type x. Note that there is no need for a transformation in any of the constituent profiles, as it reduces to the constituent head form automatically. The constituents can be nested, and the constituent profile reflects this. A sentence may be defined as a specific case of a constituent profile, as it is the *only* profile which allows transformations before reductions.

---

[4]Refer to Appendix for mathematical correctness of selective transformation.

Constituent Type	Constituent Profile
Subject	$(x\kappa_1^l)(\kappa_1) \to x \; for \; x \in \{\pi, n\}$
Direct Object	$(o\kappa_2^l)(\kappa_2) \to o$
Predicate	$(p\kappa_i^l)(\kappa_i) \to p \; for \; i \in [3,6]$
Nominal Relations	$(\rho)(\rho^r x) \to x \; for \; x \in \{n, o, p\}$ $(n)(n^r \rho)(\rho^r x) \to x \; for \; x \in \{n, o, p\}$
Verb Forms	$([x^r]^+ s\alpha^l)(\alpha\tau^l)(\tau) \to ([x^r]^+ s) \; for \; [x] \in \{n, o, p\}$ $([x^r]^+ s\tau^l)(\tau) \to ([x^r]^+ s) \; for \; [x] \in \{n, o, p\}$
Sentence	$(n)([x])^+([x^r]^+ n^r s) \to s \; for \; [x] \in \{o, p\}$

Table 3: Constituent Profiles for Hindi

Two-step reduction can be achieved as follows:

- **Type the sentence**: This allows the recognition of all possible constituent profiles, as well as conflicts with the constituent profiles.

- **Isolate and reduce constituents**: The constituents are mapped to the constituent profiles, and reduced accordingly.

- **Replace reduced forms in the sentence**: The constituents, once reduced, are placed back into the order in which they occurred in the original sentence. The sentence form should resemble the "sentence" profile.

- **Transform and reduce**: The sentence is then transformed and reduced according to the rules of transformation, as has been done above.

An example of two-step reduction for the sentence *raam ne gend ko balle se maara thaa* (Ram hit the ball with a bat) would be as follows:

Step 1:

$$\underline{(n\kappa_1^l)(\kappa_1)} \; \underline{(o\kappa_2^l)(\kappa_2)} \; \underline{(p\kappa_3^l)(\kappa_3)(p^r o^r n^r s\tau^l)(\tau)}$$

Step 2: $(n\kappa_1^l)(\kappa_1) \to n$, according to the subject constituent profile. Similarly, $(o\kappa_2^l)(\kappa_2) \to o$ and $(p\kappa_3^l)(\kappa_3) \to p$ are also valid reductions according to the object and predicate profiles. There is also the $([x^r]^+ n^r s\tau^l)(\tau) \to ([x^r]^+ n^r s)$, which is a valid verb form reduction.

Step 3: $(n)(o)(p)(p^r o^r n^r s)$ is obtained, which fits the sentence profile.

Step 4: $(n)(o)(p)(p^r o^r n^r s) \to s$, which is the required reduction

An incorrect reduction can be recognized easily. Given the example that was provided in Section 4.2 *tinaa gaanaa ne gaayaa*. After step 1, the following is obtained:

$$\underline{(n\kappa_1^l)(o)(\kappa_1)(o^r n^r s)}$$

which cannot be found in any constituent profile. Therefore, the sentence is ungrammatical, and will appropriately not be represented by the grammar

6 Word Order Alternation in English

Lambek's work in English type grammar (Lambek, 2004) and the work that has followed (Preller, 2007; Stabler, 2008) have not dealt with word order alternation in English yet. While English is a relatively fixed word order language, note that prepositional phrases and adverbial phrases are relatively free, especially with intransitive verbs. Therefore, while the default order remains "Subject-Adverb-Verb-PP", it can be seen in the following sentences that this word order can also change.

- Default (S-Adv-V-PP): "I quickly ran into the fields."

- PP-S-Adv-V: "Into the fields, I ran quickly."

- Adv-S-V-PP: "Quickly I ran into the fields."

- S-V-Adv-PP: "I ran quickly into the fields."

- S-V-PP-Adv: "I ran into the fields quickly."

To develop a robust representation of English word order, first, the initial word order constraints must be noted. The standard word order in English is SVO, which reduces to SV in the case of intransitive verbs, which is the focus of this sample. We examine the word order alternation in this fragment of English, using the methods explored in the paper.

First, the set of basic types $\{\pi, o, s, n, p\}$ has to be expanded to include types for adverbial phrase A and type for prepositional phrase ρ. The subscripts which characterize gender, number, person or tense have been ignored for this example. The determiner is considered a part of the noun phrase. Therefore, the sample sentence, in the default word order, can be typed as follows ("the fields" has been typed p):

7.
I	quickly	ran	into	the fields.
π	A	$A^r\pi^r s\rho^l$	ρp^l	p

$$(\pi)(A)(A^r\pi^r s\rho^l)(\rho p^l)(p) \to s$$

This reduction is reasonably straightforward. On changing the word order, precyclic transformations are applicable, so a similar reduction for the statement, "Quickly I ran into the fields", can be handled as follows:

8.
Quickly	I	ran	into	the fields.
A	π	$A^r\pi^r s\rho^l$	ρp^l	p

$$
\begin{aligned}
&(A)(\pi)(A^r\pi^r s\rho^l)(\rho\, p^l)(p) \\
&\to (A)(\pi)(\overline{A^r\pi^r s}) \\
&\leadsto^{ll} (A)(\pi)(\pi^r A^l s) \\
&\to (A)(A^l s) \\
&\leadsto^{rr} \overline{(A^r s^{rr})}(A) \\
&\leadsto^{ll} (s^{rr} A^l)(A) \leadsto^{ll} s
\end{aligned}
$$

The sentence "Quickly I ran the fields into" is an ungrammatical sentence and should not be reducible by the grammar. However:

9. *
Quickly	I	ran	the fields	into.
A	π	$A^r\pi^r s\rho^l$	p	ρp^l

$$
\begin{aligned}
&(A)(\pi)(A^r\pi^r s\rho^l)(p)(\rho p^l) \\
&\leadsto^{rr} (A)(\pi)(A^r\pi^r s\rho^l)(p)(p^r\rho)
\end{aligned}
$$

$$
\begin{aligned}
&\to (A)(\pi)(\overline{A^r\pi^r s}) \\
&\leadsto^{ll} (A)(\pi)(\pi^r A^l s) \\
&\to (A)(A^l s) \\
&\leadsto^{rr} \overline{(A^r s^{rr})}(A) \\
&\leadsto^{ll} (s^{rr} A^l)(A) \leadsto^{ll} s
\end{aligned}
$$

Therefore, the methods discussed in section 5 can be used to disallow this reduction.

- Using the method of restriction of pregroup grammar rules, the transformation $(\rho p^l) \leadsto^{rr} (p^r\rho)$ is disallowed. So the order of the prepositional phrase and its predicate remains the same, disallowing an ungrammatical reduction.

- Two-step reduction can be used to establish the prepositional phrase profile as $(\rho p^l)(p)$, and the sentence does not follow this profile. Therefore, further reduction is disallowed.

- Under selective transformation, the only basic type that can belong to $\mathcal{B}_{NT}$ is p. Therefore, its alternation with the type ρ is considered ungrammatical and the sentence is not reduced.

Hence, all three methods can be used to disallow the representation and reduction of ungrammatical sentences.

7 Conclusion

This paper is an attempt to formalize the syntactic notion of word order alternation using pregroup grammars by expanding on the developments in the current literature and proposing two novel methods of representing restrictions in word movement. The inspiration for this development stems from the syntactic structure of Hindi, an isolating free word order language which allows only for constituent scrambling, keeping the order of the words in the constituents the same.

In order to express the syntactic properties of Hindi, a preliminary pregroup grammar for Hindi has also been established. This pregroup grammar has been developed in a manner similar to their development in other languages, with the establishment of basic types and examples of sentences represented using the grammar. Further work can be done in the development of the pregroup grammar of Hindi, in modeling agreement rules and other aspects of the Hindi syntax.

The methods proposed include the expansion and formal representation of the method used for Sanskrit, as well as two novel approaches which are selective transformation and two-step reduction. Using examples in the paper, these methods have been applied to prove their effectiveness, and an example has also been taken from English, which does the same.

Future work in this direction could include development of pregroup representations of common cross-lingual syntactic phenomena, such as agglutenation, that would make the adaptation of pregroups to other languages easier. A more thorough grammar, based on other properties such as subject-verb agreement, verb complements and so on are other directions of developing the work.

Acknowledgements We sincerely thank the inputs and suggestions of Dr. Marie-Catherine de Marneffe. We would also like to acknowledge and thank the anonymous reviewers for their time and effort.

References

V Michele Abrusci. 1991. Phase semantics and sequent calculus for pure noncommutative classical linear propositional logic. *The Journal of Symbolic Logic*, 56(4):1403–1451.

Tafseer Ahmed, Miriam Butt, Annette Hautli, and Sebastian Sulger. 2012. A reference dependency bank for analyzing complex predicates. In *LREC*.

Bharat Ram Ambati, Samar Husain, Joakim Nivre, and Rajeev Sangal. 2010. On the role of morphosyntactic features in Hindi dependency parsing. In *Proceedings of the NAACL HLT 2010 First Workshop on Statistical Parsing of Morphologically-Rich Languages*, pages 94–102. Association for Computational Linguistics.

Daniele Bargelli and Joachim Lambek. 2001a. An algebraic approach to French sentence structure. In *International Conference on Logical Aspects of Computational Linguistics*, pages 62–78. Springer.

Donna Bargelli and Joachim Lambek. 2001b. An algebraic approach to Arabic sentence structure. *Linguistic Analysis*, 31(3):301–315.

Akshar Bharati and Rajeev Sangal. 1993. Parsing free word order languages in the Paninian framework. In *Proceedings of the 31st annual meeting on Association for Computational Linguistics*, pages 105–111. Association for Computational Linguistics.

Rajesh Bhatt, Bhuvana Narasimhan, Martha Palmer, Owen Rambow, Dipti Sharma, and Fei Xia. 2009. A multi-representational and multi-layered treebank for hindi/urdu. In *Proceedings of the Third Linguistic Annotation Workshop (LAW III)*, pages 186–189.

Lata Bopche, Gauri Dhopavkar, and Manali Kshirsagar. 2012. Grammar checking system using rule based morphological process for an indian language. In *Global Trends in Information Systems and Software Applications*, pages 524–531. Springer.

Wojciech Buszkowski. 2001. Lambek grammars based on pregroups. In *International Conference on Logical Aspects of Computational Linguistics*, pages 95–109. Springer.

Wojciech Buszkowski. 2002. Cut elimination for the Lambek calculus of adjoints.

Wojciech Buszkowski. 2003. Sequent systems for compact bilinear logic. *Mathematical Logic Quarterly: Mathematical Logic Quarterly*, 49(5):467–474.

Miriam Butt and Tracy Holloway King. 1996. Structural topic and focus without movement. In *Proceedings of the First LFG Conference*. Stanford: CSLI Publications.

Kumi Cardinal. 2002. *An algebraic study of Japanese grammar*. Ph.D. thesis, McGill University Montreal.

Claudia Casadio. 2004. Pregroup grammar. theory and applications.

Claudia Casadio. 2010. Agreement and cliticization in Italian: a pregroup analysis. In *International Conference on Language and Automata Theory and Applications*, pages 166–177. Springer.

Claudia Casadio and Jim Lambek. 2005. A computational algebraic approach to latin grammar. *Research on Language and Computation*, 3(1):45.

Claudia Casadio and Joachim Lambek. 2002. A tale of four grammars. *Studia Logica*, 71(3):315–329.

Claudia Casadio and Mehrnoosh Sadrzadeh. 2009. Clitic movement in pregroup grammar: a cross-linguistic approach. In *International Tbilisi Symposium on Logic, Language, and Computation*, pages 197–214. Springer.

Claudia Casadio and Mehrnoosh Sadrzadeh. 2014. Word order alternation in sanskrit via precyclicity in pregroup grammars. In *Horizons of the Mind. A Tribute to Prakash Panangaden*, pages 229–249. Springer.

Debasri Chakrabarti, Hemang Mandalia, Ritwik Priya, Vaijayanthi Sarma, and Pushpak Bhattacharyya. 2008. Hindi compound verbs and their automatic extraction. *Coling 2008: Companion volume: Posters*, pages 27–30.

Bob Coecke, Mehrnoosh Sadrzadeh, and Stephen Clark. 2010. Mathematical foundations for a compositional distributional model of meaning. *arXiv preprint arXiv:1003.4394*.

Julia Hockenmaier and Mark Steedman. 2007. Ccgbank: a corpus of ccg derivations and dependency structures extracted from the penn treebank. *Computational Linguistics*, 33(3):355–396.

Ayesha Kidwai. 2000. *XP-adjunction in Universal Grammar: Scrambling and binding in Hindi-Urdu*. Oxford University Press on Demand.

Aleksandra Kislak-Malinowska. 2008. Polish language in terms of pregroups. *Recent Computational Algebraic Approaches to Morphology and Syntax. Polimetrica, Milan*, pages 145–172.

J Lambek. 1999. Type grammar revisited. *Lecture notes in computer science*, pages 1–27.

Joachim Lambek. 1958. The mathematics of sentence structure. *The American Mathematical Monthly*, 65(3):154–170.

Joachim Lambek. 1997. Type grammar revisited. In *International Conference on Logical Aspects of Computational Linguistics*, pages 1–27. Springer.

Joachim Lambek. 2000. Type grammar meets German word order. *Theoretical Linguistics*, 26(1-2):19–30.

Joachim Lambek. 2004. A computational algebraic approach to english grammar. *Syntax*, 7(2):128–147.

Richard T Oehrle, Emmon Bach, and Deirdre Wheeler. 2012. *Categorial grammars and natural language structures*, volume 32. Springer Science & Business Media.

Martha Palmer, Rajesh Bhatt, Bhuvana Narasimhan, Owen Rambow, Dipti Misra Sharma, and Fei Xia. 2009. Hindi syntax: Annotating dependency, lexical predicate-argument structure, and phrase structure. In *The 7th International Conference on Natural Language Processing*, pages 14–17.

Umesh Patil, Gerrit Kentner, Anja Gollrad, Frank Kügler, Caroline Féry, and Shravan Vasishth. 2008. Focus, word order and intonation in Hindi. *Journal of South Asian Linguistics*, 1(1).

Mark Pedersen, Domenyk Eades, Samir K Amin, and Lakshmi Prakash. 2004. Relative clauses in Hindi and Arabic: A Paninian dependency grammar analysis. In *Proceedings of the Workshop on Recent Advances in Dependency Grammar*.

Anne Preller. 2007. Toward discourse representation via pregroup grammars. *Journal of Logic, Language and Information*, 16(2):173–194.

Mehrnoosh Sadrzadeh. 2007. Pregroup analysis of Persian sentences.

Mehrnoosh Sadrzadeh. 2011. An adventure into hungarian word order with cyclic pregroups. *Models, Logics, and Higher-Dimensional Categories, a tribute to the work of Michael Makkai, Centre de Recherches Mathématiques. Proceedings and Lecture Notes*, 53:263–275.

Djamé Seddah, Sandra Koebler, and Reut Tsarfaty. 2010. Proceedings of the NAACL HLT 2010 first workshop on statistical parsing of morphologically-rich languages. In *Proceedings of the NAACL HLT 2010 First Workshop on Statistical Parsing of Morphologically-Rich Languages*.

Andrew Spencer, Miriam Butt, and Tracy Holloway King. 2005. Case in Hindi. In *Proceedings of LFG*, volume 5, pages 429–446.

Edward P Stabler. 2008. Tupled pregroup grammars. *Computational and Algebraic Approaches to Natural Language, edited by Claudia Casadio and Joachim Lambek. Milano, Italia: Polimetrica*.

David N. Yetter. 1990. Quantales and (noncommutative) linear logic. *The Journal of Symbolic Logic*, 55(1):41–64.

A Appendix: The Mathematics of Selective Transformation

The operations between the sets $T(\mathcal{B}_T)$ and $T(\mathcal{B}_{NT})$ that were implemented in the paper in Section 5.2 and the non-precyclic nature of $T(\mathcal{B})$ are explained here.

Precyclic transformation was introduced in Yetter (1990), for relaxing the conditions on the cut theorem on one sided sequent calculus for pure non-commutative classical linear propositional logic. The original rules of precyclic transformation:

$$\frac{\vdash \Gamma, A}{\vdash A^{\perp\perp}, \Gamma}$$

$$\frac{\vdash A, \Gamma}{\vdash \Gamma, ^{\perp\perp} A}$$

The calculus for which this rule was applicable was called SPNCL', while the calculus where this rule was not applicable was SPNCL. In order to understand the affect of this theorem, note the cut theorem in SPNCL:

$$\frac{\vdash \Gamma_1, A, \Gamma_2 \quad \vdash \Delta_1, A^{\perp}, \Delta_2}{\vdash \Delta_1, \Gamma_1, \Delta_2, \Gamma_2}$$

$$\frac{\vdash \Gamma_1, ^{\perp} A, \Gamma_2 \quad \vdash \Delta_1, A, \Delta_2}{\vdash \Delta_1, \Gamma_1, \Delta_2, \Gamma_2}$$

if $\Delta_1 = \varnothing$ or $\Gamma_2 = \varnothing$. And the cut theorem in SPNCL', due to these rules, was reduced to:

$$\frac{\vdash \Gamma, A \quad \vdash \Delta, A^{\perp}}{\vdash \Delta, \Gamma}$$

$$\frac{\vdash \Gamma, ^{\perp} A \quad \vdash \Delta, A}{\vdash \Delta, \Gamma}$$

Precyclic pregroups are a result of a bilinear mapping of this reduction in SPNCL' to pregroups, using the interpretation map of compact bilinear logic (Buszkowski, 2003). However, note that this reduction was made to relax the constraints on cut theorem in SPNCL. Buszkowski (2002) notes that pregroups are cut eliminated, which means that all properties that can be proved using cut theorem can be proved without it. Due to this cut-elimination, in a pregroup mapped from SPNCL and one mapped from SPNCL', the adjoint behaviour is identical and therefore their concatenation and reduction do not undergo any change.

Now, the non-precyclic nature of the pregroup $T(\mathcal{B})$ is to be proved. $T(\mathcal{B})$ has been defined as $T(\mathcal{B}_T) \cup T(\mathcal{B}_{NT})$, where $T(\mathcal{B}_T)$ is the pregroup that allows for precylic transformations and $T(\mathcal{B}_{NT})$ is the pregroup that does not allow the same. Note that both SPNCL and SPNCL' are defined over the same set of sequents, but are defined using different formulae. For a formula A of $\mathscr{L}$(SPNCL) and formula B of $\mathscr{L}$(SPNCL'), the cut theorem in SPNCL' will not be applicable for a proof with both A and B, as the rule $(-)^{\perp\perp}$ cannot be used for formulae of SPNCL. Hence, given the compact map from bi-linear logic to pregroups, the analogous ll- and rr-transformations become inapplicable over a pregroup which has *any element* that does not obey precyclicity. Therefore, the union of a precyclic and a non-precyclic pregroup is a non-precyclic pregroup.

Speak Up, Fight Back!
Detection of Social Media Disclosures of Sexual Harassment

Arijit Ghosh Chowdhury*
Manipal Institute of Technology, MAHE
arijit10@gmail.com

Ramit Sawhney*
Netaji Subhas Institute of Technology
ramits.co@nsit.net.in

Puneet Mathur
MIDAS, IIIT-Delhi
pmathur3k6@gmail.com

Debanjan Mahata
Bloomberg
dmahata@bloomberg.net

Rajiv Ratn Shah
MIDAS, IIIT-Delhi
rajivratn@iiitd.ac.in

Abstract

The #MeToo movement is an ongoing prevalent phenomenon on social media aiming to demonstrate the frequency and widespread of sexual harassment by providing a platform to speak up and narrate personal experiences of such harassment. The aggregation and analysis of such disclosures pave the way to the development of technology-based prevention of sexual harassment. We contend that the lack of specificity in generic sentence classification models may not be the best way to tackle text subtleties that intrinsically prevail in a classification task as complex as identifying disclosures of sexual harassment. We propose the Disclosure Language Model, a three-part ULMFiT architecture, consisting of a Language model, a Medium-Specific (Twitter) model, and a Task-Specific classifier to tackle this problem and create a manually annotated real-world dataset to test our technique on this, to show that using a Discourse Language Model often yields better classification performance over (i) Generic deep learning based sentence classification models (ii) existing models that rely on handcrafted stylistic features. An extensive comparison with state-of-the-art generic and specific models along with a detailed error analysis presents the case for our proposed methodology.

1 Introduction

Thirty-five percent of women, including people in the LGBTQIA+ community, are globally subjected to sexual or physical assault, according to a study by UN Women [1]. With the advent of the #MeToo movement (Lee, 2018), discussions about sexual abuse have finally seen the light as compared to before, without the fear of shame or retaliation. Abuse in general and sexual harassment, in particular, is one topic that is socially stigmatized and difficult for people to talk about in both non-computer-mediated and computer-mediated contexts. The Disclosure Processes Model (DPM) (Andalibi et al., 2016) examines when and why interpersonal disclosure may be beneficial and focuses on people with concealable stigmatized identities (e.g., abuse, rape) in non-computer-mediated contexts. It has been found that disclosure of abuse has positive psychological impacts (Manikonda et al., 2016); (McClain and Amar, 2013)), and the #MeToo movement has managed to make social media avenues like Twitter a safer place to share personal experiences.

The information gathered from these kinds of online discussions can be leveraged to create better campaigns for social change by analyzing how users react to these stories and obtaining a better insight into the consequences of sexual abuse. Prior studies noted that developing an automated framework for classifying a tweet is quite challenging due to the inherent complexity of the natural language constructs (Badjatiya et al., 2017).

Tweets are entirely different from other text forms like movie reviews and news forums. Tweets are often short and ambiguous because of the limitation of characters. There are more mis-

---

* Denotes equal contribution.

[1] http://www.unwomen.org/en/what-we-do/ending-violence-against-women/facts-and-figures

Proceedings of the 2019 Conference of the North American Chapter of the Association for Computational Linguistics: Student Research Workshop, pages 136–146
Minneapolis, Minnesota, June 3 - 5, 2019. ©2017 Association for Computational Linguistics

spelled words, slangs, and acronyms on Twitter because of its casual form (Mahata et al., 2015). This motivates our study to build a medium-specific Language Model for the segregation of tweets containing disclosures of sexual harassment.

While there is a developing body of literature on the topic of identifying patterns in the language used on social media that analyze sexual harassment disclosure (Manikonda et al., 2018); (Andalibi et al., 2016), very few attempts have been made to segregate texts containing discussions about sexual abuse from texts containing personal recollections of sexual harassment experiences. Efforts have been made to segregate domestic abuse stories from Reddit by Schrading et al. (2015) and Karlekar and Bansal. However, these approaches do not take into consideration the model's domain understanding of the syntactic and semantic attributes of the specific medium in which the text is present.

In that regard, our paper makes two significant contributions.

1. Generation of a labeled real-world dataset for identifying social media disclosures of sexual abuse, by manual annotation.

2. Comparison of the proposed Medium-Specific Disclosure Language Model architecture for segregation of tweets containing disclosure, with various deep learning architectures and machine learning models, in terms of four evaluation metrics.

2   Related Work

Twitter is fast becoming the most widely used source for social media research, both in academia and in industry (Meghawat et al., 2018) (Shah and Zimmermann, 2017). Wekerle et al. (2018) have shown that Twitter is being used for increasing research on sexual violence. Using social media could support at-risk youth, professionals, and academics given the many strengths of employing such a knowledge mobilization tool. Previously, Twitter has been used to tackle mental health issues (Sawhney et al., 2018b) (Sawhney et al., 2018a) and for other social issues like detection of hate speech content online (Mathur et al., 2018). Mahata et al. (2018) have mobilized Twitter to detect information regarding personal intake of medicines. Social media use is free, easy to implement, available to difficult to access popu-

lations (e.g., victims of sexual violence), and can reduce the gap between research and practice. Bogen et al. (2018) discusses the social reactions to disclosures of sexual victimization on Twitter. This work suggests that online forums may offer a unique context for disclosing violence and receiving support. Khatua et al. (2018) have explored deep learning techniques to classify tweets of sexual violence, but have not explicitly focused on building a robust system that can detect recollections of personal stories of abuse.

Schrading et al. (2015) created the Reddit Domestic Abuse Dataset, to facilitate classification of domestic abuse stories using a combination of SVM and N-grams. Karlekar and Bansal improved upon this by using CNN-LSTMs, due to the complementary strengths of both these architectures. Reddit allows lengthy submissions, unlike Twitter, and therefore the use of standard English is more common. This allows natural language processing tools trained on standard English to function better. Our method explores the merits of using a Twitter-specific Language Model which can counter the shortcomings of using pre-trained word embeddings derived from other tasks, on a medium like Twitter where the language is informal, and the grammar is often ambiguous.

N-gram based Twitter Language Models (Vo et al., 2015) have been previously used to detect events and for analyzing Twitter conversations (Ritter et al., 2010). Atefeh and Khreich (2015) used Emoticon Smoothed Language Models for Twitter Sentiment Analysis. Rother and Rettberg (2018) used the ULMFiT model proposed by Howard and Ruder (2018) to detect offensive tweets in German. Manikonda et al. (2018) try to investigate social media posts discussing sexual abuse by analyzing factors such as *linguistic themes*, *social engagement*, and *emotional attributes*. Their work proves that Twitter is an effective source for human behavior analysis, based on several linguistic markers. Andalibi et al. (2016) attempt to characterize abuse related disclosures into different categories, based on different themes, like gender, support seeking nature, etc. Our study aims to bridge the gap between gathering information and analyzing social media disclosures of sexual abuse. Our approach suggests that the language used on Twitter can be treated as a separate language construct, with its own rules and restrictions that need to be addressed to capture subtle nuances and understand the context better.

3 Data

3.1 Data Collection

Typically, it has been difficult to extract data related to sexual harassment due to social stigma but now, an increasing number of people are turning to the Internet to vent their frustration, seek help and discuss sexual harassment issues. To maintain the privacy of the individuals in the dataset, we do not present direct quotes from any data, nor any identifying information.

Anonymized data was collected from microblogging website Twitter - specifically, content containing self-disclosures of sexual abuse from November 2016 to December 2018.

The creation of a new dataset mandates specific linguistic markers needed to be identified. Instead of developing a word list to represent this language, a corpus of words and phrases were developed using anonymized data from known Sexual Harassment forums [2] [3] [4].

User posts containing tags of *metoo, sexual violence* and *sexual harassment* were also collected from microblogging sites like Tumblr and Reddit. For e.g., subreddits like *r/traumatoolbox, r/rapecounseling, and r/survivorsofabuse.* Then the TF-IDF method was applied to these texts to determine words and phrases (1-grams, 2-grams and 3-grams) which frequently appeared in posts related to sexual harassment and violence. Finally, human annotators were asked to remove terms from this which were not based on sexual harassment, as well as duplicate terms. This process generated 70 words/phrases which were used as a basis for extraction of tweets.

The public Streaming API was used for the collection and extraction of recent and historical tweets. These texts were collected without knowing the sentiment or context. For example, when collecting tweets on the hashtag #metoo, it is not known initially whether the tweet has been posted for sexual assault awareness and prevention, or if the person is talking about their own experience of sexual abuse, or if the tweet reports an incident or a news report.

---

[2] http://www.aftersilence.org/
[3] https://pandys.org/
[4] http://isurvive.org/

was assaulted	*molested me*
raped me	*touched me*
groped	*I was stalked*
forced me	*#WhyIStayed*
#WhenIwas	*#NotOkay*
abusive	*relationship*
drugged	*underage*
inappropriate	*followed*
boyfriend	*workplace*

Table 1: Words/Phrases linked with Sexual Harassment

3.2 Data Annotation

Then, text posts equaling 5117 in all were collected which were subsequently human annotated. The annotators included Clinical Psychologists and Academia of Gender Studies. All the annotators had to review the entire dataset. The tweets were segregated based on the following criteria.

Is the user recollecting their personal experience of sexual harassment?

Every post was scrutinized and carefully analyzed by three independent annotators $H1$, $H2$ and $H3$ due to the subjectivity of text annotation. Ambiguous posts were set to the default level of *Non-Disclosure.*

The following annotation guidelines were followed.

- The default category for all posts is Non-Disclosure.

- The text is marked as Disclosure if it explicitly mentions a personal abuse experience; e.g., *"I was molested by my ex-boyfriend"*

  e.g., *"I was told by my boss that my skirt was too distracting."*

- Posts which mentioned other people's recollections were not marked as Disclosure; e.g.*"My friend's boss harassed her"*

- If the tone of the text is flippant. e.g.*"I can't play CS I got raped out there hahaha"*, then it is marked as Non-Disclosure

- Posts related to sexual harassment related news reports or incidents, e.g., *"Woman gang-raped by 12 men in Uttar Pradesh"*, are marked as Non-Disclosure.

- Posts about sexual harassment awareness e.g.*"Sexual assault and harassment are unfortunately issues that continue to plague our college community."*, are marked as Non-Disclosure.

Finally, after an agreement between the annotators (Table 4), 1126 tweets in the dataset (22% of the dataset) were annotated as Self-Disclosure with an average value of Cohen Kappas inter-annotator agreement $\kappa = 0.83$, while the rest fell into the category of Non-Disclosure. The imbalance of the dataset is encouraged to represent a realistic picture usually seen on social media websites. Our dataset is made publicly available [5], following the guidelines mentioned in Section 7 to facilitate further research and analysis on this very pertinent issue.

4 Methodology

4.1 Preprocessing

The following preprocessing steps were taken as a part of noise reduction: Extra white spaces, newlines, and special characters were removed from the sentences. All stopwords were removed. Stopwords corpus was taken from NLTK and was used to eliminate words which provide little to no information about individual tweets. URLs, screen names, hashtags(#), digits (0-9), and all Non-English words were removed from the dataset.

4.2 The Disclosure Language Model (DLM)

Previous studies show that traditional learning methods such as manual feature extraction or using representation learning methods followed by a linear classifier have been inefficient in comparison to recent deep learning methods (Khatua et al., 2018). Bag-of-words approaches tend to have a high recall but lead to high rates of false positives because lexical detection methods classify all messages containing particular terms only. Following this stream of research, our work considers deep learning techniques for the detection of social media disclosures of sexual harassment.

CNNs also have been able to generate state of the art results in text classification because of their ability to extract features from word embeddings (Kim, 2014). Recent approaches that concatenate embeddings derived from other tasks with the input at different layers (Maas et al. (2011)) still

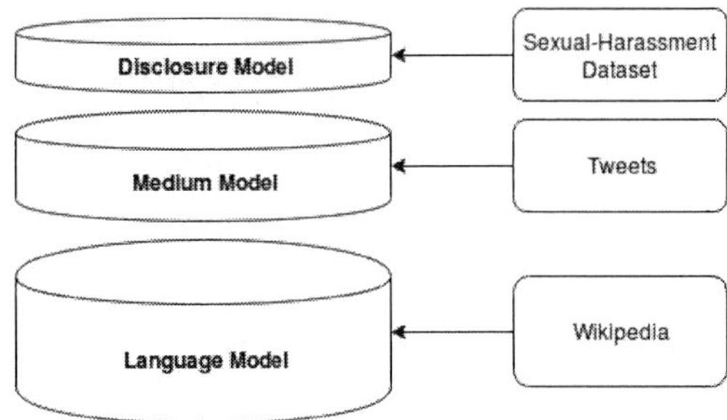

Figure 1: The Disclosure Language Model Overview

train from scratch and treat pre-trained embeddings as fixed parameters, limiting their usefulness.

We propose a three-part Disclosure Classification method, based on the Universal Language Model Fine-tuning (ULMFiT) architecture, introduced by (Howard and Ruder, 2018) that enables robust inductive transfer learning for any NLP task, akin to fine-tuning ImageNet models: We use the 3-layer AWD-LSTM architecture proposed by Merity et al. (2017) using the same hyperparameters and no additions other than tuned dropout hyperparameters. Dropouts have been successful in feed-forward and convolutional neural networks, but applying dropouts similarly to an RNNs hidden state is ineffective as it disrupts the RNNs ability to retain long-term dependencies, and may cause overfitting. Our proposed method makes use of DropConnect (Merity et al., 2017), in which, instead of activations, a randomly selected subset of weights within the network is set to zero. Each unit thus receives input from a random subset of units in the previous layer. By performing dropout on the hidden-to-hidden weight matrices, overfitting can be prevented on the recurrent connections of the LSTM.

4.3 Classification

For every tweet $t_i \in D$, in the dataset, a binary valued value variable y_i is used, which can either be 0 or 1. The value 0 indicates that the text belongs to the Non-Disclosure category while 1 indicates Disclosure.

The training has been split into three parts as shown in $Figure 1$.

- **Language Model (LM)** - This model is trained from a large corpus of unlabeled data. In this case, a pre-trained Wikipedia Language Model was used.

---

[5] github.com/ramitsawhney27/NAACLSRW19meToo

Disclosure
 # WhenIWas 15 I was molested by my best friend
I was sexually assaulted by my step brother in 2009.
At 8 years old, an aldult family member sexually assaulted me.
I was 7 the first time I was sexually assaulted.
I was sexually assaulted by at least 3 different babysitters by the time I was 6 years old.

Table 2: Human Annotation examples for Self Disclosure.

Non-Disclosure
Sexual assault and harassment are unfortunately issues that continue to plague our community.
Trying to silence sexual assault victims is another one. The list goes on and on
Then call for people that cover up sexual assault like Jim Jordan to resign???
sexual assault on public transport is real
agreed! metoo is not just exclusively for women!

Table 3: Human Annotation examples for Non Disclosure

	H1	H2	H3
H1	–	0.74	0.88
H2	0.74	–	0.86
H3	0.88	0.86	–

Table 4: Cohen's Kappa for Annotators H_1, H_2, and H_3

Layer	Howard Dropout
Input	0.25
General	0.1
LSTM Internal	0.2
Embedding	0.02
Between LSTM Layers	0.15

Table 5: Dropout used by Howard and Ruder (2018)

- **Medium Model (MM)** - The Language Model is used as the basis to train a Medium Model (MM) from unlabeled data that matches the desired medium of the task (e.g., forum posts, newspaper articles or tweets). In our study the weights of the pre-trained Language Model are slowly retrained on a subset of the Twitter Sentiment140 dataset [6]. This augmented vocabulary improves the model's domain understanding of Tweet syntax and semantics.

- **Disclosure Model (DM)** - Finally, a binary classifier is trained on top of the Medium Model from a labeled dataset. This approach

facilitates the reuse of pre-trained models for the lower layers.

5 Experiment Setup

5.1 Baselines

To make a fair comparison between all the models mentioned above, the experiments are conducted with respect to specific baselines.

Schrading et al. (2015) proposed the Domestic Abuse Disclosure (DAD) Model using the 1, 2, and 3-grams in the text, the predicates, and the semantic role labels as features, including TF-IDF and Bag of Words.

Andalibi et al. (2016) used a Self-Disclosure Analysis (SDA) Logistic Regression model with added features like TF-IDF and Char-N-grams, to characterize abuse-related disclosures by analyzing word occurrences in the texts.

In the experiments, we also evaluate and compare our model with several widely used baseline methods, mentioned in Table 6.

A small subset (10%) of the dataset is held back for testing on unseen data.

5.2 DLM Architectures and Parameters

Our method uses the Weight Dropped AWD-LSTM architecture used by , using the same hyperparameters and no additions other than tuned dropout hyperparameters. Embedding size is 400, the number of hidden activations per layer is 1150, and the number of layers used is 3. Two linear blocks with batch normalization and dropout have

---

[6]https://www.kaggle.com/Jazzanova/sentiment140

Architecture	Specification
RNN (Liu et al., 2016)	Can efficiently represent more complex patterns than the shallow neural networks.
LSTM (Wang et al., 2018)	LSTMs are able to capture the long-term dependency among words in short texts.
Bi-LSTM (Tai et al., 2015)	At each time step, the hidden state of the Bidirectional LSTM is the concatenation of the forward and backward hidden states.
GRU (Rana, 2016):	Simplified variation of the LSTM. Combines the forget and input gates into a single update gate.
CNN (Kim, 2014)	Utilize layers with convolving filters that are applied to local features.
Very Deep-CNN (Conneau et al., 2016)	Operate directly at the character level and use only small convolutions and pooling operations.
Char-CNN (Zhang et al., 2015)	The model can understand abnormal character combinations and new languages.
fastText Bag of Tricks (Joulin et al., 2017)	Word features are averaged together to form sentence representations.
HATT (Yang et al., 2016):	Two levels of attention mechanisms applied at the word-and sentence-level.
DP CNN (Johnson and Zhang, 2017)	Low-complexity word-level CNN that can detect long associations.
R-CNN (Lai et al., 2015)	Uses a recurrent structure to capture contextual information when learning word representations.
CNN-LSTM (Zhou et al., 2015)	Utilizes CNN to extract higher-level phrase representations, which are fed into an LSTM.
A-CNN-LSTM (Yuan et al., 2018)	Combined C-LSTM model with additional attention mechanisms.
openAI-Transformer (Vaswani et al., 2017)	Generative pre-training and discriminative fine-tuning of a language model for a specific task.

Table 6: Baseline Specifications

Model	Medium	Type	
Language Model	Wikipedia	1,000,000,000	Unlabeled
Medium Model	Twitter	100,000	Unlabeled
Disclosure Model	Twitter	5117	Labeled

Table 7: Training Data Overview

been added to the model, with rectified linear unit activations for the intermediate layer and a softmax activation at the last layer.

The models use different configurations for back-propagation through time (BPTT), learning rate (LR), weight decay (WD), dropouts, cyclical learning rates (CLR) (Smith (2017)) and slanted triangular learning rates (STLR) (Howard and Ruder (2018)). Additionally, gradient clipping (Pascanu et al. (2013) has been applied to some of the models. The RNN hidden-to-hidden matrix uses a weight dropout for all the models. We train the models for 15 epochs.

For the CLR the four parameters are maximum

Architecture	Accuracy	Precision	Recall	F1
DAD Model	0.91	0.90	0.91	0.90
SDA Model	0.90	0.87	0.90	0.88
Word-CNN	0.92	0.68	0.95	0.79
LSTM	0.92	0.70	0.98	0.81
RNN	0.93	0.86	0.95	0.90
GRU	0.87	0.47	0.80	0.59
VD-CNN	0.93	0.89	0.90	0.89
CL-CNN	0.92	0.70	0.91	0.79
fastText-BOT	0.87	0.70	0.80	0.74
HATT	0.93	0.93	0.95	0.93
Bi-LSTM	0.93	0.86	0.98	0.91
RCNN	0.90	0.86	0.90	0.87
DP-CNN	0.93	0.90	0.90	0.90
CNN-LSTM	0.94	0.93	0.94	0.94
Attentional Bi-LSTM	0.93	0.90	0.98	0.93
A-CNN-LSTM	0.94	0.92	**0.98**	0.94
openAI-Transformer	0.95	0.94	0.96	0.94
DLM	**0.96**	**0.95**	0.97	**0.96**

Table 8: Comparison with baselines in terms of four evaluation metrics

to minimum learning rate divisor, cooldown percentage, maximum momentum and minimum momentum in that order. For the STLR the parameters are maximum to minimum learning rate divisor and cut fract. Cut fract is the fraction of iterations we increase the LR. To obtain a sensible learning rate, the learning rate finder (LRF) introduced by Smith (2017) was used. The hyperparameters are directly transferred from (Howard and Ruder, 2018).

- **Language Model (LM)** - Batch Size $\rightarrow$ 32, BPTT $\rightarrow$ 70, Gradient Clipping $\rightarrow$ (0.4, 0.12), STLR ratio $\rightarrow$ 32, cut fract $\rightarrow$ 0.1, CLR $\rightarrow$ (10, 10, 0.95, 0.85), Weight Dropout $\rightarrow$ 0.5, LR $\rightarrow$ 0.0001, Weight Decay $\rightarrow$ 0.0000001. The Adam optimizer is used.

- **Medium Model (MM)** - Batch Size $\rightarrow$ 32, BPTT $\rightarrow$ 70, Weight Decay $\rightarrow$ 0.0000001. The model is gradually unfrozen (Howard and Ruder (2018)) by unfreezing the last layer first and then unfreezing all subsequent layers. STLR ratio $\rightarrow$ 32 and a cut fract $\rightarrow$ 0.5 were used after the last layer was unfrozen, and an STLR ratio $\rightarrow$ 20 and a cut fract $\rightarrow$ 0.1 was used when all layers were unfrozen.

- **Disclosure Model (DM)** - Learning Rate $\rightarrow$ 0.3, Batch Size $\rightarrow$ 52, BPTT $\rightarrow$ 70, Weight Decay $\rightarrow$ 0.0000001, Cyclical Learning Rates $\rightarrow$ (10, 10, 0.98, 0.85) are used. The model is gradually unfrozen layer by layer with the same hyper-parameters applied to each layer. The Howard dropouts are applied with a multiplier of 1.8 and no gradient clipping is applied. The Adam optimizer is used.

6 Results and Analysis

6.1 Performance

Table 8 describes the performance of the baseline classifiers as well as the deep learning models based on four evaluation metrics.

The Disclosure Language Model outperforms all baseline models, including RNNs, LSTMs, CNNs, and the linear DAD and SDA models. The A-CNN-LSTM and the Hierarchical Attention Model has a high recall due to its ability to capture long term dependencies better. The attention mechanism allows the model to retain some crucial hidden information when the sentences are quite long. GRUs perform poorly as they are unable to learn some latent features of the sequence that are not directly tied to the elements of the sequence. VD-CNN models typically require a large dataset for effective feature extraction. Nine layers were used, as going deeper decreased the accuracy. Short-cut connections tend to help reduce degradation. CL-CNNs may generate unusual words as they would suffer from a higher perplexity due to the nature of prediction (character-by-character). Also, longer training time can lead to vanishing gradients. The fastText model can generate embeddings quicker but performs similarly to the Char-CNN model.

The AWD-LSTM architecture used in the Disclosure Language Model can avoid catastrophic forgetting. The main benefit, however of the ULMFiT based Disclosure Language Model is that it can perform classifier re-training with a minimal amount of data. The openAI-Transformer model comes a close second in terms of performance. The results show that augmenting the training data with additional domain-specific data (i.e., Tweets) helps to obtain better F1-scores for the segregation of tweets containing instances of personal experiences of sexual harassment.

6.2 Error Analysis

An analysis has been done to show which texts lead to erroneous and a possible explanation of why that might have been the case.

- **Non-Serious -** *"I got raped at FIFA the last time I played lol"* has a flippant tone. However, the model predicted this as Disclosure because of lack of more contextual information.

- **Third person quote -** *"I was followed and harassed by two guys on my way back home last night." This is what my friend had to say after spending one day in Baja.* Here someone is referring to another person's recollection. However, this text contains all the linguistic markers associated with assault disclosure.

- **Uncertainty-** 1.*"He was my teacher and I was 12. #metoo"*.

  2. *"I too am a metoo survivor"*

  Here, the system cannot pick up the context as there is no explicit mention of assault or harassment.

- **Unfamiliarity-** *"I was walking home, and I saw in broad daylight a man walking towards me furiously rubbing his privates looking at me"*. The current dataset lacks in terms of a broad range of phrases that can imply sexual harassment.

- **First person account-** *"senatorcollins i beg you for my 12 year old daughter who was sexually assaulted by her teacher please do not vote yes on kavanaugh"*. The sentence, although in the first person, refers to someone else's experience.

- **Tweets based on a specific current event-** *"I believe Dr. Ford because the same thing happened to me"*. The user assumes that a majority of the readers will be able to gather context from the amount of information provided. However, the system is unable to pick up this nuance because of lack of information about current events.

7 Ethical Considerations

Human language processing, and human language touches many parts of life, these areas also have an ethical dimension. For example, languages define linguistic communities, so inclusion and bias become relevant topics. Based on the issues highlighted in (Schmaltz (2018)), we address these as:

- **Privacy:** Individual consent from users was not sought as the data was publicly available and attempts to contact the author for research participation could be deemed coercive and may change user behavior.

- **Fairness, Bias & Discrimination:** The exhaustive nature of training data introduces bias in terms of how representative the dataset and hence the trained model is of an underlying community. While it's not possible to capture all demographics, we try to maximize our coverage by building our dataset in two phases by first developing a lexicon from various microblogging sites.

- **Interpretation:** Although our work attempts to analyze aspects of users' nuanced and complex experiences, we acknowledge the limitations and potential misrepresentations that can occur when researchers analyze social media data, particularly data from a vulnerable population or group to which the researchers do not explicitly belong. The main aim of this study was to determine whether it was possible to categorize tweets in this way, rather than to assume the coding was accurate immediately.

8 Conclusion and Future Work

In this work, we proposed a Disclosure Language Model, a three-part ULMFiT architecture, for the task of analyzing disclosures of sexual harassment on social media. On a manually annotated real-world dataset, created in two steps to capture a broad demographic, our systems could often achieve significant performance improvements over (i) systems that rely on handcrafted textual features and (ii) Generic deep learning based systems. An extensive comparison shows the merit of using Medium-Specific Language Models based on an AWD-LSTM architecture, along with an augmented vocabulary which is capable of representing deep linguistic subtleties in the text that pose challenges to the complex task of sexual harassment disclosure. Our future agenda includes: (i) developing a medium-agnostic model robust to the changes in linguistic styles over various forms of social media, (ii) exploring the applicability of our analysis and system to identifying patterns and potential prevention and (iii) applying social network analysis to leverage community interaction and get an overall better understanding.

References

Nazanin Andalibi, Oliver L Haimson, Munmun De Choudhury, and Andrea Forte. 2016. Understanding social media disclosures of sexual abuse through the lenses of support seeking and anonymity. In *Proceedings of the 2016 CHI Conference on Human Factors in Computing Systems*, pages 3906–3918. ACM.

Farzindar Atefeh and Wael Khreich. 2015. A survey of techniques for event detection in twitter. *Computational Intelligence*, 31(1):132–164.

Pinkesh Badjatiya, Shashank Gupta, Manish Gupta, and Vasudeva Varma. 2017. Deep learning for hate speech detection in tweets. In *Proceedings of the 26th International Conference on World Wide Web Companion*, pages 759–760. International World Wide Web Conferences Steering Committee.

Katherine Bogen, Kaitlyn Bleiweiss, and Lindsay M. Orchowski. 2018. Sexual violence is notokay: Social reactions to disclosures of sexual victimization on twitter. *Psychology of Violence*.

Alexis Conneau, Holger Schwenk, Loïc Barrault, and Yann Lecun. 2016. Very deep convolutional networks for text classification. *arXiv preprint arXiv:1606.01781*.

Jeremy Howard and Sebastian Ruder. 2018. Fine-tuned language models for text classification. *arXiv preprint arXiv:1801.06146*.

Jeremy Howard and Sebastian Ruder. 2018. Universal Language Model Fine-tuning for Text Classification. *arXiv e-prints*, page arXiv:1801.06146.

Rie Johnson and Tong Zhang. 2017. Deep pyramid convolutional neural networks for text categorization. In *Proceedings of the 55th Annual Meeting of the Association for Computational Linguistics (Volume 1: Long Papers)*, volume 1, pages 562–570.

Armand Joulin, Edouard Grave, Piotr Bojanowski, and Tomas Mikolov. 2017. Bag of tricks for efficient text classification. In *Proceedings of the 15th Conference of the European Chapter of the Association for Computational Linguistics: Volume 2, Short Papers*, pages 427–431. Association for Computational Linguistics.

Sweta Karlekar and Mohit Bansal. Unc chapel hill 1swetakar, mbansall@ cs. unc. edu.

Aparup Khatua, Erik Cambria, and Apalak Khatua. 2018. Sounds of silence breakers: Exploring sexual violence on twitter. pages 397–400.

Yoon Kim. 2014. Convolutional neural networks for sentence classification. *arXiv preprint arXiv:1408.5882*.

Siwei Lai, Liheng Xu, Kang Liu, and Jun Zhao. 2015. Recurrent convolutional neural networks for text classification. In *Twenty-ninth AAAI conference on artificial intelligence*.

Bun-Hee Lee. 2018. # me too movement; it is time that we all act and participate in transformation. *Psychiatry Investigation*, 15(5):433–433.

Pengfei Liu, Xipeng Qiu, and Xuanjing Huang. 2016. Recurrent neural network for text classification with multi-task learning. *arXiv preprint arXiv:1605.05101*.

Andrew L Maas, Raymond E Daly, Peter T Pham, Dan Huang, Andrew Y Ng, and Christopher Potts. 2011. Learning word vectors for sentiment analysis. In *Proceedings of the 49th annual meeting of the association for computational linguistics: Human language technologies-volume 1*, pages 142–150. Association for Computational Linguistics.

Debanjan Mahata, Jasper Friedrichs, Rajiv Ratn Shah, and Jing Jiang. 2018. Detecting personal intake of medicine from twitter. *IEEE Intelligent Systems*, 33(4):87–95.

Debanjan Mahata, John R Talburt, and Vivek Kumar Singh. 2015. From chirps to whistles: discovering event-specific informative content from twitter. In *Proceedings of the ACM web science conference*, page 17. ACM.

Lydia Manikonda, Ghazaleh Beigi, Subbarao Kambhampati, and Huan Liu. 2018. *metoo Through the Lens of Social Media*, pages 104–110.

Lydia Manikonda, Venkata Vamsikrishna Meduri, and Subbarao Kambhampati. 2016. Tweeting the Mind and Instagramming the Heart: Exploring Differentiated Content Sharing on Social Media. *arXiv e-prints*, page arXiv:1603.02718.

Puneet Mathur, Rajiv Shah, Ramit Sawhney, and Debanjan Mahata. 2018. Detecting offensive tweets in hindi-english code-switched language. In *Proceedings of the Sixth International Workshop on Natural Language Processing for Social Media*, pages 18–26.

Natalie McClain and Angela Frederick Amar. 2013. Female survivors of child sexual abuse: Finding voice through research participation. *Issues in Mental Health Nursing*, 34(7):482–487.

Mayank Meghawat, Satyendra Yadav, Debanjan Mahata, Yifang Yin, Rajiv Ratn Shah, and Roger Zimmermann. 2018. A multimodal approach to predict social media popularity. In *2018 IEEE Conference on Multimedia Information Processing and Retrieval (MIPR)*, pages 190–195. IEEE.

Stephen Merity, Nitish Shirish Keskar, and Richard Socher. 2017. Regularizing and optimizing lstm language models. *arXiv preprint arXiv:1708.02182*.

Stephen Merity, Nitish Shirish Keskar, and Richard Socher. 2017. Regularizing and Optimizing LSTM Language Models. *arXiv e-prints*, page arXiv:1708.02182.

Razvan Pascanu, Tomas Mikolov, and Yoshua Bengio. 2013. On the difficulty of training recurrent neural networks. In *International Conference on Machine Learning*, pages 1310–1318.

Rajib Rana. 2016. Gated recurrent unit (gru) for emotion classification from noisy speech. *arXiv preprint arXiv:1612.07778*.

Alan Ritter, Colin Cherry, and Bill Dolan. 2010. Unsupervised modeling of twitter conversations. In *Human Language Technologies: The 2010 Annual Conference of the North American Chapter of the Association for Computational Linguistics*, pages 172–180. Association for Computational Linguistics.

Kristian Rother and Achim Rettberg. 2018. Ulmfit at germeval-2018: A deep neural language model for the classification of hate speech in german tweets.

Ramit Sawhney, Prachi Manchanda, Puneet Mathur, Rajiv Shah, and Raj Singh. 2018a. Exploring and learning suicidal ideation connotations on social media with deep learning. In *Proceedings of the 9th Workshop on Computational Approaches to Subjectivity, Sentiment and Social Media Analysis*, pages 167–175.

Ramit Sawhney, Prachi Manchanda, Raj Singh, and Swati Aggarwal. 2018b. A computational approach to feature extraction for identification of suicidal ideation in tweets. In *Proceedings of ACL 2018, Student Research Workshop*, pages 91–98.

Allen Schmaltz. 2018. On the utility of lay summaries and ai safety disclosures: Toward robust, open research oversight. In *Proceedings of the Second ACL Workshop on Ethics in Natural Language Processing*, pages 1–6.

Nicolas Schrading, Cecilia Alm, Ray Ptucha, and Christopher Homan. 2015. An analysis of domestic abuse discourse on reddit. pages 2577–2583.

Rajiv Shah and Roger Zimmermann. 2017. *Multimodal analysis of user-generated multimedia content*. Springer.

Leslie N Smith. 2017. Cyclical learning rates for training neural networks. In *Applications of Computer Vision (WACV), 2017 IEEE Winter Conference on*, pages 464–472. IEEE.

Kai Sheng Tai, Richard Socher, and Christopher D Manning. 2015. Improved semantic representations from tree-structured long short-term memory networks. *arXiv preprint arXiv:1503.00075*.

Ashish Vaswani, Noam Shazeer, Niki Parmar, Jakob Uszkoreit, Llion Jones, Aidan N Gomez, Łukasz Kaiser, and Illia Polosukhin. 2017. Attention is all you need. In *Advances in Neural Information Processing Systems*, pages 5998–6008.

Duc-Thuan Vo, Vo Thuan Hai, and Cheol-Young Ock. 2015. Exploiting language models to classify events from twitter. *Computational intelligence and neuroscience*, 2015:4.

Jenq-Haur Wang, Ting-Wei Liu, Xiong Luo, and Long Wang. 2018. An lstm approach to short text sentiment classification with word embeddings. In *Proceedings of the 30th Conference on Computational Linguistics and Speech Processing (RO-CLING 2018)*, pages 214–223.

Christine Wekerle, Negar Vakili, Sherry Stewart, and Tara Black. 2018. The utility of twitter as a tool for increasing reach of research on sexual violence. *Child abuse neglect*, 85.

Zichao Yang, Diyi Yang, Chris Dyer, Xiaodong He, Alex Smola, and Eduard Hovy. 2016. Hierarchical attention networks for document classification. In *Proceedings of the 2016 Conference of the North*

American Chapter of the Association for Computational Linguistics: Human Language Technologies, pages 1480–1489.

Hang Yuan, Jin Wang, and Xuejie Zhang. 2018. Ynu-hpcc at semeval-2018 task 11: Using an attention-based cnn-lstm for machine comprehension using commonsense knowledge. In *Proceedings of The 12th International Workshop on Semantic Evaluation*, pages 1058–1062.

Xiang Zhang, Junbo Zhao, and Yann LeCun. 2015. Character-level convolutional networks for text classification. In *Advances in neural information processing systems*, pages 649–657.

Chunting Zhou, Chonglin Sun, Zhiyuan Liu, and Francis Lau. 2015. A c-lstm neural network for text classification. *arXiv preprint arXiv:1511.08630*.

SNAP-BATNET: Cascading Author Profiling and Social Network Graphs for Suicide Ideation Detection on Social Media

Rohan Mishra[*]
Delhi Technological University
rohan.mishra1997@gmail.com

Pradyumna Prakhar Sinha[*]
Delhi Technological University
pradyumna_bt2k15@dtu.ac.in

Ramit Sawhney
Netaji Subhas Institute of Technology
ramits.co@nsit.net.in

Debanjan Mahata
Bloomberg
dmahata@bloomberg.net

Puneet Mathur
MIDAS, IIIT-Delhi
pmathur3k6@gmail.com

Rajiv Ratn Shah
MIDAS, IIIT-Delhi
rajivratn@iiitd.ac.in

Abstract

Suicide is a leading cause of death among youth, and the use of social media to detect suicidal ideation is an active line of research. While it has been established that these users share a common set of properties, the current state-of-the-art approaches utilize only text-based (stylistic and semantic) cues. We contend that the use of information from networks in the form of condensed social graph embeddings and author profiling using features from historical data can be combined with an existing set of features to improve the performance. To that end, we experiment on a manually annotated dataset of tweets created using a three-phase strategy and propose SNAP-BATNET, a deep learning based model to extract text-based features and a novel Feature Stacking approach to combine other community-based information such as historical author profiling and graph embeddings that outperform the current state-of-the-art. We conduct a comprehensive quantitative analysis with baselines, both generic and specific, that presents the case for SNAP-BATNET, along with an error analysis that highlights the limitations and challenges faced paving the way to the future of AI-based suicide ideation detection.

1 Introduction

Suicide is among the top three causes of death among youth worldwide. According to a WHO report[1], almost one million people die from suicide annually and 20 times more people attempt suicide. Therefore, suicide causes a global mortality rate of 16 per 100,000, and there is one attempt every 3 seconds on average (Radhakrishnan and Andrade, 2012). Moreover, the effect of it on friends and family members are often devastating (E. Clark and D. Goldney, 2000). What compounds the issue is that while it is preventable and, early detection is crucial in effective treatment, there is a lot of social stigma related to it which prevents people from disclosing their thoughts and seeking professional help. It has been found that people suffering from suicidal ideation make use of social media networks to share information about their mental health online (Park et al., 2012) with many having disclosed their suicidal thoughts and plans (Prieto et al., 2014). Therefore it is a pressing issue to be able to utilize the signals available on social media in order to identify individuals who suffer from *suicide ideation* in an automated manner and offer them the required help and treatment.

There exists an active field of research in the field of suicidal ideation detection (O'Dea et al., 2015; Sawhney et al., 2018a) that are able to extract meaningful patterns of behavior from users of social media in order to predict suicidal behavior. These have utilized the information presented in the text of the posts that were shared and utilized both traditional as well as deep learning methods. A rich body of literature exists to show the influence of social interactions of at-risk individuals for their effective detection and treatment. However, to the best of our knowledge, no advances have been made to include information from social engagement, ego networks and other user attributes

---

* Denotes equal contribution.

[1] https://www.who.int/mental_health/prevention/suicide/suicideprevent/

Proceedings of the 2019 Conference of the North American Chapter of the Association for Computational Linguistics: Student Research Workshop, pages 147–156
Minneapolis, Minnesota, June 3 - 5, 2019. ©2017 Association for Computational Linguistics

which we hypothesize would help us in being able to detect suicidal behavior better. Since the interaction of a person with their social surrounding in the form of author profiling from historical tweets and social graph based information can give us a plethora of information about their mental health (Luxton et al., 2012), we explore the usage of author profiling and other features to detect the presence of suicide ideation in tweets better.

Our contributions to the field are as follows -

1. Creation of a significantly large manually annotated dataset for detection of patterns in suicidal behavior in social media along with historical tweet data and social network graphs which will be made publicly available after anonymization keeping all ethical considerations in mind.

2. Proposing *SNAP-BATNET (Social Network Author Profiling - BiLSTM Attention NETwork)*, a feature stacking based architecture that uses novel handcrafted features: *author profiling, historical stylistic features, social network graph embeddings* and *tweet metadata* with an ablation study for validation.

3. Conducted an extensive quantitative comparison with several traditional and state-of-the-art baselines along with an in-depth error analysis to highlight the challenges faced.

2 Related Work

2.1 Suicidal Ideation Detection

There have been certain advances in the usage of social media to automatically detect cases of suicidal ideation in the past (Sawhney et al., 2018a; De Choudhury et al., 2013; Benton et al., 2017). Cavazos-Rehg et al. (2016) performed a content-based analysis on a small number of depression related tweets to derive certain qualitative insights into the behavior of users displaying suicidal behavior but did not propose any automated solution for the task of detection. Sawhney et al. (2018a) prepared a manually annotated dataset of tweets and proposed a set of features to be used to improve classifier performance but included only text-based features which limits the performance of the classifiers. De Choudhury et al. (2013) developed a crowd-sourced set of patients diagnosed with Major Depressive Disorder(MDD) and used their social media posting through the course of a

year to establish a set of signals to help predict depression before its onset. Benton et al. (2017) utilized a novel multitask learning framework to predict atypical mental health conditions with a scope of predicting suicidal behavior but included only text-based features for their multi-task framework.

Furthermore, there have been several forays into tweet classification that utilize a similar set of signals for other applications such as detection of abuse, cyberbullying and hate speech (Mathur et al., 2018b), (Mathur et al., 2018a). Waseem and Hovy (2016) used a public dataset and used a collection of features to show the usefulness of gender-based and location-based information in improving the effectiveness of classifiers. Gambäck and Sikdar (2017) developed a CNN model that used both character n-grams and word2vec features in order to improve the classifier performance greatly. Badjatiya et al. (2017) made use of the same benchmarking dataset, provided a set of baselines and used a combination of randomly initialized embeddings along with LSTM and Gradient Boosting Decision Trees to achieve state of the art performance.

2.2 Author Profiling

The inclusion of author based information has been explored in some tasks related to natural language processing. Waseem and Hovy (2016) utilized gender and location-based information along with text-based features to achieve superior performance. Johannsen et al. (2015) used similar features for syntactic parsing. While it is accepted that such demographic features may improve performance, it is often not possible to extract such features from social media websites like Twitter since this information is often unavailable and unreliable. This has spawned an exciting line of research that makes use of a social graph of interaction between users to derive information about the user. Applications extract information about each user by representing each user as a node in a social graph and creating low dimensional representations usually induced by neural architecture (Grover and Leskovec, 2016; Qiu et al., 2018).

The application of such graph-based features overcomes the limitation caused by unavailability. Mishra et al. (2018); Qian et al. (2018) use such social graph based features to gain considerable improvement in the task of abuse detection. Tasks like sarcasm detection also gain improvement by using such features(Amir et al., 2016).

3 Data

The unavailability of a public dataset for performing benchmark tests, motivated us to develop our own dataset of considerable size in order to validate our hypothesis. We would like to make our dataset, lexicon, and embeddings public to the research community after making it anonymous and keeping all ethical considerations in mind to improve AI-based suicide prevention and analysis[2].

The dataset generation was a two-phase process: (i) A lexicon of suicidal phrases was generated (ii) Tweets were scraped using the lexicon and, historic tweets and social engagement data was gathered for each of the users.

3.1 Developing a Lexicon of Suicidal Phrases

In order to scrape tweets to create the dataset, a lexicon of phrases which could indicate suicidal ideation was created. The top posts, most of which are much larger than tweets, were scraped from three different forums which have an abundance of posts with suicidal ideation. These are *r/suicidalthoughts* [3] (top 100), *r/suicidewatch*[4](top 100) and *takethislife.com* [5] (top 200). Pytextrank [6] is a python module which implements a ranking model for text processing (Mihalcea and Tarau, 2004). This was used to rank and gather the list of the most prominent phrases from these posts. A manual filtering pass was also done to remove posts with little or no suicidal ideation information. The resulting list had 143 phrases such as *hit life, think suicide, wanting to die, suicide times, last day, feel pain point, alternate life, time to go, beautiful suicide, hate life.* Furthermore, the lexicon was extended by using the lexicon shared in (Sawhney et al., 2018a).

3.2 Data Collection

Collecting tweets: For each phrase in the curated lexicon, tweets were scraped using the Twitter REST API[7]. A total of 48,887 tweets were

---

[2]https://github.com/ramitsawhney27/
NAACLSRW19Suicide
[3]https://www.reddit.com/r/
suicidalthoughts/
[4]https://www.reddit.com/r/
SuicideWatch/
[5]https://www.takethislife.com
[6]https://pypi.org/project/pytextrank/
[7]https://developer.twitter.com/en/
docs.html

tweet_id	text
hashtags	user_mentions
user_id	retweet_count
favorite_count	

Table 1: Dataset fields.

Graph Type	Edge Represents	Sparsity (10^{-5})	Avg Degree
quotes	A quoted B	0.570	0.185
mentions	A mentioned B	2.780	0.905
repliedTo	A replied to B	1.755	0.571
follower	A follows B	1.587	0.516

Table 2: Graph comparisons(A and B represent users along an edge in the graph).

obtained. Furthermore, retweets and non-English language tweets were removed. A manual check was done to remove the tweets (around 3000) which were trivially non-suicidal. The final dataset has 34,306 tweets. Each tweet in the dataset is described by the fields given in Table 1.

Data for Author Profiling: For the 34,306 tweets in the dataset, there are 32,558 unique users. For each of these users, the tweet timeline (previous 100 tweets or as many available) was scraped. Texts from historical tweets were combined for each of the users to generate the historical corpus for author profiling.

Social Graphs: The engagement between the users from the dataset was captured in the form of social graphs where the users were represented as vertices and edges denoted the relationships. Table 2 shows the different graphs constructed corresponding to four different relationships and also the statistical comparisons between them.

For the *Follower Graph*, follower lists were scraped for each of the users while for the other three graphs, tweets from the dataset and the historical collection were crawled through.

3.3 Data Annotation

Two annotators, who are students in clinical psychology adept in using social media on a daily basis, were provided with the guidelines to label the tweets as used in (Sawhney et al., 2018b). The guidelines were based on the following classification system -

1. **Suicidal intent present**

   - Posts where suicide plan and/or previous attempts are discussed.

- Text conveys a serious display of suicidal ideation.
- Posts where suicide risk is not conditional unless some event is a clear risk factor eg:depression, bullying, etc.
- Tone of text is sombre and not flippant.

2. **Suicidal intent absent**

   - Posts emphasizing on suicide related news or information.
   - Posts containing no reasonable evidence that the risk of suicide is present; includes posts containing song lyrics, etc.
   - Condolences and awareness posts.

An acceptable Cohen's Kappa score was found between the two annotations (**0.72**). In cases of ambiguity in labeling or conflicts in merging, the default class 0 (non-suicidal) was assigned. The resulting dataset had 3984 suicidal tweets (12% of the entire dataset).

4 Methodology

The overall methodology is split into three phases: *preprocessing of data, extraction of features* and finally *evaluation of models and feature sets.*

4.1 Preprocessing

Due to the unstructured format of the text used in social media, a set of filters were employed to reduce the noise while not losing useful information.

1. A tweet-tokenizer was used [8] to parse the tweet and replace every username mentions, hashtags, and urls with <mention>, <hashtag>and <url>respectively.

2. The tokenized text then underwent stopword removal and was used as an input to Word-Net Lemmatizer provided by nltk(Bird and Loper, 2004).

3. Using Lancaster Stemmer, provided by nltk(Bird and Loper, 2004) stemmed text was also generated to be used as inputs for some feature extraction methods.

4.2 Feature Extraction

The features extracted from the data set can be broadly classified into four types: *Text-based features, tweet metadata features, User Historical tweets features and Social Graph-based features.*

Text Based Features

- *TF-IDF*: Term Frequency-Inverse Document Frequency was used with the unigrams and bigrams from the stemmed text, using a total of 2000 features chosen by the tf-idf scores across the training dataset. The tf-idf scores were l2 normalized.

- *POS*: Parts of Speech counts for each lemmatized text using The Penn Tree Bank(Marcus et al., 1993) from the Averaged Perceptron Tagger in nltk is used to extract 34 features.

- *GloVe Embeddings*: The word embeddings for each word present in the pre-trained GloVe embeddings trained on Twitter (Pennington et al., 2014) were extracted, and for each tweet, the average of these is taken.

- *NRC Emotion*: The NRC Emotion Lexicon (Mohammad and Turney, 2013) is a publicly available lexicon that contains commonly occurring words along with their affect category (anger, fear, anticipation, trust, surprise, sadness, joy, or disgust) and two polarities (negative or positive). The score along these 10 features was computed for each tweet.

- *LDA*: Topic Modelling using the probability distribution over the most commonly occurring 100 topics was used as a feature for each tweet. LDA features were extracted by using scikit-learn's Latent Dirichlet Allocation module (Pedregosa et al., 2011). Only those tokens were considered which occurred at least 10 times in the entire corpus.

Tweet Metadata Features: The count of hashtags, mentions, URLs, and emojis along with the retweet count and favorite count of every tweet was extracted and used as a feature to gain information about the tweets response by the authors environment.

User Historical tweets: To gain information about the behavior of the author and their stylistic choices, a collection of their tweets were preprocessed, and stylistic and semantic features such as the averaged GloVe embeddings, NRC sentiment scores and Parts of Speech counts were extracted.

Social Graph Features: Grover and Leskovec (2016) describe an algorithm *node2vec* for converting nodes in a graph (weighted or unweighted) into feature representations.This method has been employed by Mishra et al. (2018) in the task of abuse detection in tweets. *node2vec* vectors were generated for each of the graphs as introduced in Section 3.2.

5 Baselines

A set of baselines that reflect the current state-of-the-art approaches in short text classification were established. These include methods that use traditional learning algorithms as well as deep learning based models.

- **Character n-gram + Logistic Regression**: Character n-gram with Logistic Regression in the range (1,4) has often been used effectively for classification and works as a strong baseline (Waseem and Hovy, 2016; Badjatiya et al., 2017; Mishra et al., 2018).

- **Bag of Words + GloVe + GBDT**: A Bag of Words(BoW) corpus was generated with unigram and bigram features, the averaged pre-trained GloVe embeddings were then used on a Gradient Boosting Decision Tree which incrementally builds in stage-wise fashion. It is used as a baseline in (Badjatiya et al., 2017).

- **GloVe + CNN**: A CNN architecture inspired from (Kim, 2014; Badjatiya et al., 2017) was used with filter sizes (3,4,5).

- **GloVe + LSTM**: An LSTM with 50 cells was used along with dropout layers ($p = 0.25$ and 0.5, preceding and following, respectively).

- **ELMo**: Tensorflow Hub [9] was used to get ELMo(Peters et al., 2018) embeddings which are known to have an excellent performance in several fields including sentiment analysis and text classification.

- **USE** - The Universal Sentence Encoder (Cer et al., 2018) encodes text into high dimensional vectors that can be used for tasks like text classification, semantic similarity, and clustering. Tensorflow Hub was used to get sentence encoding. Each tweet was converted encoded onto a dense 512 feature space.

- **Sawhney C-LSTM**: We replicated the C-LSTM architecture used in (Sawhney et al.,

2018a) which uses CNN to capture local features of phrases and RNN to capture global and temporal sentence semantics.

- **R-CNN**: Recurrent Convolutional Neural Networks as proposed by (Lai et al., 2015) make use of a recurrent structure to capture contextual information as far as possible when learning word representations.

6 Methodology: SNAP-BATNET

6.1 Graph Embeddings

As discussed in the previous sections, social graphs were constructed for author profiling which could capture demographic features and improve the performance of the classifier. Four such weighted and undirected graphs were constructed: *Follower Graph, Mentions Graph, RepliedTo Graph* and *Quotes Graph*. All the self-loops were removed from the graphs, as they do not contribute to suicide-related communication features.

To obtain the author profiles, the nodes in the graphs were converted into feature representation using *node2vec* (Grover and Leskovec, 2016). *node2vec* works on the lines of word2vec and determines the context of the nodes by looking into their neighborhoods in the graph. It constructs a fixed number of random walks of constant length for each of the nodes to define the neighborhood of the nodes. The random walks are governed by the parameters p *(return parameter)* and q *(in-out parameter)* which have the ability to fluctuate the sampling between a depth-first strategy and a breadth-first strategy.

node2vec by itself does not generate embeddings for solitary nodes which comprised about $2/3^{rd}$ of the total nodes. As per the empirical rule of normal distribution, 99.73% of the values lie within three standard deviations of the mean. To isolate the solitary nodes from the remaining ones, a random vector was generated three standard deviations away from the mean and was assigned to them.

Embeddings were generated for both weighted and unweighted graphs and were individually studied for the classification task. The number of dimensions and the number of epochs was set to 200 and 10 respectively. A stratified 5-fold grid search was carried out on the hyperparameters - *p, q, walk-length, window-size*. It was found that the default values for p and q(1 and 1) along with

[9] https://tfhub.dev/

Combination	F1	AP
Follower+Mentions (CG)	0.808	0.203
Follower+RepliedTo (CG)	0.806	0.196
Mentions+RepliedTo (CG)	0.803	0.197
Follower+Mentions + RepliedTo (CG)	0.807	0.201
Follower+Mentions + RepliedTo (CE)	**0.849**	**0.268**

Table 3: Graph combination results(CG-Combining graphs, CE-Combining embeddings) with weighted F1 and area under precision recall curve.

the combination of walk length 10 and window-size 5 performed best. This performance of short walks can be attributed to the sparse nature of the graphs. It was determined that unweighted graphs performed better and were used for generating combined social graph embeddings.

Combining Graph Embeddings: *Quotes Graph* was discarded from any further study owing to its individual performance in contrast with the other graphs. Its poor performance can be attributed to its statistics as given in the table 2. The rest of the graphs were combined followed two methods: by combining graphs or by combining embeddings using a deep learning approach. The resulting embeddings were trained using a Balanced Random Forest classifier. These results are shown in Table 3.

For generating these combined embeddings, a deep learning model as shown in Figure 1 was designed to be trained on the dataset. After the training, the concatenation layer was picked up as the embedding for the combination, and this was generated for all the users. These embeddings were then used in an LR classifier and a balanced random forest classifier. The results from the balanced random forest classifier were superior and were further used for feature stacking as mentioned in Section 6.2. *SNAP-BATNET* uses Follower, Mention and RepliedTo embeddings combined using the deep learning approach to generate social graph based features.

6.2 Feature Stacking

The competing systems make use of the text based features for classification. To leverage the availability of different kinds of information in form of tweet metadata, historical author profiling and social graph based embeddings so as to overcome the unavailability of a predefined lexico-semantic pattern in the text, methods of combining infor-

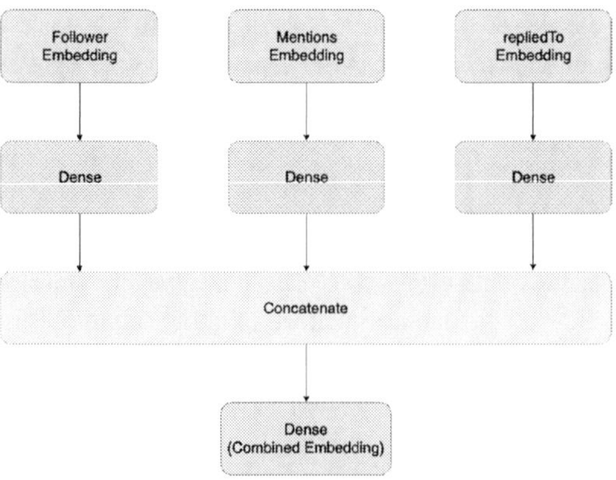

Figure 1: Combining graph embeddings.

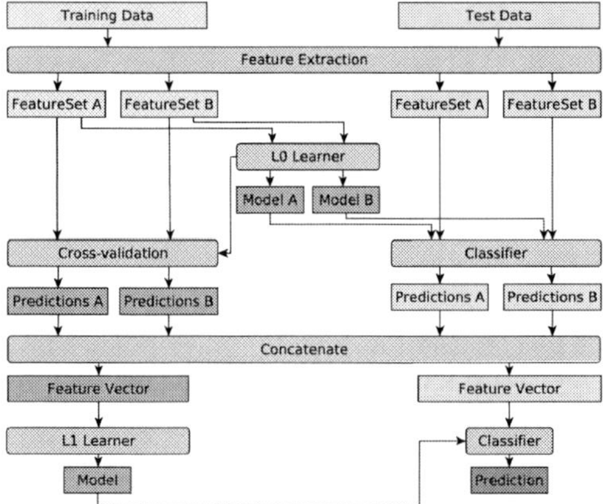

Figure 2: Feature Stacking: A meta-learning approach (figure taken from (Lui, 2012)).

mation were explored. While tweet metadata is sparse, social graph based embeddings are dense in nature.

Initially, concatenation was used, and several models were tried by performing ablation studies. It was observed that the performance of the classifiers did not change significantly and in some cases deteriorated as features were concatenated. Therefore, it was reasoned that the feature sets should be combined in a way that would have the ability to join them related to their relative importance and also allow learning of non-linear relationships between them. Instead of using concatenation which proved to be ineffective or relative weighing, which is cumbersome, we used a meta learning approach inspired from (Lui, 2012).

One major difference between (Lui, 2012) and our approach is that while it uses Logistic Regression as weak learner for each feature set, different weak learners depending on the feature set or

Model	F1	AP	F1	AP	F1	AP	F1	AP
	Text Based		**+ Tweet Metadata**		**+ Author Profiling**		**+ Graph**	
FeatStackLR	.891	.641	.893	.640	.894	.643	.896	.671
Char ngram+ LR	.892	.646	.910	.653	.912	.647	**.915**	**.679**
BoWV+GloVe+GBDT	.897	.567	.896	.534	.897	.542	.899	.584
GloVe+CNN	.908	.619	.910	.619	.910	.623	.913	.644
GloVe+LSTM	.908	.612	.906	.613	.907	.617	.910	.642
USE	.915	.669	.916	.667	.916	.666	.914	.663
ELMo	.913	.650	.894	.629	.909	.629	.911	.623
Sawhney-C-LSTM	.915	.662	.915	.662	.916	.661	.912	.687
RCNN	.921	.704	.919	.705	.920	.706	.923	.726
SNAP-BATNET	.923	.709	.925	.707	.925	.708	**.926**	**.726**

Table 4: Results with weighted F1 and area under precision recall curve.

baseline models were employed in our approach. The weak learners were chosen by using grid search over { *Logistic Regression, Balanced Random Forest Classifier, SVM* }. For each of the baselines, features from tweet metadata, historical author profiling, and social graph embeddings were combined using Feature Stacking. Logistic Regression was used as L1 learner since stacked LR is theoretically closer to a neural network and can help introduce non-linearity between the features (Dreiseitl and Ohno-Machado, 2002).

Our model *SNAP-BATNET* uses feature stacking with different L0 learners to combine the feature sets pertaining to text-based information(BiLSTM+Attention), tweet metadata information(Logistic Regression), historical author profiling(Logistic Regression) and social graph embeddings(Balanced Random Forest Classifier). Furthermore, a simple architecture(*FeatStackLR*) is proposed that uses Logistic Regression as both L0 and L1 learners. An ablation study of the handcrafted feature sets was carried out using *FeatStackLR*, which is shown in Table 5. The addition of GloVe based embedding leads to an improvement in results as these embeddings encode semantic information that is missing from statistical features.

7 Experiments and Results

7.1 Experimental Setup

All the experiments were conducted with a train-test split of 0.2. The hyperparameters for each learner were calculated by using a 5-fold stratified cross-validation grid search. The CNN and

Features	F1	AP
TF-IDF + EMB + POS + LDA + NRC	**0.891**	**0.641**
TF-IDF + EMB + POS + LDA	0.891	0.640
TF-IDF + EMB +POS	0.890	0.641
TF-IDF + EMB	0.890	0.641
TF - IDF	0.888	0.618

Table 5: Ablation study (measured using weighted F1 score and area under Precision-Recall curve).

LSTM architectures used 200-dimensional GloVe embeddings pre-trained on Twitter corpus using the Adam optimizer and were run for 10 epochs. The models were implemented in Keras with a Tensorflow Backend. In CNN and LSTM models, 0.1 of the training data was held out as validation data to prevent the model from overfitting. Each baseline model uses Feature Stacking and is used as a L0 learner to extract text-based features to be combined with other feature sets such as tweet metadata, historical author profiling and finally social graph embeddings.

7.2 Results

Zhang and Luo (2018) describe the lacunae of reporting metrics such as micro F1, Precision or Recall provided in cases of highly imbalanced datasets such as Abuse Detection. In order to properly gauge the ability of a system to detect suicidal ideation from tweets, we report the F1, Precision and Recall scores on a per class basis in Table 4. The results in Table 6 include the weighted F1 Score along with the area under the

Models and Classes		Text Based			+ Metadata			+ Author Profiling			+ Graph		
		P	R	F	P	R	F	P	R	F	P	R	F
FeatStackLR	0	.97	.89	.93	.97	.90	.93	.97	.90	.93	.97	.90	.93
	1	.47	.75	.57	.47	.74	.58	.47	.76	.58	.48	.77	.59
Char n-gram +LR	0	.97	.89	.93	.95	.94	.95	.95	.94	.95	.96	.94	.95
	1	.47	.77	.58	.57	.63	.60	.58	.63	.60	**.59**	**.66**	**.62**
BoWV + GloVe + GBDT	0	.92	.98	.95	.94	.94	.94	.94	.94	.94	.95	.94	.94
	1	.71	.32	.44	.52	.53	.52	.52	.53	.53	.52	.58	.55
GloVe +CNN	0	.94	.97	.95	.95	.96	.95	.95	.96	.95	.95	.96	.95
	1	.64	.47	.55	.60	.55	.57	.61	.54	.57	.62	.56	.59
GloVe +LSTM	0	.94	.97	.95	.95	.94	.95	.95	.94	.95	.95	.95	.95
	1	.65	.46	.54	.56	.59	.58	.56	.59	.58	.58	.60	.59
Universal Sentence Encoder	0	.94	.97	.95	.96	.94	.95	.96	.94	.95	.96	.94	.95
	1	.65	.54	.59	.58	.68	.63	.59	.66	.63	.57	.69	.62
ELMo	0	.94	.98	.96	.97	.90	.93	.94	.97	.95	.96	.94	.95
	1	.70	.46	.56	.48	.73	.58	.64	.48	.55	.57	.64	.60
Sawhney- C-LSTM	0	.94	.98	.96	.94	.96	.95	.94	.97	.96	.96	.93	.95
	1	.70	.48	.57	.64	.56	.59	.67	.53	.59	.55	.72	.63
RCNN	0	.95	.96	.96	.96	.95	.95	.96	.95	.95	.96	.96	.96
	1	.65	.62	.63	.62	.66	.64	.61	.66	.64	.64	.66	.65
SNAP-BATNET	0	.95	.97	.96	.95	.97	.96	.95	.97	.96	.95	.96	.96
	1	.71	.55	.62	.69	.60	.64	.68	.61	.64	**.68**	**.62**	**.65**

Table 6: Results with precision, recall and F1 score on a per class basis.

Precision-Recall Curve.

It was observed that adding features such as social graph embeddings, historical author profiling, and tweet metadata led to a considerable improvement in the performance of the classifiers since each feature set encodes a different kind of information that gives the resulting models more adept at the task of classification. As per our hypothesis, the addition of social graph embeddings led to significant improvement in performance across all baseline models. There was an increase in the recall value which is desirable because the reduction of false negatives was more important than the reduction of false positives. Among the traditional classifiers, character n-gram with Logistic Regression performed the best. Moreover, the use of LSTMs in the model such as Sawhney-C-LSTM, RCNN, and SNAP-BATNET improved the classifier performance. This can be reasoned by the effectiveness of LSTM in capturing long term dependencies. Among all the deep learning models, SNAP-BATNET, when combined with all other feature sets using Feature Stacking, performed the best outperforming the current state-of-the-art, i.e., Sawhney-C-LSTM.

7.3 Error Analysis

Here we go through some examples posed challenges to highlight limitations and future scope.

1. **Subtle indication**: *"Death gives meaning to life"* contains subtle indications of suicidal behavior but caused ambiguity between annotators and was not detected by the model.

2. **Sarcasm**: *"I want to f**king kill myself lol xD "* is one of the several examples where the frivolity of the tweet couldn't be determined.

3. **Quotes and Lyrics**: *"Better off Dead Sleeping With Sirens; I'm as mad, and I'm not going to take this anymore!"* are song lyrics and movie dialogues which the annotators were able to identify but the model could not as it lacked real-world knowledge.

8 Conclusion

This paper explores the use of information from the behavior of users on social media by using features such as text-based stylistic features in combination with historical tweets based profiling and social graph based embeddings. We develop a manually annotated dataset on detection of suicidal ideation in tweets, a set of handcrafted features were extracted which were utilized by a set of traditional and state of the art deep learning based models and a quantitative comparison was carried out which validated the hypothesis of the effectiveness of social graph based features and author profiling in suicidal behavior detection with our proposed SNAP-BATNET model, particularly in improving recall. An extensive error analysis and comparison with baselines presents the case for our methodology.

In the future, this work can be extended by exploiting multi-modalities in the data in the form of images, videos, and hyperlinks. Multi-modal approaches have extensively been used for various tasks like predicting social media popularity (Meghawat et al., 2018; Shah and Zimmermann, 2017). Another interesting aspect would be to adapt the pipeline described in this paper to different problems like identifying mentions of personal intake of medicine in social media (Mahata et al., 2018b,a).

References

Silvio Amir, Byron C Wallace, Hao Lyu, and Paula Carvalho Mário J Silva. 2016. Modelling context with user embeddings for sarcasm detection in social media. *arXiv preprint arXiv:1607.00976*.

Pinkesh Badjatiya, Shashank Gupta, Manish Gupta, and Vasudeva Varma. 2017. Deep learning for hate speech detection in tweets. In *Proceedings of the 26th International Conference on World Wide Web Companion*, pages 759–760. International World Wide Web Conferences Steering Committee.

Adrian Benton, Margaret Mitchell, and Dirk Hovy. 2017. Multi-task learning for mental health using social media text. *arXiv preprint arXiv:1712.03538*.

Steven Bird and Edward Loper. 2004. Nltk: the natural language toolkit. In *Proceedings of the ACL 2004 on Interactive poster and demonstration sessions*, page 31. Association for Computational Linguistics.

Patricia A Cavazos-Rehg, Melissa J Krauss, Shaina Sowles, Sarah Connolly, Carlos Rosas, Meghana Bharadwaj, and Laura J Bierut. 2016. A content analysis of depression-related tweets. *Computers in human behavior*, 54:351–357.

Daniel Cer, Yinfei Yang, Sheng-yi Kong, Nan Hua, Nicole Limtiaco, Rhomni St John, Noah Constant, Mario Guajardo-Cespedes, Steve Yuan, Chris Tar, et al. 2018. Universal sentence encoder. *arXiv preprint arXiv:1803.11175*.

Munmun De Choudhury, Michael Gamon, Scott Counts, and Eric Horvitz. 2013. Predicting depression via social media. *ICWSM*, 13:1–10.

Stephan Dreiseitl and Lucila Ohno-Machado. 2002. Logistic regression and artificial neural network classification models: a methodology review. *Journal of biomedical informatics*, 35(5-6):352–359.

Sheila E. Clark and Robert D. Goldney. 2000. The impact of suicide on relatives and friends. *The international handbook of suicide and attempted suicide*, pages 467–484.

Björn Gambäck and Utpal Kumar Sikdar. 2017. Using convolutional neural networks to classify hatespeech. In *Proceedings of the First Workshop on Abusive Language Online*, pages 85–90.

Aditya Grover and Jure Leskovec. 2016. node2vec: Scalable feature learning for networks. In *Proceedings of the 22nd ACM SIGKDD international conference on Knowledge discovery and data mining*, pages 855–864. ACM.

Anders Johannsen, Dirk Hovy, and Anders Søgaard. 2015. Cross-lingual syntactic variation over age and gender. In *Proceedings of the Nineteenth Conference on Computational Natural Language Learning*, pages 103–112.

Yoon Kim. 2014. Convolutional neural networks for sentence classification. *arXiv preprint arXiv:1408.5882*.

Siwei Lai, Liheng Xu, Kang Liu, and Jun Zhao. 2015. Recurrent convolutional neural networks for text classification. In *AAAI*, volume 333, pages 2267–2273.

Marco Lui. 2012. Feature stacking for sentence classification in evidence-based medicine. In *Proceedings of the Australasian Language Technology Association Workshop 2012*, pages 134–138.

David D Luxton, Jennifer D June, and Jonathan M Fairall. 2012. Social media and suicide: a public health perspective. *American journal of public health*, 102(S2):S195–S200.

Debanjan Mahata, Jasper Friedrichs, Rajiv Ratn Shah, and Jing Jiang. 2018a. Detecting personal intake of medicine from twitter. *IEEE Intelligent Systems*, 33(4):87–95.

Debanjan Mahata, Jasper Friedrichs, Rajiv Ratn Shah, et al. 2018b. # phramacovigilance-exploring deep learning techniques for identifying mentions of medication intake from twitter. *arXiv preprint arXiv:1805.06375*.

Mitchell P Marcus, Mary Ann Marcinkiewicz, and Beatrice Santorini. 1993. Building a large annotated corpus of english: The penn treebank. *Computational linguistics*, 19(2):313–330.

Puneet Mathur, Ramit Sawhney, Meghna Ayyar, and Rajiv Shah. 2018a. Did you offend me? classification of offensive tweets in hinglish language. In *Proceedings of the 2nd Workshop on Abusive Language Online (ALW2)*, pages 138–148.

Puneet Mathur, Rajiv Shah, Ramit Sawhney, and Debanjan Mahata. 2018b. Detecting offensive tweets in hindi-english code-switched language. In *Proceedings of the Sixth International Workshop on Natural Language Processing for Social Media*, pages 18–26.

Mayank Meghawat, Satyendra Yadav, Debanjan Mahata, Yifang Yin, Rajiv Ratn Shah, and Roger Zimmermann. 2018. A multimodal approach to predict social media popularity. In *2018 IEEE Conference on Multimedia Information Processing and Retrieval (MIPR)*, pages 190–195. IEEE.

Rada Mihalcea and Paul Tarau. 2004. Textrank: Bringing order into text. In *Proceedings of the 2004 conference on empirical methods in natural language processing*.

Pushkar Mishra, Marco Del Tredici, Helen Yannakoudakis, and Ekaterina Shutova. 2018. Author profiling for abuse detection. In *Proceedings of the 27th International Conference on Computational Linguistics*, pages 1088–1098.

Saif M Mohammad and Peter D Turney. 2013. Nrc emotion lexicon. *National Research Council, Canada*.

Bridianne O'Dea, Stephen Wan, Philip J Batterham, Alison L Calear, Cecile Paris, and Helen Christensen. 2015. Detecting suicidality on twitter. *Internet Interventions*, 2(2):183–188.

Minsu Park, Chiyoung Cha, and Meeyoung Cha. 2012. Depressive moods of users portrayed in twitter. In *Proceedings of the ACM SIGKDD Workshop on healthcare informatics (HI-KDD)*, volume 2012, pages 1–8. ACM New York, NY.

Fabian Pedregosa, Gaël Varoquaux, Alexandre Gramfort, Vincent Michel, Bertrand Thirion, Olivier Grisel, Mathieu Blondel, Peter Prettenhofer, Ron Weiss, Vincent Dubourg, et al. 2011. Scikit-learn: Machine learning in python. *Journal of machine learning research*, 12(Oct):2825–2830.

Jeffrey Pennington, Richard Socher, and Christopher Manning. 2014. Glove: Global vectors for word representation. In *Proceedings of the 2014 conference on empirical methods in natural language processing (EMNLP)*, pages 1532–1543.

Matthew E. Peters, Mark Neumann, Mohit Iyyer, Matt Gardner, Christopher Clark, Kenton Lee, and Luke Zettlemoyer. 2018. Deep contextualized word representations. In *Proc. of NAACL*.

Víctor M Prieto, Sergio Matos, Manuel Alvarez, Fidel Cacheda, and José Luís Oliveira. 2014. Twitter: a good place to detect health conditions. *PloS one*, 9(1):e86191.

Jing Qian, Mai ElSherief, Elizabeth M Belding, and William Yang Wang. 2018. Leveraging intra-user and inter-user representation learning for automated hate speech detection. *arXiv preprint arXiv:1804.03124*.

Jiezhong Qiu, Yuxiao Dong, Hao Ma, Jian Li, Kuansan Wang, and Jie Tang. 2018. Network embedding as matrix factorization: Unifying deepwalk, line, pte, and node2vec. In *Proceedings of the Eleventh ACM International Conference on Web Search and Data Mining*, pages 459–467. ACM.

Rajiv Radhakrishnan and Chittaranjan Andrade. 2012. Suicide: an indian perspective. *Indian journal of psychiatry*, 54(4):304.

Ramit Sawhney, Prachi Manchanda, Puneet Mathur, Rajiv Shah, and Raj Singh. 2018a. Exploring and learning suicidal ideation connotations on social media with deep learning. In *Proceedings of the 9th Workshop on Computational Approaches to Subjectivity, Sentiment and Social Media Analysis*, pages 167–175.

Ramit Sawhney, Prachi Manchanda, Raj Singh, and Swati Aggarwal. 2018b. A computational approach to feature extraction for identification of suicidal ideation in tweets. In *Proceedings of ACL 2018, Student Research Workshop*, pages 91–98.

Rajiv Shah and Roger Zimmermann. 2017. *Multimodal analysis of user-generated multimedia content*. Springer.

Zeerak Waseem and Dirk Hovy. 2016. Hateful symbols or hateful people? predictive features for hate speech detection on twitter. In *Proceedings of the NAACL student research workshop*, pages 88–93.

Ziqi Zhang and Lei Luo. 2018. Hate speech detection: A solved problem? the challenging case of long tail on twitter. *arXiv preprint arXiv:1803.03662*.

Author Index

Agarwal, Sumeet, 103
Ahamad, Afroz, 53

Balazs, Jorge, 110
Bhanu Murthy, Neti Lalita, 77
Bordia, Shikha, 7
Bowman, Samuel R., 7

Chen, Jiyu, 43

Dammalapati, Samvit, 103
Debnath, Alok, 125
DiPadova, Anthony, 92
Dzendzik, Daria, 1

Foster, Jennifer, 1

Ghosh Chowdhury, Arijit, 136
Gupta, Sarah, 92

Han, Wen-Bin, 35
Hedderich, Michael A., 29
Hirasawa, Tosho, 86

Kabbara, Jad, 71
Kando, Noriko, 35
Kim, Hwa-Yeon, 97
Kim, Young-Kil, 97
Klakow, Dietrich, 29
Komachi, Mamoru, 86

Li, Jiatong, 22

Mahata, Debanjan, 136, 147
Malapati, Aruna, 77
Manning, Emma, 61
Mathur, Puneet, 136, 147
Matsumura, Yukio, 86
Matsuo, Yutaka, 110
Mei, Qiaozhu, 22
Mishra, Rohan, 147
Morabia, Keval, 77
Munot, Rushab, 16

Nenkova, Ani, 16

Paul, Debjit, 29

Prakhar Sinha, Pradyumn, 147

Rajkumar, Rajakrishnan, 103
Ratn Shah, Rajiv, 136, 147
Roh, Yoon-Hyung, 97

Samant, Surender, 77
Sawhney, Ramit, 136, 147
Shrivastava, Manish, 125
Singh, Mittul, 29

Verspoor, Karin, 43
Vogel, Carl, 1

Wang, Yue, 22

Xu, Hua, 22

Yamagishi, Hayahide, 86

Zhai, Zenan, 43
Zheng, Kai, 22

Association for Computational Linguistics
209 N. Eighth Street
Stroudsburg, Pennsylvania 18360

ISBN 978-1-5108-8756-5